THE
PUSHCART
BOOK OF ESSAYS

The
Pushcart
Book of Essays

The best essays from a quarter-century of The Pushcart Prize

Anthony Brandt

PUSHCART PRESS
Wainscott, New York

Essays are reprinted with permission
of authors, or their agents or publishers.
Rights revert on publication.

For information address:
Pushcart Press
PO Box 380
Wainscott, New York 11975

distributed by W.W. Norton & Co.

INTRODUCTION

THE LAST TWENTY-FIVE YEARS have seen a remarkable rebirth of both the art and the prestige of the essay and it has been the good fortune of the annual Pushcart Prize collection, now entering its twenty-sixth year, to coincide with this rebirth, and record it. Read through the essays in Pushcart's twenty-five volumes and you can see it happening. In the mid-1970s the great majority of the essays that were then appearing in what were still called the "little magazines" were literary criticism, mostly written by academics. Some of the best of this work wound up in the Pushcart Prize—pieces by Lewis Hyde on John Berryman; Robert Hass on Robert Lowell; Frank Kermode on literature's institutional base; William Harmon on Louis Zukofsky; and more. But it was hard to find any other kind of essay. There were very few memoirs, even fewer essays on the natural world, almost none of those meditative, half-philosophical short pieces in the style of the traditional "pure" essay, the essay as Montaigne wrote it, and Plutarch before him.

By the mid-1980s all of this had changed. Most of the literary explication that had dominated magazines like *Partisan Review* and the *Chicago Review* and the rest and had set the tone for literary life in this country had disappeared. Under the influence of postmodernism, French literary theory, feminist and Marxist theory, academics in literary studies had abandoned their interest in reaching the public that keeps up with new writing and turned to producing the unreadable and impenetrable professional pieces that have transformed the publications of the Modern Language Association, among many others, into a vast and inhospitable desert of jargon. The New Critics, who had thrived in *Partisan Review* and other little

5

magazines in the 1930s and '40s and '50s, had died or slipped away, leaving no heirs. Gone, too, were Lionel Trilling, Randall Jarrell, Edmund Wilson, cultural middlemen who connected readers with the difficult work of modernism.

Whether the decline of the literary essay created a vacuum, or other kinds of essays were simply due for a revival, is impossible to say. It may be that the essay's flexibility as a form and its short length are peculiarly attractive to an era in which the ancient institutional order of the arts has collapsed—in which pop culture, that is, has come to be taken seriously, commercialization has grown out of control, and poetry and the novel, the traditional high-status genres in writing, seem to have run out of oomph. The essay is sufficiently flexible as to seem beyond genre, or as Roland Barthes once said to precede genre, to stand as the primitive first expression of the imagination.

Whatever the case, an army of essayists has marched over the hills and set up camp in the literary magazines. Joan Didion, Tom Wolfe, and the rest of the New Journalists had already loosened up the form of the reporting piece and personalized it, freeing journalism from the putative neutrality that had always been its burden and its ideal and turning it more essayistic in the process. Edward Hoaglund was winning a name with nature essays; Annie Dillard won a Pulitzer Prize for hers. If there was no more literary criticism to be had, small press publications would now run personal essays, memoirs, think pieces. The NEA started giving grants to practitioners of "creative nonfiction" alongside their grants to poetry and fiction writers, as if the essay were equal in status to these other forms. The writing schools began teaching the subject. The first of Robert Atwan's series, *The Best American Essays*, appeared in 1986. The essay had suddenly, unexpectedly come into its own.

It has been great fun watching this rebirth take place and my own good fortune to be in a position to watch it. I became the "essays editor" of the Pushcart Prize in 1986, at Bill Henderson's request; the number of essays nominated every year was becoming overwhelming and he had no time to go through them all. I still remember the first carton of essays he brought me—some 250 of them, from perhaps a hundred publications, of which we could run at the most ten. Intimidating. But the idea from the beginning has been to pick only the best and the best tends to stand out, first word to last, which has made the task less difficult. Great writing is always rare. That's a fact that an editor learns very quickly. And finding it is always exciting. The impact some of the pieces in this volume had on me the first time I read them remains with me to this day and rereading them to select the best for this volume has been a kind of celebration. Yeats remarked once that he knew a poem was good when it made him want to rush to a rack of weapons and grab a sword. Great writing seizes you that way, you react to it viscerally, in the gut; you are moved, you burst into tears. Or a kind of hush settles over you. Wow! Whew! If it didn't do that to me as a reader, it didn't get in.

What did get in inescapably reflects my own taste and it would be pointless to make apologies for it. When so few essays can be reprinted and there are so many to choose from, one's standards tend to become higher and higher the more one reads. Readability is one such standard and that tended to exclude essays that were avant-garde simply for the sake of being avant-garde. There were, however, very few of those. There were far more complaints of one kind or another, and a certain amount of whining in essay form. Whining never made it, but complaints, like Phillip Lopate's marvelously irritable "Against 'Joie de vivre'," did, if they were eloquent. Essays written from anywhere inside the many forms of political correctness did not make it. If the essay should be anything it should be open-minded, and open-mindedness is precisely what an exclusively ideological politics excludes. There were, sadly, a great many essays of this type, essays that assumed the virtues of victimization only because the writer was a woman, or a homosexual, or belonged to some other professionally oppressed group. Which is not to say that political essays were forbidden. I remember including a Wendell Berry essay in one of the volumes because he managed somehow to energize a style full of abstract words, making them come alive; somehow he made the flat style passionate, made it eloquent. Berry is, of course, an old-fashioned Jeffersonian democrat who believes in the preservation of small-scale farming for lots of good reasons, but in the face of over-whelming odds. It was not his message that attracted me, however, but his manner. He can be a powerful writer. That's what I looked for: power.

I would call this power aesthetic if the word "aesthetic" were not so loaded these days. In the current academic orthodoxy, "aesthetic" is a code word for implementing the political status quo. The idea is

7

that the "beauty" of works of art serves to distract, deliberately or not, the reader or the viewer or listener from the way in which the ruling class exploits and oppresses whole other classes of people, as well as from the way in which the work of art in question reinforces that exploitation, whatever its ostensible subject may be. Such an attitude misses the real tenor of true aesthetic response, which is always tuned to something deep in our humanity, something I am tempted to call divine. It is not beauty that so moves us, it is the power in beauty. I remember seeing *King Lear* in New York many years ago, Paul Scofield in the title role, and weeping like a child at the end. Wow! Whew! Aristotle would have said that it was pity and fear that I was feeling, and the release of these emotions. I think that's only half of it, and the lesser half. The greater half is glory, which is full of terror and exaltation at once; for this is writing that reaches us where we live and die, reaches what is common to us all; this is where we deal with the fundamental things, the fates we cannot escape, the follies we commit, the mortal, fallen creatures that we are. Not to recognize this about great writing, not to *feel* it, is to have declared oneself already more than a little incomplete inside. Great writing is rare but one test of it is that it tests us as well, tests the level of our responses to it; it finds out who we are, passes over us like a hurricane to see how deep our roots really go.

But can an *essay* be great writing? Is the form up to that? If the essays in this book are any evidence, I would say the answer is yes. It's a question of power and some of these essays are extraordinarily powerful: Susan Bergman on her father's homosexuality; Sara Suleri on the life lived by her female relatives in Pakistan; Marvin Bell explaining in his deceptively good-natured way why writing poetry is a life and not a career; Thomas Lynch on being both a poet and an undertaker: all of it sings. Andre Dubus' piece on teaching Hemingway, however short, is quite simply and unmistakably a work of art, and a great one. Read great writing and the question of its status as a form disappears. As always it is mastery of the language that counts, and these are masters. I for one am glad to have them among us, grateful for the resurgence of this form that they might use it.

Let us remember as well what has made the resurgence of the essay possible in the first place: the labor and the perseverance of the mostly anonymous editors and publishers who finance and run the small presses, more or less without thanks, because they themselves have felt the power of great writing, and understand its necessity. I

also want to thank Bill Henderson, whose own remarkable perseverance with the Pushcart Prize (in the face of overwhelming odds) deserves the highest praise. In the politics of culture his is the purest of
projects, for it is wholly dedicated to the common reader and the
common good.

Anthony Brandt

THE ESSAYS

EL HUITLACOCHE, "THE MAN WHO INVENTED THE
AUTOMATIC JUMPING BEAN."
   Bilingual Review   15

JOHN BALABAN, "DOING GOOD."
   Hudson Review   26

VINE DELORIA, "CIVILIZATION AND ISOLATION."
   North American Review   39

LESLIE FIEDLER, "LITERATURE AND LUCRE:
   A MEDITATION."
   Genre   50

CLARK BLAISE, "MEMORIES OF UNHOUSEMENT,
   A MEMOIR."
   Salmaqundi   62

JOYCE CAROL OATES, "NOTES ON FAILURE."
   Hudson Review   86

TERRENCE DES PRES, "SELF/LANDSCAPE/GRID."
   New England Review and Breadloaf Quarterly   101

DONALD HALL, "POETRY AND AMBITION."
   Kenyon Review   111

DONALD BARTHELME, "NOT-KNOWING."
   Georgia Review   129

ELIOT WEINBERGER, "PAPER TIGERS."
   Sulfur   144

PHILLIP LOPATE, "AGAINST 'JOIE DE VIVRE'."
   Ploughshares   159

SARA SULERI, "EXCELLENT THINGS IN WOMEN."
   Raritan   178

WILLIAM KITTREDGE, "REDNECK SECRETS."
    Graywolf   195

SEAMUS HEANEY, "ATLAS OF CIVILIZATION."
    Parnassus: Poetry in Review   204

FRANKLIN BURROUGHS, "A SNAPPING TURTLE IN
    JUNE."
    Georgia Review   220

SUSAN BERGMAN, "ANONYMITY."
    North American Review   240

NAOMI SHIHAB NYE, "MAINTENANCE."
    Georgia Review   252

PHILIP LEVINE, "MINE OWN JOHN BERRYMAN."
    Gettysburg Review   262

LARS EIGHNER, "ON DUMPSTER DIVING."
    Threepenny Review   287

PERDITA SCHAFFNER, "A DAY AT THE ST. REGIS
    WITH DAME EDITH."
    American Scholar   300

ROBERT HASS, "WALLACE STEVENS."
    Threepenny Review   309

MARVIN BELL, "HOMAGE TO THE RUNNER:
    BLOODY BRAIN WORK."
    American Poetry Review   320

BRENDA MILLER, "A THOUSAND BUDDHAS."
    Georgia Review   328

LOUISE ERDRICH, "SKUNK DREAMS."
    Georgia Review   337

VICKI HEARNE, "OYEZ A BEAUMONT."
    Raritan   348

IRMA WALLEM, "SEX."
    Zyzzyva   354

THOMAS LYNCH, "JESSICA, THE HOUND, AND THE
    CASKET TRADE."
    Witness   361

CHARLES SIMIC, "NEW YORK DAYS, 1958–1964."
  Gettysburg Review   371
LEWIS HYDE, "TWO ACCIDENTS: REFLECTIONS ON
  CHANCE AND CREATIVITY."
  Kenyon Review   384

ANDRE DUBUS, "A HEMINGWAY STORY."
  Kenyon Review   404

DANIEL HENRY, "A MURDER OF CROWS."
  Northern Lights   412

PAULA FOX, "BORROWED FINERY."
  Threepenny Review   418

EMILY HIESTAND, "NEON EFFECTS."
  Southwest Review   425

BRETT LOTT, "TOWARD HUMILITY."
  Fourth Genre   436

GARY FINCKE, "THE CANALS OF MARS."
  Shenandoah   456

THE MAN WHO INVENTED THE AUTOMATIC JUMPING BEAN

essay by "EL HUITLACOCHE"

from BILINGUAL REVIEW/LA REVISTA BILINGUE

MY DAD INVENTED THE FIRST authentic wormless Mexican jumping bean with an empty Contac capsule and a ball of mercury he siphoned off a store-bought thermometer. He did it for potential profit in Ciudad Juárez in 1953 in a high-rise complex that the government built for *el pueblo* out of prefab concrete and reenforced plastic girders. They named it Huertas de Netzhualcoyotl after the Aztec poet-king.

It was a big seller all over Mesoamérica. I saw it in the heart of Aztlán, through the frosted glass of a candy store window in Alamogordo on Christmas eve. Big novelty! All-purpose wormless jumping bean! Never dies or runs out on you! Works on body heat! It was one of those candy stores that the Coca Cola company moves into in a heavy way. They put up all your signs for you. They tack up tantalizing murals of cheeseburgers and coke. Above the counter the name of the store and the proprietor is in lights with two psychedelic Coca Cola imprints on either side, like Christ between his thieves. They only let you sell Coke.

I saw them in the hands of *esquintles* on the Mexican *altiplano* and even in the capital. The jobbers on Correo Mayor sold them by the gross to the peddlers, hustlers and other street people. Years later on one of my wanderings I spotted them in the renowned Quetzaltenango market in Guatemala. An old Indian woman in her shawl had them stacked up in symmetrical mounds like *frijoles pintos*. She looked like one of those sibyline old *indigenas* from whom one might expect sage or psychedelic advice. I questioned her. "Mother! What do you sell here? Mexican jumping beans?" But she paid me no heed. She sat there, mute and sassy, receiving the indrawn vision.

Not that my old man made a *centavo* from his invention. That day in '53 he came home from across the border with only about fifteen Delco batteries in his pickup. Competition was getting brutal. And what with the invention of aluminum cans . . . He had himself two Carta Blancas, scratched himself here and there; then came an inspiration. From the souvenir shelf he took the miniature Empire State building that he had bought on Times Square after the War (fighting for Tío Sam was the thing to do in those days) and carefully removed the thermometer from the tower. Then he came out of the john with a Contac capsule that he had emptied. He split the thermometer and tapped the jelly-like mercury. He made a ball from the mercury and slid it into the capsule. He held the capsule tight between his palms. He looked like he was hiding a cigarette butt from the vicissitudes of the wind. Then he let it go on the table. Mother of God! Did it jump! My father, who was fond of scientific discourse (he could expound at length about the notion of sufficiency in scientific theory) explained that it was the heat of his palms that turned the mercury to frenzied bubbling and made the capsule bounce and teeter as if there were a drunken worm in it.

Two days later he produced a refined version with the capsule painted pretty like an easter egg. He showed it to this *compadre*, Chalo, who knew a jobber in El Paso. ¡*Qué amigazo!* They went to see the jobber. The jobber went to see a plastics manufacturer, a man with great metal presses and centrifuges to force molten plastic into little cavities.

There were endless delays, boredom, abulia. My father quickly got fed up with waiting and decided to invent something else. He put together a plastic submarine out of a Revell box, bored two holes into it and filled them with hoses. He pumped air in and out with a hand pump. The sub went up and down "like magic." With the other pump he fired a dart-like torpedo out of the submarine's hulk. The ship was not a total success. A little rough water in the bathtub and the sub would roll over like a dead bullhead on the Rio Grande. "It's the balance," my dad said. "The balance has to be perfect. The tolerances are too fine. After all, plastic weighs nothing. You'd have to be a *real engineer* to solve it."

My father didn't consider himself a "real" engineer. He was smart enough to know that he was some sort of claptrap genius, and also to know he had no credentials. Maybe he considered himself on a par with a "jailhouse" lawyer. He used the adjective "real" like a scourge and a vision.

About six months later we spotted my baby sister, Conchita, playing with one of those merry, lifeless beans. My dad turned from his domino game and glared at her with malevolence. "Where'd you get that!"

Conchita began to quiver. "I traded it at school for two clear marbles!"

"They have them at school!"

"Yes."

"Everybody has them?"

And so it was finished with the automatic jumping beans. Except for the *malestar* that it left in my father's gut. He didn't really care about the royalties that he had fantasized over. He just wished more people knew who the real inventor was. We never talked or told anyone else about it. We made ourselves forget.

That was one thing I couldn't tolerate about my father. We were witness to a succession of unprincipled ruses that were played upon my father's person to the discredit of the family honor. Part of it was that fatalism characteristic of papi's generation, that passive resignation and acceptance of "reality." That was difficult to stomach, yet certainly not unique; it was the norm, therefore tolerable. To this my father added a boundless and totally unfounded faith in people. He was an ingenue, a trusting child, a father to all his charges. And

17

what's more, men, including confidence men, had confidence in him.

How my old man had faith! And he'd been in and out of so many operations. He had scoured the Southwest for old batteries to haul across the border to transform into lead ingots and sell back to the Americans; he had stamped out Jesus Christs on metal plate, struck Virgin Marys from rubber molds, learned the ins and outs of libraries in order to invent a process to detin cans; he had set diamonds, manufactured brass buttons for the armed forces, designed costume jewelry, set up a nickel-plating bath, run a route of gumball machines, managed a *molino de nixtamal* for tortillas, bought a chicken farm (without having read Sherwood Anderson), gone to school at the Polytechnic, bred rabbits, trained geese to be industrial watch dogs, raised a family and invented the automatic jumping bean. He trained scores of young men in the techniques of lathes, presses, files and baths. He was able to initiate not a few followers into the mysteries of the electro-mechanical creed. But after his accident with the sodium hydroxide he shut himself in. Now and then one of his former disciples would come over with a six pack to pay his respects. These men would be foremen at the mine at Smeltertown or supervisors of the toaster assembly line at the Magic Chef complex. Papi was pleased with his pupils but he used them as case studies—fox and crow style—to prove his point that my brother and I had to get college degrees as engineers. "There's no other way," my dad told us continually. "You have to have a passport."

In some circles my father was considered a soft touch. The chicken farm went broke after my father hired an *holgazán* with no experience "*y unos heuvos de plomo.*" A year after he convinced *el patrón* to get into the detinning business, everybody was privy and there were eight detinners in Juárez alone. Besides, they started coming out with the aluminum can. The geese functioned beautifully but he couldn't convince enough people to accept the idea. The War was over and nobody needed brass buttons. After a while his eyesight wasn't so good and he couldn't set diamonds. The big companies didn't like the idea of him moving into religious jewelry, so they muscled him out at the retail level. The United States customs officials raised the tariff on lead ingots. The gumballs got all sticky inside their machines in the Juárez corn dough. He never was able to graduate from the Polytechnic—after eight years of going at

18

night he was doing an isometric drawing of a screw and he stopped and said he wouldn't. We ate lots of rabbit and someone went ahead and manufactured automatic jumping beans without infbrming my father.

I spent five years in college; for three of those I tried to be an engineer. Go be an engineer! Get thee to an engine! My father would pin my shoulders to the wall and lecture me with manic glee. Me and my younger brother would not only be engineers—but metallurgists! He feared for his poor Mexico-Americanized sons, alloys of detinned beer cans. Appreciable schizophrenes. Unable to speak a tongue of any convention, they gabbled to each other, the younger and the older, in a papiamento of street *caliche* and devious calques. A tongue only Tex-Mexs, wetbacks, *tirilones*, *pachucos* and *pochos* could penetrate. Heat the capsule in the palm of your hand and the mercury begins seesawing and the capsule hops. Those were his sons, transplanted, technocratic, capsular Mexican jumping beans without the worm. He believed in education and a free press. Would society listen to reason?

My father liked to walk in the barrio and as *hijo major* it was my privilege to be at his side. We'd walk down the main drag, past the *chicharroneria ("sin pelos, ¿eh?")* where the pork rind hung to dry, and past the *molino de nixtamal* where at six in the morning you could queue up for the *masa* that came out like sausage from the funnel and was molded into a ball and sold like a pumpkin on a scale. Invariably we'd look at what was doing at the movies but we never went in. It would be either a Mexican flick like *Ustedes los ricos* or *Nosotros los pobres* with Pedro Infante or Jorge Negrete, or a World War II *gringada* with Spanish subtitles. John Garfield scowling like a Protestant moralist with a tommy gun emerging from his *vientre*. We would wind up at my father's favorite *tortera*, El Mandamás del Barrio. My dad would have a short beer and I'd wolf down some *nieve de mamey*. Then followed a half-hour rap between papi and the braggadocio owner, don Ernesto. They would share their mutual entrepreneurial visions. Going home my father could become very moody. He would compart his frustrations and his hopes. He made me feel like a true *varón* and I would listen to and guard his words jealously and, from the time I was twelve, with intense anguish. My father usually couched his ambitions in terms of money or some other material objective (*dólares* vs *dolores*). But it was transparent even to a youngster that his true goals were more

19

intangible. He spoke of handing down an inheritance or heritage to his sons, a patrimony, a family business, the establishment of a new order. This pleased me. What I feared was his attribution of responsibility. His resentments had become self-directed; he blamed himself for his failures, he knew he was a brilliant man and yet, somehow his objectivity about the physical world had become perversely countervailed by a totally immoderate estimation of his position in it. Perhaps it was his pride and hunger for recognition that accounted for his overweening hunger for blame. Even his accident at the detinning plant he figured, along with the insurance companies, as some "act of God." My father had no sense of being suppressed, he believed in his freedom of action to a degree that, at the age of twelve, imbued me with fearful trembling for my own personal accountability. He pressed his sons hard on the school issue. School didn't matter to him particularly as a medium of factual knowledge (much less wisdom); he pushed it on us as a means of attaining the necessary credentials, *un pasaporte* was the term he used with blind naivete for the connotations of his choice. School, or rather, graduation and the diploma were a passport into America. It permitted the bearer to travel the road royal.

One evening as usual, my father was questioning me with meticulous detail about my schoolwork. I told him that tomorrow I would have to crucify a frog. It was for junior high biology and sad and dreadful. For two weeks Maestro Rodríguez, a maestro fiercely loved by me, had been methodically outlining with a piece of yellow chalk on a slate board, the life mechanisms of the green frog. I had committed the life to memory, consuming him organ by organ. Tomorrow I was to force him open. After the frog was dunked in anesthesia I was to nail him to a piece of plywood. That was the crucifixion part, his little limbs completely distended so that the torso would be exposed to the public, scientific eye. A disturbing image which my father relished; a frog pinned like a man or boy with arms and legs stretched out on the edges of a raft, belly up on the infinite green sea . . . And then I would use the stainless steel razor to cut the frog into twin symmetries. I was to remove and label the liver, the heart, the brain. I was required to identify the optic nerve.

That evening my father had more than one short beer at El Mandamás del Barrio and I had more than one *nieve* in order to sweeten my mouth. We were troubled and enchanted by the imagery of pollywog martyrdom. When we went home my father was more moody than usual. He looked like a sullen, pathetic victim. The honor in his jaw had softened and he almost seemed to be pouting. He transmitted to me an uncontrollable trembling and a fear for my life and integrity. The most dreadful thing was that none of it could hinder me or make a difference. In the morning I would put on my blue school uniform and go to my biology class and do what I must do.

One day in college I was staggering around the stacks and fell across Jung's *Psychology and Alchemy* and I had an inkling of what my papi's metallurgy was all about. Alchemy: The transformation of dross into gold and the fashioning of the gold into a higher, purer meaning. The goose that laid the golden egg. Out of your ass, man! I spent three years in college dunning the physical world for a sense of reality. I learned all about the acids, bases and salts. They took on a moral connotation for me. But I never could get much realization from the natural world. I preferred reading a novel or loving a woman. At that time my father was *semi-retirado*. His face had been disfigured by a geyser of caustic soda when the detinning bath blew. For over six months something had been going awry with the bath. Every three or four weeks there would be this awful rumbling and out of the tank 10 feet long by 10 feet wide would spout a geyser of boiling caustic soda and tin slush. My father was very concerned. The workers were coming on the job with heavy rubber tarpaulins close at hand. There was muttering that this was hazardous work and they should get a raise. My dad walked around with a yellow pad; he kept scribbling numbers. Every day he dropped his plumb line into the foul-smelling tank and took a reading of the solution level. He was convinced that the variation in the buildup of incrustation at the bottom of the tank had led to substantial variations in temperature within the solution. When the temperature differences became too extreme: the geyser effect. He advised that the tank be drained and that the incrustations be scraped from the bottom so that the solution would receive uniform heat. But *el patrón* wouldn't hear of it. There was too fierce a competition for the scarce tin cans. If they were out of business for two, three weeks, they'd never get back on beam. What they had to do was plumb the tank for all it was worth and when she blew, *¡que se joda!* If necessary they would go back to old batteries and lead ingots. One day my father was standing over the tank with his plumb line. He looked like a little bronze boy fishing in a vat of vaporous split-pea soup. Suddenly, without warning, the physical world spat up at him. He took a sop of alkaline base right on the head. Very funny! just like Laurel and Hardy. What the hell, there's only a finite number of tin cans anyway. Besides, my dad would never have to worry anymore that he was being discriminated against merely because he was Hispanic.

After the accident papi mostly stayed at home, although he was known to beat it out occasionally to Chalo's for *un partidito de dominó*. He gave up his vocation as *subpatrón*, a teacher, trainer and overseer of men. He claimed he wasn't up to breaking in new men with his face disfigured as it was. He wouldn't be able to face the *chisme* and derision of resentful ingenues. He had taken it on himself and it made him lose his confidence. Now and then he'd get an inspiration and rush to his closet which he had fashioned into a shop and work over a virgin hunk of metal with his press and files.

Chalito and I went to college where after many peripeteias I eventually majored in sociology. In the afternoon my brother and I ran the gumball route for *el patrón*. In our pickup we wandered through all the good and bad-ass neighborhoods of El Paso and Ciudad Juárez. Everywhere we stopped a horde of expectant *esquintles* descended on us. *"¡Ahí vienen los chicleros! Dame un chicle, ¿no?"*

My old man made it easier for the gumball business when he invented some kind of corn oil to spray on the gumballs so they wouldn't stick to the glass or to each other. On the other hand, it was our solemn duty to fix the charms to the glass sides of the machine so they couldn't fall down the gum slot and requite some grimy-pawed tot in his vision of hitting the *gordo* from a magnanimous vending machine. My dad even discovered that it was easier to give the storeowner's 15% cut of the sales by weight rather than having to count out all the money. Some storeowners were not so certain, however, about the reliability of mass in the physical world and they needed constant convincing that weight and count were equivalent. Every once in a while they'd "keep us honest" by making us count the money too.

It was a tolerable life and when I graduated from college my father was present in his dark blue suit and dark tie (the combo he reserved for a funeral) feeling proud and tender and somewhat ill at ease about his scarred, reprehensible face. He poured me a tequila with his own hand and made me lick the salt from his own wrist. "You've made something of yourself!" he told me. He was not too sure about the nature of these "social" sciences but he was confident that the degree would satisfy the contingencies of the "real" world. When he died, perhaps from boredom, loneliness and a thwarted imagination, he laid a heavy rap on me. He said I was the oldest and therefore I inherited the responsibilities. I should see to it that the family was kept intact, go about the unfinished business of establishing some solid, familiar enterprise, a patrimony.

If I did not forgive my father his naive belief in his omnipotence then I would have succumbed to his logic and in condemning him would validate his credo of an ultimate, personal accountability. The vicious circle; the double bind. It is better to forgive him and lay the blame on a myopic, racist society that would have granted a white Anglo of his talents an adequate station in life. This position too has its fearful hazards for it alienates me from my father's vision and his wishes. Pater noster. His love for and exuberant response to the world pose a momentous challenge. His younger son made it as an engineer. He works for General Dynamics where he helps design submarines.

He was a man who inspired confidence. . . I prefer to fix him as he was when I was twelve. It was long before the vat full of sodium hydroxide had turned eccentric and he was at his height of virility and joy. One golden afternoon after school I went down to the detinning plant and peered through the fence at the scrap metal yard. The yard was one square kilometer wide and filled to the brim with b illiant metal. It was a splendid day and my father had decided to do some physical work with his men. He sported a magnificent Zapatista mustache. He had taken off his shirt and his bronze chest and arms rippled with muscles as he dug into a mound 8 feet high of shimmering scrap and filled a massive wire cage. He looked like bronze Neptune with his trident or maybe like a revolutionary poster of an industrial worker emanating joyous aggression. The workers were laughing and marvelling as he filled the wire cage in six minutes and then attached it to the crane that hauled it to the tank of caustic soda. I wanted to go inside the yard but I was fearful because papi's trained geese honked militantly at me from the other side of the fence. At that time I was about the same height as these ferocious bull geese and a week earlier one had pecked me on the cheek. Neither the bruise nor the moral outrage had healed. Finally the geese became distracted by a stray dog and I made a dash for it. My father greeted me with delight as if I were a creature unique, a novelty. We went to the furnace where they melted the batteries. He knew the furnace fascinated me. He let some of the molten lead down the channel and into the ingot molds. Molten lead does not look base at all but rather like fine Spanish silver. We inspected the artisans who fashioned the soles for *huaraches* out of old rubber tires. We checked out the rabbits who also lived in the yard. There was a white fluffy one I enjoyed petting and laying on certain prepubertal fantasies.

During the break the young macho workers would place a narrow board 10 feet long by 10 inches wide across the steaming and bubbling vat of caustic soda. The brackish vat looked like a place on Venus where Flash Gordon might land and the machos liked to reassure themselves by walking over the board they had laid across the corrosive brew. My father did not approve of this practice. As a man of responsibility and devout observer of the physical world he believed to the utmost in the principles of safety. Unfortunately the young workers did not share his sense of caution and they played their little game. That day they invited a brand-new worker to walk his way across the board, just in order to verify his machismo. This worker did so without the slightest hesitation. He walked across once and was rewarded with the promise of a free beer. He walked over again and received another free beer. He was supremely confident. He went over again and stumbled into the vat. The worker had heavy rubber boots but before he could catch his balance he went in over the knee and the solution filled up his boot. The workers were hollering and my father came running with a fire extinguisher filled with neutralizer. They got the worker's boot off and a patch of skin from the man's calf came peeling off with the boot. My father foamed what was left of the leg and wrapped a blanket around it.

The ambulance seemed to never come. For me and perhaps for others present the young worker had somehow been transformed and transported to an inhuman category. He was no longer like me, he was something alien, revolting and mortifying, something with which I could no longer identify. But my father held him in his arms and comforted him. The young worker was in such intense pain and shock that he could not scream. He whispered to my father if he would be short a leg. My father was too committed a realist to deny it. He clenched the young man's hand in his own. He talked to the worker about the dignity of work. He told the worker that the leg

24

didn't matter, that maybe he wasn't *el patrón* but he was *el subpat-ron* and after he was well he would see to it that there was work for him.

My question is: Why wasn't papi recognized as the inventor of the wormless bean and other joyous novelties?

1977

DOING GOOD

by JOHN BALABAN

from THE HUDSON REVIEW

PERHAPS THE CRUELEST THING the North Vietnamese did to Americans, which we will hold against them even more bitterly than our defeat, is their failure, after their victory, to bathe South Vietnam in blood. We needed a bloodbath, for even though we had lost the war, we could say that we had tried to save our half of the country from barbarous slaughter. Now it is harder to excuse the horrible things which we did in Vietnam.

If we sanctioned evil acts because they seemed to serve a greater good, perhaps we ought to forget them. The war is over. We could forget them if only we weren't so capable of performing them again, for even at the close of the war, with still another President making the decisions, we confused doing good with our own vague self-interest and the result once again was further suffering for others and increased moral confusion for ourselves. When defeat was clear, we baby-lifted hundreds of infants to save them from communist barbarism. Children who were left temporarily in orphanages were packed off to the United States. Brothers and sisters were separated and sent to unaware families thousands of miles apart. We never asked ourselves how these Asian, Eurasian and black Asian children would fare as adolescents and adults. We needed them immediately, like extras in a movie. Two scenes from our last venture at doing good in Vietnam are memorable: President Ford cradling an infant at the door of an Air Force plane (which had flown into Vietnam with arms and had flown out with babies) and an Air Force medic "giving an orphan its first drink in the U.S." (by squirting a hypodermic of Coca-Cola into its open mouth). We jammed the telephone lines with our requests for these children; when the adults came, we didn't like it.

Vietnam confused us. Most of us meant well. I am still sorting out my own involvement which began one warm afternoon in the spring of 1967 when I returned to my apartment from Widener library and encountered circumstances which more or less urged me to go: Plodding along with bookbag weighted with Middle Scots and Old English texts—the focus of my attention during my first year of graduate study at Harvard—with eyes itchy in the sunlight and shoulders stooped from reading too much, I came across a large crowd outside of Lowell House. They were students mostly and they were waiting to speak to Secretary of Defense Robert McNamara, who was talking to a small group of undergraduates while in Cambridge as a guest of the new Kennedy Institute. At that time, you remember, the Johnson Administration still got away with saying very little about the war. On this occasion, McNamara had been petitioned to speak to the academic community, which in Boston, with its several hundred colleges and junior colleges, is quite large. To make his position easier, some of his fellow guests at the Institute offered to share a platform with him. He refused. When I got to Lowell House perhaps five hundred persons were milling about. An SDS fellow was haranguing the crowd with a bull horn, but generally it was pleasant and amiable. Far down Mt. Auburn Street a bedsheet with an unintelligible protest was hung from a third-story window.

27

The tune and some of the words of "Mack the Knife" floated towards the crowd.

When McNamara did emerge, it was from a side exit into a narrow street to which the crowd rushed and, perhaps unintentionally, blocked his car. The Secret Service looked menaced and started pushing people out of the way. I stood behind an ABC camera team where it seemed safe and looked at the Secretary as he sat in his car. After a few minutes he got out and got up on the roof of his car, buckling the roof with a crackle which he ignored. The crowd hushed. He said, "I'll give you four minutes, then I must leave." He began, "When I was a student in California, I was as radical as you." The crowd groaned. "But there was one difference . . . I was more polite." The crowd booed. Someone yelled, "Fuck you!" Another yelled, "Murderer!" The cameras whirred. The sound man winked triumphantly at the camera man. McNamara was helped down by an agent and was driven off. Harvard apologized publicly.

And so I can thank Harvard and McNamara for my going to Vietnam, for both in their contrary ways had aroused in me an interest in *veritas*. During the following week, filled with decision, I wrote a poem about my going which was printed in the *American Scholar*, renewed an application that I had made more than a year earlier with the International Voluntary Services, and, even more to the point, I began dickering with my Pennsylvania draft board about trading in my student deferment for a conscientious objector rating on terms that would allow me to work in Vietnam as a civilian and without supervision.

My draft board, a group of old men who seemed frightened that I might make a speech, hearing that I was dropping my student deferment to perform good works in Vietnam, made me a conscientious objector in a four-minute hearing taken up mostly by my stating my name, by my swearing on the Bible, and by my answering "yes" when asked if I really intended to go to Vietnam. My hearing was so short that I thought they had turned me down out of hand. I had constructed answers regarding the sanctity of all life above the bird level (I still fished, and hunted grouse), and I was ready to reply that the Supreme Being was a kind of gas permeating the universe with goodliness and creation, but they did not ask one question.

In July, 1967, I arrived in Vietnam. In a few months, I was to teach at the University of Can Tho in the Mekong Delta as a volunteer with the International Voluntary Services, a kind of peace corps hired by the U.S. Agency of International Development to teach English, hand out seeds, and to relocate refugees. On the ride into Saigon from Tan Son Nhut airport, my white suit, which clothed slim confidence, was grimed with crankcase oil from the floor bed of the truck that ferried sixty of us new volunteers to a suffocating dormitory on the outskirts of town where idle small arms fire riddled one's sleep from dusk to dawn. My comrades were very keen on helping Vietnamese and seemed to suffer from none of the ambiguities that were aroused in me at the sight of all those ammo dumps and fighter-bombers at the airport; my comrades were missionaries and they found *virtus*, if not *veritas* in wretched food, stopped toilets, and sleepless nights. After some weeks of delay in Saigon, during which I tried to learn Vietnamese (my first words were "no" and "boiled water, please"), I flew to the center of the Delta where I taught descriptive linguistics. Soon I had my doubts that I was doing anybody any good, except by helping to keep a few Vietnamese draft dodgers in class and off the battlefields. And there was the worry that I was taking a job away from a Vietnamese instructor and putting him on the battlefield. And who could I help by deceiving these young people into believing that Americans could be as nice as I? Didn't I owe it to them to come to class drunk, loud, and lecherous? I only worried about these things for a few months. In February, the 1968 Tet Offensive began and the University and my house beside it were bombed by Americans and South Vietnamese.

This gave me a chance to do some *immediate* good which, of course, is the best kind because it comes without hesitation, is perfectly human to perform, and is immediately rewarding both to the receiver and to the giver. At the beginning of the Offensive, while there was fighting in the streets, and planes and Cobra helicopters were strafing overhead, I volunteered with three other young Americans to work in the general hospital. In the central courtyard of the hospital, whole families, shredded up and bleeding, lay moaning in the dirt or on reed mats under the broiling sun. My next door neighbor, raving himself, attended his delirious wife whose head was filled with slivers of shrapnel from a mortar that strayed into our dooryard as she peeked out during a lull. A teenage girl, still in the light cotton pajamas that Vietnamese wear around the house, had thrown her body over her old father because he was cold, because he was dying. A little boy thrashed about and would not be consoled by some adults because his ear drums were blown out and he could only hear pain. There were hundreds of such people. There were no doctors. In the U.S. I had talked about the war; marched against the war; I had lived in Vietnam eight months, and up until that moment I knew nothing about the war.

As the four of us stepped by the bodies and into the corridor leading to the surgery room, we met six or so heavily-armed American officers. They were military doctors, and with the fighting close by and the Vietnamese staff having already left, they were leaving too. They agreed to stay and operate if we would agree to serve as nurses and guards. So for a week, I gave blood (one unit), carried bodies, living and dead, learned how to clean and dress wounds, charged myself with closing the eyes of the dead (discharging myself from this duty when a number of stiffened eyelids refused to shut), and guarded the operating room as bullets made a sieve of the water tower near which I sat with a Red Cross band on my arm and a submachine gun in my hands. Without a guard, the surgeons wouldn't operate. If the surgeons didn't operate, many would die. Without medical stores, Vietcong soldiers would die too. To my shame and growing confusion (I had wanted to help *save* lives but I wanted the Vietcong to win) I was proposing to try to kill any that might get over the eight-foot stucco wall that surrounded the compound. Fortunately for me, none tried. Nonetheless, my sacrifice was marred. And the next day, while smuggling a sandwich to a Vietnamese friend who was holed up in a garage because he wasn't uniformed and might well have been shot in the mayhem on the streets, I got hit by a fingernail of shrapnel from a U.S. cluster bomb. After a few months of teaching and few days of doing good, all I wanted was to go home. If I could do anyone any good, it would be in the United States and not in Vietnam where do-gooder politics were mere pretension.

That spring I quit the International Voluntary Services and got a job as a field representative for the Committee of Responsibility to Save War-Injured Children. COR was a small organization among the hundreds of foreign voluntary agencies comprised of teams of Americans, French, English, Swiss, Germans, Japanese, Iranians, Spanish, Filipinos, Koreans, and some do-gooders from the UNESCO. There were Quakers, Baptists, Seventh-Day Adventists, Mennonites, Brethren, and all kind of Catholics, all doing good in some direct way by building hospitals and clinics, training nurses and doctors, doing specialized surgeries on brains, bones, eyes, and skins, making prosthetic limbs, and giving away blankets, food, vitamins, maternity kits, surgical equipment, clothing, vaccines, and medicines. Among this army of do-gooders there were legions of vampires who thrived on the war in separate, personal, and peculiar ways. G.I.'s betrayed their sense of this with their instant distrust of anyone who came to Vietnam of his own choosing. (Partly because of their suspicion and resentment, I avoided G.I.'s. I did not trust them either. Early on I had met a Navy medic who proudly showed me "V.C. ears" in a mason jar of formaldehyde. And, often, as I was hitch-hiking a ride or freeloading in a mess hall, I would talk to soldiers whose conversation centered on their urethral drips, and often they wanted, understandably enough, my assurance that killing Vietnamese was O.K. Twice, I called home to my parents to relay a message to the parents of a soldier I had just met, but generally I avoided soldiers because, very simply, it made my survival all the harder when I thought of the victimizer as victim too). Anyway, I also learned to suspect do-gooders, remembering the young American Medical Association volunteers who had come to experiment at surgeries they wouldn't dare perform on an American; the U.S. AID boozer escaping a rotten marriage; the French priest who finagled a law, in this country of Buddhists, that would give relief supplies only to Catholics; the sad, homely Englishwoman who hung around orphanages to cradle dying children, victims like herself; the Quaker who had come to adopt orphans for American families but who spent himself righteously tongue-lashing sullen bureaucrats until they froze him out of the country; the young IVS volunteer whose holiest mission was to become a Vietnamese; and his spiritual twin, the young volunteer, a shy twit among Americans, who became a powerful whore-master among slum-bound Vietnamese; the professional New York woman reporter of human interest stories who shed compassion on Vietnamese and acid and barbs on other journalists, a woman who, brilliant, bitter, raw-nerved and awkward, used Vietnam to explain her life; the Baptist missionary who preached relentless anti-Communism to his captive, refugee fiefdom near Danang; the radicals and doves who spent their obligatory week in Saigon so they could summon the cameras when they arrived back home; and remembering myself, the anonymous hero, the sensitive witness, morality's spy among the Nazis, the saver of lives, and in other self-congratulating guises.

31

For a period of six months I began each day by carrying a couple of raw eggs to Nhi Dong Children's Hospital for a 12-year old boy who had so many open wounds that he was dying of protein loss. Then I would go to the Ministry of Interior to sit all day, usually, in clerks' offices until one official found time to decide on the children's passport papers, papers that I had brought to his desk from another's desk, papers that I would carry to other desks. This was called "walking the papers." I was exhausted at the end of a day of doing good; my rage smouldered at the bureaucrats' distance from the war and at the Americans (this kind of work made one feel *above* nationality) who had maimed those innocent victims or had left them sick and homeless. At first the work had a very right feeling: children, like the boy with multiple wounds, had their lives saved. But generally I was worn out. How much good did it do? (This is the question that will ruin a do-gooder, if he asks it of himself). I ran around for six months comforting children and their families, placating hospital personnel about the beds we were taking up with our cases, ingratiating myself with boozy bureaucrats, hamstering my way through the Ministries, and making myself ridiculous by trying to browbeat the U.S. Embassy into pressuring the Saigon government into speeding up the evacuation process. At the end of six months, I put thirteen children on an airplane for hospital care in the U.S., and then headed out to the provinces to take on more cases. Thirteen, out of how many thousands?

Still, as I saw it, the Committee of Responsibility had a moral edge on the other groups because it provided some Vietnamese children with extensive medical care in the U.S. while remaining politically clear of the Saigon government. The idea was that if even a handful of war-injured children were to appear in a dozen or so American cities, then the American people would be so undeniably confronted, shocked and outraged that they would stop the war. The proposition held a basic, simple belief in the wellsprings of human goodness. My disappointment was inevitable.

Even if our proposition held, it wasn't as easy as bringing a child to the U.S., inviting the press to the airport, patching the kid up and then sending him home, as agreed, to his family (don't think we didn't anguish over sending the kids home to the war; our sense of good just wasn't sufficient for kidnapping). The only children that we were permitted to evacuate were the most severe cases for whom no one could even dare pretend that help could be gotten in Vietnam.

They required long term treatment, perhaps a dozen or so more surgeries and physical rehabilitation. They stayed a long time. Funny things happened to a few of them. The little ones started to forget their language after their Vietnamese convoyeuses returned home after three months. And while we all knew that once learned, a language could never really be forgotten and could easily be re-learned, especially by a child, still it was unsettling. Some of the teenagers tried to become Americans. They strutted before adults and competed nastily with other children, learned loud manners and ordered their nurses about. Some of them got greedy, for they were flooded with gifts by the good-willed who chanced to meet them. In Boston, when a kindly woman met a boy who had lost three limbs in a mining incident, she took off an $18,000 necklace and wanted to give it to him. In Vietnam I had to keep asking myself, "Now, is it better for a child here to die or be maimed for life or to risk his being screwed up by well-intentioned people back home?"

In May, 1969, as well as traveling to the provinces seeking evacuations, I was also returning children to their families. At the end of May two boys returned, Huynh Duc, 15 years old, and Ho Bau, 11. Duc was around the fiftieth child that COR had treated. There were, of course, thousands of civilians wounded every year, despite Robert McNamara's 1967 estimate of some one hundred and twenty (which was based on the number of compensations *paid* at that time by the Department of Defense). Duc had suffered an open fracture of his right forearm from gunshot wounds which also required below-the-knee amputation of both his legs at the Danang General Hospital where we found him in 1968. Through the recommendation of Dr. Phung Tuan Hanh, a general surgeon at the hospital, Duc was sent to Hawaii for treatment at Kauikeolani Children's Hospital and the Shriner's Hospital for Crippled Children. Ho Bau also had been evacuated from the Danang Hospital on Dr. Hanh's recommendation, for Hanh would sometimes initiate on behalf of a family the detailed evacuation papers—which involved thirty-five copies for some forms and trips to four Ministries and the U.S. Embassy. With a broad smile he would say, "It's legal and it's right. These are all my children," gesturing to the ward where the patients were crowded two and three to a bed. "These are all my relatives." Just the same I knew we were kidnapping a few, but just the same—and this was the one measure that saved me from total bewilderment in this business of doing good—they would have died. Bau would have died. In

June, 1968, about the time of the My Lai massacre, he was burned by napalm dropped from a plane in a Free Strike Zone near his house while he was playing with some other kids. He suffered third degree burns over 25% of his body, right arm, left and right legs. In the U.S. we had gotten him treatment in Boston at Massachusetts General Hospital and the Shriner's Hospital for Crippled Children. While in the U.S. Bau received a few letters from his mother (his father was dead). Miss Bui Thi Khuy, the 22-year old woman who served as his companion, translated them as best she could:

Duc, Duc, Feb. 5, 1969

Dear Son,

Bau, we received many letters from you. But we couldn't send you a letter. Bau, I know that you are alone in the different people and country. I remember every day and night very very much. Each time I call your name in my heart, I feel sadness and I don't know whom I will talk to. The War separated us. The war took my good son away. Because the situation of the War, so I must carry on. The first and last letter I send to you. I don't know what I tell you. I always pray God protects and gives you the good health. After you will return and live together with us. On that time the peace will come to my heart. Now I don't know when you come back. Today I write a letter let you know that we are well. Please write to me when you receive this letter. Miss Khuy, we are thankful and send you the best regards. Please our family send the best regards and thankful to Bau's foster parents for us. We will never forget them for their kindness to our son. Miss Khuy, please help my son write a letter for us.

Bau's Mother
NGUYEN THI XUMG
DUC DUC Tinh Quang Nam
South Vietnam.

Now three months later, with Miss Khuy, who had returned to Vietnam and who would soon take another group of children back to the U.S., I met the boys when they got off the plane in Saigon. Bau, except for his slightly scarred face, looked like a normal eleven-year-old who had just taken a long plane ride; tired, a little spaced out; wide-eyed at being in Vietnam. He was very happy to see Miss Khuy. Duc, his hair thickly oiled, wearing a long-sleeved white shirt and a tie with a bright stickpin, arrived with two mammoth suit-

34

cases, a Pan Am bag, and a crated pedal sewing machine. He would not speak Vietnamese, he hoped our house had a T.V., and said that he only intended to stay three months, for he would be returning to live in Hawaii. As proof that his return was already in the works, he produced a card showing his honorary membership in the Coast Guard Club of Hawaii.

At our house, for the next few days Duc complained that his stumps were sore from the chafing of his artificial limbs and that he couldn't eat Vietnamese food. When he started to hang in his room and play with his radios and watches, I began taking him out to lunch at working class restaurants in Saigon. Once some people snickered at his dressing like a middle-aged bureaucrat. Finally he gradually sold off most of his junk. And when gradually he found that Vietnam looked "a lot like Kailua," I decided it was time to get him home. Duc and Bau—who had meanwhile introduced Batman to the neighborhood kids—both lived in Duc Duc (Virtuous Teaching), a small village in the contested mountainous region of Quang Nam province.

Miss Khuy, Bau, Duc and I flew, with all their luggage, to Danang. At the hospital Dr. Hanh examined them with pleasure and had Duc walk about on his new legs. Duc walked proudly and without a waver. From Danang we had to take a U.S. Army Blackcat Huey helicopter for the road to Hoi An had been cut. Huey helicopters fly with their doors open and hold about six passengers besides the pilot, co-pilot, and gunner, who sits behind a big machine gun on a pivot post. Over the ocean the gunner opened up at the water. I couldn't see anything; maybe he was shooting at a whale. The noise was deafening. I suspected that he was firing to see the scare on Miss Khuy's face. From Hoi An we took another helicopter that was resupplying Marine field units patroling near Duc Duc. We flew for about thirty minutes over cratered fields, defoliated mountain forests and shining river loops. When we got to the village and hovered about a sea of brown thatch houses swelled by homes of new refugees, I wondered how we would find the boys' homes, for in a Vietnamese village there are no street names or addresses, and we had just a few hours before the supply helicopter would return; if we missed it we would have to spend the night, either in the village, which would not be safe for me, or in the Marine camp, which got mortared nearly every night and which would have been pretty rough on Miss Khuy.

35

Bau said he lived under a big pine tree. With all the luggage bouncing around on the rutted roads, we drove around in a jeep until we spotted, sure enough a large pine tree. Bau's mother was at market. His old grandmother was there and she hugged him and seemed bewildered as the rest of us as we waited for his mother to return. A crowd of neighbors gathered. I asked Bau where the place was where he had been wounded; he pointed to an area about seventy-five yards from where we were standing. That was the Free Strike Zone. Anyone could be shot there at any time.

While Miss Khuy was talking to the grandmother and Duc was chafing to get to *his* home, Bau's mother came walking up the road. When a neighbor rushed out to tell her we were there, she threw her hands to her face and ran the thirty yards to the house, pushed through the crowd, and hugged her son. She wept and called his name. Bau looked at me, and then under the sheer weight of his mother's love, he was overwhelmed and began to cry too. Everybody was crying. Miss Khuy, who was crying (Miss Khuy, who, a week later in Saigon, was to be crushed to death by a two-ton military truck out of the control of its drunken driver), looked at me and I was crying. Bau's minutes of burning, his pain and endurance, his mother's love and the enormous distance that had separated them overwhelmed us all. After a few minutes, Miss Khuy spoke to Mrs. Xung and told her how to contact us if they needed help. Khuy gave Bau a hug and his mother some stamped, addressed envelopes.

Duc's father, Huynh Cat, who made rice paper for his living, was at their home near the market (It was in the market that Duc had been cut down with other villagers when a G.I. went crazy and opened up on the crowd.) However, Duc's mother had just gone to Danang in response to our telegram to meet us at the hospital. Seeing his father waiting for us outside their house, Duc jumped down from the back of the jeep and strode to Mr. Cat, whose smile grew wider as he saw his son grown older, looking more like his father, and walking to him.

Back in Saigon, I congratulated myself on how well it had gone. Few complications. So, we had messed with their lives . . . we had done no harm. We had done some good. As I drew my work to a close and prepared a testimony on civilian casualties for the Senate Subcommittee on Refugees, Escapees, and Civilian Casualties, I liked to consider cases like Duc and Bau. (Forgetting, as best I could, the 9-year old girl who had her nose shot off and for whom we made, in

New York, a veritable red garden hose of a replacement which closed up as soon as she returned to Vietnam.)

Some weeks before the collapse of the Saigon troops, as I was having breakfast and reading *The New York Times* just before walking up to the Penn State campus where I teach composition and poetry to students who were in junior high school when I was in Vietnam, I read on the fifth or sixth page that the village of Duc Duc had been caught in a crossfire and burned. I wondered what happened to Bau and Duc, especially Duc who can't run. At best, I could say, if they had escaped, that I had returned them home so they could become homeless. I had always known that it could happen. As I see it, there was nothing else I could have done. One must act, even if his acts fail, or, if they seem to succeed, are contaminated by other men. It is hopeless to look for personal reward in good works. This isn't a rationalization to protect oneself from disappointment. It means merely that as soon as one tries to profit personally from a good act, it is poisoned. There are no personal rewards in good works unless one is stupid (which only means "blind to consequence") in which case one's good works are more or less evil.

There is no one to talk to about this for like many who have returned from Vietnam, I have returned a foreigner, one whose experiences and emotions are honed on the edge of memories from a place Americans seldom think of or would like to forget. For some reason which I do not understand American pleas for my help make me angry. Hitchhikers and United Fund collectors annoy me. Just the other day I was flying back to New York on a crowded flight when a young woman with two small boys asked me and the woman next to me if we would change seats with her and her 8-year old son so they could be next to her other, 7-year old son. "If you don't want to, just say so," she smiled when she noted my hesitation. She was seated across the aisle, one row up; her son was at her right; the son in question was across the aisle from her, in front of me, on her left. She wanted to sit right behind him. Handbags and passengers were pushing through the aisle. I had just sat down and had gotten my luggage stowed and I did not feel like moving. I said that if she didn't mind, I would stay where I was. She said "O.K." and then, in tears, suddenly lit into me: "People today are so unfeeling, so selfish," she said. "If you had children, you would understand!" Puzzled, I looked at her. If she had reached out her arm, she could have touched her son. I thought of the children who had littered the village battle-fields to be picked up, perhaps, by U.S. helicopters, children who perhaps died on route or in field hospitals, whose parents would never know what had happened to them. I thought of the children I had evacuated, children separated from their families by years and by 10,000 miles. This American woman's distress seemed selfish and absurd, but, on her terms, reasonable. She was suffering a tragedy of a kind that I can no longer recognize. I should have been delighted that she had such a limited sense of personal tragedy, but personal tragedies are pretty easily felt, aren't they? And, more importantly, do they open up Americans to the pain of others? That we had waged war in Vietnam for ten years is evidence in response. Sorry, madam, I am an adept measurer of pain and yours doesn't count for much. I thought of explaining, but I didn't feel like it. Instead, I stiffly told her, "I understand."

1978

CIVILIZATION AND ISOLATION

by VINE DELORIA

from THE NORTH AMERICAN REVIEW

"Men can be provincial in time, as well as in place," Alfred North Whitehead once remarked. When we apply this insight to the realm of human knowledge, quite frequently we refer to the non-western peoples and point out that they have failed to keep pace with the technical developments that other peoples, particularly western peoples, have made. Thus non-western societies are considered by many social scientists as remnants of stages of human evolutionary growth struggling to reach levels of sophistication that were achieved and surpassed by Europeans many centuries ago. Rarely is the question of provinciality applied directly to western European peoples, and on those occasions we find that provinciality is applied as a criterion to determine efficiency and sophistication within the worldview of that tradition.

Provinciality, however, is a characteristic of societies and individuals who fail to conduct periodic critiques of their beliefs and who assume, with some degree of smugness, that the knowledge they possess, because it has been their possession for so long, provides the basis for intelligent existence in a world of sudden and unexpected change. Western Europeans have been so much dazzled by their own technology that they have fallen into a provinciality in regard to human knowledge so narrow as to exclude major portions of human experience. Whitehead called this attitude the "fallacy of misplaced concreteness," and he meant by this the exclusionary approach to the physical world coupled with the belief that whatever approach one did use properly excluded things that have no value.

When Native Americans have been forced to confront this attitude on the part of non-Indian neighbors we have generally come off second best. A good many factors must be included in any analysis of our failure to confront and overcome the attitude of superiority which non-Indians have thrust upon us. The most important factor would probably be the efficiency of technology which non-Indians brought with them. Marvelous instruments and tools of iron and other metals blinded us and produced an uncritical assumption that whatever the white man was doing must be based upon some superior insight into the world of nature. We forgot, to our detriment, that the first Europeans we encountered thought they were going to sail over the edge of the world, that succeeding expeditions had fantasies about Fountains of Youth, Cities of Gold, and northwest passages to Cathay.

Native Americans did not realize that Europeans felt a dreadful necessity to classify us within a view of the world already made obsolete by discovery of our continent. While we could not participate in the heated theological discussions concerning our origins —whether we derived from Noah's Ark or were survivors of the Ten Lost Tribes of Israel—we perhaps could have been more insistent on making the non-Indians provide more and better arguments for their version of world history and human knowledge. Any group that frantically dug gold in the west in order to transplant it to the east and bury it cannot be quite right and their insights cannot form the highest achievement of our species.

The world is much more sophisticated today, and groups of widely varying backgrounds can communicate with each other even though they form the minority of particular societies. Thus the modern emergence of Indian peoples and the concentration by them on revival and revitalization of culture should include a persistent emphasis on the validity of their own histories, technologies, and social and political institutions. In some measure Indian groups have already begun this process of defending and justifying cultural insights tribes have preserved over the centuries of contact with Europeans. Unfortunately, much of this activity has been phrased in an anti-white format which does not produce a justification of the Indian tradition but merely points out the inadequacies of the non-Indians. We do not take time to adapt this approach to the problem. One glance at the western democracies and we discover that the political leaders, when they are not lusting in their hearts after forbidden fruit, are demonstrating that intelligent life probably does not exist on the planet or, in the alternative, are planning ways to extinguish whatever intelligent life might accidentally arise here.

Transcending this childish tactic of accusatory relationship with the non-Indian is not difficult but it involves creating or re-creating a confidence in the Indian traditions. Such a task initially involves a determination of the techniques which Indians used to accumulate, evaluate, and perpetuate their knowledge of the world and to translate this knowledge into western terms that can speak rationally and intelligently to those people within the western cultural milieu who are prepared to listen. That is a lot of "lates," but above all it is not *too* late. So I will attempt to outline the variances which I see between the western European traditions and the Indian traditions, primarily the North American peoples, with the hopes that the differences —and there are radical differences to be seen—will be illustrated so clearly as to enable us to embark on a new interpretation of human knowledge which is not provincial in either time or space.

If I were to choose the single attribute that characterizes the western approach to human knowledge, indeed to almost all human activities, I would unhesitantly choose "isolation." In scientific and philosophical terms we are perhaps speaking of William of Occam and his famous razor which has cut the throat of more than one effort to synthesize human knowledge. Briefly, we can rephrase this doctrine as the belief that by continual subdivision of any problem we can reach a certain and ultimate knowledge. For most of the last couple centuries the scientific concern with finding the tiniest element of the atom demonstrated the potency of this belief. It also, incidentally, illustrated the basic western belief in the primacy of matter over spirit. But isolation remains the dominating attitude which western peoples have adopted toward the world. We see this approach eloquently in our political institutions and the assumption that one human being is interchangeable with another and that the conglomerate of human decisions, counted statistically, produces the proper course of action for a nation to adopt. This belief reduces wisdom to public opinion polls and produces those nasty and distasteful compromises which substitute for intelligent activities in most of the western democracies.

We find additional confirmation of this belief in isolation in the various religious traditions that are characteristic of western peoples. Almost always, in the last analyses, we find the solitary individual in the hands of an angry, or at least disgruntled, god. Even those western peoples who have rejected the traditional religious denominations of their culture have not found another approach to the religious question but have simply adopted the Oriental version of solitude, listening to one hand clapping, and other symbolic gestures, and are now contentedly recycling their own energies endlessly. Even the atheists and humanists ground their justifications in the primacy of the individual rather than the maturity of the species.

One reason for the scientific and philosophical isolation of the elements of experience is the belief, deeply held although rarely practiced, that one cannot trust sense perceptions, human emotions, or the intuitional abilities of the human personality. This article of faith must certainly go as far back as the Greek philosophers and the prophetic movement in Israel, but was not a dominating factor in western existence until the relatively late period when Descartes, Leibnitz, and Newton demonstrated the efficiency of the mathematical descriptions of the physical world. Since that time western peoples have increasingly depended upon mathematics for their analyses and insights of nature. The approach has proven spectacular in the physical sciences, particularly physics, and the technology that has been produced as a by-product of physical theory has only served to entrench in western minds the belief that mathematics is the proper description of reality. So influential is this attitude that in the last century we have seen the development of social sciences which seem to suggest that statistical truth is equivalent to ultimate reality. The social sciences now insist that all human activities can be described as functions of complicated formulas. I have seen this attitude applied to elections in the United States, but I have generally rejected that approach and bet on the people who counted the votes rather than on those statistics which projected who would vote. Mayor Richard Daley of Chicago, now deceased, never failed me in this respect.

As mathematics has been more influential in representing the scientific quest, and as the scope of human knowledge has expanded, the old tendency toward isolation has produced a strange phenomenon in which human knowledge is divided into separate categories variously called disciplines, fields of study, or what have you. As sciences have given rise to subgrouping of knowledge and specialties have been developed, knowledge itself has suffered a fragmentation and the sole guarantee of the validity of knowledge has been in the similarity of techniques employed to accumulate and interpret data. Briefly, even this field of methodology has degenerated as the various disciplines have moved away from each other, so that the sole criterion of truth today seems to lie in the sincerity of the researcher and his or her relative status within the specific field of endeavor. Sincerity is no guarantee of anything except an emotional state and quite often not much of a characterization even of that.

Isolation, in the oriental context, seems to be the isolation of emotions and personality, but in the western context can only be understood if seen in the context of the physical universe conceived as a giant machine that operates according to certain immutable laws. Conceiving physical reality as if it were a machine not only squeezes emotions and intuitions out of the data but introduces into the data the belief that the unusual cannot occur. Casuality becomes the primary mode of interpreting data and eventually becomes the manner in which people describe a situation, so that even observations of events become incomplete and only the mechanical aspects of the happening are reported.

When this attitude emerges in the field of history its effect is to reduce the intensity of experience and homogenize human activities so that everything can be classified under the same categories of interpretation. History becomes at first a chronology and eventually a trivial commentary that has no criteria by which factors are described or understood. Most contemporary interpretations of world history are simply the imposition of uniformitarian principles on factual data that has been emptied of any human content. Ultimately, history becomes a collection of data of what we would like to believe about the world as dictated by the ideals we hold, rather than even an accurate chronology of what actually happened. We become helpless integers involved in a process over which we have no control and with respect to which we have little understanding.

Perhaps the final consequence of approaching the world with the intent to isolate and thereby achieve dominance over things is the belief that the way we see things is the proper manner of describing them. Thus we approach and reuinite with the original contention that we are dealing with the fallacy of misplaced concreteness. But we have not engaged in a reasoning process as much as taken a tour around the intellectual and conceptual universe of the western European to illustrate the various modes that this basic error can take. A few illustrations may be in order, to demonstrate both the provinciality of the western attitude and the manner in which Indians and dissatisfied non-Indians can begin to move away from this mooring and expand the horizons of all concerned. The treatment of non-western peoples, particularly North American Indian peoples, provides a perfect setting in which we can examine the manner of escape.

The Europeans, arriving in North America, discovered a people that had no written language, laws, religions, or customs, yet governed themselves so well that the American constitutional fathers were encouraged by Benjamin Franklin to model themselves after the Iroquois League when they came to devise a constitution. Europeans, looking at Indian societies, decided that these people lived in savagery because they had no written rules and regulations to govern them. Here we find the intense desire to objectify, to render human activities to mechanical form, and to accord respect by discovering similarity and homogeneity. Finding a qualitative difference between Indians and themselves, the Europeans promptly characterized the North American peoples as a lawless breed devoid of the attributes of civilized society. A great many wrongs were done to Indians because non-Indians believed them to be without laws and therefore unable to make intelligent or just decisions regarding their lives.

All of these beliefs about Indians changed as social science became more influential in western society and more sophisticated in its

44

observations. In 1926, with the publication of Malinowski's famous book, *Crime and Custom in Savage Society,* which demonstrated that customs could be as restrictive and socially integrating as written codes and laws, the perception of people made a radical shift and Indians were considered savages because they were so tightly bound by custom and lacked the freedom of western democratic peoples. How a whole race could shift in one century from most lawless to most law-bound remained a mystery to the Indians who came into contact with western intellectual history, but it should have been an indication to non-Indians that all was not well with the western way of perceiving human activities.

This example illustrates that much of what western peoples have understood as knowledge is simply a reorientation, within their own framework, of the thesis used to interpret phenomena, and is not a corresponding development in the phenomena itself. Even more, the example indicates that no final statement, and perhaps no reliable statement, can ever be made concerning knowledge of the world. There is always another viewpoint by which interpretations of data can be made and when this situation becomes entrenched in the academic worldview of a culture, inevitably the reality that it describes becomes a verbal or mental reality. When phenomena do not fulfill our expectations, they are disregarded, downgraded, or derided and the opportunity to come to grips with another facet of reality escapes us.

When we turn to the North American Indian worldview we discover an entirely different perspective on the world. Instead of isolating things, Indians encompassed them; togetherness, synthesis, and relatedness characterized their experiences of the universe. The ordinary distinctions between mind and matter, human and other life forms, nature and human beings, and even our species and the divinity were not considered valid ways of understanding experience. Life was a complex matrix of entities, emotions, revelations, and cooperative enterprises and any abstraction was considered stupid and dangerous, destructive of spirit and reductionist in the very aspects that made life important. A great many non-Indians have intuited this "togetherness" from observing Indians and reading of the "Indian way," but have failed to understand the remarkable system of relationships which undergirds a seemingly innocent and simple life.

Relatedness is a much better description of the Indian way of looking at the world. Here we are not describing a comparative knowledge in which no absolute value exists. Indeed, all values are absolute because they are experiences and because they deal with specific relationships between specific individuals. A good example of this specificity is the manner in which the Osage Indians fed themselves. In the early spring they would plant their corn along the bottomlands of the Missouri River about the place where St. Louis is today. After they had sown their crop they would depart for the far Rocky Mountains in Colorado and Wyoming to do their summer hunting. The Osage would spend most of the summer in the high mountains hunting deer, buffalo, antelope and other large game animals, and they would dry their meat in the sun, making it suitable for preservation.

In the middle of July they would begin to examine one of the mountain flowers and when this flower began to turn to seed they would know that it was time to begin their journey back to their winter homes. They would pack up their summer's hunting surplus and return to Missouri where their corn would now be ready for the harvest. Such behavior may seem the utmost of simplicity except that to accomplish such a task required that the Osage know the relationships of plants, animals, and lands over a distance of some 1,000 miles and know these complex relationships so well that they could transfer an abstract sense of time, time in the sense of organic growth, from plant to plant over that distance and use the growth of a mountain plant as a gauge or calendar for their corn.

Here we have no general knowledge, no principles valid in all cases, no knowledge that can be tested in the laboratory. We have a knowledge totally unlike western scientific knowledge and yet an understanding of great profundity. Within this scope of knowledge we have an intuitive understanding of the spiritual nature of life which enables people to act in a purposive and predictive sense. Classifications, in this system of thinking, defy western categorization; they are not deductive and cannot be reached through any complicated logical path. Yet they exist and serve amazingly well in determining how a specific people will relate to an environment. Thus if we can learn anything from this example the first lesson must be that classifications, as we have been used to them in the western schemata of knowledge, are useless when we approach a more intimate relationship with the universe.

The hallmark of relatedness or synthesis is experience rather than

46

interpretation. In the synthetic process we first experience the unity of existence and then, upon reflection and further experience, we begin to separate elements of that experience into useful categories of knowledge in which similarities and intimacies are the most important criteria. For that reason most Indian classifications of birds, animals, reptiles, and other life forms begin with the activities of these creatures and seek to identify similar purposive behaviors. Simple morphology, as western peoples have conceived the organic world, have little part in the Indian format; when they do, the morphological features that are chosen are understood as indicating similarity of temperament, not evolutionary origins. Thus our species, birds, and bears are considered to be the "two-leggeds," and we behave in many respects as if we were a single species. A good Indian medicine man can conduct a sophisticated tour of human and animal personality by describing the traits that convinced Indians long ago that the "two-leggeds" were a specific group.

The shift from isolating things to relating them involves the recognition of a different form of preserving knowledge. When we isolate and then interpret phenomena, our basic intent is to derive principles from which we can predict future behavior, illustrate mechanical operations, or analyse into further component parts. Our interpretation and rearrangement of data is most important. In the tradition which relates everything in specific terms the immediate experience is most critical and everything is oriented toward a preservation of the exact conditions under which something happened. Little effort is devoted to rearranging the elements of the incident or experience, for it was the uniqueness of that particular experience that first attracted us and made it seem important. Thus the tradition seeks to preserve as accurately as possible everything that took place.

When we look at the traditions of the North American peoples we discover that they have carried down over the generations many accounts of phenomena we would consider amazing today. The Ojibway of western Ontario, for example, relate stories of the water monster who lived in the lakes and rivers and tipped over the canoes of the unwary and unlucky. Pictures of this creature are liberally scattered over much of Ontario and eastern Canada. The Sioux also relate the story of water monsters and their description correlates to an astounding degree with the Ojibway tale. Further west the Indians of the Pacific Northwest have traditions that the lakes of the region were formerly much larger and contained monsters who stirred the waves unmercifully whenever humans ventured out on the water. A correlation of all accounts, of petroglyphs and pictographs of the various tribes, and an acknowledgment that this particular set of stories is always intimately tied to specific lakes should be sufficient to inform us that at one time within the memory of these tribes, a different and perhaps more spectacular form of life inhabited this continent. If we use our imaginations we can see in this tradition the presence of the group that we have always called "dinosaurs."

Now to suggest that human beings have been living in North America since the Mesozoic is radical only when we restrict our interpretation of human knowledge to that already accumulated by western peoples through the process of isolating elements of experience. The suggestion seems less radical when we remember that the oral traditions do not seek to interpret as much as they attempt to recall and remember precisely the unusual events of the past. The possibility that these stories contain the elements of past experiences is heightened considerably when we view contemporary research on the dinosaurs and discover that the latest and most precise interpretation of this group conceives them as warmblooded, bearing their young live, and traveling in herds, all characteristics of mammals and not reptiles, and possessing behavior patterns not unlike those which the Indian water monster tales relate.

What are we to do when a tradition which has always been seen by western peoples as primitive and superstitious now threatens to become an important source in a new and important revolution in paleontology? Are there other important areas of experience that have been preserved by oral traditions that have been neglected or discarded by the scientific mind because of the all-consuming goal of achieving truth by the isolation of elements of experience? Here we have a dilemma of major proportions which strikes the western mind at precisely the most vulnerable point. Isolation has not produced truth as much as it has produced specialists who studiously avoid synthesis in favor of a continuing subdivision of information into increasingly separated disciplines. We finally arrive at the fundamental question underlying the scope of human knowledge: is truth divisible into categories or is it synthetic, incorporating all aspects of experience and understanding?

The present situation calls for a sense of maturity between cultures that no other period of human history has required. We must now begin to transcend all other parochial considerations in our understanding and move forward into a new period of synthesis in which all information is brought into a coherent whole. Alfred North Whitehead remarked rather casually in *Science and the Modern World* that "it takes a very unusual mind to undertake the analysis of the obvious." Now the obvious always refers to those things that are so commonly accepted as to be considered beyond serious consideration by scholars. So the task of moving human knowledge forward has generally fallen to the amateur, to those who simply wish to know, and to the humble souls who refuse to surrender an idea to the guardians of human knowledge, the academics; those souls who understand knowledge as the possession of the whole human species and not the plaything of the specialist.

North American peoples have an important role to play in the determination of knowledge in the future. They represent thousands of years of experience in living on this continent and their customs and traditions, the particular and sometimes peculiar ways they have of approaching problems, of living, and of protecting the lands, are not simply the clumsy adjustments of primitives but the seasoned responses of people who synthesized and summarized the best manner of adapting themselves to the world in which they lived. Insofar as their insights can be translated into principles which can reorient western thinking, scientific and social, and insofar as North American peoples can understand their own traditions and abide by them, to that degree we can produce a more sophisticated, humane, and sensible society on this continent.

So the provinciality of which Whitehead speaks is really the provincial manner in which we today look at the experiences and memories of our ancestors and define the history of our species and planet. World history, Arnold Toynbee once remarked, is a parochial affair comparable to a map of the Mediterranean area being considered a true and accurate map of the world. Human knowledge cannot be provincial, but must enclose the planet and render an accurate account of its nature and growth. We are today on the threshhold of a new era in which this task will be accomplished— and it is perhaps the most exciting time of any that our species has experienced. Let us have the emotional and intellectual maturity to bring it to pass.

1979

LITERATURE AND LUCRE: A MEDITATION

by LESLIE A. FIEDLER

from GENRE

IT SEEMS TO ME ODD that I have never before, in my long life as a maker and teacher of fictions, talked from a public platform or written for publication about literature and lucre; and even odder that I feel so ill at ease attempting it for the first time. I am not suggesting that I do not ordinarily associate money with the arts I practice and for which I am these days more often than not paid. Indeed, I can scarcely separate the one from the other; since from the moment I was possessed (at age six or seven) by the desire to become a writer, I have been aware that the process—in our society at least—is inextricably involved with making money. Please understand. By "becoming a writer" I do not mean just

50

getting out on to paper what I could no longer contain in my bursting heart and head, which is to fully consummated writing mere masturbation or *ejaculatio praecox*. What I yearned for was to be published, to be read, "to be great, to be known" (in the words of a poem by Stephen Spender which I have never forgotten), to open communication with an audience, to exist for others: utterly alien others, bound to me—unlike family or friends—only after the fact of having read me.

How hypothetical that audience, those alien others might remain, and consequently how unreal, impalpable the recognition, honor and love, I did not at first realize. To be sure, there are occasional letters of response, reviews in the press, even—if one lives long enough—testimonials and ceremonies. But for a long time, money (that one fiction of universal currency) is the only, and indeed always remains the most reliable, token that one has in fact touched, moved, shared one's most private fantasies with the faceless, nameless "you" to whom the writer's all-too-familiar "I" longs to be joined in mutual pleasure. "I stop somewhere waiting for you," is a sentence not just from Walt Whitman's but every writer's love letter to the world. It is only when the first royalty check arrives in the mail (an answer as palpable as a poem) that the writer begins to suspect that the "you" he has had to invent in his lonely chamber, in order to begin writing at all, is real; and that therefore his "I" (not the "I" to which like everyone else he is born, but the fictive "I" which he, in order to be a writer, must create simultaneously with the "you") is real, too.

But this means, as all writers know, though most of us (including me) find it hard to confess, that literature, the literary work, remains incomplete until it has passed from the desk to the market place; which is to say, until it has been packaged, huckstered, hyped and sold. Moreover, writers themselves (as they are also aware) remain reluctant virgins, crying to the world. "Love me! Love me!", until, as the revealing phrase of the trade has it, they have "sold their first piece." What scorn, therefore, the truly published, fully consummated writer has for those *demi-vierges* who publish themselves—turning in spinsterish despair to (again the customary phrase is significant) "Vanity Presses."

The fully published writer, however, feels not just scorn for the half-published and pity for the unpublished, but a kind of guilt, rather like the guilt of those who live by tourism or selling their own bodies. In his case as in theirs, that guilt breeds a kind of resentment against the intermediaries and accomplices who have made possible what he himself has desired. Just as the Western organizers of Rodeo Days hate dudes, or whores and gigolos their pimps, johns and aging benefactors, the commercially successful writer hates agents, editors, publishers, reviewers and the M.C.'s of T.V. Talk Shows—hates finally the poor audience itself for buying what has been offered for sale. That guilt and resentment I must admit I share, though by admitting it I compound my plight. But this surely is one of the reasons why, as I began by confessing, I feel ill at ease in approaching the subject so innocently proposed by the organizers of this symposium. I spoke the general version of this meditation in a setting which both symbolized and aggravated that guilt and resentment, since I had been paid to attend and testify; and I was present therefore, perhaps, not *just* for the sake of the lucre involved, but for that reason among others.

Indeed, I should like to think that the subject which I am treating is one so important to me and the community to which I belong that sooner or later I would have felt obliged to deal with it, even if somebody paid me *not* to do so. But this has not been my fate, so how can I be sure? In any case, here I am taking it up once more in print and for further payment, continuing communication much as I began it: not as one talks (or writes) to an old friend, or even to some one he sits beside on a plane, at a bar; but because there is a contract between us, because we are joined briefly by a cash nexus. In some sense, this, if not quite falsifies, at least uncomfortably modifies the nature of our discourse, creating real possibilities of distrust and misunderstanding. I have been paid to talk and write, while you have paid to listen and read. You, therefore, as you should, feel free, if I do not keep up my end of the bargain, neither entertain nor enlighten you, let's say, to grumble and complain: but *not*, in any case, to get your money back—not from me. It is a strange business, in which I am an entrepreneur, or rather a non-entrepreneur, guaranteed against risk.

But this is precisely the situation in which I have written and spoken for all of my professional life: as a novelist, poet, teacher, scholar and critic-pedagogue. Like other critic-pedagogues, I am not only paid for public performance; but I get free books for which other people pay hard cash, and am invited to attend without paying admission plays and movies for which others must buy tickets at the box-office. Moreover, I and my peers, or at least those among us who have access to commercial journals, are rewarded for a second time by being paid for registering in print our opinions of those books, movies and plays: opinions which *must* be (I sometimes uncomfortable suspect) radically different from the responses of those we address, precisely because having paid their way into the theatre, they have an investment to protect.

Even scholar-pedagogues who, out of a snobbishness desire to remain "pure," refuse to publish in paying journals like *The New York Times Book Review, The Times Literary Supplement* or, God forbid, *Esquire* and *Playboy* (in all of which, I must confess, I have appeared), cannot really escape the commercial trap. Unless willing to perish, they must publish *somewhere*; if only in subsidized journals of high prestige and low readability, like the PMLA, to which I have never contributed. But the readership of such journals consists not just of specialists in certain fields (unlike the readers of popular magazines, more inclined to disapprove than approve what they have paid for), but also the Promotion and Tenure committees of the Universities to which the contributors belong. Such committees will, on the basis of such articles, grant them tenure or promotion: thus guaranteeing that they will be paid more for repeating in the classroom what they have already published, or rehearsing what they hope to publish next. Eventually, moreover, such articles are gathered together, revised and expanded to make scholarly books, which have to be subsidized either by their authors or the schools in which they teach, since they are bought only by University Libraries, from whose shelves (a recent study has discovered) some seventy percent of them are *never* taken out.

Nonetheless, when these already over-subsidized pedagogues have persisted long enough in producing goods for which there is a reward but no market, they are likely to receive Grants and Fellowships, the most prestigious funded from carefully invested money, originally accumulated by Robber Barons like the Rockefellers, the Guggenheims and the Fords—which is to say, the filthiest American lucre of all. Furthermore, when they have attained seniority and prestige (or sometimes long before, while they are still only needy and promising) they may be asked to compile, collaborate in or merely lend their names to Freshman Texts. Carefully tailored to maximum classroom demand as determined by market analysts, such texts are the academic equivalents of block-busting best-sellers by Jacqueline Susann, or Harold Robbins, Think, for instance, of Brooks' and Warren's inordinately successful *Understanding Poetry,* at once smugly elitist and happily profitable.

But this is not better, after all, than "selling out to Hollywood" like that backsliding Ivy League Professor, Erich Segal; or leaving the respectable sponsorship of Princeton University Press for the fleshpots of Simon and Schuster, who are not only the publishers of my own most recent book, but (I reassure myself) of Joseph Heller's *Catch-22,* a novel "taught" by some of my anti-commercial colleagues. Indeed, many, perhaps the great majority of the books taught by even the most snobbish and genteel among us were written by men shamelessly involved with the marketplace: Shakespeare, Richardson, Balzac, Dickens, Mark Twain, Scott Fitzgerald, Faulkner, Hemingway, and Arthur Miller, Norman Mailer and Saul Bellow, to name only the first that come to mind. Morever, in the last three or four decades, many writers we "require" in class have compounded their complicity by themselves becoming teachers, i.e., secondary as well as primary hucksters.

But, I remind myself, only a generation or two ago "serious" creative writers (the heirs of Modernist elitism and Marxist politics) considered employment in the university—that front for what our own students were still calling in the sixties "the industrial-military complex"—a kind of "selling-out" comparable to taking a job with an advertising agency or MGM or Henry Luce: a search for low-level security in place of high-risk ventures in the arena of High Culture. Not in Grub Street, be it understood, but in Bohemia; that anti-Market Place, in which, after the invention of the Avant Garde and the raising of the slogan *"Epatez la bourgeoisie,"* "true artists" were imagined as starving, while pseudoartists flourished.

Even in the hey-day of Modernism, the legend of *la vie de Bohème* did not deceive everyone. Sigmund Freud, for instance, remained faithful enough to the Reality Principle to argue that *all* artists were driven by fantasies of becoming beloved, famous and rich. And George Bernard Shaw, always the enemy of pious hypocrisy, ironically made the same point in his famous argument with Samuel Goldwyn over the filming of *My Fair Lady,* a musical based on his *Pygmalion*. "The trouble," he is reputed to have said, "is that you, Mr. Goldwyn, think about nothing but art, while all I think of is money." He is less likely to have been influenced by Freud, however, than by his true-blue English predecessor, Dr. Samuel Johnson, who is on record as believing that money is the "purest" of all motives for writing; by which I presume he meant it is the truest, the least likely to be mere cant and self-deceit. In any case, I remember both Shaw and Johnson each time I enter a group of strangers engaged in passionate debate, and discover that if they are discussing literature, nine times out of ten they turn out to be business men, but if they are talking about money, they are likely to be writers.

In America, however—perhaps precisely because among us commerce is offically more honored than art—our eminent writers have not typically spoken with equal candor on the subject of literature and lucre. Certainly, the great novelists of the mid-nineteenth century, celebrated in F. O. Matthiessen's *The American Renaissance* and D. H. Lawrence's *Studies in Classic American Literature,* have chosen self-pity over irony or frankness in talking about their relationship to the marketplace. The classic statement is Melville's, "Dollars damn me . . . all my books are botches. . . ." And implicit in this melancholy cry from the heart is a belief, as strong and pertinacious as any myth by which we live, that the authentic writer is neither drawn to nor confirmed in his vocation by the hope of marketplace success, the dream of becoming rich and famous; but can only be seduced by lucre, led to betray or prostitute his talent.

Paradoxically, American culture came of age at the very moment when old aristocratic sponsors of the arts were being replaced by the mass audience and the masters of the new media, who profit by responding to its taste. The first of these media was print, and the first truly popular genre, the Novel. But this is also the American form *par excellence*, invented even as we were inventing our Republic; and in it, the first American authors achieved fame for themselves and the culture which nurtured them. A commodity, mass produced and mass distributed, it offered its practitioners the possibility of growing rich as well as famous. But from the start, that possibility remained more promise than fact, at least for writers like Charles Brockden Brown, Edgar Allan Poe, Nathaniel

55

Hawthorne and Herman Melville, who thought of themselves as producing "literature."

Before the first of these sophisticated novelists (all male) had begun to write, "best sellers" were already being turned out by other more naive, less pretentious authors (largely female), whose taste and fantasy coincided with that of the popular audience, itself largely female. Even over the long haul, the books loved by most Americans who read anything between covers at all have not been *Moby Dick* and *The Scarlet Letter* nor even *Huckleberry Finn*, which live now chiefly as assigned reading in classrooms, but a series of deeply moving though stylistically undistinguished fictions, which begins with Susanna Rowson's *Charlotte Temple*, reaches a nineteenth-century high-point with Harriet Beecher Stowe's *Uncle Tom's Cabin* and a twentieth-century climax with Margaret Mitchell's *Gone With the Wind*. The last, though never approved by "serious" critics and seldom required in "serious" courses in literature, is still sold in paperback reprints; and, translated into the newer, more popular post-Gutenburg media of film and T.V., is probably known to a larger world-wide audience than any other American fiction.

For a century and a half, those writers among us who aspire to critical acclaim and an eternal place in libraries, have therefore felt compelled to struggle not just for their livelihood but for their very existence against the authors of "best sellers," whom they secretly envy and publicly despise. This cultural warfare may seem at first glance a struggle of the poor against the rich, the failed against the successful. But the situation is more complex than this since in terms of culture rather than economics, art novelists and their audience "fit though few" constitute a privileged, educationally-advantaged minority; while popular novelists and their mass readership remain a despised *lumpen* minority, whose cultural insecurity is further shaken when their kids learn in school to question their taste.

The struggle of High Art and Low is, moreover, a battle of the sexes. Referring to the writers who had preempted the paying audience before he ever entered the scene, Nathaniel Hawthorne called them a "damn'd mob of scribbling women." And, indeed, from Mrs. Rowson to Jacqueline Susann, the authors of monumental, long-lasting popular successes have continued to come from the sex which thinks of itself as otherwise exploited, oppressed, dominated in a patriarchal society. Unlike other oppressive minorities, however (white slave owners, for example), it is possible for both males and the cultural elite to contend, with a certain superficial plausibility, that they are victims rather than victimizers. And, indeed, both primary and secondary literature in the United States, the novels and poems of which we are most proud and the critical autobiographical works written on them, reflect the myth of the "serious" writer as an alienated male, condemned to neglect and poverty by a culture simultaneously commercialized and feminized.

There are prototypes of this myth in remotest antiquity: the legend of Euripides, for instance, first avant-garde artist in the West, having been hunted to death by a pack of angry women (or, alternatively, dogs); while behind even that is the primal image of Dionysus, torn to pieces by Bacchantes, eager to still his singing and exact revenge for their slighted sex. It is Poe, however, who first embodies that image for the American imagination, at least as he has been re-interpreted for us by French poets of the *décadence*, Baudelaire and Mallarmé, who celebrated him as a *poète maudit, "un Byron egaré dans le nouveau monde."* But even earlier, Poe had collaborated, as it were, with his friend-enemy Rufus Griswold to create a demi-fictional portrait of himself as a dope-ridden alcoholic, dying in the streets of Baltimore after a long starvation and neglect in an environment hostile to art.

That image of the true artist destroyed by a money-grubbing society, though originally the hybrid offspring of Southern American self-hated and the French contempt for everything in our culture except its presumed victims, throve in the New World. Reembodied generation after generation, it is most notably exemplified after Poe by Herman Melville, whom we rejoice to imagine drudging away his last unhappy years in the Custom House, unpublished, unhonored, forgotten; and Scott Fitzgerald, dying in shabby surroundings in a Hollywood which preferred Mammon to literature, and had no sense that this failed alcoholic scriptwriter was destined to outlive in glory the most celebrated producers, directors and actors of his time. That Poe and Melville and Fitzgerald failed not because they despised lucre and shunned the marketplace, but precisely because they were so desperately committed to the American dream of "making it," the legend does not permit us to remember.

We really know that Fitzgerald began by producing best-selling novels and peddling hastily written short stories to family magazines at prices which mounted with his fame; and that he ended by squandering away a larger fortune than ordinary Americans can imagine earning in a lifetime of backbreaking work. Poe, too, though never as successful, even momentarily, spent his brief career as a hack-writer and editor of commercial literary journals in pursuit of the common reader and the quick buck. Indeed, the fantasies which drove them both are betrayed in stories like Poe's "The Goldbug" and Fitzgerald's "A Diamond as Big as the Ritz"— the dream of innocently acquiring guilty treasure, and the nightmare of losing everything.

Similarly, the mad, metaphysical quest of Melville's *Moby Dick* begins as a carefully planned commercial venture, with Ishmael bargaining for his fair share of the profits. And why not—in light of the fact that Melville's mad, metaphysical career began with the best seller, *Typee.* Indeed, he never ceased trying to recapture his initial rapport with the popular audience. Even *Pierre*, whose underlying theme is the plight of the alienated artist in America, he assured his publisher (and perhaps believed himself) was "a rural bowl of milk," i.e., a domestic romance as palatable to the large female audience as to the somewhat smaller male one who had admired his adventure stories.

The pathos of such writers, whether they ended in insanity and withdrawal like Melville or in premature death like Poe and Fitzgerald, is not that they nobly refused to provide what the marketplace demanded, but that they tried to do so and failed. But this is not the story which the American mass audience likes to be told, since they need to be assured that the writers they choose only posthumously to honor (if not read) in some sense died for their sins: their lack of sensibility, mindless pursuit of profit, indifference to art—but not to artists, particularly failed ones, after they are dead. Realizing how in our world nothing succeeds like failure—certain lesser writers, from Rufus Griswold to Budd Schulberg, have produced parasitic best sellers about the tragic fates of Poe and Fitzgerald.

It may have been booze that destroyed Poe or Fitzgerald, but the great public prefers to believe they did it with their little hatchets—thus feeling at once powerful and guilty: a potent emotional mix for all true Americans. Certainly, we do not seem to derive as much satisfaction from contemplating the careers of eminent writers who have made it, dying, like Harriet Beecher Stowe, honored and rich—though cheerfully batty. It is, for instance, Mark Twain's final loneliness and melancholia we prefer to dwell on, or his many failures along the way. Yet though Twain went bankrupt as often as any other capitalist entrepreneur of the Gilded Age, at the end he was able to support a splendiferous house, and a set of bad habits which compelled him to smoke forty Havana cigars a day and to drink enough Old Grandad to send him to bed insensible night after night. He had finally grown so wealthy, indeed, that the only people he felt he could talk to as equals were Henry Rogers, Vice President of Standard Oil, and Andrew Carnegie, whom he addressed as "St. Andrew" in letters signed "St. Mark."

Ironically, his fortune was based on the continuing success of *Huckleberry Finn,* which is to say, the classic version of the American antisuccess story. We are asked to love Huck (and to prove our love by buying the book in which he appears) for running away, not just from school, church and family, but money as well: that guilty-innocent treasure which he and Tom had stumbled on at the end of *Tom Sawyer,* but which he, unlike Tom and the hero of Poe's "The Gold Bug," ultimately rejects. What Twain never wrote was a fictional account of a boy like himself, who, instead of "lighting out for the territory ahead of the rest," stayed home, grew up (as he would not let Tom grow up), permitted himself to be "civilized" by his wife and daughter; and at last got rich by writing about another eternal child who made all the opposite choices. Before the middle of the twentieth century, in fact, there is no respectable American book which portrays sympathetically an author who made good. Even Horatio Alger's disreputable juveniles, though they portray striking it rich as a truly Happy Ending, deal with boys who rose from rags to riches by becoming not writers but merchants or bankers.

Only in the last decade of this century did it become possible, first in fact, then in fiction, for a novelist highly regarded by critics (Norman Mailer is an example) to become wealthy long before his

59

death by having his books chosen as major Book Club Selections; then signing million dollar paperback contracts; and finally appearing on T.V. Talk Shows, where (becoming, as it were, his own Griswold or Schulberg) he played the mythological role of the writer for the benefit of an audience which had not read, never would read his work. Even novelists who shun all publicity, like J. D. Salinger and Thomas Pynchon, accumulate royalties comparable to those earned by such critically despised darlings of the populace as Harold Robbins and Jacqueline Susan. Only Saul Bellow, however, Nobel Prize Winner and Laureate of the New Conservatism, has thus far dared translate this new-style Happy Ending from life to literature. And this is perhaps why his *Humboldt's Gift* has been universally (willfully, I suspect) misunderstood by its critics.

It seems, at first, a rather conventional elegy for a *poète maudit:* the last, somewhat improbable heir to the tradition of Poe, Melville and Fitzgerald, reborn this time as a failed New York Jewish intellectual—a super-articulate, self-defeating *luftmensch,* who has died abandoned and penniless before the action of the novel begins. It has been suggested by many, including Bellow himself, that the model for Humboldt was the poet, Delmore Schwartz, who had indeed come to such a shabby end. But while there is a great deal of Schwartz in Humboldt, he is finally the portrait not of any single individual but of a whole generation of Jewish-American losers: including, surely, Bellow's one-time guru and life-long friend, Issac Rosenfeld, also dead before reaching forty, his handful of stories and essays remembered by a shrinking handful of aging admirers; and perhaps Lenny Bruce as well, that hipster and stand-up comedian who O.D.'d in 1966. Reading of Humboldt's fate, I cannot, in any case, help thinking of *all* those mad, bright young Jewish Americans, still caught up in the obsolescent myth of the Artist as Victim, and dead before they had lived long enough to realize, like Bellow, that in prosperous America it was no longer necessary to end as a Beautiful Loser.

In any case, Bellow's book is called not *Humboldt* but *Humboldt's Gift;* and the recipient of that gift, that not-so-beautiful Winner, Charlie Citrine, is its real hero. For a little while, Citrine (who at times seems scarcely distinguishable from his author) finds in Humboldt's death and his own survival, an occasion for guilt—the guilt we have long been trained to think of as the inevitable accompaniment of making it. But in the end, he succeeds in convincing himself that Humboldt has died for him, that all such losers die for all winners; leaving us as a heritage not empty regrets but a saleable story: his story once, our story now, the book we are reading. Properly exploited, that story can (in the fiction we read) be sold to the movies, or (in the larger world outside) clinch for its author the Nobel Prize; make us survivors, in short, rich enough to meet the obligations of the prosperous living: alimony, mortgage payments, credit card debits, fifty percent income taxes. And if we weep a little, remembering those others whom we loved and betrayed and by whose death we profited, we can (as the old saying has it) cry all the way to the bank.

1981

61

MEMORIES OF UNHOUSEMENT, A MEMOIR

by CLARK BLAISE

from SALMAGUNDI

I.

Before the Interstate system obliterated the old America, you used to come upon them at country cross-roads: clusters of white arrows tipped in black, pointing in every direction. Somewhere on the Plains you would see it, slow down, and be thrilled: *Denver 885*, it would say, or *New Orleans 1045*, or better yet, *Los Angeles 2000*. How they got there, who decided on the city and the mileage, I'll never know. Perhaps they had taken over from the whitewashed rocks, the dabs of tar, left by earlier waves of lost, impatient travelers, when twenty or thirty miles a day was more than fair measure. Nowadays, the green mirror-studded billboards conspire to keep our minds on the effortlessly attainable, the inevitable. No more than two destinations, they seem to say, don't tease us with prospects greater than our immediate ambition. *Glens Falls*, the one nearest to me now says *Saratoga Springs 18*.

We are deprived of that special thrill when our destination, our crazy, private destination, made its first appearance in one of those black-tipped clusters. No reason at all that on a road between Chicago and Madison, just outside Beloit, Wisconsin, WINNIPEG should miraculously appear. Yet in 1949 when I was nine and guiding my father on our longest trip home, it did. Nine hundred miles in a '47 Chevy, with its split windshield, high fenders and curved chrome bars over the dashboard radio, for my salesman-father was a typical, fifteen-hour long haul. But for old-times' sake he'd break journey in Detroit Lakes, he said. Detroit Lakes, in northern Minnesota, was where they'd honeymooned in 1939. Up there in the headwaters of the Mississippi is where I was conceived, I suppose.

I was born in Fargo, North Dakota, in 1940. Along with Roger Maris and William Gass and Larry Woiwode. In that *Ragtime* spirit that haunts us all, I sometimes think of my mother pushing the pram, of Mrs. Woiwode pushing hers, of little Roger Maris, then six, dashing past us, bat on shoulder. Billy Gass, a bifocular teenager, squints a moment at these figures of life, then returns to the ice castle of his imagination. "The Pedersen Kid" crystallizing even then. *Beyond the Bedroom Wall* gurgles in his stroller. Babe Ruth's assassin takes a few mean cuts. I am the only Canadian writer born in Fargo, North Dakota.

There is nothing obscure, really, about Fargo. In 1977, at a cocktail party in New Delhi, India, I found myself talking to an agreeable, white-haired American with a professional manner, the U.S. Agricultural attache. My India-born wife was serving that year as the director of a Canadian academic-exchange program. She was a quasi-diplomat.

"I consider myself half a Canadian, really," he said.

"I'm more than half American myself," I replied.

We shared a smile, wondering who would explain himself first. "I was born in North Dakota," I said. Then, covering my tracks, I added, "My parents had just emigrated."

"I was about to say almost the same thing. Where in North Dakota?"

"Fargo."

"Amazing."

He was the first North Dakotan I had ever met. "What year would that have been,' he asked. "Forty, forty-one?"

"April, 1940."

"I was just finishing my M.A. at North Dakota State that spring. My wife was an O.B. nurse."

Parallel lives were beginning to converge, as though a collision course, plotted by children on separate planets, had suddenly become inevitable. We said together, "St. John's Hospital."

I added, "Dr. Hanna."

He called his wife over. As she put her drink down and turned to join us, he said, "How would you like to meet the first person you ever saw?"

We always returned to Winnipeg whenever my father ran out of work. Or when unmentionable things occurred. We had left Pittsburgh in 1945, Cincinnati in 1943, Fargo in 1942, and—a week before—Leesburg, Florida. Everytime we left, we headed back to Winnipeg, my mother's city.

My father was from the village of Lac Megantic, a few mountain ridges north of Maine, directly south of Quebec City. Winnipeg must have been a torture to him. I remember him, slicing luncheon meats in an upstairs bedrom in my grandmother's house, sipping beer and smoking Canadian cigarettes whose cork-tips inflamed his lips, next to a leaking window; he never spoke of his dislikes. He never warned us. He merely acted without apology. He was probably not entirely sane.

Once in Pittsburgh, in an outburst that still lies blottered somewhere, he'd discovered a fellow-salesman sneaking back to the floor just minutes after ducking out for lunch. While my father supposedly ate—he had a weakness for restaurants, for sitting at a table and being served, a leisurely lunch bespoke respectability—the other salesman let himself out of the men's room cubicle, where he'd downed a sandwich, and let himself back on the floor. He'd intended a clear hour to himself, writing up every sale and crediting himself with every commission. The rules dictate full credit to the lone name on the final bill. It discourages lunch-hours, among other things.

My father was hiding in the other cubicle. He came back and found the scab writing up one of his juicier sales. My father, even at his most sociopathic, could be a charming man. I came to fear those eruptions of charm. Frenchmen, as Quebeckers of his generation were usually called ("Hey, Frenchie!") are often very charming. Especially to Americans. My father looked more Jewish than French, more gypsy than Jew. He spoke furniture-yiddish and ring-Italian. I am his genetic miscue. Though always impeccably dressed—his code was as inflexible as an autodidact's stiff vocabulary—he appears to me now, two years dead, in a bandana and earrings, a billowing black shirt and dark, baggy pants, tucked

64

into his greasy boots. There should be a tribe, somewhere, that combines all his somber talents.

My father possessed—or, rather, it possessed him—a murderous temper. He had pounded out twenty victories in three weight-divisions, in two countries, under various names that served him like flags of convenience, until finally being hammered himself by an eventual champion. Thereafter he'd confined his skills to Canada's most successful export industry, helping assure the delivery of Montreal's finest whiskey to parched, Prohibition-dry New York. I learned all this later from his last wife, a cautious woman with police connections in Pittsfield, Massachusetts. She'd had his record routinely checked, after marrying him and growing suspicious. Fifty years ago, or longer now, he'd "been known" to every policeforce between Troy and Burlington. No gesture in the universe is ever lost. They never pinned murder on him, but there had been assault and manslaughter and even an accessory charge, later dropped. He was in the hospital by then, bounced between surgery and intensive care; legs gone, lungs clotted, a face reduced to that sloping nose and fleshy, slightly-folded ears.

The charm and the sledge-hammer. It is 1945, a year I cannot believe I've lived through. We are on the fifth floor of the Pittsburgh Sears, during the putative lunch-break of two very hungry salesmen. My father called his colleague over. He asked him to bring the order book. He smiled so graciously at the customers, his customers from a missed supper the night before, that they were reassured. *No, no*, he grinned, *quite all right*.

The order book was long and narrow and thick. Gripped at its bound end and then snapped against a flat object, it emitted a sharp, satisfying crack, like a solid jab or a clean base hit. The flat, astonished cheek of the salesman was such a surface and my father tatooed each cheek as though they'd been the alternate sides of a small punching bag, until, even with slaps, a cheek like a leather bag can gradually unravel.

That finished him with Sears and for awhile, banished him from the States. We crossed into Canada at Niagara Falls that midnight and were in Winnipeg three days later. That was the earlier time, 1945. Canada was still at War, the same war that (I was told) had sent us to North Dakota in 1939. Canada, part of Britain's war effort, would be on the front lines as soon as the Luftwaffe finished mopping up. German U-Boats already controlled the Gulf of St.

Lawrence. The French islands of St. Pierre and Miguelon, off the coast of Newfoundland, were rebelling against the Vichy regime; no one knew how long that would last, a fog-bound Casablanca. Newfoundland and Labrador, British crown colonies and still ten years away from joining Canada, would of course be ceded to the Nazis, just like the Channel Islands. The Frenchies in Quebec refused to fight an English War; Adrien Arcand and his brownshirts were poised for a *putsch*, whenever Hitler ordered it. Which left Ontario, in 1939 and '40, feeling itself in the probable frontline of combat, with Lindbergh-style collaborationists controlling the States, the *Bunds* of Buffalo stirring up border-hate. I'd never been in a War. In Pittsburgh of 1945, I didn't feel part of a War, not like Winnipeg.

My father, a French-Canadian, never even considered fighting an English war. By his lights, justly so. He was barely over-age for the American draft. Brawny, steel-making Pittsburgh had been a good place for a salesman to sit out the hostilities. But for that unprincipled salesman and my father's temper, we might have stayed; no gesture in the universe escapes consequence.

This is my first memory: the soldiers at Canadian customs, their jaunty berets. The smell of a different tobacco in the air. My uncle in his Colonel's khaki, the Passchendaele medals on his chest, smoking thick pieces of glass for me and my cousins. The scientists of the free world had gathered in Winnipeg in 1945 for a spectacular view of a solar eclipse. I remember my twin cousins, limber girls of eight, doing backward flips all around my grandmother's house.

II.

For most Canadians the differences between their country and the United States are minimal. The majority of English-speaking Canadians cross the border without papers, taking their places in the United States (we like to think) as nobler sorts of Americans. More respectful, less bumptious, better educated. Lofty types, a touch disdainful; Galbreaths all. We queue up, we don't litter. Compare any large Canadian city with an American counterpart: the difference is obvious and public pride is deeply layered. If we saw anything drop from a car window, or onto the sidewalk, my mother would mutter, "Americans!" There is something to it. Most public facilities in the United States resemble relics from a combat zone. It's hard for Canadians to avoid a little smugness, even those who emigrate.

But there is another kind of Canadian; smaller in number but infinitely richer in influence, who pounces upon every distinction, magnifies it and cherishes the disparity. It might be said that he keeps alive a certain Confederation Flame, for without his voice, Canada would certainly yield to profit and convenience and become, officially, a clean and prosperous corner of the United States. It might be said they are the reason Canada was created and the reason it still exists: to draw fine distinctions, to show that individual liberty and the pursuit of happiness is not the only reason for existing as a nation. To many Canadians, the American is a person who doesn't hesitate shooting a stranger for running over his lawn, for honking at a red light. These Canadians prefer their quiet, more authoritarian country, the sovereignty of parliament and not the litigious individual. They read Canadian magazines and sometimes British, they go only to movies listed as "Canadian or Foreign"; thus acknowledging the peculiar status of things American, they watch (and listen) exclusively to the CBC. Mention "the States" to them and you might pull a blank. "I was in Fargo once," a cousin might say. "Small town. Ugly."

"New York? God, no thanks. You can get killed there."

The only Canadians I know who genuinely *like* the United States are of course the French-speakers. And for good reason. The French-Canadian, when he leaves home on this continent, is tolerated only in the United States. In Toronto, I have heard the familiar retort, "Speak White!" I've seen my (one-time) fellow Torontonians demand of young Quebec tourists, chatting away on the immaculate Toronto subway, to *please* remember where they are; that so much jabbering in French is giving everyone a headache and no matter what Trudeau is trying to do to the country it won't work because it was settled when Wolfe defeated Montcalm and affirmed when they hanged Louis Riel and they ought to hang Rene Levesque too. On Prince Edward Island, in a tourist home modelled on Anne of Green Gables, the landlady, in showing us our rooms and remarking on my Quebec license plates (but not on my French name) confided in me, "the white man built this country! What are the French trying to do?"

At Old Orchard Beach, *l'etat Maine*, or in many parts of south

Florida, America has capitulated to the French fact. Commercial greed, a tradition of tolerance, or simple confidence conspire to make French a conquering language. And all winter long, the tanned Quebecois flock back to Dorval Airport in the most outrageous motley of straw hats and Palm Beach T-shirts, straw bags stuffed with grapefruit. The last Americans. Levesque said as much, appealing to Americans for support: I am the George Washington of my people. I hear more *joual* on the streets of New York than in Toronto.

When my father quit the liquor-escorting business, after deserting his first two wives, he found himself in depression-cold Montreal, thirty-seven, unskilled though not untalented. He'd always sold things, apart from special services, and now he offered his salesmanship to the T. Eaton Company, then considered the world's largest department store. Montreal was Canada's most important city. If wealth had been preserved in those desperate years, it was to be found in the English community of Montreal, a minority of the population with a corner on nearly all its commercial holdings.

My father spoke good English. After all, he'd been up and down the Hudson Valley both as a fighter and as a smuggler and most of his family, by this time, had settled in Manchester, New Hampshire and Fall River, Massachusetts. It was fluent English, the way Trudeau's and Levesque's is fluent, but it was different from his French. A little coarser, with damns and hells when he didn't need them, and other words inappropriate to their context. In English he could be emphatic but not always convincing. At the same time, his childhood and adolescent French had deserted him. He had underworld French, but in truth he had no language, no voice; only expletives. It came as a shock to me, towards the very end of his life, when in a wheelchair he visited us in Paris and confided, "If I went back to Montreal I could speak French again. A couple of months and I could speak it as good as you."

The point is this. First, by unstated rules, and then by directive, he was not permitted to serve English-speaking customers. For him, it would be the priests and nuns, the spinsters with anglicized taste, the maids and charladies of Cote-des-Neiges and Westmount wealth. Whenever the blustery, regimental sorts with their Great War medals still on their blazer pockets came in, my father was instructed to call Mr. Fraser to come over and help, and eventually, write up the sale. I enter the story only because the interior decorator, to whom he once complained, spoke to the manager. She seemed to be a fair-minded woman, educated, European-trained, and from the West. In 1939 she became his third wife, and they headed off to Winnipeg, and from Winnipeg my father wrote letters and Sears of Fargo gave him a chance. They went to Detroit Lakes to celebrate.

My first long exposure to Canada took place ten years later, following one of my father's failures in the southern part of the United States. Oh, I know what drives a Canadian, especially a French-speaking one, farther and farther south, until he can go no further! Warmth. Heat. *Look, son, how it shimmers!* Light as thick as syrup bouncing off our car. Seat leather that sizzles. *Ouch!* my mother cried. Oh, give me a home where the highway ahead looks wet twelve months a year! He was made for swimming trunks; a dark man with an hourglass build who could sleep all day in the sun and glow like walnut at night. Mosquitoes found him unappealing. Women did not. There were so many I lost count, once I learned how to measure them. The only truth I have to go on is that *any* woman he talked to outside of the strictest necessity: any waitress, any bank-teller, any secretary, any neighbor—any woman whose first name he knew (or denied knowing)—was also his part-time companion. Otherwise, he avoided women all together. What could he possibly talk about?

We'd driven up from Florida. Those clustered signposts served us well: *Atlanta 605. New Orleans 590.* We were tearing around America, rolling double-sixes around the old Monopoly board. One day for Florida, another for Georgia. Then they came fast: Tennessee, Kentucky, Indiana, Illinois, and before the half-week was out, that sign in Beloit: *Winnipeg 945.* We were in the green and watery states now, in the lee of Canada: Wisconsin and Minnesota. We were in Fargo for an afternoon and I wandered down the main street of my, and Roger's hometown. He was fifteen now; prime for scouting. We drove past the house we'd lived in, that spring of 1940: Fifth Street, S. E.

They identified the next door neighbor's house for me; we knocked but no one was home. Their name was Hinckle. Mr. Hinckle, back in the summer and fall of 1940, had loved to hold me (my father did not); the only infant-pictures I have were taken by

Mr. Hinckle, or by his wife while I was in his arms. A great many years later, in 1973, I published a book of short stories in Canada which, by luck, was reviewed in the Minneapolis *Tribune*. A line in the review moved me, and I repeat it here: "by opening himself to us, he makes it possible for us to better know ourselves." And a few weeks later I received, forwarded by my publisher, a letter from a nursing home in St. Paul, from Mrs. Hinckle, writing in a firm hand, asking if I had possibly been born in Fargo in 1940. She'd never had children, but she'd always thought herself a mother to me. Mr. Hinckle would have been so happy to read this marvelous review. It was in one of those stories that I had written, *no gesture in the universe is ever lost*, in a context that I had tried to make absurd. Now I know that it is the core of all my beliefs.

III

That afternoon in Fargo as I walked on Fifth Street, S.E., feeling attached to the concrete that had possibly supported my pram and to the trees that had, years earlier, bloomed in Mrs. Hinckle's lens, a car slowed down and a window unrolled. Those were Manitoba windows, with their inside sheets of frost-free plastic, and I responded to them as emblems of an even earlier, purer hometown than Fargo. Winnipeg was where all my mother's memories came to rest, where my grandparents and all my relatives lived, and it being only five hours away, it was the city where I would be spending that night and, for all I knew, the rest of my life.

"Sonny?" the driver asked. A resonant, kindly, crinkly, northern voice. He had sandy hair and a reddish moustache. No Americans wore moustaches in those days, except cads and lovers in Hollywood movies. Thirty years ago, Canadians really looked and sounded different, surrogates of Britain, even in border-state situations. (I realize now that *of course*, especially in border confrontations with the United States, Canadians enjoy their only dominance: the might of Vancouver, Calgary, Winnipeg, Toronto and Montreal, exerted against the puny, unpeopled northern fringes of Washington, Montana, North Dakota, and upstate New England. The only exceptions were Detroit and Buffalo, and even there Canadians felt a moral smugness.) I knew which side of this particular border I belonged on.

"Sonny?"

"Yessir?" I answered, still the obedient, drawling Southern boy.
"You from around here?"

Judging from the way my cousins were about to receive me,
pretending (I thought) not to understand a word I said, I must have
answered, *"Ah wuz boned raht cheach."*

"Then pardon my French but where the Hell is the Moorhead
Bridge?"

Moorhead, Minnesota, faces Fargo from across the Red River.
My mother had had her first labor pains on that bridge, where she
walked every day. She'd made it sound (as she always did, in all
her stories) an exciting chase, which side got an agent to her first.
I'd felt myself competed for: the underpopulated hunger of North
Dakota against the progressive Sky Blue Waters of Minnesota. A
North Dakota birth was just right for me: manageably modest, yet
special. Minnesota was too important, too American, it mattered
too much in the American scheme of things. If I had to be born an
American, let it be North Dakota.

And then it just spilled out. "Y'all lookin for St. Boniface,
aincha?"

The driver's head sort of rested, rolling slightly, on the edge of
the window, unable to compute, precisely, what had just been
heard. St. Boniface was the French-speaking twin city of Winnipeg, just across this same Red River. The river only divided states
in America; in Canada it symbolized infinitely more. My cousins in
Winnipeg had never crossed the river except to skim far eastward,
into the fishing waters of the Whiteshell, near Kenora. Whenever
my father visited Winnipeg, he found many reasons to go over to
St. Boniface and he often took me with him. Winnipeg was that
kind of city to me; a macrocosm of my family, a microcosm of the
country, achingly close yet out of reach from the town of my birth.

"Did you *hear* that?" the man was asking, turning to his wife and
elderly passengers in the back seat. *St. Boniface* and snorts of
laughter. "Yes, son. How do I get to your St. Boniface?"

Of course I didn't have the slightest notion. If we were on Fifth,
I reasoned, the numbers probably got smaller as they approached
the water. My own street ran slightly downhill; I pointed the car
straight ahead.

My parents came along shortly. We drove down the main street,
visited Sears—the agent of our Americanization—and then we
were gone again, following the river north to Grand Forks, and

71

eventually, Pembina, the border, and Emerson, where Canada started. Like many children, I suppose, I held my breath till we crossed the border and inhaled deeply of Canadian air, convinced it was something purer than the stuff I'd just expelled.

Of all the distinctions I have invented in my life, (and come to believe in, with the force of myth), the differences between Canada and the United States—so frail in reality, so inconsequential in the consciousness of America or the world or even most Canadians—is still my last, my most important illusion. It matters, or it mattered until very recently, that a border exists. That people so similar should be formed in different ways. That because I inherited those differences, I should have something special to say on both sides of the border. Through my childhood and adolescence and well into my adulthood, to the ragged fringe of middle age, the faith in a Canada being of a different order of history, experience and humanity, granted me an identity. It was never easy to claim it, but I never doubted it was there, and that I belonged to it. And because of having an identity there, it seemed that I had a prior understanding of Canadian temperament. My humor was Canadian humor. Even with an absurd, rural Florida accent, things I said in Canada, to Canadians, were invariably appreciated, understood on several levels, inflated beyond my own understanding. Canada cultivated an unused part of me that America had never touched. The significant blob of otherness in my life has always been Canada; it sits like a helmet over the United States, but I was the only person who felt its weight.

North, North, North: that glorious direction. The provincial bison-shield of Manitoba, the narrow highway that cut through the wheatfields on the left and the French-speaking hamlets along the river on our right, their lone church-steeples gleaming (to my mother's disgust) higher than the bluffs that hid the rest of the town, and seeming even taller than the wheat elevators that stretched westward, each of them announcing a calloused, sun-reddened Protestant town. And then, the highway divided, trolley tracks appeared, and we were in Winnipeg.

I think often of the compass points. Like the arrow-clusters at cramped country crossroads, the cardinal directions all move me; I dream restless dreams of that *setting out* feeling, of entering a highway for what you know to be a long drive, and reading that first, firm, challenge to the continent. *East*. And I would see fishing boats and a pounding rocky surf and the great cities and I would think (in my southern, and mid-western days) *yes*, that's the best direction. East for me. Culture, history, people, excitement, sophistication. But then, on my only trip to California, undertaken with a group of high school seniors from Pittsburgh, I thrilled to those days of unbroken signposts: *West, West, West,* and even when the land was flat or Appalachian-rolling, I'd be thinking of buttes and mesas and sawtooth mountains and I'd think of getting properly lost in all that space, and feeling free. Well, this was *North:* this was just about as far North as anyone could imagine; watery and glistening and cold, as though the sign itself should be read under a stream of icy water; I think of North and I think of Hamm's Beer and Land o'Lakes butter and of the lakes and pure forests of the Canadian shield, that area that stops just a few hours east of Winnipeg, where town names again turn French and people along the highway are unmistakably Indian.

Most of my life has been spent on the southern fringes of the shield and though my opinion of its charms has changed—it is time again for heat—it is still the direction that defines me. North. Northern. I like the northern winter not because of sportiness in me or delight in the bracing qualities of a stern climate, but merely for its obliging me to stay indoors. North gives justification for the torpid side of my personality (that I'm on best terms with) to take over.

I think that is why SOUTH has no charm for me at all; it is the only cardinal point that fails to conjure an unreal, dreamlike essence of itself. When I think of the north Florida and south Georgia I knew, I remember only walls of leggy pine with slash marks on their trunks, hung with resin buckets, and I remember the Coke machines in country gas stations where for a nickel I could lift a heavy metal lid (I can remember the first whiff of that cold, moist air, I remember the pleasure of trailing my fingers in that iced water), spot a bottle cap in one of the metal tracks and glide it along to the spring-catch my nickel had released. And I can remember draining those stubby little Coke bottles with their raised, roughened letters on the side, always checking the bottom to see where it had been bottled, how far it had come, though nearly all were good ol' bottles from Plant City and Orlando. Well,

73

all I remember of *South* is sand and heat and thirst and skies and the color of sweaty undershirts, spotted with buzzards.

IV.

On Wolseley Drive in Winnipeg, on the banks of the Assiniboine, my grandparents had their house. Three hours away, my aunt and uncle had an even larger home, with a basement full of hunting rifles, decoys, canoes and kayaks, and a special room for a billiards table. Since my uncle was in those days a writer and commercial artist as well as president of the Wheat Pool—and was soon to become Winnipeg's best-known television personality—and my aunt was a broadcaster, they had studios and libraries on their second floor. The third floor held guest rooms and an attic full of bundled magazines going back to the beginning of *National Geographic* and *Readers' Digest,* as well as the splashy American weeklies like *Life* and *Saturday Evening Post.* They kept the hunting and fishing magazines, and everything Canadian, particularly everything relating to the Prairies and especially Manitoba. Nothing important had ever been thrown out. The house was virtually a computer, although means of retrieval were still a little primitive.

That house, and their lives, represented something to me called Canada, that was more than merely attractive; it was compelling. In the various towns and cities of my first ten years, we had always lived in small apartments carved out of old servants' quarters, on the fringe of other people's families, and we always seemed to be sharing some vital function of other people's lives. Kitchens, bathrooms, entrances, hall-ways, washing facilities. Maybe that's why, in years to come when we finally rented our own duplexes, my father celebrated by roaming around in his boxer shorts all day Sunday and from the moment he returned home. I used to wonder about that. In my favorite TV show, "Father Knows Best", Robert Young ("Jim Anderson") always came home in a suit and changed to an elbow-patched tweed or corduroy jacket. Whatever it was, Canada, by virtue of its cool, English houses and its politeness and its streetcars and its formalities and its formidable understanding of everything going on in the world, as well as in the city, was a more interesting place to live than America. It was certainly more

74

complicated, with French instructions running down the sides and backs of every food package. My parents had moved back to Canada at a time when its differences from the United States were unforced but extreme; whatever seemed foreign to me on a perceptual level was nevertheless perfectly comprehensible on a level of precognition. Or, to put it in the terms I would later live by, Canada was a novel that others found dull and difficult, but that I found interesting and accessible from the beginning. You could say that my life was a dissertation on the subject of Canada and the United States, and what it is like, being a part of both.

I visited my aunt and uncle every day and shot pool in the basement by myself or with my cousin. My parents and I stayed at my grandmother's and between the houses and the school, I became a Canadian.

My grandmother was a classic of the grandmother type; too old to have a life of her own, but young enough to manage the lives of several others. She was small but sturdy, she had wit and a deadpan delivery that was the first to ever "get me going" as she put it—the first person subtler than my comprehension. She had taken up driving and a wee bit of smoking and drinking (the sign of an amateur in these matters: she kept her cigarettes loose in an old sugarbowl in the kitchen cupboard, and she would smoke a cigarette only at predictable times of morning and evening and when the dough was rising after a first good punch-down).

My grandfather, when awake, was the focus of our awareness, though not of our attention. While he was up, we all kept an eye on him. He was classically senile: a bald, tall, stooped old patriarch, a one-time doctor, a breeder of flowers and fruit trees and an importer of draft horses, the consolidator of an insurance group—a man of great substance in Western Canada. Up on the second floor, in the room occupied by my parents and me, I would read the volumes of Who's Who in Western Canada that told my grandfather's tale ("The Luther Burbank of Canada"), and I never tired of reading the biographies of him in the Canadian Readers' Digest, the Who's Who and all the profiles in the various medical and insurance journals. Canada's best-known novelist of that time and place, Frederick Philip Grove, had even based a novel on him. From those biographies I learned the name of the various prize-winning peaches and apples he'd introduced, the prize-winning horses he'd bred and I learned to feel a touch of family pride whenever we passed an office of the Wawanesa Mutual, the insurance company he had headed. *Everyone* in Winnipeg seemed to be famous, all of my relatives had wealth and power and visibility; casual visitors to my uncle's house turned out to be cabinet ministers, American governors, authors. When I walked down the street with my aunt or uncle, people stopped and often turned around to watch as they walked by. After the bruised, violent anonymous lives we'd lived in those mildewed Southern towns, Winnipeg was like a jolt of pure, cold oxygen, the only place left in the world that conformed to the notions of reality I'd gotten from reading and from my own intense imagining.

At the age of seventy-five, my grandfather was merely a disturbing presence. He was strong and stern and he kept himself busy through a ten-hour workday in his old study and sometimes in the living room, underlining every sentence in every book and magazine in the house. He did not know his name, or that of his wife and daughters (he'd had nine daughters and one son, and all five of the survivors visited regularly except the son in Toronto, and my mother). His memory had deserted him while he was in his early fifties, and as a doctor he'd recognized—it had been his father's fate as well—and had gotten out of medicine, and cut back on the insurance. He'd retired, physically exhausted, with a heart condition. The insurance company had treated him generously. His faculties continued to fail. He was apparently alert enough, in 1940, when my mother brought me up from Fargo for my first visit, to feel the bumps on my head and declare, "Don't worry, Annie, this boy will never be a fighter." So far as I can determine, he never spoke to me, or of me, again. His heart repaired itself, as it often does in bodies suddenly relieved of stress, and he had his work, the underlining of every word in the *Free Press* and *Tribune*, and all those stacks of magazines. That was my Canada and that was my grandfather's house: a place where everything was intact and even madness could be quietly accommodated. There was, in fact, only one thing that could not be housed, because he was not organically a part of it, and that was my father.

"See what *he* wants," my grandmother would ask, not unkindly. She was as afraid of giving offense as my father was; therefore they worked out elaborate systems of mutual avoidance. He rarely came downstairs. Whenever he did, an aroma of tobacco preceded him by at least a minute, and my grandfather would lay his pencil down, carefully marking his place in the work still before him, stand, and—high, quivering voice fierce with rage—order him out. "How dare you, sir, walk across my carpet with your dirty workman's boots? Out, Out, I say!" My father, in Winnipeg, never went outside in the winter, and was always in slippers. My grandfather was furious, muttering , "the cheek, the gall! I will report this insolence to Stewart, don't think I won't!" That would be the sign for my mother, first, to interpose herself. "It's all right, daddy, he's Leo, your son-in-law." Stewart had been a stable-hand, imported from Scotland like all the Clydesdales. Now my grandfather was in a proper Victorian rage, throwing my mother aside, "I don't know why you're shielding him, Lillie, but I'm getting to the bottom of this. I won't rest—" by which time my father had sneaked back up the stairs, cursing to himself and my grandfather would be left standing, hands clenched, undecided over the next challenge. All the women in his life were "Lillie," my grandmother's name, except my grandmother, who was usually just "mother." After he died, at the age of eighty-two, my grandmother had her own few bad years, heaping invectives on her husband, not for those last twenty inglorious years, but for the years of his magnificent achievement, the *Who's Who* years. Who, or what, to believe? Even as I write this, my own mother is close to enacting the dramas of her parents, and as I reach back into these events of thirty years ago, I'm aware that truth is simply a matter of framing and reframing. I've chosen to believe certain versions, I've rejected others. I too was blessed with a gifted memory and I've worn it down by now to something dull and ordinary and I fear that the family disease awaits me.

When my grandfather's fists unclenched he'd go back to the chair and begin the assault on a new column of print.

The winter of 1950 was one of the snowiest in Winnipeg history. It would lead to a flood that is still remembered, to sandbags in my aunt's and grandmother's backyards, to those canoes and kayaks pushing off directly from the driveway and bringing relief a few blocks downstream. And, as the head of the Red Cross, it would be my aunt's finest hour: in the pictures we were sent (by that time we too had pushed off; they caught up with us in Cleveland, in a rooming house on Euclid Avenue), my aunt and uncle would be bundled in their parkas, under helmets with the Red Cross painted on the sides, and it would remind me of British Air Raid wardens.

77

The pictures were grainy, black and white, some of them smeared from rainwater on the lenses (a beautiful, accidental effect; what would be its equivalent in language?). I should like that talent—to capture activity, strain, sleeplessness, peril, the direction of a thousand lives and millions of dollars, and the muddy, ice-choked river racing by the fixed point of my grandmother's backyard, tossing boulders of ice, houses, trucks, with the fury of a horizontal Niagara.

That would be the spring. Right now, it is still a hard, Siberian winter day. Winnipeg exists, paradoxically, by virtue of its relative mildness, its southern latitude. Southern only for Canada; America had abandoned any attempt to colonize the lands north of the Twin Cities. Winnipeg should not exist, except as an urban planner's act of defiance, an experiment on the heartless Russian model. But it does exist, as Edmonton exists, as Montreal exists, and the effects of that anomaly—the intense self-consciousness, the isolation , the pride, the shame and absurdity of carrying on normal life at forty below zero—creates a population that fills the studios and board-rooms and lecture halls of Canada with so much talent that old Winnipeggers form a kind of talent-Mafia in Toronto. Some drained south, the Monty Halls and David Steinbergs and Erving Goffmans, but most defied the dominant pulls of the continent and headed East. Winnipeg, meaning "muddy water," is built on one of the very few north-flowing rivers in North America. Maybe there's more of a social component to geology than we had ever suspected.

The people of the city are proud of their winters, proud of their simple survival. They were afraid of softness, at least in my mother's family, and they were constantly headed deeper North, as though to test themselves, as though Winnipeg represented some degenerate, sub-tropical fringe of sybaritic abandonment. My cousins began their kayaking at ten or so, portaging to rivers and lakes right to the shores of Hudson's Bay. They had a farm in the Sand Hills in the western part of the province, where they grew flax and ran trap lines, and in the fall I went with them— Florida child that I was then, accent and all—and learned to shoot at an early enough age to avoid the normal hesitancies and sentimentalities of the urban academic. I learned to hunt like a farmer, like a competitor and protector; I concentrated on gophers and red-winged blackbirds.

V.

One Saturday deep in the winter of 1949-50, my grandmother asked me to go up to Portage Avenue to see Mr. McArdle and to bring back the meat-order, which she was phoning in. I was given directions to find the shop, but no money. From what I could see, no money ever entered or left my grandmother's house. Accounts were rendered, usually in person, by well-dressed men who waited in the parlor. Tea and biscuits would be served. My grandfather would be on good behavior, looking from face to face, following conversations, or so it seemed, laughing when others laughed. Sundays would bring visits of an elderly threesome of spinster sisters, "The Bonnycastle Girls," who dressed in sybillant black satins, who exuded the kinds of perfume associated with toilet waters and colognes, something closer to a "scent" than a "fragrance," like a liquified powder. They had visited my grandmother every Sunday for the past forty years, although no one (on our side, at least) was quite prepared to explain to me if they were friends from a different time and place, or relatives, or perhaps, inherited obligations, the weekly visit a form of interest on an unpayable capital. I joined the group enthusiastically smiling and following faces much like my grandfather, until one day when I got too close and detected odors under the cologne and realized something disagreeable was being hidden; there was, in fact, no attempt being made to attract.

I walked up Stiles to McArdle's. The street was packed with white-frame houses behind their deeply snowy yards. I am reminded now, in their winter settings, of a street like an occluded lower jaw, all the way up to Portage Avenue. One long block under the winter sun, in the winds of thirty-five below. "It's nippy outside. Bundle up. Don't tarry," said my grandmother.

I have seen most of the world's major cities by now, but Portage Avenue in the early Fifties remains for me something special, like a Russian movie, molded on a scale of epic tedium that nevertheless achieves a certain indifferent weight. If we could rid our minds of notions of charm and beauty and still be receptive to urban grandeur, then Portage Avenue, the east-west axis of Winnipeg and half the province of Manitoba, would stand as a model. It was conceived on a scale of spaciousness in keeping with the open fields and possibly in revenge for the two thousand miles of crabbed forest at its back. It was wide, straight, and flat, and down

79

its middle in its own private *maidan,* rolled the endless herd of rumbling streetcars. Standing at Stiles, I could look a couple of miles to the west, the buildings showing not a single variation in height and not a single uniformity of design, and spot, *in embryo* as it were, the line of streetcars that would be passing me in the next half hour. Since no one could stand outside more than ten minutes anyway, it was most compassionate of the transport commission to flood the rails with more cars than any city had a right to expect. That was my Winnipeg; a city of prompt and endless convenience.

I presented my request to the aproned, blood-stained, gray-haired man with the scholarly glasses. "What would it be, now?" he asked, the voice foreign yet attractive to me, able to squeeze out twice as many words per second as my slow, hateful speech. I was working on reducing my accent, for I knew from overhearing my parents in their bed that we were finished in the South anyway. I hoped we'd never leave Winnipeg. I was getting more "ays" and fewer "uhs" into every line, though I still couldn't force myself into Canadian pronunciations of *zed* and *shedule*. Canadian spellings all looked right to me; "honour" seemed a graver concept with its extra vowel intact.

"I've come for the meat order," I said.

"I can see that."

"My grandmother called you."

He squinted. Obviously he was expected to know every child in his square mile. "And who might she be, now?"

I gave the name.

His face broke into a *Saturday Evening Post* cover of recognition. The bushy white eyebrows shot up, the rimless glasses slipped, the lips formed an "Oh!" and fell, arms outstretched, against his countertop, as though doing a cheating, standing push-up.

"Why, it's the wee bairn! Why dinja say, lad? You're the wee American bairn she's been talking about. What's your name again?"

"Clark."

"Clar-r-r-k." he rolled the name like a large, succulent, chocolate-covered cherry. "Now isn't that fine! Clarrrk is music to my ears, it is."

It was a name I despised, and had paid for repeatedly in Southern schools. Clark Bars and Clark Kent and Clark Gable were the extent of my visibility in the American world, and to be named after any of them, as they all assumed I had, was an assault on the rituals of Southern dignity. I realize now that a name like Clark, in those years, was a tribal name—there were two Clarks (first names) and innumerable Clarkes (last name) in the school I now attended, including a teacher, and some of them conformed to my notion of what Clarks inevitably were like. Clarks in America had all been wounded, and they bore their wounds with minimal grace. In Canada they competed with Icelandics for places on the hockey team.

I was, however, even in Winnipeg, a little uneasy with my last name, which was clearly unique—Blais—and which added unpronouncibility to the earlier charge of exploitativeness. I couldn't understand why we didn't spell it "Blaze" since that was the way it usually came out, though I'd heard through my father that it was really an unpleasant little burp of a name, a little like "Bligh" and sometimes "Blay", so that there was no consistency to it, not even a spelling that conformed in any way to its sound. It didn't help matters that I couldn't pronounce my own name; it seemed a minimal expectation in one who took some pride in his academic achievements. My first name outweighed my second name, with its crispness and neat, hard bracketing of a single vowel with two of the most forceful consonant-clusters in the English language. That first name of mine was like an ice-cube; the last name was a head-cold. It had seemed to me, at eight and nine and ten, that the greatest mystery in the world, and the greatest potential for terror, were locked in the letters of my two names. I spent hours in my grandfather's old study, now a laundry room, using his old doctor's fountain pen-set and his old stacks of prescription pads, practicing signatures that would eliminate that last sound from my name.

"How is the old gentleman?" asked Mr. McArdle.

"Just fine."

"A bit of a handful now and then, I reckon. He likes to go for his strolls, y'know. In the summer, of course."

"He's fine."

"But a great man, in his time."

I deposited the "wee gift" that my grandmother had bundled for me: two thick slices of her fresh cracked-wheat bread, separated by waxed paper from a savory, crusty meat. These were unknown foods to me.

"Steak and kidney pie, ay, laddie?" In my previous life as a Southerner, carrying gifts to tradesmen was unthinkable (so was the idea of a special butchershop in those small Florida towns we'd inhabited; my mother had gone to the town's lone chain-store outlet, around back where the black people had their service-window opening onto the alley by the garbage cans, to ask for items that were our meat-staples but which were cat-food or "nigger food" down there—liver, kidneys, sweetbreads, and above all, tongue, her favorite, and my lunch-time sandwich, which could make my classmates retch as I bit into it).

"I have the order," he told me. "I was going to drop it off myself later on, when Cam comes in. My son, Campbell."

I nodded.

"How are your cousins? Fine lads. Clar-r-r-k's my name, too. Clarrrk McArrrdle. Clark's historically a MacArthur, you know. Like that Yankee general. The MacArthur tartan is one we can wear. What's your last name? I don't believe they ever told me."

I told him.

He frowned, screwed up his jolly old elf's face, as though preparing for some ultimate test of strength. But his voice came out muted, almost choked.

"You're an American lad, you say."

"Yes, sir."

"I've never in all my born days heard a name like that. You don't look a Chink. Are you sure you got it right?"

I told him it was my name as best I could pronounce it. He took it, as I half-intended, as approximating "Bligh."

"That's a very sorry name, if you ask me," he said. He stabbed at a piece of my grandmother's pie. "English to boot."

"No sir," I charged. "It's Canadian. French-Canadian, actually."

And here, in a butcher shop on Portage Avenue, I stepped ever so briefly behind the veil, out of the tribal tent, into the special solitude of Canadian life. The butcher's face was simply blank. It registered nothing; as though I'd not even come in or had not been seen. I had meant to say, *naw, it's not one of those foreign British things* . . . it's Canadian. My relatives maintained a discreet silence on things American, but for British institutions they manifested a keen dislike. Whenever the BBC news came on, every day at noon, beginning as it always did with an upper-class twit intoning news of the Royal Family, such as "The King today . . ."

my cousin would pipe up, ". . . cut a long, wet one in the Royal Crapper," or some such; it was still an era when Canadian nationalists looked to America for a counter-weight to the British presence. And definitely I was not an American, if you could overlook my accent. I am grandma's boy, and the Old Gentleman's grandson, and I've come to take my place here, trading steak and kidney pie for a few hand-picked lobes of glistening calves' liver. And I can prove I belong; I've got a Canadian name. The only words I knew with "Canadian" in them had "French-" in front of them. It went with "Canadian" the way "early" and "All-" went with "American," as a completion, an intensification of an otherwise ungraspable concept.

"No one ever said that," said the butcher. He moved behind the counter as though the floor were spread with coals; he jabbed out liver from a porcelain tray with a normal dinner fork, and then let it slide off the fork onto waxed paper, with a look that hovered on disgust.

"Understand me, Master Clarrrk," he said. "I have nothing in the world against you parrsonally. But I canna abide the French, as a race. They should stay in St. Bonny and not go mucking with the white races. That's my final warrd on the subject." He wrapped the liver in a purplish, brown paper and tied it neatly with cords. "Good day, lad," he said. "My best to the old folks."

VI.

Up on the second floor, in the bedroom we had converted to an apartment, with a hotplate for my father's coffee and a small skillet for my mother's eggs—the smoke-filled haven of my father—a small drama was being enacted that would alter all our lives. My mother had reactivated her old teacher's permit and was, by now, substituting on a near-daily basis in various parts of the city. I was in school, struggling to overcome the deficiencies of a rural Southern background; thanks to family connections, I was not routinely demoted two grades (as was the case with American transfers), and was managing, with after school tutoring, to make a successful transition to the world of ink and nibs, formulas, and long compositions. I was singing British folk songs instead of Military Service Hymns: no one sang "O, Canada!" louder than I, every morning in the hall. And for the first time, I was enjoying my classmates. In

Florida, students were to be tolerated or avoided while pursuing the fugitive pleasures of the text. Here, there was no schoolyard fighting, despite the tempting target I must have offered. The captains of the various team-sports—most of them imposing Icelandic boys with names like Thordarson and Thorlakson—would choose me first, simply because I was obviously the worst. Selections were made in ascending order of competence. They took time to teach me the unfamiliar games, British Bulldog and broom hockey, and would even stop the action if they saw I was too hopelessly out of place.

No one could have been more displaced than my father. He'd ask me when it was safe to go downstairs and to slip outside (this necessitated checking on my grandfather and enduring his scolding for having snuck into the house from "the stables"). Whenever I'm sitting on a bus these days and see a passenger still outside, devouring the stub of a cigarette and then filling his lungs with a final drag before stepping aboard—to let it out all over the bus—I think back to my father and the way he transformed that house into a Saturday night tavern simply by coming downstairs. My grandmother smoked her cigarettes with barely any smoke, let alone after-smell.

He had been going to St. Boniface, and to the furniture stores in the Jewish North End of Winnipeg, the parts of town rich in contacts for the life he knew. Like my mother, he had a transferable skill. He worked a few days, and decided things were too slow, too old-fashioned. He didn't know the Canadian furniture scene anymore, and the American brands, when carried, were far too expensive. Of course he didn't mention anything to us about working or about looking for other work. That wouldn't be his style.

One day after school I went upstairs to read old magazines and the *Who's Who*. My father was there (he rarely was), at his place by the window, looking out on the snowy roof, up Stiles Street to Portage, in the distance. On his knees was a letter. On the window ledge were some notebook pages he must have stolen from me. When he saw me, he folded the letter back in the envelope. I tried to show I wasn't interested, but a small suitcase on the bed was packed.

I went over to my cousin's to shoot pool. My grandfather was sleeping; my father would have no trouble. I couldn't imagine where we'd be going next, but *West*, I remember excited me. I felt ready for it now.

I played pool till the phone rang. My aunt called me from the head of the stairs, "Clark, your mother."

No, I said, I hadn't seen him. I didn't know anything about it. She was crying. What can I *tell* them? she cried. I was looking for an apartment for us, she said. *We agreed; we'd try to settle down.*

He was gone, all right. Shirts, suits, shoes, and car: the salesman's clearing-out. My mother was already reframing it for her mother's and sister's sake: "Leo decided he could do better in the States. He's following a lead in . . . (I made it up: Denver) . . . Denver. He'll send for us when he locates an apartment." I even believed in Denver; I looked up a city-map and tried to memorize the grid. Years later, pursuing my own studies of another Franco-American whose life—given a different dominance in our family—I might have crossed, I again encountered those heroic late-forties and 1950 Denver streets of Neal Cassady and Jack Kerouac; madness to push this further, though a message to me seems to linger. Kerouac and Cassady were my father's world, the one he never escaped, and he died back inside it, in New Hampshire, as desolately as Kerouac did in his mother's transplanted Lowell kitchen in Florida. His father's name was Leo.

On the sheet of notebook paper, I found drafts of a letter to us that was never, finally, left. It said more or less what we expected; he'd gotten a lead, it looked good, and he trusted himself to make a better personal impression than he could in a letter mailed from Winnipeg. If he got it, we'd live better than we ever had. My mother, too, gazed out over the roof, down Stiles, at that one; no need to say the obvious.

She didn't notice the rest of the page, which wasn't a proper letter at all. It was a page of signature. His signature. *Lee Blaise*, it said, up and down several rows. Then, Lee R. Blaise, up and down many more.

"Lee Blaise," I said to myself. Yes, Yes. Clark Blaise. It looked right. It balanced. It was anchored.

1983

85

NOTES ON FAILURE

by JOYCE CAROL OATES

from THE HUDSON REVIEW

> To Whom the Mornings stand for Nights
> What must the Midnights—be!
> —Emily Dickinson

IF WRITING QUICKENS ONE'S SENSE OF LIFE like falling in love, like being precariously in love, it is not because one has any confidence in achieving *success,* but because one is most painfully and constantly made aware of *mortality:* the persistent question being, Is this the work I fail to complete, is this the "posthumous" work that will draw forth so much pity . . .?

The practicing writer, the writer-at-work, the writer immersed in his or her project, is not an entity at all, let alone a person, but some curious mélange of wildly varying states of mind, clustered toward what might be called the darker end of the spectrum: indecision, frustration, pain, dismay, despair, remorse, impatience, outright failure. To be honored in midstream for one's labor would be ideal, but impossible; to be honored after the fact is always too late, for by then another project has been begun, another concatenation of indefinable states. Perhaps one must contend with vaguely warring personalities, in some sort of sequential arrangement?—perhaps premonitions of failure are but the soul's wise economy, in not risking hubris?—it cannot matter, for, in any case, the writer, however battered a veteran, can't have any real faith, any absolute faith, in his stamina (let alone his theoretical "gift") to get him through the ordeal of *creating*, to the plateau of *creation*. One is frequently asked whether the process becomes easier, with the passage of time, and the reply is obvious—*Nothing gets easier with the passage of time, not even the passing of time*.

The artist, perhaps more than most people, inhabits failure, degrees of failure and accommodation and compromise: but the terms of his failure are generally secret. It seems reasonable to believe that failure may be a truth, or at any rate a negotiable fact, while success is a temporary illusion of some intoxicating sort, a bubble soon to be pricked, a flower whose petals will quickly drop. If despair is—as I believe it to be—as absurd a state of the soul as euphoria, who can protest that it feels more substantial, more reliable, less out of scale with the human environment—? When it was observed to T. S. Eliot that most critics are failed writers, Eliot replied: "But so are most writers."

Though most of us inhabit degrees of failure or the anticipation of it, very few persons are willing to acknowledge it, out of a vague but surely correct sense that it is not altogether American to do so. *Your standards are unreasonably high, you must be exaggerating, you must be of a naturally melancholy and saturnine temperament* . . . From this pragmatic vantage point "success" itself is but a form of "failure," a compromise between what is desired and what is attained. One must be stoic, one must develop a sense of humor. And, after all, there is the example of William Faulkner who considered himself a failed poet; Henry James returning to prose fiction after the conspicuous failure of his playwriting career; Ring Lardner writing his impeccable American prose because he despaired of writing sentimental popular songs; Hans Christian Andersen perfecting his fairy tales since he was clearly a failure in other genres—poetry, playwriting, life. One has only to glance at *Chamber Music* to see why James Joyce specialized in prose.

Whoever battles with monsters had better see that it does not turn him into a monster. And if you gaze too long into an abyss— the abyss will gaze back into you. So Nietzsche cryptically warns us: and it is not implausible to surmise that he knew, so far as his own battles, his own monsters, and his own imminent abyss were concerned, much that lay before him: though he could not have guessed its attendant ironies, or the ignoble shallowness of the abyss. Neither does he suggest an alternative.

The spectre of failure haunts us less than the spectre of failing— the process, the activity, the absorbing delusionary stratagems. The battle lost, in retrospect, is, after all, a battle necessarily lost to time: and, won or lost, it belongs to another person. But the battle in the process of being lost, each gesture, each pulsebeat . . . This is the true abyss of dread, the unspeakable predicament. *To Whom the Mornings stand for Nights,/What must the Midnights—be!*

But how graceful, how extraordinary these pitiless lines, written by Emily Dickinson some four years earlier, in 1862:

> The first Day's Night had come—
> And grateful that a thing
> So terrible—had been endured—
> I told my Soul to sing—
>
> She said her Strings were snapt—
> Her bow—to Atoms blown—
> And so to mend her—gave me work
> Until another Morn—
>
> And then—a Day as huge
> As Yesterdays in pairs,
> Unrolled its horror in my face—
> Until it blocked my eyes—
>
> My Brain—begun to laugh—
> I mumbled—like a fool—
> And tho' 'tis Years ago—that Day—
> My Brain keeps giggling—still.
>
> And Something's odd—within—
> That person that I was—
> And this One—do not feel the same—
> Could it be Madness—this?

Here the poet communicates, in the most succinct and compelling imagery, the phenomenon of the ceaseless process of *creating*: the instruction by what one might call the ego that the Soul "sing," despite the nightmare of "Yesterdays in pairs"—the valiant effort of keeping language, forging language, though the conviction is overwhelming that "the person that I was—/And this One—do not feel the same." (For how, a scant poem later, *can* they be the same?) And again, in the same year:

> The Brain, within its Groove
> Runs evenly—and true—
> But let a Splinter swerve—
> 'Twere easier for You—
>
> To put a Current back—
> When Floods have slit the Hills—
> And scooped a Turnpike for Themselves—
> And trodden out the Mills—

The Flood that is the source of creativity, and the source of self-oblivion: sweeping away, among other things, the very Soul that would sing. And is it possible to forgive Joseph Conrad for saying, in the midst of his slough of despair while writing *Nostromo*—surely one of the prodigious feats of the imagination, in our time—that writing is but the "conversion of nervous force" into language?—so profoundly bleak an utterance that one supposes it must be true. For, after all, as the busily productive Charles Gould remarks to his wife, a man must apply himself to *some* activity.

Even that self-proclaimed "teacher of athletes," that vehement rejector of "down-hearted doubters . . ./Frivolous, sullen, moping, angry, affected, dishearten'd, atheistical," that Bard of the American roadway who so wears us out with his yawp of barbaric optimism, and his ebullient energy—even the great Whitman himself confesses that things are often quite different, quite different indeed. When one is alone, walking at the edge of the ocean, at autumn, "held by this electric self out of the pride of which I utter poems"—

> O baffled, balk'd, bent to the very earth,
> Oppressed with myself that I have dared to open my mouth,
> Aware now that amid all that blab whose echoes recoil upon me I
>   have not once had the least idea who or what I am,
> But that before all my arrogant poems the real Me stands yet
>   untouch'd, untold, altogether unreach'd,

Withdrawn far, mocking me with self-congratulatory signs and
　　bows,
With peals of distant ironical laughter at every word I have
　　written
Pointing in silence to these songs, and then to the sand beneath.
　　　　　　　　　　　　—"As I Ebb'd with the Ocean of Life"

Interesting to note that these lines were published in the same
year, 1860, as such tirelessly exuberant and more "Whitmanesque"
poems as "For You O Democracy," "Myself and Mine" ("Myself
and mine gymnastic ever,/To stand the cold or heat, to take good
aim with a gun, to sail a/boat, to manage horses, to beget superb
children"), and "I Hear America Singing." More subdued and
more eloquent is the short poem, "A Clear Midnight," of 1881,
which allows us to overhear the poet in his solitude, the poet no
longer in the blaze of noon on a public platform:

This is thy hour O Soul, thy free flight into the wordless,
Away from books, away from art, the day erased, the lesson
　　done,
Thee fully forth emerging, silent, gazing, pondering the themes
　　thou lovest best,
Night, sleep, death and the stars.

One feels distinctly honored, to have the privilege of such
moments: to venture around behind the tapestry, to see the
threads in their untidy knots, the loose ends hanging frayed.

Why certain individuals appear to devote their lives to the
phenomenon of interpreting experience in terms of structure, and
of language, must remain a mystery. It is not an alternative to life,
still less an escape from life, it *is* life: yet overlaid with a peculiar
sort of luminosity, as if one were, and were not, fully inhabiting the
present tense. Freud's supposition—which must have been his
own secret compulsion, his sounding of his own depths—that the
artist labors at his art to win fame, power, riches, and the love of
women, hardly addresses itself to the fact that, such booty being
won, the artist often intensifies his effort: and finds much of life,
apart from that effort, unrewarding. Why, then, this instinct to
interpret; to transpose flickering and transient thoughts into the

relative permanence of language; to give oneself over to decades of obsessive labor, in the service of an elusive "transcendental" ideal, that, in any case, will surely be misunderstood?—or scarcely valued at all? Assuming that all art is metaphor, or metaphorical, what really *is* the motive for metaphor?—is there a motive?—or, in fact, metaphor?—can one say anything finally, with unqualified confidence, about any work of art?—why it strikes a profound, irresistible, and occasionally life-altering response in some individuals, yet means very little to others. In this, the art of reading hardly differs from the art of writing, in that its most intense pleasures and pains must remain private, and cannot be communicated to others. Our secret affinities remain secret even to ourselves . . . we fall in love with certain works of art, as we fall in love with certain individuals, for no very clear motive.

In 1955, in the final year of his life, as profusely honored as any writer in history, Thomas Mann wryly observed in a letter that he had always admired Hans Christian Andersen's fairy tale, "The Steadfast Tin Soldier." "Fundamentally," says Mann, "it is the symbol of my life." And what is the "symbol" of Mann's life? Andersen's toy soldier is futilely in love with a pretty dancer, a paper cut-out; his fate is to be cruelly, if casually, tossed into the fire by a child, and melted down to the shape "of a small tin heart." Like most of Andersen's tales the story of the steadfast tin soldier is scarcely a children's story, though couched in the mock-simple language of childhood; and one can see why Thomas Mann felt such kinship with it, for it begins: "There were once five and twenty tin soldiers, all brothers, for they were the offspring of the same old tin spoon. Each man shouldered his gun, kept his eyes well to the front, and wore the smartest red and blue uniform imaginable. . . . All the soldiers were exactly alike with one exception, and he differed from the rest in having only one leg. For he was made last, and there was not quite enough tin left to finish him. However, he stood just as well on his one leg as the others did on two. In fact he was the very one who became famous."

Is the artist secretly in love with failure, one might ask.

Is there something dangerous about "success," something finite and limited and, in a sense, historical: the passing over from *striving*, and *strife*, to *achievement*—? One thinks again of

Nietzsche, that most profound of psychologists, who tasted the poisonous euphoria of success, however brief, however unsatisfying: beware the danger in happiness! *Now everything I touch turns out to be wonderful. Now I love any fate that comes along. Who would like to be my fate?*

Yet it is perhaps not failure the writer loves, so much as the addictive nature of incompletion and risk. A work of art acquires, and then demands, its own singular "voice"; it insists upon its integrity; as Gide in his Notebook observed, the artist needs "a special world of which he alone has the key." That the fear of dying or becoming seriously ill in midstream is very real, cannot be doubted: and if there is an obvious contradiction here (one dreads completion; one dreads the possibility of a "posthumous" and therefore uncompleted work), that contradiction is very likely at the heart of the artistic enterprise. The writer carries himself as he would carry a precarious pyramid of eggs, because he is, in fact, a precarious pyramid of eggs, in danger of falling at any moment, and shattering on the floor in an ignoble mess. And he understands beforehand that no one, not even his most "sympathetic" fellow writers, will acknowledge his brilliant intentions, and see, for themselves, the great work he would surely have completed, had he lived.

An affinity for risk, danger, mystery, a certain derangement of the soul; a craving for distress, the pinching of the nerves, the not-yet-voiced; the predilection for insomnia; an impatience with past selves and past creations that must be hidden from one's admirers—why is the artist drawn to such extremes, why are we drawn along with him? Here, a forthright and passionate voice, from a source many would think unlikely:

> There are few of us who have not sometimes wakened before dawn, either after one of those dreamless nights that make us almost enamoured of death, or one of those nights of horror and misshapen joy, when through the chambers of the brain sweep phantoms more terrible than reality itself, and instinct with that vivid life that lurks in all grotesques, and that lends to Gothic art its enduring vitality. . . . Veil after veil of thin dusky gauze is lifted, and by degrees the forms and colors of things

92

are restored to them, and we watch the dawn remaking the world in its antique pattern. The wan mirrors get back their mimic life. . . . Nothing seems to us changed. Out of the unreal shadows of the night comes back the real life that we had known. We have to resume it where we had left off, and there steals over us a terrible sense of the necessity of the continuance of energy in the same wearisome round of stereotyped habits, or a wild longing, it may be, that our eyelids might open some morning upon a world that had been refashioned anew in the darkness . . . a world in which the past would have little or no place, or survive, at any rate, in no conscious form of obligation and regret. . . . It was the creation of such worlds as these that seemed to Dorian Gray to be the true object . . . of life.

That this unmistakably heartfelt observation should be bracketed, in Wilde's great novel, by chapters of near-numbing cleverness, and moralizing of a Bunyanesque—a truly medieval—nature, does not detract from its peculiar poignancy: for here, one feels, Wilde is speaking without artifice or posturing; and that Dorian Gray, freed for the moment from his somewhat mechanical role in the allegory Wilde has assembled, to explain himself to himself, has in fact acquired the transparency—the invisibility—of a mask of our own.

As the ancient legend instructs us, Medusa, the image-bearing goddess of Greek mythology, could not be encountered directly by the hero Perseus, for her power was such that she turned everyone who gazed upon her into stone. (The Gorgon, Medusa, had once been a beautiful woman who had been transformed into a monster—with wings, glaring eyes, tusk-like teeth, and those famous serpents for hair.) Only through shrewd indirection, by means of a polished shield, could she be approached in order to be slain—that is, "conquered" by a mortal man.

Medusa—Perseus—the polished shield: one is led to read the tale as a cautionary parable, which tells us that the inchoate and undetermined event, the act without structure, without the necessary constraint (and cunning) of the human imagination, is too brutal—because too inhuman?—to be borne. Perseus, aided by Athene, conquers the barbaric in nature, and in his own nature, by means of *reflection*.

The demonic flood of emotion represented by Medusa is, then, successfully subdued by the stratagems of restraint, confinement, indirection, craftiness, patience—which is to say, by a kind of art: the deliberate artfulness that substitutes intellectual caution for the brashness of primitive instinct. So art labors to give *meaning* to a profusion of *meanings:* its structures—inevitably "exclusive," and therefore inevitably "unjust"—provide a way of seeing with the mind's eye that is unquestionably superior to the eye itself.

(And if Medusa were not terrible of aspect, threatening both sanity and life, who, one wonders, would trouble to gaze upon her? It is precisely the risk she represents, the grave danger, that makes her a Muse.)

Will one fail is a question less apposite, finally, than *can one succeed?*—granted the psychic predicament, the addiction to a worldly skepticism that contrasts (perhaps comically) with the artist's private system of customs, habits, and superstitious routines that constitutes his "working life." (A study should really be done of artists' private systems—that cluster of stratagems, both voluntary and involuntary, that make daily life navigable. Here we would find, I think, a bizarre and ingenious assortment of Great Religions in embryo—a system of checks and balances, rewards, and taboos, fastidious as a work of art. *What is your work-schedule*, one writer asks another, never *What are the great themes of your books?*—for the question is, of course, in code, and really implies *Are you perhaps crazier than I?—and will you elaborate?*)

How to attain a destination is always more intriguing (involving, as it does, both ingenuity and labor) than *what* the destination finally is. It has always been the tedious argument of moralists that artists appear to value their art above what is called "morality": but is not the artist by definition an individual who has grown to care more about the interior dimensions of his art than about its public aspect, simply because—can this be doubted?—he spends all his waking hours, and many of his sleeping hours, in that landscape?

The curious blend of the visionary and the pragmatic that characterizes most novelists is exemplified by Joyce's attitude toward the various styles of *Ulysses*, those remarkable exuberant self-parodying voices: "From my point of view it hardly matters whether the technique is 'veracious' or not; it has served me as a bridge over which to march my eighteen episodes, and, once I have got my troops across, the opposing forces can, for all I care, blow the bridge sky-high." And though critics generally focus upon the ingenious relationship of *Ulysses* to the *Odyssey*, the classical structure was one Joyce chose with a certain degree of arbitrariness, as he might have chosen another—*Peer Gynt*, for instance; or *Faust*. That the writer labors to discover the secret of his work is perhaps the writer's most baffling predicament, about which he cannot easily speak: for he cannot write the fiction without becoming, beforehand, the person who *must* write that fiction; and he cannot be that person, without first subordinating himself to the process, the labor, of creating that fiction . . . Which is why one becomes addicted to insomnia itself, to a perpetual sense of things about to fail, the pyramid of eggs about to tumble, the house of cards about to be blown away. Deadpan, Stanislaus Joyce noted in his diary, in 1907: "Jim says that . . . when he writes, his mind is as nearly normal as possible."

But my position, as elaborated, is, after all, only the reverse of the tapestry.

Let us reconsider. Isn't there, perhaps, a very literal advantage, now and then, to failure?—a way of turning even the most melancholy of experiences inside-out, until they resemble experiences of *value*, of *growth*, of *profound significance*? That Henry James so spectacularly failed as a playwright had at least two consequences: it contributed to a nervous collapse; and it diverted him from a career for which he was unsuited (not because he had a too grandly "literary" and ambitious conception of the theatre but because, in fact, his theatrical aspirations were so conventional, so trivial)—thereby allowing him the spaciousness of relative failure. The public catastrophe of *Guy Domville* behind him, James writes in his notebook: "I take up my *own* old pen again—the pen of all my old unforgettable efforts and sacred struggles. To myself— today—I need say no more. Large and full and high the future still opens. It is now indeed that I may do the work of my life. And I will." *What Maisie Knew, The Awkward Age, The Ambassadors,*

The Wings of the Dove, The Golden Bowl—the work of James's life. Which success, in the London theatre, would have supplanted—or would have made unnecessary.

Alice James, the younger sister of William and Henry, was born into a family in which, by Henry's admission, "girls seem scarcely to have had a chance." As her brilliant *Diary* acknowledges, Alice made a career of various kinds of failure: the failure to become an adult; the failure to become a "woman" in conventional terms; the failure to realize her considerable intellectual and literary gifts; the failure—which strikes us as magnificently stubborn—to survive. (When Alice discovered that she had cancer of the breast, at the age of 43, she wrote rhapsodically in her diary of her great good fortune: for now her long and questionable career of invalidism had its concrete, incontestable, deathly vindication.)

Alice lies on her couch forever. Alice, the "innocent" victim of fainting spells, convulsions, fits of hysteria, mysterious paralyzing pains, and such nineteenth-century female maladies as nervous hyperesthesia, spinal neurosis, cardiac complications, and rheumatic gout. Alice, the focus of a great deal of familial attention; yet the focus of no one's interest. Lying on her couch she does not matter in the public world, in the world of men, of history. She does not count; she *is* nothing. Yet the *Diary*, revealed to her brothers only after her death, exhibits a merciless eye, an unfailingly accurate ear, a talent that rivals "Harry's" (that is, Henry's) for its astuteness, and far surpasses his for its satirical and sometimes cruel humor. Alice James's career invalidism deprives her of everything; yet, paradoxically, of nothing. The triumph of the *Diary* is the triumph of a distinct literary voice, as valuable as the voice of Virginia Woolf's celebrated diaries.

> I think if I get into the habit of writing a bit about what happens, or rather what doesn't happen, I may lose a little of the sense of loneliness and isolation which abides with me. . . . Scribbling my notes and reading [in order to clarify] the density and shape the formless mass within. Life seems inconceivably rich.

Life seems inconceivably rich—the sudden exclamation of the writer, the artist, in defiance of external circumstances.

The invalid remains an invalid. She dies triumphantly young. When a nurse wishes to commiserate with her about her predicament, Alice notes in her diary that destiny—any destiny—because it *is* destiny—is fascinating: thus pity is unnecessary. One is born not to suffer but to negotiate with suffering, to choose or invent forms to accommodate it.

Every commentator feels puritanically obliged to pass judgment on Alice. As if the *Diary* were not a document of literary worth; as if it doesn't surpass in literary and historical interest most of the publications of Alice's contemporaries, male or female. This "failure" to realize one's gifts may look like something very different from within. One must remember that, in the James family, "an interesting failure had more value than too-obvious success"—as it does to most observers.

In any case Alice James creates "Alice," a possibly fictitious person, a marvelous unforgettable voice. It is Alice who sinks unprotesting into death; it is Alice who says: "I shall proclaim that anyone who spends her life as an appendage to five cushions and three shawls is justified in committing the sloppiest kind of suicide at a moment's notice."

In Cyril Connolly's elegiac "war-book" *The Unquiet Grave, A Word Cycle by Palinurus* (1945), the shadowy doomed figure of Palinurus broods upon the melancholic but strengthening wisdom of the ages, as a means of "contemplating" (never has the force of that word been more justified), and eventually rejecting, his own suicide. Palinurus, the legendary pilot of Aeneas, becomes for the thirty-nine-year-old Connolly an image of his own ambivalence, which might be termed "neurotic" and self-destructive—unless one recalls the specific historical context in which the idiosyncratic "word cycle" was written, between the autumn of 1942 and the autumn of 1943, in London. *The Unquiet Grave* is a journal in perpetual metamorphosis; a lyric assemblage of epigrams, reflections, paradoxes, and descriptive passages; a commonplace book in which the masters of European literature from Horace and Virgil to Goethe, Schopenhauer, Flaubert, and beyond, are employed, as voices in Palinurus' meditation. Palinurus suffered a fate that, in abbreviated form, would appear to cry out for retribution, as well as pity:

Palinurus, a skillful pilot of the ship of Aeneas, fell into the sea in his sleep, was three days exposed to the tempests and waves of the sea, and at last came to the sea shore near Velia, where the cruel inhabitants of the place murdered him to obtain his clothes: his body was left unburied on the seashore.

(Lemprière)

Connolly's meditation upon the temptations of death takes the formal structure of an initiation, a descent into hell, a purification, a cure—for "the ghost of Palinurus must be appeased." Approaching forty, Connolly prepares to "heave his carcass of vanity, boredom, guilt and remorse into another decade." His marriage has failed; the France he has loved is cut off from him, as a consequence of the war; it may well be that the world as he has known it will not endure. He considers the rewards of opium-smoking, he broods upon the recent suicides of four friends, he surrenders his lost Eden and accommodates himself to a changed but evidently enduring world. The word cycle ends with an understated defense of the virtues of happiness, by way of a close analysis of Palinurus' complicity in his fate:

> As a myth . . . with a valuable psychological interpretation, Palinurus clearly stands for a certain will-to-failure or repugnance-to-success, a desire to give up at the last moment, an urge toward loneliness, isolation, and obscurity. Palinurus, in spite of his great ability and his conspicuous public position, deserted his post in the moment of victory and opted for the unknown shore.

Connolly rejects his own predilection for failure and self-willed death only by this systematic immersion in "Palinurus' " desire for the unknown shore: *The Unquiet Grave* achieves its success as a unique work by way of its sympathy with failure.

Early failure, "success" in being published of so minimal a nature it might be termed failure, repeated frustrations may have made James Joyce possible: these factors did not, at any rate, humble him.

Consider the example of his first attempt at a novel, *Stephen Hero*, a fragmented work that reads precisely like a "first novel"—

ambitious, youthful, flawed with the energies and native insights of youth, altogether conventional in outline and style, but, one would say, "promising." (Though conspicuously less promising than D. H. Lawrence's first novel *The White Peacock*.) Had Joyce found himself in a position to publish *Stephen Hero*—had his other publishing experiences been less disheartening—he would have used the material that constitutes *A Portrait of the Artist as a Young Man*; and that great novel would not have been written. As things evolved, Joyce retreated, and allowed himself ten years to write a masterpiece: and so he rewrote *Stephen Hero* totally, using the first draft as raw material upon which language makes a gloss. *Stephen Hero* presents characters and ideas, tells a story: *A Portrait of the Artist* is about language, *is* language, a portrait-in-progress of the creator, as he discovers the range and depth of his genius. The "soul in gestation" of Stephen Dedalus gains its individuality and its defiant strength as the novel proceeds; at the novel's conclusion it has even gained a kind of autonomy—wresting from the author a *first-person* voice, supplanting the novel's strategy of narration with Stephen's own journal. Out of unexceptional and perhaps even banal material Joyce created one of the most original works in our language. If the publication of *Dubliners* had been less catastrophic, however, and a clamor had arisen for the first novel by this "promising" young Irishman, one might imagine a version of *Stephen Hero* published the following year: for, if the verse of *Chamber Music* (Joyce's first book) is any measure, Joyce was surely not a competent critic of his own work at this time; and, in any case, as always, he needed money. If *Stephen Hero* had been published, *Portrait* could not have been written; without *Portrait*, its conclusion in particular, it is difficult to imagine the genesis of *Ulysses* . . . So one speculates; so it seems likely, in retrospect. But James Joyce was protected by the unpopularity of his work. He enjoyed, as his brother Stanislaus observed, "that inflexibility firmly rooted in failure."

The possibilities are countless. Can one imagine a D. H. Lawrence whose great novel *The Rainbow* had enjoyed a routine popular fate, instead of arousing the most extraordinary sort of vituperation ("There is no form of viciousness, of suggestiveness, that is not reflected in these pages," said a reviewer for one publication; the novel, said another reviewer, "had no right to exist"); how then could *Women in Love*, fueled by Lawrence's rage

99

and loathing, have been written? And what of the evangelical *Lady Chatterley's Lover*, in its several versions? In an alternative universe there is a William Faulkner whose poetry (variously, and ineptly, modelled on Swinburne, Eliot, and others) was "successful"; there is a Faulkner whose early, derivative novels gained him a substantial public and commercial success. Imitation Hemingway in *Soldiers' Pay*, imitation Huxley in *Mosquitoes*—with the consequence that Faulkner's own voice might never have developed. (For when Faulkner needed money—and he always needed money—he wrote as rapidly and as pragmatically as possible.) That his great, idiosyncratic, difficult novels—*The Sound and the Fury, As I Lay Dying, Light in August, Absalom, Absalom!*—held so little commercial promise allowed him the freedom, the spaciousness, one might even say the privacy, to experiment with language as radically as he wished: for it is the "inflexibility" of which Stanislaus Joyce spoke that genius most requires.

But the genius cannot know that he is a genius—not really: he has hopes, he has premonitions, he suffers raging paranoid doubts, but he can have, in the end, only himself for measurement. Success is distant and illusory, failure one's loyal companion, one's stimulus for imagining that the next book will be better—for, otherwise, why write? The impulse can be made to sound theoretical, and even philosophical, but it is, no doubt, as physical as our blood and marrow. *This insatiable desire to write something before I die, this ravaging sense of the shortness and feverishness of life, make me cling . . . to my one anchor*—so Virginia Woolf, in her diary, speaks for us all.

1983

SELF/LANDSCAPE/GRID

by TERRENCE DES PRES

from NEW ENGLAND REVIEW AND BREAD LOAF QUARTERLY

> *Miller owns this field, Locke that, and Manning the woodland beyond. But none of them owns the landscape. There is a property in the horizon which no man has but he whose eye can integrate all the parts, that is, the poet.*
>
> *—Emerson*

> *Every appearance in nature corresponds to some state of mind. . . .*
>
> *—Emerson*

I LIVE IN UPSTATE NEW YORK, rural countryside and lovely hills, a place my neighbors like to call "the village." It's small, quiet, great for raising kids. Forty miles to the north, however, lies Griffiss Airforce Base, known locally as Rome, because Rome is the town the base uses. Out of there fly the B-52's that control our part of the sky. There too the Pentagon keeps its brood of cruise missiles. So nobody doubts, in this part of the country, that Rome (when it happens) will be the spot where the warheads hit. At one time we thought that the Russians had size but no technical finesse. That gave us a stupid sort of hope. An overshot might land on our heads, but if incoming missiles fell short, they would come down way north, maybe on Edmund Wilson's old stone house in Talcottville, and we, at least, would be well out of range. Now we are told that the Soviets have refined their delivery. Their guidance systems are on target, not least because the Russians have used American technology, computers, micro-chips, ball-bearings, made and sold by American firms. That, no matter how we look at it, is ugly news. And with Rome at the nub of a nuclear arc, we are resigned in our knowledge that things will start exactly forty miles away. How far the firestorm will reach is what we mainly wonder. We don't know, but we are counting on these upstate hills to block the worst of the blast. If the horizon works in our favor, we shall then have time to consider the wind. In the meantime, B-52's cross and recross above us. They gleam with their nuclear payload. Two or three are up there always, and once I counted thirteen. The air is creased with vapor trails, and in the afternoons, when the sun starts down, the sky looks welted with scars.

That, anyway, is the prospect I share with my neighbors, our part of the nuclear grid. Not a landscape of the mind, no inner weather sort of scene, it's just life's natural place for those who live here. Even so, the bombers overhead keep me reminded that this landscape possesses, or is possessed by, some other will, some demonic grand design or purpose not at all my own. Nor would that kind of death be mine. An all-at-once affair for almost everyone is how that death would come, impersonal but still no accident. That way of dying would be the ultimate instance of political intrusion, for that is what has brought us to this pass, politics, and by political intrusion I mean the increasing unsettlement and rending of our private lives by public force. We do what we can as citizens, but when it comes to nuclear war we can't do much. The hazard is before us and won't budge. How to live with it is our problem, and some of us, at least, resort to magic. We turn to words which give the spirit breathing space and strength to endure. As in any time of ultimate concern, we call on poetry.

I can read *Ecclesiastes* or *King Lear* for a language equal to extremity, but such language isn't of my time, not of my landscape perhaps I should say. I find a little of what I need in poets like Akhmatova or Mandelstam or Milosz, but American poetry? and among poets of the present generation? Not much, in fact hardly anything. I'm writing in early February (1983) and I've just gone through the recent issue of *American Poetry Review*, which offers forty-eight poems by twenty-one poets. Some few good poems, but only two touch upon our nuclear fate, which leaves forty-six in worlds elsewhere. In "Against Stuff" Marvin Bell follows the possibility—this is a night-thoughts poem—that all our forms and habits, including those of poetry itself, may have been wrong, wrong enough to bring us to "the coming instantaneous flaming" of

102

all creatures and things "which could not suffer/that much light at one time." The poem spreads disquiet and resists reply, and in the following lines the pun on "not right" keeps the poet honestly uncertain:

> and, if we are shortly to find ourselves
> without beast, field or flower,
> is it not right that we now prepare
> by removing them from our poetry?

Under nuclear pressure, should poetry contract its domain? The other poem in *APR*, Maxine Kumin's "You Are In Bear Country," moves with wit and nice inevitability to the imagined moment when the grizzly attacks—and then jumps to this question in italics:

> *Is death*
> *by bear to be preferred*
> *to death by bomb?*

The question seems to intrude out of nowhere, and the poet closes by answering yes. The point, I presume, is that any thought of death, even one so unlikely, recalls the nuclear alternative. And grotesque though it would be, death "by bear" does seem preferable, one's own at least, and natural, part of the order of things and an order, too, as timeless as the wilderness. Bizarre consolations, but once the nuclear element intrudes, these are the sorts of ludicrous lengths to which we feel pushed. And the either/or is not even a choice, but only a preference. The absence of *a* and *the* before *bear* and *bomb* suggests two categories of death, only one of which is humanly acceptable.

After *APR* I went on to *Poetry*, where there was nothing relevant, and after that I rummaged randomly through the library's stock of recent journals and magazines, all I could manage in two afternoons. I am sure I read more than two hundred poems, most of them quite short, some very good, but none informed by nuclear awareness. I realize, of course, that any successful poem must authorize itself, must utter its world with self-certainty, but even so, reading so many poems one after the other left me rather shocked by the completeness, the sealed-up way these poems deny the knowledge or nearness of nuclear threat. The other striking thing about most of these poems was their sameness, and especially the meagerness. These observations are not original, of course. Lots of poetry gets written and published in America just now, and if one reads even a small but steady portion of it, one starts to see that the current talk about a "crisis" in our poetry is not unfounded. The trivialization, the huddled stance, the seemingly deliberate littleness of so much poetry in the last few years— how shall we account for it?

Perhaps the rise of the "work-shop" poem has had something to do with it. Maybe also the new careerism among younger poets bent on bureaucratic power in the universities; those who, as Marx would say, have gone over to the management. And surely the kind of literary criticism now in vogue, hostile to the integrity of language, doesn't help. But these are as much symptoms as causes, and the larger situation comes down to this: In a time of nuclear threat, with absolutely everything at stake, our poetry grows increasingly claustrophilic and small-themed, it contracts its domain, it retires still further into the narrow chamber of the self; and we see in this not only the exhaustion of a mode and a tradition, but also the spectacle of spirit cowed and retreating.

The retreat has been swift because American practice invites it. Founded on Emersonian principles, our poetry has drawn much of its strength from an almost exclusive attention to self and nature. Typically we have conceived of the self *as* a world rather than of the self *in* the world. Things beyond the self either yield to imagination or else they don't matter, and the world becomes a store of metaphor to be raided as one can. The "strong" poet turns any landscape to private use, and solipsism wins praise as the sign of success. Emerson didn't invent these attitudes, but he was good at summing them up. "Every natural fact is a symbol of some spiritual fact," he wrote, and "the Universe is the externization [sic] of the soul." Thus the road was open for Whitman and poets to come, and thus Emerson delivered his mandate: "Know then that the world exists for you," and "Build therefore your own world." Partly, this is the mythology of our national experience, with its determination to deny social-political limits and focus instead on individual destiny. Partly, too, this is the American brand of Romanticism, part of a larger movement that on the continent peaked in its influential French example. Baudelaire called the world a "forest of symbols," and Mallarmé thought that everything

104

external, *la cité, ses gouvernements, le code,* could be dismissed as *le mirage brutal.*

Stated thus, the whole business seems outlandish—but not really. The Emersonian mandate supports maximum belief in the poet's potency, not in itself a bad thing. Then, too, poets in our century have held some very odd convictions, Yeats for example, or for that matter, Merrill. But in one respect there is no doubting: American poetry has rejected history and politics on principle. Despite Lowell's example and more recent exceptions like Rich and Forché, our poets in the main have been satisfied to stick with Emerson, and few would find anything to take exception with in the following lines from Emerson's *Ode:*

> I cannot leave
> My honeyed thought
> For the priest's cant,
> Or statesman's rant.
>
> If I refuse
> My study for their politique,
> Which at the best is trick,
> The angry Muse
> Puts confusion in my brain.

American contempt for politicians runs deep. As a sort of common-sense cynicism it allows us to go untroubled by crime in high places and, more to the point, it bolsters our belief that personal life exists apart from, and is superior to, political force and its agencies. But also, as Gunnar Myrdal demonstrated in *An American Dilemma,* our sort of political cynicism goes hand in hand with a remarkably durable idealism. We take for granted that governments are corrupt, then feel that some other power, providential and beyond the meddling of men, governs our destiny finally. Where there's a will there's a way, and everything comes right in the end. But does it? Even without the Bomb to put such faith into question, Emerson's example—Poland, for God's sake!— invites scepticism:

> The Cossack eats Poland,
> Like stolen fruit;

Her last noble is ruined,
Her last poet mute:
Straight, into double band
The victors divide;
Half for freedom strike and stand:—
The astonished Muse finds thousands at her side.

The Muse might well be befuddled, given the logic of Emerson's syntax. But of course, Emerson's faith in the future—disaster compensated by renewal—can't mean much to us. With the advent of the nuclear age there is no assurance that anything will remain for the phoenix to rise from.

We have fallen from the Garden, and the Garden itself—nature conceived as an inviolate wilderness—is pocked with nuclear waste and toxic dumps, at the mercy of industry, all of it open to nuclear defilement. Generations come and go, but that *the earth abideth forever* is something we need to feel, one of the foundations of poetry and humanness, and now we are not sure. That is the problem with nuclear threat, simply as threat; it undermines all certainty, and things once absolute are now contingent. To feel that one's private life was in the hands of God, or Fate, or even History, allowed the self a margin of transcendence; the dignity of personal life was part of a great if mysterious Order. But now our lives are in the hands of a few men in the Pentagon and the Kremlin, men who, having affirmed that they would destroy us to save us, have certified their madness—and yet their will determines our lives and our deaths. We are, then, quite literally enslaved, and assuming that this bothers poets no less than the rest of us, why do they so seldom speak of it? It is not too much to say that most poetry in America is written against experience, against first feelings and needs. Whether the Emersonian tradition is a trap or a last-ditch defense is perhaps a moot point. But the poetry of self still predominates, with nature as its cornerstone, despite Los Alamos, a lovely spot in the mountains.

Nuclear wipe-out is possible, perhaps probable, and every day I talk with people who are convinced it will happen. No soul is free of that terror, nor of that knowledge; and simply as a state of mind or way of knowing, it drastically alters how we receive and value our experience. Birth, for example, or one's own death; surely having children troubles us in ways not known before, and we need to feel that each of us shall have a death of his or her own, simply in order to feel fully possessed of our lives. These are common feelings, and it's clearer than it used to be that no man (no, nor woman neither) is an island. Our surface lives are individual and unique, but human existence itself—the being that all of us share and feel threatened—gives us our most important sense of ourselves and, I should also think, gives poetry its most significant themes. Can it be, then, that the shallowness of recent poetry reveals a desperate clinging to the surface?

I do *not* ask for poems directly about the Bomb or the end of the world, although with the Bell poem in *APR* as evidence, a theme of this kind can be as legitimate as any other. I don't expect poems of protest or outrage or horror either, although again, I can't see that they would hurt. I do, however, try to keep in mind that some subjects are more human, and more humanly exigent than others—Forché on Salvador compared to Leithauser on dandelions— and also that poets are often scared off by subjects which, precisely because of the fear, signal a challenge worth the risk. But what I'd mainly hope to see, in this case, is poetry that probes the impact of nuclear threat, poetry informed by nuclear knowing, poems that issue from the vantage of a self that accepts its larger landscape, a poetic diction testing itself against the magnitude of our present plight, or finally just poems which survive their own awareness of the ways nuclear holocaust threatens not only humankind but the life of poetry itself.

Nature, for example, remains the mainstay of our poetry. Natural imagery makes us trust the poem, suggests a permanence at the root of things, and every poem about nature bears somewhere within it the myth of renewal and rebirth. But from the nuclear perspective, these ministrations falter. Permanence? Rebirth? Emerson's response to nature was genuinely poetic, and the measure of our present loss may be judged by the degree of nostalgia rather than assent we feel when he says: "In the woods, we return to reason and faith. There I feel that nothing can befall me in life,—no disgrace, no calamity (leaving me my eyes), which nature cannot repair." Well, his notion of calamity isn't ours. And nature, for all its proven renovative power, could never repair the worst that might befall us. Nature suffers the same division we observe in ourselves and in the landscape generally. We are what we are, yet some deep part of selfhood has been invaded by forces

107

wholly alien to personal being, political forces of which the worst is nuclear threat. In the same way, the landscape belongs to us and yet it does not. This concrete place we share is also a site on the nuclear grid. And when, therefore, Emerson tells us that "Every appearance in nature corresponds to some state of mind," we must inquire not only What state of mind? but also Whose mind?

No doubt the crews in the bombers are bored. And no doubt bureaucratic haggling keeps the commander of the base in Rome bogged down in mindless detail. The chiefs in the Pentagon, on the other hand, definitely share a state of mind which must, now and then, get rather dizzy with the glamour of their global strategy. What the Russians have in mind we don't know. But for all of them, we and the landscape are expendable; to think that way, after all, is their job. We cannot say, then, that the landscape corresponds to their minds and to ours in the same way. Rather, what expresses their state of mind, provokes and negates our own. In a traditional landscape, points of correspondence for us would be, among other things, the sky's infinity and the sense of permanence arising from the land itself. But exactly this kind of metaphor-making has been undermined by the transformation of the landscape into a sector on the grid. Or we might look at it this way: the military state of mind becomes an alien element *in* the landscape as we behold it, the B-52's, the proximity of the missile site, the grid and its planners. These forces have broken into our world, they have defiled its integrity, and the new points of correspondence between ourselves and the landscape are the condition of vulnerability and the threat of terminal defacement. Self and world, nature and landscape, everything exists in itself *and* as acceptable loss on the nuclear grid.

I've gone on at length about the landscape in my part of the country to suggest what Emerson's poetic principle—"Every appearance in nature corresponds to some state of mind"—might mean in the nuclear age. Every person has his or her own place, of course, and in a country as vast as ours the variety of landscape must be nearly infinite. The kinds of personal vision to which a landscape corresponds must also, then, be fairly limitless. But all vision converges in the fact that every landscape is part of the nuclear grid. I have the air base in Rome to remind me of this, whereas people living in, say, New York City are reminded by the city itself—its status as a prime target; the difficulty of maintaining life-support systems, water, energy, even in normal times; traffic's five o'clock entrapment every afternoon, not to mention the way the city is mocked by officials in Washington who suggest that in the event of an alert, nine million people will please evacuate the area. Then too, there are the nuclear power plants nearby; these are also targets, and when hit will spout radiation like the fourth of July. The citizenry can always avail itself of shovels, as another Washington wit has proposed, but no, there's no real hope. So that landscape too has its message.

Meanwhile, poets write about "marshes, lakes and woods, Sweet Emma of Preservation Hall, a Greek lover, an alchemist, actresses, fairy tales, canning peaches in North Carolina," stuff like that, to quote from the ad for a recent anthology. The apology for poems of this kind (triviality aside) is that by celebrating modest moments of the human spectacle—little snaps of wonder, bliss or pain—poetry implicitly takes its stand against the nuclear negation. To say Yes to life, this argument goes, automatically says No to the Bomb. And yes, a grain of truth sprouts here. I expect many among us read poetry that way in any case. The upshot, however, is that poets can go on producing their vignettes of self, pleased to be fighting the good fight without undue costs—except *the* cost, which is the enforced superficiality, the required avoidance of our deeper dismay.

Nuclear threat engenders cynicism, despair, allegiance to a mystique of physical force, and to say No to such destructive powers requires an enormously vehement Yes to life and human value. What's called for, in fact, is the kind of poetry we once named "great," and my suspicion is that today the will to greatness is absent. Great poems, Wordsworth's or Whitman's for example, confront their times; they face and contain their own negation. The human spirit draws its strength from adversity, and so do poems. Examples like *The Prelude* and *Song of Myself* incorporate and thereby transcend that which, if they ignored it, would surely cancel their capacity for final affirmation. And having mentioned poems of this calibre, I might also add that the "American sublime," as critics call it, has been missing in our poetry at least since late Stevens. The sublime, as observers like Burke and Kant and Schopenhauer insist, arises from terror, terror beheld and resisted,

109

the terror of revolution for Wordsworth, of the abyss for Whitman, of nuclear annihilation for any poet today who would make a language to match our extremity.

I can see, though, why we try to avoid what we know. Terror will flare up suddenly, a burst of flame in the chest, and then there is simply no strength. Other times the mind goes blank in disbelief. The temptation to retreat is always with us, but where can we go, where finally? Sometimes I let it all recede, let silence be enough, and go for a walk through the fields and apple hedge above my house. The horizon then is remarkably clear, the sky is still its oldest blue. Overhead, the planes are half a hemisphere ahead of their thunder. It's hard not to think of them as beautiful, sometimes; humankind took so long to get up there. I wind my way through milkweed in the meadow and remember how Emerson, crossing an empty field, felt glad to the brink of fear. We know what he means, the elation that sweeps through us at such moments. And then I think of Osip Mandelstam and an old Russian proverb; life, he wrote, is not a walk across a field. We know what he means too, the inhuman hardship of centuries, the modern horror of being stalked to death. But it's all of this, isn't it? the grimness and the glory. Why should we think to keep them apart? We fear, maybe, that dread will undermine our joy, and often it does. To keep them wed is poetry's job. And now that the big salvations have failed us, the one clear thing is that we live by words.

1984

POETRY AND AMBITION

by DONALD HALL

from THE KENYON REVIEW

1. I SEE NO REASON to spend your life writing poems unless your goal is to write great poems.

An ambitious project—but sensible, I think. And it seems to me that contemporary American poetry is afflicted by modesty of ambition—a modesty, alas, genuine . . . if sometimes accompanied by vast pretense. Of course the great majority of contemporary poems, in any era, will always be bad or mediocre. (Our time may well be characterized by more mediocrity and less badness.) But if failure is constant the types of failure vary, and the qualities and habits of our society specify the manners and the methods of our failure. I think that we fail in part because we lack serious ambition.

2. If I recommend ambition, I do not mean to suggest that it is easy or pleasurable. "I would sooner fail," said Keats at twenty-two, "than not be among the greatest." When he died three years later he believed in his despair that he had done nothing, the poet of "Ode to a Nightingale" convinced that his name was "writ in water." But he was mistaken, he was mistaken. . . . If I praise the ambition that drove Keats, I do not mean to suggest that it will ever be rewarded. We never know the value of our own work, and everything reasonable leads us to doubt it: for we can be certain that few contemporaries will be read in a hundred years. To desire to write poems that endure—we undertake such a goal certain of two things: that in all likelihood we will fail, and that if we succeed we will never know it.

Every now and then I meet someone certain of personal great-ness. I want to pat this person on the shoulder and mutter comforting words: "Things will get better! You won't always feel so depressed! Cheer up!"

But I just called high ambition sensible. If our goal in life is to remain content, *no* ambition is sensible. . . . If our goal is to write poetry, the only way we are likely to be *any* good is to try to be as great as the best.

3. But for some people it seems ambitious merely to set up as a poet, merely to write and to publish. Publication stands in for achievement—as everyone knows, universities and grant-givers take publication as achievement—but to accept such a substitution is modest indeed, for publication is cheap and easy. In this country we publish more poems (in books and magazines) and more poets read more poems aloud at more poetry readings than ever before; the increase in thirty years has been tenfold.

So what? Many of these poems are often *readable*, charming, funny, touching, sometimes even intelligent. But they are usually brief, they resemble each other, they are anecdotal, they do not extend themselves, they make no great claims, they connect small things to other small things. Ambitious poems usually require a certain length for magnitude; one need not mention monuments like *The Canterbury Tales*, *The Faerie Queene*, *Paradise Lost*, or *The Prelude*. "Epithalamion," "Lycidas," and "Ode: Intimations of Immortality" are sufficiently extended, not to mention "The Garden" or "Out of the Cradle. . . ." Not to mention the poet like Yeats whose briefer works make great connections.

I do not complain that we find ourselves incapable of such achievement; I complain that we seem not even to entertain the desire.

4. Where Shakespeare used "ambitious" of Macbeth we would say "over-ambitious"; Milton used "ambition" for the unscrupulous overreaching of Satan; the word describes a deadly sin like "pride." Now when I call Milton "ambitious" I use the modern word, mellowed and washed of its darkness. This amelioration reflects capitalism's investment in social mobility. In more hierarchal times pursuit of honor might require revolutionary social change, or

murder; but Protestantism and capitalism celebrate the desire to rise.

Milton and Shakespeare, like Homer, acknowledge the desire to make words that live forever: ambitious enough, and fit to the O.E.D.'s first definition of "ambition" as "eager desire of honor"— which will do for poets and warriors, courtiers and architects, diplomats, Members of Parliament, and Kings. Desire need not imply drudgery. Hard work enters the definition at least with Milton, who is ready "To scorn delights, and live laborious days," to discover fame, "the spur, that last infirmity of noble minds." We note the infirmity who note that fame results only from laborious days' attendance upon a task of some magnitude: when Milton invoked the Heavenly Muse's "aid to my adventurous song," he wanted merely to "justify the ways of God to men."

If the word "ambitious" has mellowed, "fame" has deteriorated enough to require a moment's thought. For us, fame tends to mean Johnny Carson and *People* magazine. For Keats as for Milton, for Hector as for Gilgamesh, it meant something like universal and enduring love for the deed done or the song sung. The idea is more classic than Christian, and the poet not only seeks it but confers it. Who knows Achilles' valor but for Homer's tongue? But in the 1980s—after centuries of cheap printing, after the spread of mere literacy and the decline of qualified literacy, after the loss of history and the historical sense, after television has become mother of us all—we have seen the decline of fame until we use it now as Andy Warhol uses it, as the mere quantitative distribution of images. . . . We have a culture crowded with people who are famous for being famous.

5. True ambition in a poet seeks fame in the old sense, to make words that live forever. If even to entertain such ambition reveals monstrous egotism, let me argue that the common alternative is petty egotism that spends itself in small competitiveness, that measures its success by quantity of publication, by blurbs on jackets, by small achievement: to be the best poet in the workshop, to be published by Atheneum, to win the Pulitzer or the Nobel. . . . The grander goal is to be as good as Dante.

Let me hypothesize the developmental stages of the poet.
At twelve, the American poet-to-be is afflicted with generalized

113

ambition. (Robert Frost wanted to be a baseball pitcher and a United States senator: Oliver Wendell Holmes said that *nothing* was so commonplace as the desire to appear remarkable; the desire may be common but it is at least essential.) At sixteen the poet reads Whitman and Homer and wants to be immortal. Alas, at twenty-four the same poet wants to be in the *New Yorker*.

There is an early stage when the poem becomes more important than the poet; one can see it as a transition from the lesser egotism to the greater. At the stage of lesser egotism, the poet keeps a bad line or an inferior word or image because *that's the way it was: that's what really happened*. At this stage the frail ego of the author takes precedence over art. The poet must develop, past this silliness, to the stage where the poem is altered for its own sake, to make it better art, not for the sake of its maker's feelings but because decent art is the goal. Then the poem lives at some distance from its creator's little daily emotions; it can take on its own character in the mysterious place of satisfying shapes and shapely utterance. The poem freed from its precarious utility as ego's appendage may possibly fly into the sky and become a star permanent in the night air.

Yet, alas, when the poet tastes a little fame, a little praise. . . . Sometimes the poet who has passed this developmental stage will forget duty to the art of poetry and again serve the petty egotism of the self. . . .

Nothing is learned once that does not need learning again. The poet whose ambition is unlimited at sixteen and petty at twenty-four may turn unlimited at thirty-five and regress at fifty. But if everyone suffers from interest, everyone may pursue disinterest.

Then there is a possible further stage: when the poet becomes an instrument or agency of art, the poem freed from the poet's ego may entertain the possibility of grandeur. And this grandeur, by a familiar paradox, may turn itself an apparent 180 degrees to tell the truth. Only when the poem turns wholly away from the petty ego, only when its internal structure fully serves art's delicious purposes, may it serve to reveal and envision. "Man can *embody* truth"—said Yeats; I add the italic—"he cannot *know* it." Embodiment is art and artfulness.

When Yeats was just south of fifty he wrote that he "sought an

114

image not a book." Many aging poets leave the book behind to search for the diagram, and write no more poetry than Michael Robartes who drew geometrical shapes in the sand. The turn toward wisdom—toward gathering the whole world into a book—often leaves poetry behind as a frivolity. And though these prophets may delight in abstract revelation, we cannot follow them into knowing, who followed their earlier embodiments. . . . Yeats' soul knew an appetite for invisibility—the temptation of many—but the man remained composite, and although he sought and found a vision he continued to write a book.

6. We find our models of ambition mostly from reading.

We develop the notion of art from our reading. When we call the poem more important than ourselves, it is not that we have confidence in *our* ability to write it; we believe in *poetry*. We look daily at the great monuments of old accomplishment and we desire to add to their number, to make poems in homage to poems. Old poems that we continue to read and love become the standard we try to live up to. These poems, internalized, criticize our own work. These old poems become our Muse, our encouragement to song and our discouragement of comparison.

Therefore it is essential for all poets, all the time, to read and reread the great ones. Some lucky poets make their living by publicly reacquainting themselves in the classroom with the great poems of the language. Alas, many poets now teach nothing but creative writing, read nothing but the words of children . . . (I will return to this subject).

It is also true that many would-be poets lack respect for learning. How strange that the old ones read books. . . . Keats stopped school when he has fifteen or so; but he translated the *Aeneid* in order to study it and worked over Dante in Italian and daily sat at the feet of Spenser, Shakespeare, and Milton. ("Keats studied the old poets every day / Instead of picking up his M.F.A.") Ben Jonson was learned and in his cups looked down at Shakespeare's relative ignorance of ancient languages—but Shakespeare learned more language and literature at his Stratford grammar school than we acquire in twenty years of schooling. Whitman read and educated himself with vigor; Eliot and Pound continued their studies after stints of graduate school.

On the other hand, we play records all night and write unambitious poems. Even talented young poets—saturated in S'ung, suffused in Sufi—know nothing of Bishop King's "Exequy." The syntax and sounds of one's own tongue, and that tongue's four-hundred-year-old ancestors, give us more than all the classics of all the world in translation.

But to struggle to read the great poems of another language—*in* the language—that is another thing. We are the first generation of poets not to study Latin; not to read Dante in Italian. Thus the puniness of our unambitious syntax and limited vocabulary.

When we have read the great poems we can study as well the lives of the poets. It is useful, in the pursuit of models, to read the lives and letters of the poets whose work we love. Keats's letters, heaven knows.

7. In all societies there is a template to which its institutions conform, whether or not the institutions instigate products or activities that suit such a pattern. In the Middle Ages the Church provided the model, and Guilds and secret societies erected their colleges of cardinals. Today the American industrial corporation provides the template, and the university models itself on General Motors. Corporations exist to create or discover consumers' desires and fulfill them with something that satisfies briefly and needs frequent repetition. CBS provides television as Gillette supplies disposable razors—and, alas, the universities turn out degree-holders equally disposable; and the major publishers of New York City (most of them less profitable annexes of conglomerates peddling soap, beer, and paper towels) provide disposable masterpieces.

The United States invented mass quick-consumption and we are very good at it. We are not famous for making Ferraris and Roll Royces; we are famous for the people's car, the Model T, the Model A—"transportation," as we call it: the particular abstracted into the utilitarian generality—and two in every garage. Quality is all very well but it is *not* democratic; if we insist on hand-building Rolls Royces most of us will walk to work. Democracy demands the interchangeable part and the worker on the production line; Thomas Jefferson may have had other notions but de Tocqueville was our prophet. Or take American cuisine: it has never added a

116

sauce to the world's palate, but our fast-food industry overruns the planet.

Thus: our poems, in their charming and interchangeable quantity, do not presume to the status of "Lycidas"—for that would be elitist and un-American. We write and publish the McPoem—*ten billion served*—which becomes our contribution to the history of literature as the Model T is our contribution to a history which runs from bare feet past elephant and rickshaw to the vehicles of space. Pull in any time day or night, park by the busload, and the McPoem waits on the steam shelf for us, wrapped and protected, indistinguishable, undistinguished, and reliable—the good old McPoem identical from coast to coast and in all the little towns between, subject to the quality control of the least common denominator.

And every year, Ronald McDonald takes the Pulitzer.

To produce the McPoem, institutions must enforce patterns, institutions within institutions, all subject to the same glorious dominance of unconscious economic determinism, template and formula of consumerism.

The McPoem is the product of the workshops of Hamburger University.

8. But before we look into the workshop, with its training program for junior poets, let us take a look at models provided by poetic heroes of the American present. The university does not invent the stereotypes; it provides technology for mass reproduction of a model created elsewhere.

Question: If you manufacture Pac-Man, or a car called Mustang, and everyone suddenly wants to buy what you make, how do you respond? Answer: You add shifts, pay overtime, and expand the plant in order to saturate the market with your product. . . . You make your product as quickly as you can manufacture it; notions of quality control do not disturb your dreams.

When Robert Lowell was young he wrote slowly and painfully and very well. On his wonderful Library of Congress LP, before he recites his early poem about "Falling Asleep over the Aeneid," he tells how the poem began when he tried translating Virgil but produced only eighty lines in six months, which he found disheartening. Five years elapsed between his Pulitzer book *Lord Weary's*

117

Castle, which was the announcement of his genius, and its under-rated successor *The Mills of the Kavanaghs*. Then there were eight more years before the abrupt innovation of *Life Studies*. *For the Union Dead* was spotty, *Near the Ocean* spottier, and then the rot set in.

Now, no man should be hanged for losing his gift, most especially a man who suffered as Lowell did. But one can, I think, feel annoyed when quality plunges as quantity multiplies: Lowell published six bad books of poems in those disastrous last eight years of his life.

(I say "bad books" and would go to the stake over the judgment, but let me hasten to acknowledge that each of these dreadful collections—dead metaphor, flat rhythm, narcissistic self-exploitation—was celebrated by leading critics on the front page of the *New York Times Book Review* and the *New York Review of Books* as the greatest yet of uniformly great emanations of great poetical greatness, greatly achieved. . . . But one wastes one's time in indignation. Taste is always a fool.)

John Berryman wrote with difficult concentration his difficult, concentrated *Mistress Bradstreet;* then he eked out 77 *Dream Songs*. Alas, after the success of this product he mass-produced *His Toy His Dream His Rest*, 308 further dream songs—quick improvisations of self-imitation, which is the true identity of the famous "voice" accorded late Berryman-Lowell. Now Robert Penn Warren, our current grand old man, accumulates another long book of poems every year or so, repeating himself instead of rewriting the same poem until it is right—hurry, hurry, hurry—and the publishing tribe celebrates these sentimental, crude, trite products of our industrial culture.

Not all poets overproduce in a response to eminence: Elizabeth Bishop never went on overtime; T. S. Eliot wrote bad plays at the end of his life, but never watered the soup of his poems; nor did Williams nor Stevens nor Pound. Of course everyone writes some inferior work—but these poets did not gush out bad poems late in their lives when they were famous and the market required more products for selling.

Mind you, the workshops of Hamburger University turned out cheap, ersatz Bishop, Eliot, Williams, Stevens, and Pound. All you want. . . .

9. Horace, when he wrote the *Ars Poetica*, recommended that poets keep their poems home for ten years; don't let them go, don't publish them until you have kept them around for ten years: by that time, they ought to stop moving on you; by that time, you ought to have them right. Sensible advice, I think—but difficult to follow. When Pope wrote "An Essay on Criticism" seventeen hundred years after Horace, he cut the waiting time in half, suggesting that poets keep their poems for five years before publication. Henry Adams said something about acceleration, mounting his complaint in 1912; some would say that acceleration has accelerated in the seventy years since. By this time, I would be grateful—and published poetry would be better—if people kept their poems home for eighteen months.

Poems have become as instant as coffee or onion soup mix. One of our eminent critics compared Lowell's last book to the work of Horace, although some of its poems were dated the year of publication. Anyone editing a magazine receives poems dated the day of the postmark. When a poet types and submits a poem just composed (or even shows it to spouse or friend) the poet cuts off from the poem the possibility of growth and change; I suspect that the poet *wishes* to forestall the possibilities of growth and change, though of course without acknowledging the wish.

If Robert Lowell, John Berryman and Robert Penn Warren publish without allowing for revision or self-criticism, how can we expect a twenty-four-year-old in Manhattan to wait five years—or eighteen months? With these famous men as models, how should we blame the young poet who boasts in a brochure of over four hundred poems published in the last five years? Or the publisher, advertising a book, who brags that his poet has published twelve books in ten years? Or the workshop teacher who meets a colleague on a crosswalk and buffs the backs of his fingernails against his tweed as he proclaims that, over the last two years, he has averaged "placing" two poems a week?

10. Abolish the M.F.A.! What a ringing slogan for a new Cato: *Iowa delenda est!*

The workshop schools us to produce the McPoem, which is "a mold in plaster, / Made with no loss of time," with no waste of effort, with no strenuous questioning as to merit. If we attend a workshop we must bring something to class or we do not contribute. What kind of workshop could Horace have contributed to, if he kept his poems to himself for ten years? No, we will not admit Horace and Pope to our workshops, for they will just sit there, holding back their own work, claiming it is not ready, acting superior, a bunch of *elitists.* . . .

When we use a metaphor, it is useful to make inquiries of it. I have already compared the workshop to a fast food franchise, to a Ford assembly line. . . . Or should we compare Creative Writing 401 to a sweatshop where women sew shirts at an illegally low wage? Probably the metaphor refers to none of the above, because the workshop is rarely a place for starting and finishing poems; it is a place for repairing them. The poetry workshop resembles a garage to which we bring incomplete or malfunctioning homemade machines for diagnosis and repair. Here is the homemade airplane for which the crazed inventor forgot to provide wings; here is the internal combustion engine all finished except that it lacks a carburetor; here is the rowboat without oarlocks, the ladder without rungs, the motorcycle without wheels. We advance our nonfunctional machine into a circle of other apprentice inventors and one or two senior Edisons. "Very good," they say; "it *almost* flies. . . . How about, uh . . . how about *wings?*" Or, "Let me just show you how to build a carburetor. . . ."

Whatever we bring to this place, we bring it soo soon. The weekly meetings of the workshop serve the haste of our culture. When we bring a new poem to the workshop, anxious for praise, others' voices enter the poem's metabolism before it is mature, distorting its possible growth and change. "It's only when you get far enough away from your work to begin to be critical of it yourself"—Robert Frost said—"that anyone else's criticism can be tolerable. . . ." Bring to class only, he said, "old and cold things. . . ." Nothing is old and cold until it has gone through months of drafts. Therefore workshopping is intrinsically impossible.

It is from workshops that American poets learn to enjoy the embarrassment of publication—too soon, too soon—because *making public* is a condition of workshopping. This publication exposes oneself to one's fellow-poets only—a condition of which poets are perpetually accused and frequently guilty. We learn to write poems that will please not the Muse but our contemporaries, thus poems that resemble our contemporaries' poems—thus the recipe for the McPoem. . . . If we learn one thing else, we learn to publish promiscuously; these premature ejaculations count on number and frequency to counterbalance ineptitude.

Poets who stay outside the circle of peers—like Whitman, who did not go to Harvard; like Dickinson for whom there was no tradition; like Robert Frost, who dropped out of two colleges to make his own way—these poets take Homer for their peer. To quote Frost again: "The thing is to write better and better poems. Setting our heart when we're too young on getting our poems appreciated lands us in the politics of poetry which is death." Agreeing with these words from Frost's dour middle-age, we need to add: and "setting our heart" when we are old "on getting our poems appreciated" lands us in the same place.

11. At the same time, it's a big country. . . .

Most poets need the conversation of other poets. They do not need mentors; they need friends, critics, people to argue with. It is no accident that Wordsworth, Coleridge, and Southey were friends when they were young; if Pound, H.D., and William Carlos Williams had not known each other when young, would they have become William Carlos Williams, H.D., and Pound? There have been some lone wolves but not many. The history of poetry is a history of friendships and rivalries, not only with the dead great ones but with the living young. My four years at college overlapped with the undergraduates Frank O'Hara, Adrienne Rich, John Ashbery, Robert Bly, Peter Davison, L. E. Sissman, and Kenneth Koch. (At the same time Galway Kinnell and W. S. Merwin attended Princeton.) I do not assert that we resembled a sewing circle, that we often helped each other overtly, or even that we *liked* each other. I do assert that we were lucky to have each other around for purposes of conversation.

We were not in workshops; we were merely attending college. Where else in this country would we have met each other? In France there is an answer to this question and it is Paris. Europe goes in for capital cities. Although England is less centralized than France or Romania, London is more capital than New York, San

Francisco, or Washington. While the French poet can discover the intellectual life of his times at a café, the American requires a degree program. The workshop is the institutionalized café.

The American problem of geographical isolation is real. Any remote place may be the site of poetry—imagined, remembered, or lived in—but for almost every poet it is necessary to live in exile before returning home—an exile rich in conflict and confirmation. Central New Hampshire or the Olympic Peninsula or Cincinnati or the soybean plains of western Minnesota or the lower East Side may shine at the center of our work and our lives; but if we never leave these places we are not likely to grow up enough to do the work. There is a terrible poignancy in the talented artist who fears to leave home—defined as a place *first* to leave and *then* to return to.

So the workshop answers the need for a café. But I called it the *institutionalized* café, and it differs from the Parisian version by instituting requirements and by hiring and paying mentors. Workshop mentors even make assignments: "Write a persona poem in the voice of a dead ancestor." "Make a poem containing these ten words in this order with as many other words as you wish." "Write a poem without adjectives, or without prepositions, or without content. . . ." These formulas, everyone says, are a whole lot of fun. . . . They also reduce poetry to a parlor game; they trivialize and make safe-seeming the real terrors of real art. This reduction-by-formula is not accidental. We play these games *in order* to reduce poetry to a parlor game. Games serve to democratize, to soften, and to standardize; they are repellent. Although in theory workshops serve a useful purpose in gathering young artists together, workshop practices enforce the McPoem.

This is your contrary assignment: be as good a poet as George Herbert. Take as long as you wish.

12. I mentioned earlier the disastrous separation, in many universities, of creative writing and literature. There are people writing poetry—teaching poetry, studying poetry—who find reading *academic*. Such a sentence sounds like a satiric invention; alas, it is objective reporting.

Our culture rewards specialization. It is absurd that we erect a barrier between one who reads and one who writes, but it is an absurdity with a history. It is absurd because in our writing our standards derive from what we have read, and its history reaches back to the ancient war between the poets and the philosophers, exemplified in Plato's "Ion" as the philosopher condescends to the rhapsode. In the thirties poets like Ransom, Tate, and Winters entered the academy under sufferance, condescended to. Tate and Winters especially made themselves academically rigorous. They secured the beachheads; the army of their grandchildren occupies the country: often grandsons and daughters who write books but do not read them.

The separation of the literature department from the writing department is a disaster; for poet, for scholar, and for student. The poet may prolong adolescence into retirement by dealing only with the products of infant brains. (If the poet, as in some schools, teaches literature, but only to writing students, the effect is better but not much better. The temptation exists then to teach literature as craft or trade; Americans don't need anyone teaching them trade.) The scholars of the department, institutionally separated from the contemporary, are encouraged to ignore it. In the ideal relationship, writers play gadfly to scholars, and and scholars help writers connect to the body of past literature. Students lose the writer's special contribution to the study of literature. Everybody loses.

13. It is commonplace that, in the English and American tradition, critic and poet are the same person—from Campion to Pound, from Sidney to Eliot. This tradition started with controversies between poets over the propriety of rhyme and English meter, and with poets' defense of poetry against Puritan attack. It flourished, serving many purposes, through Dryden, Johnson, Coleridge, Wordsworth, Keats in his letters, Shelley, Arnold. . . . Although certain poets have left no criticism, there are *no* first-rate critics in the English tradition who are not also poets—except for Hazlitt. The poet and the critic have been almost continuous, as if writing poetry and thinking about it were not discrete activities.

When Roman Jakobson—great linguist, Harvard professor—was approached some years ago with the suggestion that Vladimir Nabokov might be appointed professor of Slavic, Jakobson was skeptical; he had nothing against elephants, he said, but he would not appoint one professor of zoology.

Oh, dear.

The analogy compares the elegant and stylish Nabokov—novelist in various languages, lepidopterist, lecturer, and critic—to the great, gray, hulking pachyderm, intellectually noted *only* for memory. . . . By jokes and analogies we reveal ourselves. Jakobson condescends to Nabokov—just as Plato patted little Ion on his head, just as Sartre makes charitable exception for poets in *What is Literature?*, just as men have traditionally condescended to women and imperialists to natives. The points are clear: 1) "Artists are closer to nature than thinkers; they are more instinctive, more emotional; they are childlike." 2) "Artists like bright colors; artists have a natural sense of rhythm; artists screw all the time." 3) "Don't misunderstand. We *like* artists . . . in their place, which is in the zoo, or at any rate outside the Republic, or at any rate outside tenured ranks."

(One must admit, I suppose, that poets often find themselves in tenured ranks these days. But increasingly they enter by the zoo entrance, which in our universities is the department of creative writing.)

Formalism, with its dream of finite measurement, is a beautiful arrogance, a fantasy of materialism. When we find what's to measure and measure it, we should understand style-as-fingerprint, quantifying characteristic phonemic sequence . . . or whatever. But it seems likely that we will continue to intuit qualities, like degrees of intensity, for which objective measure is impossible. Then hard-noses will claim that only the measurable exists—which is why hard-nose usually means soft-head.

Once I audited a course of Jakobson's, for which I am grateful; the old formalist discoursed on comparative prosody, witty and energetic and learned, giving verbatim examples from Urdu and fifty other languages, exemplifying the multiplicity of countable noise. The journey was marvelous, the marvel diminished only a little by its terminus. The last lecture, pointed to for some weeks, turned out to be a demonstration, from an objective and untraditional approach, of how to scan (and the scansion was fine, and it was the way one scanned the poem when one was sixteen) of Edgar Poe's "The Raven."

14. A product of the creative writing industry is the writerly newsletter which concerns itself with publications, grants, and

124

jobs—and with nothing serious. If poets meeting each other in 1941 discussed how much they were paid a line, now they trade information about grants; left wing and right united; to be Establishment is to have received an N.E.A. grant; to be anti-Establishment is to denounce the N.E.A. as a conspiracy. . . . Like Republicans and Democrats, all belong to the same capitalist party.

Poets and Writers publishes *Coda*, with chatty articles about self-publication, with lists of contests and awards. It resembles not so much a trade journal as a hobbyist's bulletin, unrelievedly cheerful, relentlessly trivial. The same organization issues the telephone-book, *A Directory of American Poets*, "Names and addresses of 1,500 poets. . . ." The same organization offers T-shirts and bookbags labeled "Poets and Writers."

Associated Writing Programs publishes *A.W.P. Newsletter*, which includes one article each issue—often a talk addressed to an A.W.P. meeting—and adds helpful business aids: The December 1982 issue includes advice on "The 'Well Written' Letter of Application," lists of magazines requesting material ("The editors state they are looking for 'straightforward but not inartistic work' "), lists of grants and awards ("The annual HARRY SMITH BOOK AWARD is given by COSMEP to . . ."), and notices of A.W.P. competitions and conventions. . . .

Really, these newsletters provide illusion; for jobs and grants go to the eminent people. As we all know, eminence is arithmetical: it derives from the number of units published times the prestige of the places of publication. People hiring or granting do not judge quality—it's so subjective!—but anyone can multiply units by the prestige index and come off with the *product*. Eminence also brings readings. Can we go uncorrupted by such knowledge? I am asked to introduce a young poet's volume; the publisher will pay the going rate; but I did not know that there was a going rate. . . . Even blurbs on jackets are commodities. They are exchanged for pamphlets, for readings; reciprocal blurbs are only the most obvious exchanges. . . .

15. Sigh.

If it seems hopeless, one has only to look up in perfect silence at the stars . . . and it *does* help to remember that poems are the stars, not poets. Of most help is to remember that it is possible for people to take hold of themselves and become better by thinking. It is also necessary, alas, to *continue* to take hold of ourselves—if we are to pursue the true ambition of poetry. Our disinterest must discover that last week's nobility was really covert rottenness, etcetera. One is never free and clear; one must work continually to sustain, to recover. . . .

When Keats in his letters praised disinterestedness—his favorite moral idea, destroyed when it is misused as a synonym for lethargy (on the same day I found it misused in the *New York Times, Inside Sports*, and the *American Poetry Review*), he lectured himself because he feared that he would lose it. (Lectures loud with moral advice are always self-addressed.) No one is guiltless of temptation, but it is possible to resist temptation. When Keats worried over his reputation, over insults from Haydon or *The Quarterly*, over Shelley's condescension or Wordsworth's neglect, he reminded himself to cultivate disinterest; to avoid distraction and to keep his eye on the true goal, which was to become one of the English Poets.

Yeats is responsible for a number of the stars in the sky, and when we read his letters we find that the young man was an extraordinary trimmer—soliciting reviews from Oscar Wilde and flattering Katherine Tynan, older and more established on the Celtic turf. One of the O.E.D.'s definitions of ambition, after "eager desire of honor," is "personal solicitation of honor." When he wrote, "I seek an image not a book," he acknowledged that as a young man he had sought a book indeed. None of us, beseeching Doubleday or Pittsburgh, has ever sought with greater fervor.

And Whitman reviewed himself, and Roethke campaigned for praise like a legislator at the state fair, and Frost buttered Untermeyer on both sides. . . . (Therefore let us abjure the old saw that self-promotion and empire-building mean bad poetry. Most entrepreneurs are bad poets—but then, so are most poets.) Self-promotion remains a side-issue of poetry and ambition. It *can* reflect a greed or covetousness which displaces the grand ambition—the kind of covetousness which looks on the life lived only as a source of poems; "I got a poem out of it." Or it can show only the trivial side of someone who, on other occasions, makes great art. At any rate, we should spend our time worrying not about other people's bad characters, but our own.

Finally, of course, I speak of nothing except the modest topic: how shall we lead our lives? I think of a man I admire as much as anyone, the English sculptor Henry Moore, eighty-four as I write these notes, eighty when I spoke with him last. "Now that you are eighty," I asked him, "would you tell me the secret of life?" Being a confident and eloquent Yorkshireman, Moore would not deny my request. He told me:

"The greatest good luck in life, for *anybody,* is to have something that means *everything* to you . . . to do what you want to do, and to find that people will pay you for doing it . . . *if* it's unattainable. It's no good having an objective that's attainable! That's the big thing: you have an ideal, an objective, and that objective is unreachable. . . ."

16. There is no audit we can perform on ourselves, to assure that we work with proper ambition. Obviously it helps to be careful; to revise, to take time, to put the poem away; to pursue distance in the hope of objective measure. We know that the poem, to satisfy ambition's goals, must not express mere personal feeling or opinion—as the moment's McPoem does. It must by its language make art's new object. We must try to hold ourselves to the mark; we must not write to publish or to prevail. Repeated scrutiny is the only method general enough for recommending. . . .

And of course repeated scrutiny is not foolproof; and we will fool ourselves. Nor can the hours we work provide an index of ambition or seriousness. Although Henry Moore laughs at artists who work only an hour or two a day, he acknowledges that sculptors can carve sixteen hours at a stretch for years on end—tap-tap-tap on stone—and remain lazy. We can revise our poems five hundred times; we can lock poems in their rooms for ten years—and remain modest in our endeavor. On the other hand, anyone casting a glance over biography or literary history must acknowledge: some great poems have come without noticeable labor.

But as I speak I confuse realms. Ambition is not a quality of the poem but of the poet. Failure and achievement belong to the poet, and if our goal remains unattainable, then failure must be standard. To pursue the unattainable for eighty-five years, like Henry Moore, may imply a certain temperament. . . . If there is no method of work that we can rely on, maybe at least we can encourage in ourselves a temperament that is not easily satisfied.

Sometime when we are discouraged with our own work, we may notice that even the great poems, the sources and the standards, seem inadequate: "Ode to a Nightingale" feels too limited in scope, "Out of the Cradle" too sloppy, "To His Coy Mistress" too neat, and "Among Schoolchildren" padded. . . .

Maybe ambition is appropriately unattainable when we acknowledge: *No poem is so great as we demand that poetry be.*

1984

NOT-KNOWING

by DONALD BARTHELME

from THE GEORGIA REVIEW

LET US suppose that someone is writing a story. From the world of conventional signs he takes an azalea bush, plants it in a pleasant park. He takes a gold pocket watch from the world of conventional signs and places it under the azalea bush. He takes from the same rich source a handsome thief and a chastity belt, places the thief in the chastity belt and lays him tenderly under the azalea, not neglecting to wind the gold pocket watch so that its ticking will, at length, awaken the now-sleeping thief. From the Sarah Lawrence campus he borrows a pair of seniors, Jacqueline and Jemima, and sets them to walking in the vicinity of the azalea bush and the handsome, chaste thief. Jacqueline and Jemima have just failed the Graduate Record Examination and are cursing God in colorful Sarah Lawrence language. What happens next?

Of course, I don't know.

It's appropriate to pause and say that the writer is one who, embarking upon a task, does not know what to do. I cannot tell you, at this moment, whether, Jacqueline and Jemima will succeed or fail in their effort to jimmy the chastity belt's lock, or whether the thief, whose name is Zeno and who has stolen the answer sheets for the next set of Graduate Record Examinations, will pocket the pocket watch or turn it over to the nearest park employee. The fate of the azalea bush, whether it will bloom or strangle in a killing frost, is unknown to me.

A very conscientious writer might purchase an azalea at the Downtown Nursery and a gold watch at Tiffany's, hire a handsome thief fresh from Riker's Island, obtain the loan of a chastity belt from the Metropolitan, inveigle Jacqueline and Jemima in from Bronxville, and arrange them all under glass for study, writing up the results in honest, even fastidious prose. But in so doing he places himself in the realm of journalism or sociology. The not-knowing is crucial to art, is what permits art to be made. Without the scanning process engendered by not-knowing, without the possibility of having the mind move in unanticipated directions, there would be no invention.

This is not to say that I don't know anything about Jacqueline or Jemima, but what I do know comes into being at the instant it's inscribed. Jacqueline, for example, loathes her mother, whereas Jemima dotes on hers—I discover this by writing the sentence that announces it. Zeno was fathered by a—what? Polar bear? Roller skate? Shower of gold? I opt for the shower of gold, for Zeno is a hero (although he's just become one by virtue of his golden parent). Inside the pocket watch there is engraved a legend. Can I make it out? I think so: *Drink me*, it says. No no, can't use it, that's Lewis Carroll's. But could Zeno be a watch-swallower rather than a thief? No again, Zeno'd choke on it, and so would the reader. There are rules.

Writing is a process of dealing with not-knowing, a forcing of what and how. We have all heard novelists testify to the fact that, beginning a new book, they are utterly baffled as to how to proceed, what should be written and how it might be written, even though they've done a dozen. At best there's a slender intuition, not much greater than an itch. The anxiety attached to this situation is not inconsiderable. "Nothing to paint and nothing to paint with," as Beckett says of Bram van Velde. The not-knowing is not simple, because it's hedged about with prohibitions, roads that may not be taken. The more serious the artist, the more problems he takes into account and the more considerations limit his possible initiatives—a point to which I shall return.

What kind of a fellow is Zeno? How do I know until he's opened his mouth?

"Gently, ladies, gently," says Zeno, as Jacqueline and Jemima bash away at the belt with a spade borrowed from a friendly park employee. And to the park employee: "Somebody seems to have lost this-here watch."

Let us change the scene.

Alphonse, the park employee from the preceding episode, he

who lent the spade, is alone in his dismal room on West Street (I could position him as well in a four-story townhouse on East Seventy-second, but you'd object, and rightly so, verisimilitude forbids it, nothing's calculated quicker than a salary). Alphonse, like so many toilers in the great city, is not as simple as he seems. Like those waiters who are really actors and those cab drivers who are really composers of electronic music, Alphonse is sunlighting as a Parks Department employee although he is, in reality, a literary critic. We find him writing a letter to his friend Gaston, also a literary critic although masquerading pro tem as a guard at the Whitney Museum. Alphonse poises paws over his Smith-Corona and writes:

Dear Gaston,

Yes, you are absolutely right—Postmodernism is dead. A stunning blow, but not entirely surprising. I am spreading the news as rapidly as possible, so that all of our friends who are in the Postmodernist "bag" can get out of it before their cars are repossessed and the insurance companies tear up their policies. Sad to see Postmodernism go (and so quickly!). I was fond of it. As fond, almost, as I was of its grave and noble predecessor, Modernism. But we cannot dwell in the done-for. The death of a movement is a natural part of life, as was understood so well by the partisans of Naturalism, which is dead.

I remember exactly where I was when I realized that Postmodernism had bought it. I was in my study with a cup of tequila and William Y's new book, *One-Half*. Y's work is, we agree, good—*very* good. But who can make the leap to greatness while dragging after him the burnt-out boxcars of a dead aesthetic? Perhaps we can find new employment for him. On the roads, for example. When the insight overtook me, I started to my feet, knocking over the tequila, and said aloud (although there was no one to hear), "What? Postmodernism, too?" So many, so many. I put Y's book away on a high shelf and turned to the contemplation of the death of Plainsong, A.D. 958.

By the way: Structuralism's tottering. I heard it from Gerald, who is at Johns Hopkins and thus in the thick of things. You don't have to tell everybody. Frequently,

131

idle talk is enough to give a movement that last little "push" that topples it into its grave. I'm convinced that's what happened to the New Criticism. I'm persuaded that it was Gerald, whispering in the corridors.

On the bright side, one thing that is dead that I don't feel too bad about is Existentialism, which I never thought was anything more than Phenomenology's bathwater anyway. It had a good run, but how peeving it was to hear all those artists going around talking about "the existential moment" and similar claptrap. Luckily, they have stopped doing that now. Similarly, the Nouveau Roman's passing did not disturb me overmuch. "Made dreariness into a religion," you said, quite correctly. I know this was one of your pared-to-the-bone movements and all that, but I didn't even like what they left out. A neat omission usually raises the hairs on the back of my neck. Not here. Robbe-Grillet's only true success, for my money, was with *Jealousy*, which I'm told he wrote in a fit of.

Well, where are we? Surrealism gone, got a little sweet toward the end, you could watch the wine of life turning into Gatorade. Sticky. Altar Poems—those constructed in the shape of an altar for the greater honor and glory of God—have not been seen much lately: missing and presumed dead. The Anti-Novel is dead; I read it in the *Times*. The Anti-Hero and the Anti-Heroine had a thing going which resulted in three Anti-Children, all of them now at M.I.T. The Novel of the Soil is dead, as are Expressionism, Impressionism, Futurism, Imagism, Vorticism, Regionalism, Realism, the Kitchen Sink School of Drama, the Theatre of the Absurd, the Theatre of Cruelty, Black Humor, and Gongorism. You know all this; I'm just totting up. To be a Pre-Raphaelite in the present era is to be somewhat out of touch. And, of course, Concrete Poetry—sank like a stone.

So we have a difficulty. What shall we call the New Thing, which I haven't encountered yet but which is bound to be out there somewhere? Post-Postmodernism sounds, to me, a little lumpy. I've been toying with the Revolution of the Word, II, or the New Revolution of the Word, but I'm afraid the Jolas estate may hold a copyright. It should have the word *new* in it somewhere. The New Newness? Or maybe the Post-New? It's a problem. I await your comments and suggestions. If we're going to slap a saddle on this rough beast, we've got to get moving.

Yours,
Alphonse

If I am slightly more sanguine than Alphonse about Postmodernism, however dubious about the term itself and not altogether clear as to who is supposed to be on the bus and who is not, it's because I locate it in relation to a series of problems, and feel that the problems are durable ones. Problems are a comfort. Wittgenstein said, of philosophers, that some of them suffer from "loss of problems," a development in which everything seems quite simple to them and what they write becomes "immeasurably shallow and trivial." The same can be said of writers. Before I mention some of the specific difficulties I have in mind, I'd like to at least glance at some of the criticisms that have been leveled at the alleged Postmodernists—let's say John Barth, William Gass, John Hawkes, Robert Coover, William Gaddis, Thomas Pynchon, and myself in this country, Calvino in Italy, Peter Handke and Thomas Bernhard in Germany, although other names could be invoked. The criticisms run roughly as follows: that this kind of writing has turned its back on the world, is in some sense not about the world but about its own processes, that it is masturbatory, certainly chilly, that it excludes readers by design, speaks only to the already tenured, or that it does not speak at all, but instead, like Frost's Secret, sits in the center of a ring and Knows.

I would ardently contest each of these propositions, but it's rather easy to see what gives rise to them. The problems that seem to me to define the writer's task at this moment (to the extent that he has chosen them as his problems) are not of a kind that make for ease of communication, for work that rushes toward the reader with outflung arms—rather, they're the reverse. Let me cite three such difficulties that I take to be important, all having to do with language. First, there is art's own project, since Mallarmé, of restoring freshness to a much-handled language, essentially an effort toward finding a language in which making art is possible at all. This remains a ground theme, as potent, problematically, today as it was a century ago. Secondly, there is the political and social contamination of language by its use in manipulation of various kinds over time and the effort to find what might be called a "clean" language, problems associated with the Roland Barthes of *Writing Degree Zero* but also discussed by Lukács and others. Finally, there is the pressure on language from contemporary culture in the broadest sense—I mean our devouring commercial culture—which results in a double impoverishment: theft of complexity from the reader, theft of the reader from the writer.

These are by no means the only thorny matters with which the writer has to deal, nor (allowing for the very great differences among the practitioners under discussion) does every writer called Postmodern respond to them in the same way and to the same degree, nor is it the case that other writers of quite different tendencies are innocent of these concerns. If I call these matters "thorny," it's because any adequate attempt to deal with them automatically creates barriers to the ready assimilation of the work. Art is not difficult because it wishes to be difficult, but because it wishes to be art. However much the writer might long to be, in his work, simple, honest, and straightforward, these virtues are no longer available to him. He discovers that in being simple, honest, and straightforward, nothing much happens: he speaks the speakable, whereas what we are looking for is the as-yet unspeakable, the as-yet unspoken.

With Mallarmé the effort toward mimesis, the representation of the external world, becomes a much more complex thing than it had been previously. Mallarmé shakes words loose from their attachments and bestows new meanings upon them, meanings which point not toward the external world but toward the Absolute, acts of poetic intuition. This is a fateful step; not for nothing does Barthes call him the Hamlet of literature. It produces, for one thing, a poetry of unprecedented difficulty. You will find no Mallarmé in Bartlett's *Familiar Quotations*. Even so ardent an admirer as Charles Mauron speaks of the sense of alienation enforced by his work. Mauron writes: "All who remember the day when first they looked into the *Poems* or the *Divagations* will testify to that curious feeling of *exclusion* which put them, in the face of a text written with *their* words (and moreover, as they could somehow feel, magnificently written), suddenly outside their own language, deprived of their rights in a common speech, and, as it were, rejected by their oldest friends." Mallarmé's work is also, and perhaps most importantly, a step toward establishing a new ontological status for the poem, as an object in the world rather than a representation of the world. But the ground seized is dangerous ground. After Mallarmé the struggle to renew language becomes a given for the writer, his exemplary quest an imperative. Mallarmé's work, "this whisper that is so close to silence," as Marcel Raymond calls it, is at once a liberation and a loss to silence of a great deal of territory.

The silencing of an existing rhetoric (in Harold Rosenberg's phrase) is also what is at issue in Barthes's deliberations in *Writing Degree Zero* and after—in this case a variety of rhetorics seen as actively pernicious rather than passively inhibiting. The question is, what is the complicity of language in the massive crimes of Fascism, Stalinism, or (by implication) our own policies in Vietnam? In the control of societies by the powerful and their busy functionaries? If these abominations are all in some sense facilitated by, made possible by, language, to what degree is that language ruinously contaminated (considerations also raised by George Steiner in his well-known essay "The Hollow Miracle" and, much earlier, by George Orwell)? I am sketching here, inadequately, a fairly complex argument; I am not particularly taken with Barthes's tentative solutions but the problems command the greatest respect. Again, we have language deeply suspicious of its own behavior; although this suspicion is not different in kind from Hemingway's noticing, early in the century, that words like *honor, glory,* and *country* were perjured, bought, the skepticism is far deeper now, and informed as well by the investigations of linguistic philosophers, structuralists, semioticians. Even conjunctions must be inspected carefully. "I read each word with the feeling appropriate to it," says Wittgenstein. "The word 'but' for example with the but-feeling. . . ." He is not wrong. Isn't the but-feeling, as he calls it, already sending us headlong down a greased slide before we've had the time to contemplate the proposition it's abutting? Quickly now, quickly—when you hear the phrase "our vital interests" do you stop to wonder whether you were invited to the den, Zen Klan, or coven meeting at which these were defined? Did you speak?

In turning to the action of contemporary culture on language, and thus on the writer, the first thing to be noticed is a loss of reference. If I want a world of reference to which all possible readers in this country can respond, there is only one universe of discourse available, that in which the Love Boat sails on seas of passion like a Flying Dutchman of passion and the dedicated men in white of *General Hospital* pursue, with evenhanded diligence, triple bypasses and the nursing staff. This limits things somewhat. The earlier newspaper culture, which once dealt in a certain amount of nuance and zestful, highly literate hurly-burly, has deteriorated shockingly. The newspaper I worked for as a raw youth, thirty years ago, is today a pallid imitation of its former self. Where once we could put spurious quotes in the paper and attribute them to Ambrose Bierce and be fairly sure that enough readers would get the joke to make the joke worthwhile, from the point of view of both reader and writer, no such common ground now exists. The situation is not peculiar to this country. Steiner remarks of the best current journalism in Germany that, read against an average number of the *Frankfurter Zeitung* of pre-Hitler days, it's difficult at times to believe that both are written in German. At the other end of the scale much of the most exquisite description of the world, discourse about the world, is now being carried on in mathematical languages obscure to most people—certainly to me—and the contributions the sciences once made to our common language in the form of coinages, new words and concepts, are now available only to specialists. When one adds the ferocious appropriation of high culture by commercial culture—it takes, by my estimate, about forty-five minutes for any given novelty in art to travel from the Mary Boone Gallery on West Broadway to the display windows of Henri Bendel on Fifty-seventh Street—one begins to appreciate the seductions of silence.

Problems in part define the kind of work the writer chooses to do, and are not to be avoided but embraced. A writer, says Karl Kraus, is a man who can make a riddle out of an answer.

Let me begin again.

Jacqueline and Jemima are instructing Zeno, who has returned the purloined GRE documents and is thus restored to dull respectability, in Postmodernism. Postmodernism, they tell him, has turned its back on the world, is not about the world but about its

136

own processes, is masturbatory, certainly chilly, excludes readers by design, speaks only to the already tenured, or does not speak at all, but instead—

Zeno, to demonstrate that he too knows a thing or two, quotes the critic Perry Meisel on semiotics. "Semiotics," he says, "is in a position to claim that no phenomenon has any ontological status outside its place in the particular information system from which it draws its meaning"—he takes a large gulp of his Gibson— "and therefore, all language is finally groundless." I am eavesdropping and I am much reassured. This insight is one I can use. Gaston, the critic who is a guard at the Whitney Museum, is in love with an IRS agent named Madelaine, the very IRS agent, in fact, who is auditing my return for the year 1982. "Madelaine," I say kindly to her over lunch, "semiotics is in a position to claim that no phenomenon has any ontological status outside its place in the particular information system from which it draws its meaning, and therefore, all language is finally groundless, including that of those funny little notices you've been sending me." "Yes," says Madelaine kindly, pulling from her pocket a large gold pocket watch that Alphonse has sold Gaston for twenty dollars, her lovely violet eyes atwitter, "but some information systems are more enforceable than others." Alas, she's right.

If the writer is taken to be the work's way of getting itself written, a sort of lightning rod for an accumulation of atmospheric disturbances, a St. Sebastian absorbing in his tattered breast the arrows of the Zeitgeist, this changes not very much the traditional view of the artist. But it does license a very great deal of critical imperialism.

This is fun for everyone. A couple of years ago I received a letter from a critic requesting permission to reprint a story of mine as an addendum to the piece he had written about it. He attached the copy of my story he proposed to reproduce, and I was amazed to find that my poor story had sprouted a set of tiny numbers—one to eighty-eight, as I recall—an army of tiny numbers marching over the surface of my poor distracted text. Resisting the temptation to tell him that all the tiny numbers were in the wrong places, I gave him permission to do what he wished, but I did notice that by a species of literary judo the status of my text had been reduced to that of footnote.

There is, in this kind of criticism, an element of aggression that gives one pause. Deconstruction is an enterprise that announces its intentions with startling candor. Any work of art depends upon a complex series of interdependences. If I wrench the rubber tire from the belly of Rauschenberg's famous goat to determine, in the interest of a finer understanding of same, whether the tire is a B. F. Goodrich or a Uniroyal, the work collapses, more or less behind my back. I say this not because I find this kind of study valueless but because the mystery worthy of study, for me, is not the signification of parts but how they come together, the tire wrestled over the goat's hind legs. Calvin Tomkins tells us in *The Bride and the Bachelors* that Rauschenberg himself says that the tire seemed "something as unavoidable as the goat." To see both goat and tire as "unavoidable" choices, in the context of art-making, is to illuminate just how strange the combinatorial process can be. Nor was the choice a hasty one; Tomkins tells us that the goat had been in the studio for three years and had appeared in two previous versions (the final version is titled "Monogram") before it met the tire.

Modern-day critics speak of "recuperating" a text, suggesting an accelerated and possibly strenuous nursing back to health of a basically sickly text, very likely one that did not even know itself to be ill. I would argue that in the competing methodologies of contemporary criticism, many of them quite rich in implications, a sort of tyranny of great expectations obtains, a rage for final explanations, a refusal to allow a work that mystery which is essential to it. I hope I am not myself engaging in mystification if I say, not that the attempt should not be made, but that the mystery exists. I see no immediate way out of the paradox—tear a mystery to tatters and you have tatters, not mystery—I merely note it and pass on.

We can, however, wonder for a moment why the goat girdled with its tire is somehow a magical object, rather than, say, only a dumb idea. Harold Rosenberg speaks of the contemporary artwork as "anxious," as wondering: Am I a masterpiece or simply a pile of junk? (If I take many of my examples here from the art world rather than the world of literature it is because the issues are more quickly seen in terms of the first: "goat" and "tire" are standing in for pages of prose, pounds of poetry.) What precisely is it in the coming together of goat and tire that is magical? It's not the surprise of seeing the goat attired, although that's part of it. One might say, for example, that the tire *contests* the goat, *contradicts* the goat, as a mode of being, even that the tire *reproaches* the goat, in some sense. On the simplest punning level, the goat is *tired*. Or that the unfortunate tire has *been caught by* the goat, which has been fishing in the Hudson—goats eat anything, as everyone knows—or that the goat is being *consumed by* the tire; it's outside, after all, mechanization takes command. Or that the goateed goat is protesting the fatigue of its friend, the tire, by wearing it as a sort of STRIKE button. Or that two contrasting models of infinity are being presented, tires and goats both being infinitely reproducible, the first depending on the good fortunes of the B. F. Goodrich Company and the second upon the copulatory enthusiasm of goats—parallel production lines suddenly met. And so on. What is magical about the object is that it at once invites and resists interpretation. Its artistic worth is measurable by the degree to which it remains, after interpretation, vital—no interpretation or cardiopulmonary push-pull can exhaust or empty it.

In what sense is the work "about" the world, the world that Jacqueline and Jemima have earnestly assured Zeno the work has turned its scarlet rump to? It is to this vexing question that we shall turn next.

Let us discuss the condition of my desk. It is messy, mildly messy. The messiness is both physical (coffee cups, cigarette ash) and spiritual (unpaid bills, unwritten novels). The emotional life of the man who sits at the desk is also messy—I am in love with a set of twins, Hilda and Heidi, and in a fit of enthusiasm I have joined the Bolivian army. The apartment in which the desk is located seems to have been sublet from Moonbeam McSwine. In the streets outside the apartment melting snow has revealed a choice assortment of decaying et cetera. Furthermore, the social organization of the country is untidy, the world situation in disarray. How do I render all this messiness, and if I succeed, what have I done?

In a common-sense way we agree that I attempt to find verbal equivalents for whatever it is I wish to render. The unpaid bills are easy enough. I need merely quote one: FINAL DISCONNECT NOTICE. Hilda and Heidi are somewhat more difficult. I can say that they are beautiful—why not?—and you will more or less agree, although the bald statement has hardly stirred your senses. I can describe them—Hilda has the map of Bolivia tattooed on her

139

right cheek and Heidi habitually wears, on her left hand, a set of brass knuckles wrought of solid silver—and they move a step closer. Best of all, perhaps, I can permit them to speak, for they speak much as we do.

"On Valentine's Day," says Hilda, "he sent me oysters, a dozen and a half."

"He sent me oysters too," says Heidi, "two dozen."

"Mine were long-stemmed oysters," says Hilda, "on a bed of the most wonderful spinach."

"Oh yes, spinach," says Heidi, "he sent me spinach too, miles and miles of spinach, wrote every bit of it himself."

To render "messy" adequately, to the point that you are enabled to feel it—it should, ideally, frighten your shoes—I would have to be more graphic than the decorum of the occasion allows. What should be emphasized is that one proceeds by way of particulars. If I know how a set of brass knuckles feels on Heidi's left hand it's because I bought one once, in a pawnshop, not to smash up someone's face but to exhibit on a pedestal in a museum show devoted to cultural artifacts of ambivalent status. The world enters the work as it enters our ordinary lives, not as world-view or system but in sharp particularity: a tax notice from Madelaine, a snowball containing a résumé from Gaston.

The words with which I attempt to render "messy," like any other words, are not inert, rather they are furiously busy. We do not mistake the words *the taste of chocolate* for the taste of chocolate itself, but neither do we miss the tease in *taste*, the shock in *chocolate*. Words have halos, patinas, overhangs, echoes. The word *halo*, for instance, may invoke St. Hilarius, of whom we've seen too little lately. The word *patina* brings back the fine pewtery shine on the saint's halo. The word *overhang* reminds us that we have, hanging over us, a dinner date with St. Hilarius, that crashing bore. The word *echo* restores to us Echo herself, poised like the White Rock girl on the overhang of a patina of a halo— infirm ground, we don't want the poor spirit to pitch into the pond where Narcissus blooms eternally, they'll bump foreheads, or maybe other parts closer to the feet, a scandal. There's chocolate smeared all over Hilarius' halo—messy, messy. . . .

140

The combinatorial agility of words, the exponential generation of meaning once they're allowed to go to bed together, allows the writer to surprise himself, makes art possible, reveals how much of Being we haven't yet encountered. It could be argued that computers can do this sort of thing for us, with critic-computers monitoring their output. When computers learn how to make jokes, artists will be in serious trouble. But artists will respond in such a way as to make art impossible for the computer. They will redefine art to take into account (that is, to exclude) technology—photography's impact upon painting and painting's brilliant response being a clear and comparatively recent example.

The prior history of words is one of the aspects of language the world uses to smuggle itself into the work. If words can be contaminated by the world, they can also carry with them into the work trace elements of world which can be used in a positive sense. We must allow ourselves the advantages of our disadvantages.

A late bulletin: Hilda and Heidi have had a baby, with which they're thoroughly displeased, it's got no credit cards and can't speak French, they'll send it back. . . . Messy.

Style is not much a matter of choice. One does not sit down to write and think: Is this poem going to be a Queene Anne poem, a Biedermeier poem, a Vienna Secession poem, or a Chinese Chippendale poem? Rather it is both a response to constraint and a seizing of opportunity. Very often a constraint is an opportunity. It would seem impossible to write *Don Quixote* once again, yet Borges has done so with great style, improving on the original (as he is not slow to tell us) while remaining faithful to it, faithful as a tick on a dog's belly. I don't mean that whim does not intrude. Why do I avoid, as much as possible, using the semicolon? Let me be plain: the semicolon is ugly, ugly as a tick on a dog's belly. I pinch them out of my prose. The great German writer Arno Schmidt, punctuation-drunk, averages eleven to a page.

Style is of course *how*. And the degree to which *how* has become *what*—since, say, Flaubert—is a question that men of conscience wax wroth about, and should. If I say of my friend that on this issue his marbles are a little flat on one side, this does not mean that I do not love my friend. He, on the other hand, considers that I am ridden by strange imperatives, and that the little piece I gave to

141

the world last week, while nice enough in its own way, would have been vastly better had not my deplorable aesthetics caused me to score it for banjulele, cross between a banjo and a uke. Bless Babel.

Let us suppose that I am the toughest banjulele player in town and that I have contracted to play "Melancholy Baby" for six hours before an audience that will include the four next-toughest banjulele players in town. We imagine the smoky basement club, the hustling waiters (themselves students of the jazz banjulele), Jacqueline, Jemima, Zeno, Alphonse, Gaston, Madelaine, Hilda, and Heidi forming a congenial group at the bar. There is one thing of which you may be sure: I am not going to play "Melancholy Baby" as written. Rather I will play something that is parallel, in some sense, to "Melancholy Baby," based upon the chords of "Melancholy Baby"—commentary, exegesis, elaboration, contradiction. The interest of my construction, if any, is to be located in the space between the new entity I have constructed and the "real" "Melancholy Baby," which remains in the mind as the horizon which bounds my efforts.

This is, I think, the relation of art to world. I suggest that art is always a meditation upon external reality rather than a representation of external reality or a jackleg attempt to "be" external reality. If I perform even reasonably well, no one will accuse me of not providing a true, verifiable, note-for-note reproduction of "Melancholy Baby"—it will be recognized that this was not what I was after. Twenty years ago I was much more convinced of the autonomy of the literary object than I am now, and even wrote a rather persuasive defense of the proposition that I have just rejected: that the object is itself world. Beguiled by the rhetoric of the time—the sculptor Phillip Pavia was publishing a quite good magazine called *It Is,* and this was typical—I felt that the high ground had been claimed and wanted to place my scuffed cowboy boots right there. The proposition's still attractive. What's the right answer? Bless Babel.

A couple of years ago I visited Willem de Kooning's studio in East Hampton, and when the big doors are opened one can't help seeing—it's a shock—the relation between the rushing green world outside and the paintings. Precisely how de Kooning manages to distill nature into art is a mystery, but the explosive relation is there, I've seen it. Once when I was in Elaine de

142

Kooning's studio on Broadway, at a time when the metal sculptor Herbert Ferber occupied the studio immediately above, there came through the floor a most horrible crashing and banging. "What in the world is that?" I asked, and Elaine said, "Oh, that's Herbert thinking."

Art is a true account of the activity of mind. Because consciousness, in Husserl's formulation, is always consciousness *of* something, art thinks ever of the world, cannot not think of the world, could not turn its back on the world even if it wished to. This does not mean that it's going to be honest as a mailman; it's more likely to appear as a drag queen. The problems I mentioned earlier, as well as others not taken up, enforce complexity. "We do not spend much time in front of a canvas whose intentions are plain," writes Cioran, "music of a specific character, unquestionable contours, exhausts our patience, the over-explicit poem seems . . . incomprehensible." Flannery O'Connor, an artist of the first rank, famously disliked anything that looked funny on the page, and her distaste has widely been taken as a tough-minded put-down of puerile experimentalism. But did she also dislike anything that looked funny on the wall? If so, a severe deprivation. Art cannot remain in one place. A certain amount of movement up, down, across, even a gallop toward the past, is a necessary precondition.

Style enables us to speak, to imagine again. Beckett speaks of "the long sonata of the dead"—where on earth did the word *sonata* come from, imposing as it does an orderly, even exalted design upon the most disorderly, distressing phenomenon known to us? The fact is not challenged, but understood, momentarily, in a new way. It's our good fortune to be able to imagine alternative realities, other possibilities. We can quarrel with the world, constructively (no one alive has quarreled with the world more extensively or splendidly than Beckett). "Belief in progress," says Baudelaire, "is a doctrine of idlers and Belgians." Perhaps. But if I have anything unorthodox to offer here, it's that I think art's project is fundamentally meliorative. The aim of meditating about the world is finally to change the world. It is this meliorative aspect of literature that provides its ethical dimension. We are all Upton Sinclairs, even that Hamlet, Stéphane Mallarmé.

1986

143

PAPER TIGERS

by ELIOT WEINBERGER

from SULFUR

T.

The Maharajah of Rewa, according to his English Adviser, had his own method of hunting tiger:

> He found the easiest way to bag tigers was to take with him a book and a monkey on a long string. When seated in the *machan* [a platform in the trees] he would release the monkey, who immediately climbed into the top branches. He would then give the signal for the beat to start and settle down to read. As soon as the tiger approached the monkey would spot him and give the cough with which all monkeys warn the jungle folk that "Sher Khan" the tiger is on the prowl. His Highness would then quickly put down his book and pick up the rifle.

At the turning of a page, the apparition of a tiger:

Y.

Berggasse 19, March 10, 1933: H. D., one of the last patients of Freud, records her sessions with the Professor:

> Curiously in fantasy I think of a tiger. Myself as a tiger? This tiger may pounce out. Suppose it should

144

attack the frail and delicate old Professor? Do I fear my own terrors of the present situation, the lurking "beast" may or may not destroy him? I mention this tiger as a past nursery fantasy. Suppose it should actually materialize? The Professor says, "I have my protector."

He indicates Yofi, the little lioness curled at his feet.

And a few days later:

> I spoke again of our toy animals and he reminded me of my tiger fantasy. Wasn't there a story, "the woman and the tiger," he asked. I remembered "The Lady or the Tiger."

G.

A King invents a peculiar system of justice: The accused is placed in a large arena before the entire populace and must open one of two identical doors. Behind one, a tiger, which will leap out and tear the man into pieces, establishing his guilt. Behind the other, a lady "most suitable to his years and station," whom he must immediately marry as a reward for his innocence. ("It mattered not that he might already possess a wife and family, or that his affections might be engaged upon an object of his own selection. The King allowed no such subordinate arrangements to interfere with his great scheme of retribution and reward.") The accused, then, must "open either [door] he pleased, without having the slightest idea whether, in the next instant, he was to be devoured or married."

As might be expected, the King has a daughter, and she falls in love with a handsome commoner. Learning of this transgression, the King declares that the boy must be sent to the arena. For one door, the most ferocious tiger in the land is found; for the other, the most beautiful maiden—more beautiful, in fact, than the King's own daughter.

Before the trial, the wily daughter discovers the secret of the doors, and as the boy enters the arena she signals him with her right hand. He immediately opens the right door . . . But which would be worse for this "hot-blooded semi-barbaric princess": to see her beloved ripped to shreds, or happily married to a woman

145

more lovely than she? What was the meaning of her sign? Or, as the story ends: "Which came out of the opened door—the lady, or the tiger?"

E.

Frank Stockton's "The Lady, or the Tiger?," first published in *The Century Magazine* in 1882, quickly became an international obsession. At the time inconclusive endings were vexatious, not modern, and for the twenty years until his death Stockton was besieged with solutions, sequels, and threats. Among the latter, Rudyard Kipling subjected Stockton to a bit of impeccable Raj ragging, as reported by the San Francisco *Wave* in 1896:

> Stockton and Kipling met at an author's reception, and after some preliminary talk, the former remarked: "By the way, Kipling, I'm thinking of going over to India some day myself." "Do so, my dear fellow," replied Mr. Kipling, with suspicious warmth of cordiality. "Come as soon as ever you can! And, by the way, do you know what we'll do when we get you out there, away from your friends and family? Well, the first thing will be to lure you out into the jungle and have you seized and bound by our trusty wallahs. Then we'll lay you on your back and have one of our very biggest elephants stand over you and poise his ample forefoot directly over your head. Then I'll say in my most insinuating tones, 'Come now, Stockton, which was it—The Lady or the Tiger?' . . ."

And Mrs. Stockton recorded this ludicrous scene in her diary:

> Miss Evans, our niece, wrote to us that a missionary who was visiting her mission station among the Karens [a tribe in northeast Burma], told her she had just come from a distant wild tribe of Karens occasionally visited by missionaries and to her surprise was immediately asked by them if she knew who came out the door, The Lady or the Tiger? Her explanation of it was that some former visitor had read to them this story as suited to their

fancy; and as she had just come from the outside world they supposed she could tell the end of it.

Men generally favored the lady, women the tiger. An exception was Robert Browning, who declared he had "no hesitation in supposing that such a princess, under such circumstances, would direct her lover to the tiger's door." In fact, Freud's slip was to the point: it is an *and*, not an *or*, proposition. The choice between lady or tiger, "devoured or married," was to its readers hardly a choice at all. As one W. S. Hopson of San Francisco wrote in 1895:

> When my wife flies into a passion,
> And her anger waxes wroth,
> I think of the Lady and the Tiger,
> And sigh that I chose them both.

R.

A few years after Stockton's death, Elinor Glyn's *Three Weeks* (1907) was the steamy bestseller of its day, its success due largely to its famous seduction scene on a tiger-skin rug:

> Paul entered from the terrace. And the loveliest sight of all, in front of the fire, stretched at full length, was his tiger and on him—also at full length—reclined the lady . . .
> "No! You mustn't come near me, Paul . . . Not yet. You bought me the tiger. Ah that was good! My beautiful tiger!" And she gave a movement like a snake, of joy to feel its fur under her, while she stretched out her hands and caressed the creature where the hair turned white and black at the side, and was deep and soft.
> "Beautiful one! Beautiful one!" she purred. "And I know all your feelings and your passions, and now I have got your skin—for the joy of my skin." And she quivered again with a movement of a snake.

Alas, tiger's fur is short and coarse, and would make for an itchy tryst. But Glyn's book effectively played on the fusion of lady and tiger in the popular imagination. It also inspired this piece of anonymous doggerel (and mnemonic guide to proper pronunciation):

> Would you like to sin
> with Elinor Glyn
> on a tiger skin?
> Or would you prefer
> to err
> with her
> on some other fur?

T.

Tiger, woman, passion. Glyn's sin comes out of ancient tradition, for the tiger has always been first female, and later male.

The earliest recorded tigers in the West were those presented to Seleucus I (d. 280 B.C.). (Alexander of course had seen tigers in Persia.) In Latin poetry *tigris* is always feminine (the word means "arrow," and was applied to the swiftness of the animal and the river); in Roman art tigresses are nearly always portrayed. Female tiger is often paired with male lion, much as Freud's "lioness" Yofi checks H. D.'s tiger. Bacchus' chariot was drawn by such a pair. It is a distinction Keats articulates in "Hyperion" as "tiger-passioned, lion-thoughted." (Similarly, the Brontës' cats were named "Tiger" and "Keeper.") As late as the eighteenth century it was believed that the way to capture a tiger cub—the only way to get a tiger for one's menagerie—was the procedure first described by Claudian nearly two thousand years before: steal the cub and, with the tiger in pursuit, scatter mirrors in her path; her female vanity is such that she will gaze fondly in the mirror and forget about the baby.

In China the tiger was originally *yin*: associated with the underworld, and with the West (where the sun enters the underworld). In the *feng-shui* system of geomancy, it is paired with the *yang* green dragon. (The Buddhists would later reverse the genders of the tiger/green dragon pair—stressing the tiger's *yang* nobility, and pointing out, quite correctly, that tigers wear the character for "king," *wang* 王, on their foreheads). Wordsworth's description (in *The Prelude*) of Jacobin Paris as "Defenceless as a wood where tigers roam" may owe something to Virgil's characterization of Rome as "a wilderness of tigers." But both are identical to the stock

148

Chinese metaphor for a corrupt and sick society: a tiger *(yin)* in a bamboo grove *(yang)*, the dark within the light.

Most important is the Chinese tiger-monster, the *tao tie* ("the glutton") which is prominent as early as the Shang dynasty. The *tao tie* is a devourer, and almost always appears in funerary art; sometimes the burial urn itself is in the shape of a tiger. It is the earth eating the dead to provide nourishment for the living—much as the Greek word *sarcophagus* means "to eat flesh." (In the pre-Columbian Americas where there were no tigers, the jaguar was its exact equivalent: an earth-image paired in Mesoamerica with the sky-symbol of the feathered serpent, in South America commonly portrayed in burial urns. The whole city of Cuzco was originally laid out in the form of a jaguar—a kind of living necropolis, *polis* as affirmation of death and life.)

Although frequent in the early Harappan art of the Indus Valley, the tiger is rarely visible as an icon in India until its masculinization in Mughal times—quite strange, considering that Hinduism tended to find metaphysical uses for nearly every indigenous thing. In Hindu iconography it appears only occasionally as the vehicle for the Durga, the terrifying destroyer-goddess. There are, for example, no tigers in Vidyakara's *Treasury*, the great Sanskrit poetry anthology, where so much of Indian life is represented. But among the jungle tribes the tiger was an active presence as devouring mother, fecund mother. "In Akola," writes William Crooke in 1894, "the gardeners are unwilling to inform the sportsmen of the whereabouts of a tiger which may have taken up quarters in their plantation, for they have a superstition that a garden plot loses its fertility from the moment one of these animals is killed." And among the Gonds, wedding ceremonies were marked by the appearance of "two demoniacs possessed by Bagheswar, the tiger god" who "fell ravenously on a bleating kid, and gnawed it with their teeth till it expired."

Y.

Rachel Blau DuPlessis, explicating one of her own poems, writes:

> In "Crowbar," the whole argument comes to the poised
> end in the doubling of two words: *hungry* and *angry*

which grasp towards the odd *-ngry* ending they hold in common. *Hungry* meant complicit with the psychic cultural construction of beautiful, seductive and seduced women; *angry* meant critical of the same.

Hungry woman, angry woman: destroyer, devourer, nurturer: tiger images all. It is curious in this context to read Emily Dickinson's two enigmatic poems on tigers:

566

A Dying Tiger—moaned for Drink—
I hunted all the Sand—
I caught the Dripping of a Rock
And bore it in my Hand—

His Mighty Balls—in death were thick—
But searching—I could see
A Vision on the Retina
Of Water—and of me—

'Twas not my blame—who sped too slow—
'Twas not his blame—who died
While I was reaching him—
But 'twas—the fact that he was dead—

872

As the Starved Maelstrom laps the Navies
As the Vultures teased
Forces the Broods in lonely Valleys
As the Tiger eased

By but a Crumb of Blood, fasts Scarlet
Till he meet a Man
Dainty adorned with Veins and Tissues
And partakes—his Tongue

150

Cooled by the Morsel for a moment
Growns a fiercer thing
Till he esteem his Dates and Cocoa
A Nutrition mean

I, of a finer Famine
Deem my Supper dry
For but a berry of Domingo
And a Torrid Eye.

G.

There are no tigers in the Bible, and there were no tigers in medieval Europe—the bestiaries tended to classify them as birds or snakes. For nearly a thousand years, there were no tigers that look like tigers in Western art. So, when they began to be imported again into Europe from the animal market of Constantinople at the end of the fifteenth century, they were among the only creatures with no metaphysical meaning. In the absence of a fixed iconography, the West had to invent its allegorical tiger.

Shakespeare compares the murderous Queen Margaret (in *Henry VI Part 3*) to a tiger, and has Romeo express his rage in *yin* imagery:

> The time and my intents are savage-wild,
> More fierce and more inexorable far
> Than empty tigers or the roaring sea.

But he also uses the tiger in its now-familiar masculine role: symbol of military valor. (Almost all the armies of the world are decked with tiger images.) Henry the Fifth, in his "Once more unto the breach, dear friends" speech:

> But when the blast of war blows in our ears,
> Then imitate the action of the tiger:
> Stiffen the sinews, summon up the blood,
> Disguise fair nature with hard-favored rage;
> Then lend the eye a terrible aspect . . .
> Now set the teeth and stretch the nostril wide,

Hold hard the breath and bend up every spirit
To his full height! On, on you noble English . . .

E.

The Western image of the tiger was permanently altered in the
eighteenth century by the reign of the Mughal prince Tipu Sultan
(1750–99), the self-styled Tiger of Mysore and a perfect incarnation
of the perennial Orientalist nightmare of the Eastern despot.

A stern moralist, Tipu abolished polyandry and instituted his
version of Koranic law. He changed the calendar and all weights
and measures; he renamed all the cities and towns. He sponsored
the arts and commercial enterprises, reformed every detail of daily
existence from the way the markets ran to the way crops were
planted and gathered. He kept a book of his dreams. At night he
slept on the floor on a coarse piece of canvas, and each morning he
ate the brains of male sparrows for breakfast.

He commanded an army of 140,000, sworn to wipe out the
British. Prisoners were subjected to particularly grotesque torture:
boiling oil, special devices for removing noses and upper lips. In
his most brilliantly insidious punishment the enemy was turned
into the Other: British soldiers were forced to cut off their foreskins
and eat them.

He was also, in his mind, a tiger. His throne was mounted on a
full-size gilded tiger with rock-crystal eyes and teeth; its finials
were tiger heads set with rubies and diamonds; its canopy was
tiger-striped with hammered gold. His soldiers dressed in tiger-
patterned ("bubberee") jackets and kept their prisoners in tiger
cages until it was time for them to be thrown to the tigers. Their
cannons had tiger breech-blocks, their mortars were in the shape
of crouching tigers, their rifles had tiger-headed stocks and ham-
mers, their swords were engraved with tigers or forged in a striped
blend of metals. Live tigers were chained to the palace doors.
Tipu's handkerchiefs were striped; his banner read "The Tiger is
God."

All this, to put it mildly, made quite an impression in the West.
The newspapers were full of Tipu: if an elderly servant was
murdered in a siege, she was immediately transformed into four
hundred beautiful British virgins throwing themselves on swords
rather than face the ravishment of Tipu's troops. In London, Tipu

152

plays were a permanent attraction for thirty years. (The first, *Tippoo Sahib, or British Valour in India*, began running at Covent Garden on June 1, 1791. It was followed the next year by *Tippoo Sultan, or the Siege of Bangalore*.) When Tipu was finally slain and his capital, Seringpatam, captured by the British in 1798, it was cause for national celebration. Robert Ker Porter's 120-foot-long painting, "The Storming of Seringpatam," was mounted on the stage of the Lyceum, and the crowds paid a shilling each to view the great scene. Wilkie Collins in 1868 added an aura to his Moonstone by having it come from the plunder of Seringpatam, and as late as 1898 Sir Henry Newbolt had a popular schlock epic poem on Tipu's defeat.

The tiger, then, took on a fearful androgyny: a masculine military ferocity within a dark Eastern feminine otherness. The tiger was, in the words of Capt. Williamson's *Oriental Field Sports* (1807), "the mottled object of detestation": an obstacle to progress; everything that was not white, Western, male, good. Its literal and metaphorical vanquishing became a British obsession. For a century boys' stories were full of man-eating tigers. With a short leap, the word "man-eater" was soon applied to women.

R.

Blake's "tyger," according to the exegetes, stands for wrath, revolution, untamed energy and beauty, the romantic revolt of imagination against reason. Its direction is East—contrary to the Chinese, but obvious for a Westerner. It is associated with fire and smoke: "burning bright," roaming "in the redounding smoke in forests of affliction," "blinded by the smoke" issuing from "the wild furies" of its own brain. Numerous critics have pointed out that "The Tyger" of *Songs of Experience* was written in 1793, during the French Revolution. But it was also a time when the papers and theaters were crazy with tales of Tipu.

Did Blake ever see a real tiger? The Tower of London menagerie had been opened to the public in the middle of the century (price of admission: three ha'pennies or one dead dog or cat), and it frequently featured tigers. A new specimen was acquired in 1791, the year the first Tipu play opened. And when Blake lived at Fountain Court, the Strand, he could have strolled over to Pidcock's Exhibition of Wild Beasts, where tigers were often on display.

Pidcock and Blake form two sides of a tiger triangle: the third is George Stubbs, the first English painter of tigers. His *The Tyger*, as Kathleen Raine points out in *Blake and the Tradition*, was first exhibited at the Society of Artists of Great Britain in 1769, at the same time and in the same building where the twelve-year-old William Blake was studying drawing at Pars' school. (It was, by the way, Pidcock who sold Stubbs the dead tiger which the artist used for his last work, which bore the matchless title *The Comparative Anatomy of Humans, Chickens & Tigers*.)

Raine remarks on the effect that the painted tiger must have had on the boy Blake. She does not consider, however, the painting itself: Stubbs' "tyger," like all tigers he painted, is not an icon of untamed energy, but rather a recumbent, noble but cuddly, large cat. (In contrast, his lions are always portrayed committing acts of terror in a storm-tossed landscape—as in the famous *Horse Attacked by a Lion*, now at Yale; a motif Stubbs copied from Roman statuary, which was itself a copy from Scythian art.) And when Blake came to illustrate his "The Tyger" the animal was so oddly passive and sweet, almost smiling, that some friends complained. Shakespeare's hard-favored rage had been disguised by fair nature.

There is no doubt that Blake associated tigers with wrath and revolution, but it is interesting that Blake drew his physical image from Stubbs' painting and the half-dead animals in the local cages—surely he could have imagined it otherwise. (Consider the terror of his flea.) Or is Blake's (and Stubbs') tyger meant to demonstrate the possibilities latent beneath a passive exterior, as yogis traditionally sat immobile on tiger-skin mats, as the men of the industrialized West saw women: a dormant volcano? Is the tyger's blank smile its most fearful symmetry?

T.

It is quite probable that Blake had heard of the death of Sir Hector Munro's son, the most famous tiger-kills-Englishman story of the century. This account appeared in *The Gentleman's Magazine* in July 1793, the year "The Tyger" was composed:

> To describe the aweful, horrid and lamentable accident I have been an eye witness of, is impossible. Yesterday morning Mr Downey, of the [East India] Company's troops, Lieut. Pyefinch, poor Mr Munro and myself

went onshore on Saugor Island to shoot deer. We saw innumerable tracks of tigers and deer, but still we were induced to pursue our sport, and did the whole day. At about halfpast three we sat down on the edge of the jungle, to eat some cold meat sent us from the ship, and had just commenced our meal, when Mr Pyefinch and a black servant told us there was a fine deer within six yards of us. Mr Downey and myself immediately jumped up to take our guns; mine was the nearest, and I had just laid hold of it when I heard a roar, like thunder, and saw an immense tiger spring on the unfortunate Munro, who was sitting down. In a moment his head was in the beast's mouth, and he rushed into the jungle with him, with as much ease as I could lift a kitten, tearing through the thickest bushes and trees, everything yielding to his monstrous strength. The agonies of horror, regret, and, I must say fear (for there were other tigers, male and female) rushed on me at once. The only effort I could make was to fire at him, though the poor youth was still in his mouth. I relied partly on Providence, partly on my own aim, and fired a musket. I saw the tiger stagger and agitated, and cried out so immediately. Mr Downey then fired two shots and I one more. We retired from the jungle, and, a few minutes after, Mr Munro came up to us, all over blood, and fell. We took him on our backs to the boat, and got every medical assistance for him from the *Valentine* East India Main, which lay at anchor near the Island, but in vain. He lived twenty four hours in the extreme torture; his head and skull were torn and broke to pieces, and he was wounded by the claws all over the neck and shoulders; but it was better to take him away, though irrecoverable than leave him to be devoured limb by limb. We have just read the funeral service over the body, and committed it to the deep. He was an amiable and promising youth. I must observe, there was a large fire blazing close to us, composed of ten or a dozen whole trees; I made it myself, on purpose to keep the tigers off, as I had always heard it would. There were eight or ten of the natives about us; many shots had been fired at the place, and much noise and laughing at the time; but this ferocious animal disregarded all. The human mind cannot form an idea of the scene; it turned my very soul within me. The beast was about four and a half feet high, and nine long. His head appeared as large as an ox's, his eyes darting fire, and his roar, when he first seized his prey, will never be out of my recollection. We had scarcely pushed our boats from the shore when the tigress made her appearance, raging mad almost, and remained on the sand as long as the distance would allow me to see her.

This scene of the humanly unthinkable, tiger and fire, may have partially inspired Blake. It did most certainly inspire Tipu Sultan. Sir Hector, the boy's father (and ancestor of Hector Hugh Munro, "Saki," whose stories are full of animals attacking people) was the archenemy of Tipu's father, Haidar Ali. At the news of the boy's death—which Tipu gleefully interpreted as a sign that his fellow tigers were joining the struggle against the British—he ordered the construction of a large mechanical toy, now in the Victoria and Albert Museum, to commemorate the event.

It is a lifesize wooden tiger crouched on a prone Englishman. They face each other; the man's left hand touches the tiger's face. They might be mistaken for lovers, but the tiger's teeth are sunk in the man's neck. ("Tipu Sultan," after all, means "Tiger Conqueror of Passion.") Wound up, the toy, simultaneously emits roars and hideous groans. Keats, in "The Cap and Bells," called it the "Man-Tiger-Organ."

Y.

After the fall of Seringpatam, tiger-killing became the standard measure in India of a Britisher's valor and innate superiority. And after the Empire forced peaceful co-existence onto the normally warring princely states, the maharajahs could only display their power and manhood in British terms. No visit to a palace by a distinguished foreigner was complete without a tiger hunt. That the guest would be neither endangered nor disappointed, the tigers were often drugged beforehand with opium-laced meat to ensure a safe and unerring shot.

George Yule of the Bengal Civil Service killed 400 then stopped counting. Colonel Rice killed 93 in four years. Montague Gerard killed 227. The Maharajah of Surguja killed 1,150. The Maharajah Scindia killed at least 700. The guests of the Maharajah Scindia killed at least 200. The Maharajah of Gauripiur killed 500 then stopped counting.

As early as 1827, one Capt. Mundy could write, with unintentional irony:

> Thus in the space of about two hours, and within sight of the camp, we found and slew three tigers, a piece of good fortune rarely to be met with in these modern times, when the spread of cultivation, and the zeal of the English sportsmen have almost exterminated the breed of these animals.

G.

The Bali tiger: *extinct since 1975*.
The Caspian tiger: 15–20 left, *extinction inevitable*.
The Java tiger: 6–10 left, *extinction inevitable*.
The Sumatra tiger: 700–800 left, *preservation possible*.
The Siberian tiger: 180–200 left, *extinction possible*.
The Chinese tiger: 50–80 left, *extinction probable*.
The Indo-Chinese tiger: 4500–5000 left, *declining rapidly*.
The Bengal tiger: 2500 left, *preservation possible*.
Estimated population of the Bengal tiger, *c.* 1900: 40,000.
Estimated world population of tigers, *c.* 1920: 100,000.

Cleansed, the tiger appears in Eliot's "Gerontion" as Christ.

E

Tigers eat men only when they are starving or are too old or sick to catch more elusive prey. In parts of India, it is believed that man-eating tigers are not tigers at all, but men who have transformed themselves into tigers to commit, for their purposes, masked acts of murder. These counterfeit tigers, the man-eaters, are recognizable to the villagers, as they would have been to Freud: they have no tails.

R.

Jorge Luis Borges, from his half-century of blindness, writes:

> In my childhood I ardently worshiped tigers . . . I used
> to linger endlessly before their cage at the zoo; I judged
> vast encyclopedias and books of natural history by the
> splendor of their tigers. (I still remember those illustra-
> tions: I who cannot quite recall the eyes or the smile of a
> woman.)

1987

AGAINST *JOIE DE VIVRE*

by PHILLIP LOPATE

from PLOUGHSHARES

OVER THE YEARS I have developed a distaste for the spectacle of *joie de vivre*, the knack of knowing how to live. Not that I disapprove of all hearty enjoyment of life. A flushed sense of happiness can overtake a person anywhere, and one is no more to blame for it than the Asiatic flu or a sudden benevolent change in the weather (which is often joy's immediate cause). No, what rankles me is the stylization of this private condition into a bullying social ritual.

The French, who have elevated the picnic to their highest civilized rite, are probably most responsible for promoting this smugly upbeat, flaunting style. It took the French genius for formalizing the informal to bring sticky sacramental sanctity to the baguette, wine and cheese. A pure image of sleeveless *joie de vivre* Sundays can also be found in Renoir's paintings. Weekend satyrs dance and wink; leisure takes on a bohemian stripe. A decent writer, Henry Miller, caught the French malady and ran back to tell us of *pissoirs* in the Paris streets (why this should have impressed him so, I've never figured out).

But if you want a double dose of *joie de vivre*, you need to consult a later, hence more stylized version of the French myth of pagan happiness: those *Family of Man* photographs of endlessly kissing lovers, snapped by Doisneau and Boubat, not to mention Cartier-Bresson's icon of the proud tyke carrying bottles of wine. If Cartier-Bresson and his disciples are excellent photographers for all that, it is in spite of their rubbing our noses in a tediously programmatic "affirmation of life."

159

Though it is traditionally the province of the French, the whole Mediterranean is a hotbed of professional *joie de vivrism*, which they have gotten down to a routine like a crack *son et lumière* display. The Italians export *dolce far niente* as aggressively as tomato paste. For the Greeks, a Zorba dance to life has supplanted classical antiquities as their main touristic lure. Hard to imagine anything as stomach-turning as being forced to participate in such an oppressively robust, folknik effusion. Fortunately, the country has its share of thin, nervous, bitter types, but Greeks do exist who would clutch you to their joyfully stout bellies and crush you there. The *joie de vivrist* is an incorrigible missionary, who presumes that everyone wants to express pro-life feelings in the same stereotyped manner.

A warning: since I myself have a large store of nervous discontent (some would say hostility) I am apt to be harsh in my secret judgments of others, seeing them as defective because they are not enough like me. From moment to moment, the person I am with often seems too shrill, too bland, too something-or-other to allow my own expansiveness to swing into stage center. "Feeling no need to drink, you will promptly despise a drunkard" (Kenneth Burke). So it goes with me—which is why I am not a literary critic. I have no faith that my discriminations in taste are anything but the picky awareness of what will keep me stimulated, based on the peculiar family and class circumstances which formed me. But the knowledge that my discriminations are skewed and not always universally desirable doesn't stop me in the least from making them, just as one never gives up a negative first impression, no matter how many times it is contradicted. A believer in astrology (to cite another false system), having guessed that someone is a Saggitarius, and then told he is a Scorpio, says "Scorpio—yes, of course!" without missing a beat, or relinquishing confidence in his ability to tell people's signs, or in his idea that the person is somehow secretly Saggitarian.

1. The Houseboat

I remember the exact year when my dislike for *joie de vivre* began to crystallize. It was 1969. We had gone to visit an old Greek painter on his houseboat in Sausalito. Old Vartas's vitality was legendary and it was considered a spiritual honor to meet him, like getting an audience with the Pope. Each Sunday he had a sort of open house, or open boat.

My "sponsor," Frank, had been many times to the houseboat, furnishing Vartas with record albums, since the old painter had a passion for San Francisco rock bands. Frank told me that Vartas had been a pal of Henry Miller's, and I, being a writer of Russian descent, would love him. I failed to grasp the syllogism, but, putting aside my instinct to dislike anybody I have been assured I will adore, I prepared myself to give the man a chance.

Greeting us on the gang plank was an old man with thick, lush white hair and snowy eyebrows, his face reddened from the sun. As he took us into the houseboat cabin he told me proudly that he was seventy-seven years old, and gestured toward the paintings that were spaced a few feet apart, leaning on the floor against the wall. They were celebrations of the blue Aegean, boats moored in ports, whitewashed houses on a hill, painted in primary colors and decorated with collaged materials: mirrors, burlap, life-saver candies. These sunny little canvases with their talented innocence, third-generation spirit of Montmartre, bore testimony to a love of life so unbending as to leave an impression of rigid narrow-mindedness as extreme as any Savonarola. Their rejection of sorrow was total. They were the sort of festive paintings that sell at high-rent Madison Avenue galleries specializing in European schlock.

Then I became aware of three young, beautiful women, bare-shouldered, wearing white *dhotis*, each with long blond hair falling onto a skyblue halter—unmistakably suggesting the Three Graces. They lived with him on the houseboat, I was told, giving no one knew what compensation for their lodgings. Perhaps their only payment was to feed his vanity in front of outsiders. The Greek painter smiled with the air of an old fox around the trio. For their part, they obligingly contributed their praises of Vartas's youthful zip, which of course was taken by some guests as double-entendre for undiminished sexual prowess. The Three Graces also gathered the food-offerings of the visitors to make a mid-day meal.

Then the boat, equipped with a sail, was launched to sea. I must admit it gave me a spoilsport's pleasure when the winds turned becalmed. We could not move. Aboard were several members of the Bay Area's French colony, who dangled their feet over the sides, passed around bunches of grapes and sang what I imagined

161

were Gallic camping songs. The French know boredom, so they would understand how to behave in such a situation. It has been my observation that many Frenchmen and women stationed in America have the attitude of taking it easy, slumming at a health resort, and nowhere more so than in California. The émigré crew included a securities analyst, an academic sociologist, a museum administrator and his wife, a modiste: on Vartas's boat they all got drunk and carried on like redskins, noble savages off Tahiti.

Joie de vivre requires a *soupçon* of the primitive. But since the illusion of the primitive soon palls and has nowhere to go, it becomes necessary to make new initiates. A good part of the day, in fact, was taken up with regulars interpreting to firsttimers like myself certain mores pertaining to the houseboat, as well as offering tidbits about Vartas's Rabelaisian views of life. Here everyone was encouraged to do what he willed. (How much could you do on a becalmed boat surrounded by strangers?) No one had much solid information about their host's past, which only increased the privileged status of those who knew at least one fact. Useless to ask the object of this venerating speculation, since Vartas said next to nothing (adding to his impressiveness) when he was around, and disappeared below for long stretches of time.

In the evening, after a communal dinner, the new Grateful Dead record Frank had brought was put on the phonograph, and Vartas danced, first by himself, then with all three Graces, bending his arms in broad, hooking sweeps. He stomped his foot and looked around scampishly at the guests for appreciation, not unlike a monkey-grinder and his monkey. Imagine, if you will, a being whose generous bestowal of self-satisfaction invites and is willing to receive nothing but flattery in return, a person who has managed to make others buy his somewhat senile projection of indestructibility as a Hymn to Life. In no sense could he be called a charlatan; he delivered what he promised, an incarnation of *joie de vivre*, and if it was shallow, it was also effective, managing even to attract an enviable "harem" (which was what really burned me).

A few years passed.

Some Dutch TV crew, ever on the lookout for exotic bits of Americana that would make good short subjects, planned to do a documentary about Vartas as a sort of paean to eternal youth. I later learned from Frank that Vartas died before the shooting could be completed. A pity, in a way. The home movie I've run off in my head of the old man is getting a little tattered, the colors splotchy, and the scenario goes nowhere, lacks point. All I have for sure is the title: The Man Who Gave *Joie De Vivre* A Bad Name.

"Ah, what a twinkle in the eye the old man has! He'll outlive us all." So we speak of old people who bore us, when we wish to honor them. We often see projected onto old people this worship of the life-force. It is not the fault of the old if they then turn around and try to exploit our misguided amazement at their longevity as though it were a personal tour de force. The elderly, when they are honest with themselves, realize they have done nothing particularly to be proud of in lasting to a ripe old age, and then carrying themselves through a thousand more days. Yet you still hear an old woman or man telling a bus driver with a chuckle, "Would you believe that I am eighty-four years old!" As though they should be patted on the back for still knowing how to talk, or as though they had pulled a practical joke on the other riders by staying so spry and mobile. Such insecure, wheedling behavior always embarrassed me. I will look away rather than meet the speaker's eyes and be forced to lie with a smile, "Yes, you are remarkable," which seems condescending on my part and humiliating to us both.

Like children forced to play the cute part adults expect of them, some old people must get confused trying to adapt to a social role of indeterminate standards, which is why they seem to whine: "I'm doing all right, aren't I—for my age?" It is interesting that society's two most powerless groups, children and the elderly, have both been made into sentimental symbols. In the child's little hungry hands grasping for life, joined to the old person's frail slipping fingers hanging onto it, you have one of the commonest advertising metaphors for intense appreciation. It is enough to show a young child sleeping in his or her grandparent's lap to procure *joie de vivre* overload.

2. The Dinner Party

I am invited periodically to dinner parties and brunches—and I go, because I like to be with people and oblige them, even if I secretly cannot share their optimism about these events. I go, not believing that I will have fun, but with the intent of observing people who think *a dinner party* a good time. I eat their fancy

163

food, drink the wine, make my share of entertaining conversation, and often leave having had a pleasant evening. Which does not prevent me from anticipating the next invitation with the same bleak lack of hope. To put it in a nutshell, I am an ingrate.

Although I have traveled a long way from my proletarian origins and, like a perfect little bourgeois, talk, dress, act and spend money, I hold onto my poor-boy's outrage at the "decadence" (meaning, dull entertainment style) of the middle and upper-middle classes; or, like a model Soviet moviegoer watching scenes of pre-revolutionary capitalists gorging caviar, I am appalled, but I dig in with the rest.

Perhaps my uneasiness with dinner parties comes from the simple fact that not a single dinner party was given by my solitudinous parents the whole time I was growing up, and I had to wait until my late twenties before learning the ritual. A spy in the enemy camp, I have made myself a patient observer of strange customs. For the benefit of other late-starting social climbers, this is what I have observed:

As everyone should know, the ritual of the dinner party begins away from the table. Usually in the living room, hors d'oeuvres and walnuts are set out, to start the digestive juices flowing. Here introductions between strangers are also made. Most dinner parties contain at least a few guests who have been unknown to each other before that evening, but whom the host and/or hostess envision would enjoy meeting. These novel pairings and their interactions add spice to the *post-mortem:* who got along with whom? The lack of prior acquaintanceship also ensures that the guests will have to rely on and go through the only people known to everyone, the host and hostess, whose absorption of this help-lessly dependent attention is one of the main reasons for throwing dinner parties.

Although an after-work "leisure activity," the dinner party is in fact a celebration of professional identity. Each of the guests has been pre-selected as in a floral bouquet; and in certain developed forms of this ritual there is usually a cunning mix of professions. Yet the point is finally not so much diversity as commonality: what remarkably shared attitudes and interests these people from differ-ent vocations demonstrate by conversing intelligently, or at least glibly, on the topics that arise. Naturally, a person cannot discourse too technically about one's line of work, so he or she picks precisely those themes that invite overlap. The psychiatrist laments the new breed of ego-less, narcissistic patient who keeps turning up in his office—a beach bum who lacks the work ethic; the college professor bemoans the shoddy intellectual backgrounds and self-centered ignorance of his students; and the bookseller parodies the customer who pronounced "Sophocles" to rhyme with "bifocles". The dinner party is thus an exercise in locating ignorance—elsewhere. Whoever is present is *ipso facto* part of that beleaguered remnant of civilized folk fast disappearing from Earth.

Or think of a dinner party as a club of revolutionaries, a technocratic elite whose social interactions that night are a dry run for some future takeover of the State. These are the future cabinet members (now only a shadow-cabinet, alas) meeting to practice for the first time. How well they get on! "The time will soon be ripe, my friends. . . ." If this is too fanciful for you, then compare the dinner party to a utopian community, a Brook Farm supper club, where only the best and most useful community-members are chosen to participate. The smugness begins as soon as one enters the door, since one is already part of the chosen few. And from then on, every mechanical step in dinner-party process is designed to augment the atmosphere of group *amour-propre*. This is not to say that there won't be one or two people in an absolute torment of exclusion, too shy to speak up, or else suspecting that when they do, their contributions fail to carry the same weight as the others'. The group's all-purpose drone of self-contentment ignores these drowning people—cruelly inattentive in one sense, but benign in another: it invites them to join the shared ethos of success any time they are ready.

The group is asked to repair to the table. Once again they find themselves marvelling at a shared perception of life. How delicious the fish soup! How cute the stuffed tomatoes! What did you use for this green sauce? Now comes much talk of ingredients, and credit is given where credit is due. It is Jacques who made the salad. It was Mamie who brought the homemade bread. Everyone pleads with the hostess to sit down, not to work so hard—an empty formula whose hypocrisy bothers no one. Who else is going to put the butter dish on the table? For a moment all become quiet, except for the sounds of eating. This corresponds to the part in a church service which calls for silent prayer.

I am saved from such culinary paganism by the fact that food is largely an indifferent matter to me. I rarely think much about what I am putting in my mouth. Though my savage, illiterate palate has inevitably been educated to some degree by the many meals I have shared with people who care enormously about such things, I resist going any further. I am superstitious that the day I send back a dish at a restaurant, or make a complicated journey to somewhere just for a meal, that day I will have sacrificed my freedom and traded in my soul for a lesser god.

I don't expect the reader to agree with me. That's not the point. Unlike the behavior called for at a dinner party, I am not obliged sitting at my typewriter to help procure consensus every moment. So I am at liberty to declare, to the friend who once told me that dinner parties were one of the only opportunities for intelligently convivial conversation to take place in this cold, fragmented city, that she is crazy. The conversation at dinner parties is of a mind-numbing calibre. No discussion of any clarifying rigor—be it political, spiritual, artistic or financial—can take place in a context where fervent conviction of any kind is frowned upon, and the desire to follow through a sequence of ideas must give way every time to the impressionistic, breezy flitting from topic to topic. Talk must be bubbly but not penetrating. Illumination would only slow the flow. Some hit-and-run remark may accidentally jog an idea loose, but in such cases it is better to scribble a few words down on the napkin for later, than attempt to "think" at a dinner party.

What do people talk about at such gatherings? The latest movies, the priciness of things, word-processors, restaurants, muggings and burglaries, private versus public schools, the fool in the White House (there have been so many fools in a row that this subject is getting tired), the undeserved reputations of certain better-known professionals in one's field, the fashions in investments, the investments in fashion. What is traded at the dinner-party table is, of course, class information. You will learn whether you are in the avant-garde or rear guard of your social class, or, preferably, right in step.

As for Serious Subjects, dinner-party guests have the latest *New Yorker* in-depth piece to bring up. People who ordinarily would not spare a moment worrying about the treatment of schizophrenics in mental hospitals, the fate of Great Britain in the Common Market, or the disposal of nuclear wastes, suddenly find their consciences orchestrated in unison about these problems, thanks to their favorite periodical—though a month later they have forgotten all about it and are onto something new.

The dinner party is a suburban form of entertainment. Its spread in our big cities represents an insidious Fifth Column suburbanization of the metropolis. In the suburbs it becomes necessary to be able to discourse knowledgeably about the heart of the city, but from the viewpoint of a day-shopper. Dinner-party chatter is the communicative equivalent of roaming around shopping malls.

Much thought has gone into the ideal size for a dinner party—usually with the hostess arriving at the figure eight. Six would give each personality too much weight; ten would lead to splintering side-discussions; eight is the largest number still able to force everyone into the same compulsively congenial conversation. My own strength as a conversationalist comes out less in groups of eight than one-to-one, which may explain my resistance to dinner parties. At the table, unfortunately, any engrossing *tête-á-tête* is frowned upon as anti-social. I often find myself in the frustrating situation of being drawn to several engaging people, in among the bores, and wishing I could have a private conversation with each, without being able to do more than signal across the table a wry recognition of that fact. "Some other time, perhaps," we seem to be saying with our eyes, all evening long.

Later, however—to give the devil his due—when guests and hosts retire from the table back to the living room, the strict demands of group participation may be relaxed, and individuals allowed to pair off in some form of conversational intimacy. But one must be ever on the lookout for the group's need to swoop everybody together again for one last demonstration of collective fealty.

The first to leave breaks the communal spell. There is a sudden rush to the coat closet, the bathroom, the bedroom, as others, under the protection of the first defector's original sin, quit the Party apologetically. The utopian dream has collapsed: left behind are a few loyalists and insomniacs, swillers of a last cognac. "Don't leave yet," begs the host, knowing what a sense of letdown, pain and self-recrimination awaits. Dirty dishes are, if anything, a comfort: the faucet's warm gush serves to stave off the moment of anesthetized stock-taking—Was that really necessary?—in the sobering silence which follows a dinner party.

167

3. *Joie's Doppelgänger*

I have no desire to rail against the Me Generation. We all know that the current epicurean style of the Good Life, from light foods to Nike running shoes, is a result of market research techniques developed to sell "spot" markets, and, as such, a natural outgrowth of consumer capitalism. I may not like it but I can't pretend that my objections are the result of a high-minded Laschian political analysis. Moreover, my own record of activism is not so noticeably impressive that I can lecture the Sunday brunchers to roll up their sleeves and start fighting social injustices instead of indulging themselves.

No, if I try to understand the reasons for my antihedonistic biases, they come from somewhere other than idealism. It's odd, because there seems to be a contradiction between this curmudgeonly feeling inside me and my periodically strong appetite for life. I am reminded of my hero, William Hazlitt, with his sarcastic grumpy disposition on the one hand, and his capacity for "gusto" (his word, not Schlitz's) on the other. With Hazlitt, one senses a fanatically tenacious defense of his individuality and independence against some unnamed bully stalking him. He had trained himself to be a connoisseur of vitality, and got irritated when life was not filled to the brim. I am far less irritable—before others; I will laugh if there is the merest *anything* to laugh at. But it is a tense, pouncing pleasure, not one which will allow me to sink into undifferentiated relaxation. The prospect of a long day at the beach makes me panic. There is no harder work I can think of than taking myself off to somewhere pleasant, where I am forced to stay for hours and "have fun." Taking it easy, watching my personality's borders loosen and dissolve, arouses an unpleasantly floating giddiness. I don't even like water-beds. Fear of Freud's "oceanic feeling," I suppose. . . . I distrust anything which will make me pause long enough to be put in touch with my helplessness.

The other repugnance I experience around *joie-de-vivrism* is that I associate its rituals with depression. All these people sitting around a pool, drinking margaritas, they're not really happy, they're depressed. Perhaps I am generalizing too much from my own despair in such situations. Drunk, sunbaked, stretched out in a beach-chair, I am unable to ward off the sensation of being utterly alone, unconnected, cut off from the others.

An article on the Science Page of the *Times* about depression (they seem to run one every few months) described the illness as a pattern of "learned helplessness." Dr. Martin Seligman of the University of Pennsylvania described his series of experiments: "At first mild electrical shocks were given to dogs, from which they were unable to escape. In a second set of experiments, dogs were given shocks from which they could escape—but they didn't try. They just lay there, passively accepting the pain. It seemed that the animals' inability to control their experiences had brought them to a state resembling clinical depression in humans."

Keep busy, I always say. At all costs avoid the trough of passivity, which leads to the Slough of Despond. Someone—a girlfriend, who else?—once accused me of being intolerant of the depressed way of looking at the world, which had its own intelligence and moral integrity, both obviously unavailable to me. It's true. I don't like the smell of depression (it has a smell, a very distinct one, something fetid like morning odors), and I stay away from depressed characters whenever possible. Except when they happen to be my closest friends or family members. It goes without saying that I am also, for all my squeamishness, attracted to depressed people, since they seem to know something I don't. I wouldn't rule out the possibility that the brown-gray logic of depression *is* the truth. In another experiment (also reported on the Science Page), pitting "optimists" against clinically diagnosed "depressives" on their self-perceived abilities to effect outcomes according to their wills, researchers tentatively concluded that depressed people may have a more realistic, clear-sighted view of the world.

Nevertheless, what I don't like about depressives sometimes is their chummy I-told-you-so smugness, like Woody Allen fans who treat anhedonia as a vanguard position.

And for all that, depressives make the most rabid converts to *joie de vivre*. The reason is, *joie de vivre* and depression are not opposites but relatives of the same family, practically twins. When I see *joie de vivre* rituals, I always notice, like a TV ghost, depression right alongside it. I knew a man, dominated by a powerful father, who thought he had come out of a long depression occasioned, in his mind, by his divorce. Whenever I met him he would say that his life was getting better and better. Now he could run long distances, he was putting healthy food in his system, he was more physically fit at forty than he had been at twenty-five, and now he had dates, he was going out with three different women, he had a good therapist, he was looking forward to renting a bungalow in better woods than the previous summer. . . . I don't know whether it was his tone of voice when he said this, his sagging shoulders, or what, but I always had an urge to burst into tears. If only he had admitted he was miserable I could have consoled him outright instead of being embarrassed to notice the deep hurt in him, like a swallowed razor cutting him from inside. And his pain still stunk up the room like in the old days, that sour cabbage smell was in his running suit, yet he wouldn't let on, he thought the smell was gone. The therapist had told him to forgive himself, and he had gone ahead and done it, the poor shlemiehl. But tell me: why would anyone need such a stylized, disciplined regimen of enjoyment if he were not depressed?

4. In the Here-And-Now

The argument of both the hedonist and the guru is that if we were but to open ourselves to the richness of the moment, to concentrate on the feast before us, we would be filled with bliss. I have lived in the present from time to time, and I can tell you that it is much over-rated. Occasionally, as a holiday from stroking one's memories or brooding about future worries, I grant you, it can be a nice change of pace. But to "be here now" hour after hour would never work. I don't even approve of stories written in the present tense. As for poets who never use a past participle, they deserve the eternity they are striving for.

Besides, the present has a way of intruding whether you like it or not; why should I go out of my way to meet it? Let it splash on me from time to time, like a car going through a puddle, and I, on the sidewalk of my solitude, will salute it grimly like any other modern inconvenience.

If I attend a concert, obviously not to listen to the music but to find a brief breathing-space in which to meditate on the past and future, I realize that there may be moments when the music invades my ears and I am forced to pay attention to it, note after note. I believe I take such intrusions gracefully. The present is not always an unwelcome guest, so long as it doesn't stay too long and cut into our time for remembering.

Even for survival, it's not necessary to focus one's full attention on the present. The instincts of a pedestrian crossing the street in a reverie will usually suffice. Alertness is alright as long as it is not treated as a promissory note on happiness. Anyone who recommends attention to the moment as a prescription for grateful wonder is only telling half the truth. To be happy one must pay attention, but to be unhappy one must also have paid attention.

Attention, at best, is a form of prayer. Conversely, as Simone Weil said, prayer is a way of focusing attention. All religions recognize this when they ask their worshipers to repeat the name of their God, a devotional practice which draws the practitioner into a trancelike awareness of the present, and the objects around oneself. With a part of the soul one praises God, and with the other part one expresses a hunger, a dissatisfaction, a desire for more spiritual contact. Praise must never stray too far from longing, that longing which takes us implicitly beyond the present.

I was about to say that the very act of attention implies longing, but this is not necessarily true. Attention is not always infused with desire; it can settle on us most placidly once desire has been momentarily satisfied, like after the sex act. There are also periods following over-work, when the exhausted slave-body is freed and the eyes dilate to register with awe the lights of the city; one is too tired to desire anything else.

Such moments are rare. They form the basis for a poetic appreciation of the beauty of the world. However, there seems no reliable way to invoke or prolong them. The rest of the time, when we are not being edgy or impatient, we are often simply *disappointed*, which amounts to a confession that the present is not good enough. People often try to hide their disappointment—just as Berryman's mother told him not to let people see that he was bored, because it suggested that he had no "inner resources." But there is something to be said for disappointment.

This least respected form of suffering, downgraded to a kind of petulance, at least accurately measures the distance between hope and reality. And it has its own peculiar satisfactions: Why else do we return years later to places where we had been happy, if not to savor the bittersweet pleasure of disappointment?

Moreover, it is the other side of a strong, predictive feeling for beauty or appropriate civility or decency: Only those with a sense of order and harmony can be disappointed.

We are told that to be disappointed is immature, in that it presupposes having unrealistic expectations, whereas the wise man meets each moment head-on without preconceptions, with freshness and detachment, grateful for anything it offers. However, this pernicious teaching ignores everything we know of the world. If we continue to expect what turns out to be not forthcoming, it is not because we are unworldly in our expectations, but because our very worldliness has taught us to demand of an unjust world that it behave a little more fairly. The least we can do, for instance, is to register the expectation that people in a stronger position be kind and not cruel to those in a weaker, knowing all the while that we will probably be disappointed.

The truth is, most wisdom is embittering. The task of the wise person cannot be to pretend with false naiveté that every moment is new and unprecedented, but to bear the burden of bitterness which experience forces on us with as much uncomplaining dignity as strength will allow. Beyond that, all we can ask of ourselves is that bitterness not cancel out our capacity still to be surprised.

5. Making Love

If it is true that I have the tendency to withhold sympathy from those pleasures or experiences which fall outside my capabilities, the opposite is also true: I admire immoderately those things I cannot do. I've always gone out with women who swam better than I did. It's as if I were asking them to teach me how to make love. Though I know how to make love (more or less), I have never fully shaken that adolescent boy's insecurity that there was more to it than I could ever imagine, and that I needed a full-time instructress. For my first sexual experiences, in fact, I chose older women. Later, when I slept with women my own age and younger, I still tended to take the stylistic lead from them, adapting myself to each one's rhythm and ardor, not only because I wanted to be "responsive," but because I secretly thought that women—any woman—understood love-making in a way that I did not. In bed I came to them as a student; and I have made them pay later, in other ways, for letting them see me thus. Sex has always been so impromptu, so out of my control, so different each time, that even when I became the confident bull in bed I was dismayed by this surprising sudden power, itself a form of powerlessness because so unpredictable.

Something Michel Leiris wrote in his book, *Manhood,* has always stuck with me: "It has been some time, in any case, since I have ceased to consider the sexual act as a simple matter, but rather as a relatively exceptional act, necessitating certain inner accommodations that are either particularly tragic or particularly exalted, but very different, in either case, from what I regard as my usual disposition."

The transformation from a preoccupied urban intellectual to a sexual animal involves, at times, an almost superhuman strain. To find in one's bed a living, undulating woman of God knows what capacities and secret desires, may seem too high, too formal, too ridiculous or blissful an occasion—not to mention the shock to an undernourished heart like mine of an injection of undiluted affection, if the woman proves loving as well.

Most often, I simply do what the flood allows me to, improvising here or there like a man tying a white flag to a raft that is being swiftly swept along, a plea for love or forgiveness. But as for artistry, control, enslavement through my penis, that's someone else. Which is not to say that there weren't women who were perfectly happy with me as a lover. In those cases, there was some love between us outside of bed: the intimacy was much more intense because we had something big to say to each other before we ever took off our clothes, but which could now be said only with our bodies.

With other women, whom I cared less about, I was sometimes a dud. I am not one of those men who can force himself to make love passionately or athletically when his affections are not engaged. From the perplexity of wide variations in my experiences I have been able to tell myself that I am neither a good nor a bad lover, but one who responds differently according to the emotions present. A banal conclusion; maybe a true one.

It does not do away, however, with some need to have my remaining insecurities about sexual ability laid to rest. I begin to suspect that all my fancy distrust of hedonism comes down to a fear of being judged in this one category: Do I make love well? Every brie and wine picnic, every tanned body relaxing on the beach, every celebration of *joie de vivre* carries a sly wink of some missed sexual enlightenment which may be too threatening to me. I am like the prudish old maid who blushes behind her packages when she sees sexy young people kissing.

When I was twenty I married. My wife was the second woman I had ever slept with. Our marriage was the recognition that we suited one another remarkably well as company—could walk and talk and share insights all day, work side by side like Chinese peasants, read silently together like graduate students, tease each other like brother and sister, and when at night we found our bodies tired, pull the covers over ourselves and become lovers. She was two years older than I, but I was good at faking maturity; and I found her so companionable and trustworthy and able to take care of me that I could not let such a gold mine go by.

Our love-life was mild and regular. There was a sweetness to sex, as befitted domesticity. Out of the surplus energy of late afternoons I would find myself coming up behind her sometimes as she worked in the kitchen, taking her away from her involvements, leading her by the hand into the bedroom. I would unbutton her blouse. I would stroke her breasts, and she would get a look in her eyes of quiet intermittent hunger, like a German shepherd being petted; she would seem to listen far off; absent-mindedly day-dreaming, she would return my petting, stroke my arm with distracted patience like a mother who has something on the stove, trying to calm her weeping child. I would listen too to guess what she might be hearing, bird calls or steam heat. The enlargement of her nipples under my fingers fascinated me. Goose bumps either rose on her skin where I touched or didn't, I noted with scientific interest, a moment before getting carried away by my own eager-ness. Then we were undressing, she was doing something in the bathroom, and I was waiting on the bed, with all the consciousness of a sunmote. I was large and ready. The proud husband, waiting to receive my treasure. . . .

I remember our favorite position was she on top, I on the bottom, upthrusting and receiving. Distraction, absentminded-ness, return, calm exploration marked our sensual life. To be forgetful seemed the highest grace. We often achieved perfection.

Then I became haunted with images of seductive, heartless cunts. It was the era of the miniskirt, girl-women, Rudi Gernreich bikinis and Tiger Morse underwear, see-through blouses, flashes of flesh which invited the hand to go creeping under and into

174

costumes. I wanted my wife to be more glamorous. We would go shopping for dresses together, and she would complain that her legs were wrong for these new fashions. Or she would come home proudly with a bargain pink and blue felt minidress, bought for three dollars at a discount store, which my aching heart would tell me missed the point completely.

She too became dissatisfied with the absence of furtive excitement in our marriage. She wanted to seduce me, like a stranger on a plane. But I was too easy, so we ended up seducing others. Then we turned back to each other and with one last desperate attempt, before the marriage fell to pieces, sought in the other a plasticity of sensual forms, like the statuary in an Indian temple. In our lovemaking I tried to believe that the body of one woman was the body of all women, and all I achieved was a groping to distance lovingly familiar forms into those of anonymous erotic succubi. The height of this insanity, I remember, was one evening in the park when I pounded my wife's lips with kisses in an effort to provoke something between us like "hot passion." My eyes closed, I practiced a repertoire of French tongue-kisses on her. I shall never forget her frightened silent appeal that I stop, because I had turned into someone she no longer recognized.

But we were young. And so, dependent on each other, like orphans. By the time I left, at twenty-five, I knew I had been a fool, and had ruined everything, but I had to continue being a fool because it had been my odd misfortune to have stumbled onto kindness and tranquility too quickly.

I moved to California in search of an earthly sexual paradise, and that year I tried hardest to make my peace with *joie de vivre*. I was sick but didn't know it—a diseased animal, Nietzsche would say. I hung around Berkeley's campus, stared up at the Campanile tower, I sat on the grass watching coeds younger than I, and, pretending that I was still going to university (no deeper sense of being a fraud obtainable), I tried to grasp the rhythms of carefree youth; I blended in at rallies, I stood at the fringes of be-ins, watching new rituals of communal love, someone being passed through the air hand to hand. But I never "trusted the group" enough to let myself be the guinea pig; or if I did, it was only with the proud stubborn conviction that nothing could change me— though I also wanted to change. Swearing I would never learn transcendence, I hitchhiked and climbed mountains. I went to wine-tasting festivals, and also accepted the wine jug from hippie gypsies in a circle around a beach campfire, without first wiping off the lip. I registered for a Free School course in human sexual response, just to get laid; and when that worked, I was shocked, and took up with someone else. There were many women in those years who got naked with me. I wish I could remember their names. I smoked grass with them, and as a sign of faith I took psychedelic drugs, and we made love in bushes and beachhouses, as though hacking through jungles with machetes to stay in touch with our ecstatic genitals while our minds soared off into natural marvels. Such experiences taught me, I will admit, how much romantic feeling can transform the body whose nerve-tendrils are receptive to it. Technicolor fantasies of one girlfriend as a señorita with flowers in her impossibly wavy hair would suddenly pitch and roll beneath me, and the bliss of touching her naked suntanned breast and the damp black pubic hairs was too unthinkably perfect to elicit anything but abject gratitude. At such moments I have held the world in my hands and *known* it. I was coming home to the body of Woman, those globes and grasses which had launched me. In the childish fantasy accompanying one sexual climax, under LSD, I was hitting a home run, and the Stars and Stripes flying in the background of my mind's eye as I "slid into home" acclaimed the patriotic rightness of my semenal release. For once I had no guilt about how or when I ejaculated.

If afterwards, when we came down, there was often a sour air of disenchantment and mutual prostitution, that does not take away from the legacy, the rapture of those moments. If I no longer use drugs—in fact, have become anti-drug—I think I still owe them something for showing me how to recognize the all-embracing reflex. At first I needed drugs to teach me about the stupendousness of sex. Later, without them, there would be situations—after a lovely talk or coming home from a party in a taxi—when I would be overcome by amorous tropism towards the woman with me. The appetite for flesh which comes over me at such moments, and the pleasure there is in finally satisfying it, seems so just that I always think I have stumbled into a state of blessed grace. That it can never last, that it is a trick of the mind and the blood, are rumors I push out of sight.

176

To know rapture is to have one's whole life poisoned. If you will forgive a ridiculous analogy, a tincture of rapture is like a red bandana in the laundry that runs and turns all the white wash pink. We should just as soon stay away from any future ecstatic experiences which spoil everyday living by comparison. Not that I have any intention of stopping. Still, if I will have nothing to do with religious mysticism, it is probably because I sense a susceptibility in that direction. Poetry is also dangerous. All quickening awakenings to Being extract a price later.

Are there people who live under such spells all the time? Was this the secret of the idiotic smile on the half-moon face of the painter Vartas? The lovers of life, the robust Cellinis, the Casanovas? Is there a technique to hedonism that will allow the term of rapture to be indefinitely extended? I don't believe it. The hedonist's despair is still that he is forced to make do with the present. Who knows about the success rate of religious mystics? In any case, I could not bring myself to state that what I am waiting for is God. Such a statement would sound too grandiose and presumptuous, and make too great a rupture in my customary thinking. But I can identify with the pre- if not the post-stage of what Simone Weil describes:

"The soul knows for certain only that it is hungry. The important thing is that it announces its hunger by crying. A child does not stop crying if we suggest to it that perhaps there is no bread. It goes on crying just the same. The danger is not lest the soul should doubt whether there is any bread, but lest, by a lie, it should persuade itself that it is not hungry."

So much for *joie de vivre*. It's too compensatory. I don't really know what I'm waiting for. I know only that until I have gained what I want from this life, my expressions of gratitude and joy will be restricted to variations of a hunter's alertness. I give thanks to a nip in the air that clarifies the scent. But I think it hypocritical to pretend satisfaction while I am still hungry.

1987

EXCELLENT THINGS IN WOMEN

by SARA SULERI

from RARITAN A QUARTERLY REVIEW

LEAVING Pakistan was, of course, tantamount to giving up the company of women. I can only tell this to someone like Anita, knowing that she will understand, as we go perambulating through the grimness of New Haven and feeding on the pleasures of our conversational way. Dale, who lives in Boston, would also understand. She will one day write a book about the stern and secretive life of breast feeding, and is partial to fantasies that culminate in an abundance of resolution. And Fawzi, with a grimace of recognition, knows because she knows the impulse to forget.

To a stranger or an acquaintance, however, some vestigial remoteness obliges me to explain that my reference is to a place where the concept of woman was not really part of an available vocabulary: we were too busy for that concept, just living, and conducting precise negotiations with what it meant to be a sister or a child or a wife or a mother or a servant. By this point of course I am damned by my own discourse, and doubly damned when I add that yes, once in a while we naturally thought of ourselves as women, but only in some perfunctory biological way that we happened on, perchance. Or else it was a hugely practical joke, we thought, hidden somewhere among our clothes. But formulating that sentence is about as hopeless as attempting to locate the luminous qualities of an Islamic landscape, which can on occasion generate such esthetically pleasing moments of life. My audience is lost, and angry to be lost, and both of us must find some token of exchange for this failed conversation. I try to put the subject down and change its clothes, but before I know it, it has sprinted off evilly in the direction of ocular evidence. It goads me into saying, with the defiance of a plea, you did not deal with Dadi.

Dadi, my father's mother, was born in Meerut toward the end of the last century. She was married at sixteen and widowed in her thirties, and in her later years could never exactly recall how many children she had borne. When India was partitioned in August 1947, she moved her thin, pure Urdu into the Punjab of Pakistan and waited for the return of her eldest son, my father. He had gone careening off to a place called Inglestan, or England, fired by one of the several enthusiasms made available by the proliferating talk of independence. Dadi was peeved. She had long since dispensed with any loyalties larger than the pitiless give-and-take of people who are forced to live in the same place, and she resented independence for the distances it made. She was not among those who, on the fourteenth of August, unfurled flags and festivities against the backdrop of people fleeing and cities burning. About that era she would only say, looking up sour and cryptic over the edge of her Koran, and I was also burned. She was, but that was years later.

By the time I knew her, Dadi, with her flair for drama, had allowed life to sit so heavily upon her back that her spine wilted and froze into a perfect curve, and so it was in the posture of a shrimp that she went scuttling through the day. She either scuttled, or did not: it all depended on the nature of her fight with the devil. There were days when she so hated him that all she could do was lie out straight and tiny on her bed, uttering the most awful imprecations. Sometimes, to my mother's great distress, she could only berate Satan in full eloquence after she had clambered on top of the dining room table and lain there like a little moldering centerpiece. Satan was to blame: he had after all made her older son linger long enough in Inglestan to give up his rightful wife, a relative, and take up instead with a white-legged woman. He'd taken her only daughter Ayesha when Ayesha lay in childbirth. And he'd sent her youngest son to Swaziland, or Switzerland: her thin hand waved away such sophistries of name.

God she loved, understanding him better than anyone. Her favorite days were those when she could circumvent both the gar-

179

dener and my father, all in the solemn service of her God. She'd steal a knife and weedle her way to the nearest sapling in the garden, some sprightly poplar, or a eucalyptus newly planted. She'd squat, she'd hack it down, and then she would peel its bark away until she had a walking stick, all white and virgin and her own. It drove my father into tears of rage. He must have bought her a dozen walking sticks, one for each of our trips to the mountains, but it was like assembling a row of briar pipes for one who will not smoke. For Dadi had different aims. Armed with implements of her own creation, she would creep down the driveway unperceived to stop cars and people on the street, to give them all the gossip that she had on God.

Food, too, could move her to intensities. Her eyesight always took a sharp turn for the worse over meals, so that she could point hazily at a perfectly ordinary potato and murmur with an Adamic reverence, what *is* it, what *is* it called. With some shortness of manner, one of us would describe and catalog the items on the table. *Alu ka bhartha,* Dadi repeated with wonderment and joy. Yes, Saira begum, you can put some here. Not too much, she'd add pleadingly. For ritual had it that the more she demurred, the more she expected her plate to be piled with an amplitude that her own politeness would never allow. The ritual happened three times a day.

We pondered on it but never quite determined whether food or God constituted her most profound delight. Obvious problems, however, occurred on occasions which brought the two together. One was the Muslim festival called Eid, which celebrates the seductions of the Abraham story in a remarkably literal way. In Pakistan, at least, people buy sheep or goats and fatten them up for weeks with all sorts of delectables. Then, on the appointed day they're chopped, in place of sons, and neighbors graciously exchange silver trays heaped with raw and quivering meat. After Eid prayers the men come home, the animal is cooked, and shortly thereafter, they rush out of the kitchen steaming plates of grilled lung and liver, of a freshness quite superlative.

It was a freshness to which my Welsh mother did not immediately take. She observed the custom but located in it a conundrum that allowed for no ready solution. For, liberal to an extravagant degree on thoughts abstract, she found herself to be remarkably slow and squeamish on particular things. Chopping up animals for God was

180

one. She could not quite locate the metaphor, and was therefore a little uneasy. My father, the writer, quite agreed, for he was so civilized in those days.

Dadi didn't agree. She pined for choppable things. Once she made the mistake of buying a baby goat and bringing him home months in advance of Eid. She wanted to guarantee the texture of his festive flesh by a daily feeding of tender peas and ghee, or clarified butter. Ifat and Shahid and I greeted a goat into the family with boisterous rapture, and soon after, he ravished us completely when we found him nonchalantly at the clothesline, eating up Shahid's pajamas. Of course there was no fight: the little goat was our delight, and even Dadi knew there was no killing him. He became my brother's and my sister's and my first pet, and he grew huge, a big and grinning thing.

Years after, Dadi had her will. We were all old enough, she must have thought, to make the house sprawl out, abstracted, into a multitude of secrets. That was true, but still we all noticed one another's secretive ways. So my sisters and I just shook our heads when the day before Eid our Dadi disappeared. We hid the fact from my father, who at this time of life had begun to equate petulance with extreme vociferation. So we went about our jobs and were Islamic for a day. We waited to sight moons on the wrong occasions and we watched the food come into lavishment. Dried dates change shape when they are soaked in milk, and carrots rich and strange can turn magically sweet when deftly covered with green nutty shavings and smatterings of silver.

Dusk was sweet as we sat out, the day's work done, in an evening garden. Lahore spread like peace around us. My father spoke, and when Papa talked it was of Pakistan. But we were glad, then, at being audience to that familiar conversation, till his voice looked up, and failed. There was Dadi making her return, and she was prodigal. Like a question mark interested only in its own conclusions, her body crawled through the gates. Our guests were spellbound; then they looked away. For Dadi, moving in her eerie crab formations chose to ignore the hangman's rope she firmly held. And behind her in the gloaming minced, hugely affable, a goat.

That goat was still smiling the following day, when Dadi's victory meant that the butcher came and went just as he should, on Eid. Goat was killed and cooked: a scrawny beast that required much cooking and never melted into tenderness, he muscularly winked and glistened on our plates as we sat eating him on Eid. Dadi ate, that is: Papa had taken his mortification to some distant corner of the house: Ifat refused to chew on hemp: Tillat and Irfan still gulped their baby sobs over such a slaughter. Honestly, said Mamma, honestly. For Dadi had successfully cut through tissues of festivity just as the butcher slit the goat, but there was something else that she was eating with that meat. I saw it in her concentration. I know that she was making God talk to her as to Abraham, and see what she could do—for him—to sons. God didn't dare, and she ate on, alone.

Of those middle years it is hard to say whether Dadi was literally left alone or whether a quality of being apart and absorbed was always emanated by her bodily presence. In the winter, I see her alone, painstakingly dragging her straw mat out to the courtyard at the back of the house, and following the rich course of the afternoon sun. With her would go her Koran, a metal basin in which she could wash her hands, and her ridiculously heavy-spouted watering pot that was made of brass. None of us, according to Dadi, was quite pure enough to transport these particular items: the rest of the paraphernalia we could carry out. These were baskets of her writing and sewing materials and her bottle of most pungent and Dadi-like bitter oils, which she'd coat on the papery skin that held her brittle bones. And in the summer, when the night created an illusion of possible coolness, and all held their breath while waiting for a thin and intermittent breeze, Dadi would be on the roof, alone. Her summer bed was a wooden frame latticed with a sweetly smelling rope, much aerated at the foot of the bed. She'd lie there all night, until the wild monsoons would wake the lightest and the soundest sleeper into a rapturous welcome of rain.

In Pakistan, of course, there is no spring but just a rapid elision from winter into summer, which is somewhat analogous to the absence of a recognizable loneliness from the behavior of that climate. In a similar fashion it is quite hard to distinguish between Dadi with people and Dadi alone. She was just impossibly unable to remain unnoticed. In the winter, when she was not writing or reading, she would sew for her delight tiny and magical reticules out of old silks and fragments that she had saved, palm-sized cloth bags that would unravel into the precision of secret and more secret pockets. But none of them did she ever need to hide, for something of Dadi always remained intact, however much we sought to open her. Her discourse, for example, was too impervious to allow for penetration,

182

so that when one or two of us remonstrated with her in a single hour she never bothered to distinguish her replies. Instead, generic and prophetic, she would pronounce, the world takes on a single face. Must you, Dadi, I'd begin, to be halted then by her great complaint: "the world takes on a single face."

It did. And often it was a countenance of some delight, for Dadi also loved the accidental jostle with things belligerent. As she went perambulating through the house, suddenly she'd hear Shahid, her first grandson, telling me or one of my sisters that we were vile, we were disgusting women. And Dadi, who never addressed anyone of us without first conferring the title of lady, so we were Teellat begum, Nuzhat begum, Iffatt begum, Saira begum, would halt in reprimand and tell her grandson never to call her granddaughters women. What else shall I call them, men? Shahid yelled. Men, said Dadi, men. There is more goodness in a woman's little finger than in the benighted mind of man. Hear, hear, Dadi, *hanh hanh*, Dadi, my sisters cried. For men, said Dadi, shaking the name off her fingertips like some unwanted water, live as though they were unsuckled things. And heaven, she grimly added, is the thing Mohammed says (peace be upon him) lies beneath the feet of women! But he was a man, Shahid still would rage, if he weren't laughing, as all of us were laughing, while Dadi sat among us like a belle or a May queen.

Toward the end of the middle years my father stopped speaking to his mother, and the atmosphere at home appreciably improved. They secretly hit upon novel histrionics that took the place of their daily battle. Instead they chose the curious way of silent things: twice a day, Dadi would leave her room and walk the long length of the corridor to my father's room. There she just peered around the door, as though to check if he were real. Each time she peered, my father would interrupt whatever adult thing he may have been doing in order to enact a silent paroxysm, an elaborate facial pantomime of revulsion and affront. At teatime in particular, when Papa would want the world to congregate in his room for tea, Dadi came to peer her ghostly peer. Shortly thereafter conversation was bound to fracture, for we could not drown the fact that Dadi, invigorated by an outcast's strength, was sitting in the dining room and chanting an appeal: God give me tea, God give me tea.

At about this time Dadi stopped smelling old and smelled instead of something equivalent to death. It would have been easy to notice if she had been dying, but instead she managed the change as a certain gradation into subtlety, just as her annoying little stove could shift its hanging odors away from smoke and into ash. During the middle years there had been something more defined about her being, which sat in the world as solely its own context. But Pakistan was increasingly complicating the question of context, as though history, like a pestilence, was insisting that nothing could have definition outside relations to its own fevered sleep. So it was simple for my father to ignore the letters that Dadi had begun to write to him every other day, in her fine wavering script, letters of advice about the house or the children or the servants. Or she transcribed her complaint: Oh my son, Zia. Do you think your son, Shahid, upon whom God bestowed a thousand blessings, should be permitted to lift up his grandmother's chair and carry it into the courtyard, when his grandmother is seated in it? She had cackled in a combination of delight and virgin joy when Shahid had so transported her, but that little crackling sound she omitted from her letter. She ended it, and all her notes, with her single endearment. It was a phrase to halt and arrest when Dadi actually uttered it: her solitary piece of tenderness was an injunction, really, to her world. Keep on living, she would say.

Between that phrase and the great Dadi conflagration comes the era of the trying times. They began in the winter war of 1971, when East Pakistan became Bangladesh and Indira Gandhi hailed the demise of the two-nation theory. Ifat's husband was off fighting and we spent the war together with her father-in-law, the brigadier, in the pink house on the hill. It was an ideal location for anti-aircraft guns, so there was a bevy of soldiers and weaponry installed upon our roof. During each air raid the brigadier would stride purposefully into the garden and bark commands at them, as though the success of the war rested upon his stiff upper lip. Then Dacca fell, and General Yahya came on television to resign the presidency and accede defeat. Drunk, by God, barked the brigadier as we sat watching, drunk.

The following morning General Yahya's mistress came to mourn with us over breakfast, lumbering in with swathes of overscented silk. The brigadier lit an English cigarette—he was frequently known to avow that Pakistani cigarettes gave him a cuff—and bit on his moustache. Yes, he barked, these are trying times. Oh yes, Gul, Yahya's mistress wailed, these are such trying times. She gulped on her own eloquence, her breakfast bosom quaked, and then resumed authority over that dangling sentence. It is so trying, she continued, I find it so trying, it is trying to us all, to live in these trying, trying times. Ifat's eyes met mine in complete accord: mistress transmogrified to muse; Bhutto returned from the U.N. to put Yahya under house arrest and become the first elected president of Pakistan; Ifat's husband went to India as a war prisoner for two years; my father lost his newspaper. We had entered the era of the trying times.

Dadi didn't notice the war, just as she didn't really notice the proliferation of her great-grandchildren, for Ifat and Nuzzi conceived at the drop of a hat and kept popping babies out for our delight. Tillat and I felt favored at this vicarious taste of motherhood: we learned to become that enviable personage, a khala, mother's sister, and when our married sisters came to visit with their entourage, we reveled in the exercise of khala-love. I once asked Dadi how many sisters she had had. She looked up with the oceanic gray of her cataracted eyes and answered, I forget.

The children helped, because we needed distraction, there being then in Pakistan a slightly musty taste of defeat to all our activities. The children gave us something, but they also took away: they initiated a slight displacement of my mother, for her grandchildren would not speak any English, and she could not read them stories as of old. Urdu always remained a shyness on her tongue, and as the babies came and went she let something of her influence imperceptibly recede, as though she occupied an increasingly private air space. Her eldest son was now in England, so Mamma found herself living in the classic posture of an Indian woman, who sends away her sons and runs the risk of seeing them then succumb to the great alternatives represented by the West. It was a position that preoccupied her, and without my really noticing what was happening, she quietly handed over many of her wifely duties to her two remaining daughters, to Tillat and to me. In the summer, once the ferocity of the afternoon sun had died down, it was her pleasure to go out into the garden on her own. There she would stand, absorbed and abstracted, watering the driveway and breathing in the heady smell of water on hot dust. I'd watch her often, from my room upstairs. She looked like a girl.

We were aware of something, of a reconfiguration in the air, but could not exactly phrase where it would lead us. Dadi now spoke mainly to herself, and even the audience provided by the deity had dropped away. Somehow there was not a proper balance between the way things came and the way they went, as Halima the cleaning woman knew full well when she looked at me intently, asking a question that had no question in it: Do I grieve, or do I celebrate? Halima had given birth to her latest son the night her older child had died in screams of meningitis; once heard, never to be forgotten. She came back to work a week later, and we were talking as we put away the family's winter clothes into vast metal trunks. For in England, they would call it spring.

We felt a quickening urgency of change drown our sense of regular direction, as though something was bound to happen soon, but not knowing what it was that was making history nervous. And so we were not really that surprised when we found ourselves living through the summer of the trials by fire. That summer's climax came when Dadi went up in a little ball of flames. But somehow sequentially related were my mother's trip to England, to tend to her dying mother, the night I beat up Tillat, and the evening I nearly castrated my little brother, runt of the litter, serious-eyed Irfan.

It was an accident on both our parts. I was in the kitchen, so it must have been a Sunday when Allah Ditta, the cook, took the evening off. He was a mean-spirited man with an incongruously delicate touch when it came to making food. On Sunday at midday he would bluster one of us into the kitchen and show us what he had prepared for the evening meal, leaving strict and belligerent instructions about what would happen if we overheated this or dared brown that. So I was in the kitchen heating up some food, when Farni came back from playing hockey with that ominous asthmatic rattle in his throat. He, the youngest, had been my parents' gravest infant: in adolescence he remained a gentle invalid. Of course he pretended otherwise, and was loud and raucous, but it never worked.

Tillat and I immediately turned on him with the bullying litany that actually is quite soothing, the invariable female reproach to the returning male. He was to do what he hated, and stave off his disease by sitting over a bowl of camphor and boiling water, inhaling its acrid fumes. I insisted that he sit on the cook's little stool in the kitchen, holding the bowl of water on his lap, so that I could cook and Farni could not cheat and I could time each minute he should

186

sit there thus confined. We seated him and flounced a towel on his reluctant head. The kitchen jointly reeked of cumin and camphor, and he sat skinny and penitent and swathed for half a minute before begging to be done. I slammed down the carving knife and screamed *Irfan* with such ferocity that he jumped literally and figuratively quite out of his skin. The bowl of water emptied onto him, and with a gurgling cry he leapt up, tearing at his steaming clothes. He clutched at his groin, and everywhere he touched the skin slid off, so that between his fingers his penis easily unsheathed, a blanched and fiery grape. What's happening, screamed Papa from his room; what's happening, echoed Dadi's wail from the opposite end of the house. What was happening was that I was holding Farni's shoulders, trying to stop him jumping up and down, but I was jumping too, while Tillat just stood there frozen, frowning at his poor ravaged grapes.

This was June, and the white heat of summer. We spent the next few days laying ice on Farni's wounds: half the time I was allowed to stay with him, until the doctors suddenly remembered I was a woman and hurried me out when his body made crazy spastic reactions to its burns. Once things grew calmer and we were alone, Irfan looked away and said, I hope I didn't shock you, Sara. And I was so taken by tenderness for his bony convalescent body that it took me years to realize that yes, something female in me had been deeply shocked.

Mamma knew nothing of this, of course. We kept it from her so that she could concentrate on what took her back to the rocky coast-line of Wales, and to places she had not really revisited since she was a girl. She sat waiting with her mother, who was blind now and of a fine translucency, and both of them knew that they were waiting for her death. It was a peculiar posture for Mamma to maintain, but her quiet letters spoke mainly of the sharp astringent light that made the sea wind feel so brisk in Wales, and so many worlds away from the daily omnipresent weight of a summer in Lahore. And there, one afternoon, walking childless among the brambles and the furze, Mamma realized that her childhood was distinctly lost. It was not that I wanted to feel more familiar, she later told me, or that I was more used to feeling unfamiliar in Lahore. It's just that familiarity isn't important, really, she murmured absently, it really doesn't matter at all.

187

When Mamma was ready to return she wired us her plans, and my father read the cable, kissed it, then put it in his pocket. I watched him and felt startled, as we all did on the occasions when our parents' lives seemed to drop away before our eyes, leaving them youthfully engrossed in the illusion of knowledge conferred by love. We were so used to conceiving of them as parents moving in and out of hectic days that it always amused us, and touched us secretly, when they made quaint and punctilious returns to the amorous bond that had initiated the unlikely lives through which we knew them.

That summer, while my mother was away, Tillat and I experienced a new bond of powerlessness, which is the white and shaking rage of sexual jealousy in parenthood. I had always behaved toward her as a belligerent surrogate parent, but she was growing beyond that scope, and in her girlhood asking me for a formal acknowledgment of equality that I was loath to give. My reluctance was rooted in a helpless fear of what the world could do to her, for I was young and ignorant enough not to see that what I could do was worse. She went out one evening, when my father was off on one of his many trips. The house was gaping emptily, and Tillat was very late. Allah Ditta had gone home, and Dadi and Irfan were sleeping; I read, and thought, and walked up and down the garden, and Tillat was very very late. When she came back she wore that strange sheath of complacency and guilt which pleasure puts on faces very young. It smote an outrage in my heart until despite all resolutions to the contrary I heard my hiss: and where were you? Her returning look was both fearful and preening at the same time, so that the next thing to be smitten was her face. Don't, Sara, Tillat said in her superior way, physical violence is so degrading. To you, maybe, I answered, and hit her once again.

It made a sorrowful bond between us, for we both felt complicit in the shamefulness that had made me seem righteous, when I had felt simply jealous, which we tacitly agreed was a more legitimate thing to be. But we had lost something, a certain protective aura, some unspoken myth asserting that love between sisters at least was sexually innocent. Now we had to fold that vain belief away and stand in slightly more naked relation to our affection. Till then we had associated such violence with all that was outside us, as though, somehow, the more historical process fractured, the more whole we

188

would be. But now we were losing a sense of the differentiated identities of history and ourselves, and were guiltily aware that we had known it all along, our part in the construction of unreality.

By this time, Dadi's burns were slowly learning how to heal. It was she who had given the summer its strange pace by nearly burning herself alive at its inception. On an early April night Dadi awoke, seized by a desperate need for tea. It was three in the morning and the household was asleep, so she could do the great forbidden thing of creeping into Allah Ditta's kitchen and taking charge, like pixies in the night. As all of us were so bored with predicting, one of her many cotton garments took to fire that truant night. But Dadi deserves credit for her resourceful voice, which wavered out for witness to her burning death. By the time Tillat awoke and found her, she was a little flaming ball: *Dadi*, said Tillat in the reproach of sleep, and beat her quiet with a blanket. In the morning we discovered Dadi's torso had been quite consumed and nothing recognizable remained, from collarbone to groin. The doctors bade us to some decent mourning.

But Dadi had different plans. She lived through her sojourn at the hospital: she weathered her return. And then after six weeks at home she angrily refused to be lugged daily to the doctor's to get her dressings changed, as though she were a chunk of meat: Saira begum will do it, she announced. And thus developed my great intimacy with the fluid properties of human flesh. By the time Mamma left for England, Dadi's left breast was still coagulate and raw. When Farni got his burns she was growing pink and livid tightropes, strung from hip to hip in a flaming advertisement of life. And in the days when Tillat and I were wrestling, Dadi's vanished nipples started to congeal and turn their cavities into triumphant little loveknots.

I learned about the specialization of beauty from that body. There were times like love when I felt only disappointment to carefully ease the dressings off and find again a piece of flesh that would not knit, happier in the texture of a stubborn glue. But then, on some more exhilarating day, I'd peel like an onion all her bandages away and suddenly discover I was looking down at some literal tenacity, and was bemused at all the freshly withered shapes she could create. Each new striation was a triumph to itself, and when Dadi's hairless groin solidified again, and sent firm signals that abdomen must do the same, I could have wept with glee.

During her immolation, Dadi's diet underwent some curious changes. At first her consciousness teetered too much for her to pray, but then as she grew stronger it took us a while to notice what was missing: she had forgotten prayer. It left her life as firmly as tobacco can leave the lives of only the most passionate smokers, and I don't know if she ever prayed again. At about this time, however, with the heavy-handed inevitability that characterized his relation to his mother, my father took to prayer. I came home one afternoon and looked for him in all the usual places, but he wasn't to be found. Finally I came across Tillat and asked her where Papa was. Praying, she said. *Praying?* I said. Praying, she said, and I felt most embarrassed. For us it was rather as though we had come upon the children playing some forbidden, titillating game, and decided it was wisest to ignore it calmly. In an unspoken way, though, I think we dimly knew we were about to witness Islam's departure from the land of Pakistan. The men would take it to the streets and make it vociferate, but the great romance between religion and the populace, the embrace that engendered Pakistan, was done. So Papa prayed, with the desperate ardor of a lover trying to converse life back into a finished love.

And that was a change, when Dadi sewed herself together again and forgot to put back prayer into its proper pocket, for God could now leave the home and soon would join the government. Papa prayed and fasted and went on pilgrimage and read the Koran aloud with the most peculiar locutions. Occasionally we also caught him in nocturnal altercations that made him sound suspiciously like Dadi: we looked askance, but did not say a thing. And my mother was quite admirable. She behaved as though she always knew she'd wed a swaying, chanting thing, or that to register surprise would be an impoliteness to existence. Her expression reminded me somewhat of the time when Ifat was eight, and Mamma was urging her recalcitrance into some goodly task. Ifat postponed, and Mamma, always nifty with appropriate fables, quoted meaningfully: "I'll do it myself, said the little red hen." Ifat looked up with bright affection. Good little red hen, she murmured. Then a glance crossed my mother's face, a look between a slight smile and a quick rejection of eloquent response, something like a woman looking down, and then away.

She looked like that at my father's sudden hungering for God, which was added to the growing number of subjects about which we,

190

my mother and her daughters, silently decided we had no conversation. We knew that there was something other than trying times ahead and would far rather hold our breath than speculate about what other surprises the era held up its capacious sleeve. Tillat and I decided to quash our dread of waiting around for change by changing for ourselves, before destiny took the time to come our way. I moved to America and Tillat to Kuwait and marriage. To both intentions my mother said, I see, and helped us in our preparations: she knew by now her son would not return and was not unprepared to extend the courtesy of waiting to her daughters, too. We left, and Islam predictably took to the streets, threatening and shaking Bhutto's empire. Mamma and Dadi remained the only women in the house, the one untalking, the other unpraying.

Dadi behaved abysmally at my mother's funeral, they told me, and made them all annoyed. She set up loud and unnecessary lamentations in the dining room, somewhat like an heir apparent, as though this death had reinstated her as mother of the house. While Ifat and Nuzzi and Tillat wandered frozen eyed, dealing with the roses and the ice, Dadi demanded an irritating amount of attention, stretching out supine and crying out, your mother has betrayed your father; she has left him; she has gone. Food from respectful mourners poured in, cauldron after cauldron, and Dadi rediscovered a voracious appetite.

Years later, I was somewhat sorry that I heard this tale because it made me take affront. When I went back to Pakistan, I was too peeved with Dadi to find out how she was. Instead I heard Ifat tell me about standing there in the hospital, watching the doctors suddenly pump upon my mother's heart—I'd seen it on television, she gravely said, I knew it was the end. Mamma's students from the university had found the rickshaw driver who had knocked her down, pummeled him nearly to death, and camped out in our garden, sobbing wildly, all in hordes.

By this time Bhutto was in prison and awaiting trial, and General Zulu was presiding over the Islamization of Pakistan. But we had no time to notice. My mother was buried at the nerve center of Lahore, a wild and dusty place, and my father immediately made arrangements to buy the plot of land next to her grave: we are ready when you are, Shahid sang. Her tombstone bore some pretty Urdu poetry and a completely fictitious place of birth, because there were some

191

details my father tended to forget. Honestly, it would have moved his wife to say.

So I was angry with Dadi at that time, and I didn't stop to see her. I saw my mother's grave and then came back to America, and hardly reacted when, six months from then, my father called from London and mentioned that Dadi was now dead. It happened in the same week that Bhutto finally was hanged, and our imaginations were consumed by that public and historical dying. Pakistan made rapid provisions not to talk about the thing that had been done, and somehow accidentally Dadi must have been mislaid into that larger decision, because she too ceased to be a mentioned thing. My father tried to get back in time for the funeral, but he was so busy talking Bhutto-talk in England that he missed his flight. Luckily, Irfani was at home and saw Dadi to her grave.

Bhutto's hanging had the effect of making Pakistan feel quite unreliable, particularly to itself. There was a new secretiveness its landscape learned, quite unusual for a formerly loquacious place. It accounts for the fact that I have never seen my grandmother's grave, and neither have my sisters. I think we would have tried, had we been together, despite the free-floating anarchy in the air that—like the heroin trade—made the world suspicious and afraid. Now there was no longer any need to wait for change because change was all there was, and we had quite forgotten the flavor of an era that stayed in place long enough to gain a name. One morning I awoke to see that, during the course of the night, my mind had completely ejected the names of all the streets in Pakistan, as though to assure that I could not return, or that if I did, it would be returning to a loss. Overnight the country had grown absentminded, and patches of amnesia hung over the hollows of the land like fog.

But I think we would have mourned Dadi in our belated way, except that the coming year saw Ifat killed in the consuming rush of change and disbanded the company of women for all times. It was a curious day in March, two years after my mother died, when the weight of that anniversary made us all disconsolate for her quietude. I'll speak to Ifat, though, I thought to myself in America. But in Pakistan someone had different ideas for that sister of mine and thwarted all my plans. When she went walking out that warm March night a car came by and trampeled her into the ground, and then it vanished strangely. By the time I reached Lahore, a tall and slender mound had usurped the grave space where my father hoped to lie, next to the more moderate shape that was his wife. Children take over everything.

So worn by repetition we stood by Ifat's grave and took note of the narcissi, still alive, that she must have put upon my mother's on the day that she had died. It made us impatient, in a way, as though we had to decide there was never anything quite as farcical as grief, and that it had to be eliminated from our diets for good. It cut away, of course, our intimacy with Pakistan, where history is synonymous with grief and always most at home in the attitudes of grieving. Our congregation in Lahore was brief, and then we swiftly returned to a more geographic reality. We are lost, Sara, Shahid said to me on the phone from England. Yes, Shahid, I firmly said, we're lost.

Today, I'd be less emphatic. Ifat and Mamma must have honey-combed and crumbled now, in the comfortable way that overtakes bedfellows. And somehow it seems apt and heartening that Dadi, being what she was, was never given the pomposities that enter the most well meaning of farewells, but seeped instead into the nooks and crannies of our forgetfulness. She fell between two stools of grief, which is quite appropriate, since she was greatest when her life was at its most unreal. Anyway, she was always outside our ken, an anecdotal thing, neither more nor less. And so some sweet reassurance of reality accompanies my discourse when I claim that when Dadi died, we all forgot to grieve.

For to be lost is just a minute's respite, after all, like a train that cannot help but stop at way stations, in order to stage a pretend version of the journey's end. Dying, we saw, was simply change taken to points of mocking extremity; it wasn't a thing to lose us but to find us out, and catch us where we least wanted to be caught. In Pakistan, Bhutto became rapidly obsolete after a few successions of bumper harvests, and none of us can fight the ways that the names Mamma and Ifat have become archaisms and quaintnesses on our lips.

Now I live in New Haven and feel quite happy with my life. I miss of course the absence of woman, and grow increasingly nostalgic for a world where the modulations of age are as recognized and welcomed as the shift from season into season. But that's a hazard that has to come along, since I have made myself an inhabitant of a population which democratically insists that everyone from twenty-nine to fifty-six roughly occupies the same space of age. When I teach topics in third world literature, much time is lost in trying to explain that such a place is not locatable, except as a discourse of convenience. It is like pretending that history or home is real and not located precisely where you're sitting, I hear my voice quite idiotically say. And then it happens. A face, puzzled and attentive and belonging to my gender, raises its intelligence to ask why, since I am teaching third world writing, I haven't given equal space to women writers on my syllabus. I look up, the horse's mouth, a foolish thing to be. Unequal images battle in my mind for pre-cedence—there's imperial Ifat, there's Mamma in the garden and Halima the cleaning woman is there too, there's uncanny Dadi with her goat. Against all my own odds I know what I must say. Because, I'll answer slowly, there are no women in the third world.

1988

194

REDNECK SECRETS

by WILLIAM KITTREDGE

from OWNING IT ALL (Graywolf Press)

Back in my more scattered days there was a time when I decided the solution to all life's miseries would begin with marrying a nurse. Cool hands and commiseration. She would be a second-generation Swedish girl who left the family farm in North Dakota to live a new life in Denver, her hair would be long and silvery blonde, and she would smile every time she saw me and always be after me to get out of the house and go have a glass of beer with my buckaroo cronies.

Our faithfulness to one another would be legendary. We would live near Lolo, Montana, on the banks of the Bitterroot River where Lewis and Clark camped to rest on their way West, "Traveler's Rest," land which floods a little in the spring of the year, a small price to pay for such connection with mythology. Our garden would be intricately perfect on the sunny uphill side of our 16 acres, with little wooden flume boxes to turn the irrigation water down one ditch or another.

We would own three horses, one a blue roan Appaloosa, and haul them around in our trailer to jackpot roping events on summer weekends. I wouldn't be much good on horseback, never was, but nobody would care. The saddle shed would be tacked to the side of our doublewide expando New Moon mobile home, and there would be a neat little lawn with a white picket fence about as high as your knee, and a boxer dog called Aces and Eights, with a great studded collar. There would be a .357 magnum pistol in the drawer of the bedside table, and on Friday night we would dance to the music of old-time fiddlers at some country tavern and in the fall we would go into the mountains for firewood and kill two or three elk for the freezer. There would be wild asparagus along the irrigation ditches and morels down under the cottonwoods by the river, and we would always be good.

And I would keep a journal, like Lewis and Clark, and spell bad, because in my heart I would want to be a mountain man—"We luved aft the movee in the bak seet agin tonite."

WE MUST NOT gainsay such Western dreams. They are not automatically idiot. There are, after all, good Rednecks and bad Rednecks. Those are categories.

So many people in the American West are hurt, and hurting. Bad Rednecks originate out of hurt and a sense of having been discarded and ignored by the Great World, which these days exists mostly on television, distant and most times dizzily out of focus out here in Redneck country.

Bad Rednecks lose faith and ride away into foolishness, striking back. The spastic utility of violence. The other night in a barroom, I saw one man turn to another, who had been pestering him with drunken nonsense. "Son," he said, "you better calm yourself, because if you don't, things are going to get real Western here for a minute."

REAL WESTERN. Back in the late '40's when I was getting close to graduating from high school, they used to stage Saturday night prizefights down in the Veterans Auditorium. Not boxing matches but prizefights, a name which rings in the ear something like *cock-fight*. One night the two main-event fighters, always heavyweights, were some hulking Indian and a white farmer from a little dairy-farm community.

The Indian, I recall, had the word "Mother" carved on his hairless chest. Not tattooed, but carved in the flesh with a blade, so the scar tissue spelled out the word in livid welts. The white farmer looked soft and his body was alabaster, pure white, except for his wrists and neck, which were dark, burned-in-the-fields red, burnished red. While they hammered at each other we hooted from the stands like gibbons, rooting for our favorites on strictly territorial and racial grounds, and in the end were all disappointed. The white farmer went down like thunder about three times, blood snorting from his nose in a delicate spray and decorating his whiteness like in, say, the movies. The Indian simply retreated to his corner and refused to go on. It didn't make any sense.

We screeched and stomped, but the Indian just stood there looking at the bleeding white man, and the white man cleared his head and looked at the Indian, and then they both shook their heads at one another, as if acknowledging some private news they had just then learned to share. They both climbed out of the ring and together made their way up the aisle. Walked away.

Real Western. Of course, in that short-lived partnership of the downtrodden, the Indian was probably doomed to a lifetime on the lower end of the seesaw. No dairy farms in a pastoral valley, nor morning milking and school boards for him. But that is not the essential point in this equation. There is a real spiritual equivalency between Redmen and Rednecks. How sad and ironic that they tend to hit at each other for lack of a real target, acting out some tired old scenario. Both, with some justice, feel used and cheated and disenfranchised. Both want to strike back, which may be just walking away, or the bad answer, bloody noses.

NOBODY IS CLAIMING certain Rednecks are gorgeous about their ways of resolving the pain of their frustrations. Some of them will indeed get drunk in honky-tonks and raise hell and harass young men with long hair and golden earrings. These are the bad Rednecks.

Why bad? Because they are betraying themselves. Out-of-power groups keep fighting each other instead of what they really resent: power itself. A redneck pounding a hippie in a dark barroom is embarrassing because we see the cowardice. What he wants to hit is a banker in broad daylight.

But things are looking up. Rednecks take drugs; hippies take jobs. And the hippie carpenters and the 250-pound, pigtailed lumberjacks preserve their essence. They are still isolated, outrageous, lonely, proud and mean. Any one of them might yearn for a nurse, a doublewide, a blue roan Appaloosa, and a sense of place in a country that left him behind.

LIKE THE INDIAN and the buffalo on the old nickel, there are two sides to American faith. But in terms of Redneck currency, they conflict. On the one side there is individualism, which in its most

197

radical mountain-man form becomes isolation and loneliness: the standard country-and-western lament. It will lead to dying alone in your motel room: whether gored, boozed or smacked makes little difference. On the other side there are family and community, that pastoral society of good people inhabiting the good place on earth that William Bradford and Thomas Jefferson so loved to think about.

Last winter after the snowmobile races in Seeley Lake, I had come home to stand alongside my favorite bar rail and listen to my favorite skinny Redneck barmaid turn down propositions. Did I say *home?* Anyway, standing there and feeling at home, I realized that good Redneck bars are like good hippy bars: they are community centers, like churches and pubs in the old days, and drastically unlike our singles bars where every person is so radically on his or her own.

My skinny barmaid friend looked up at one lumberjack fellow, who was clomping around in his White logger boots and smiling his most winsome. She said, "You're just one of those boys with a sink full of dishes. You ain't looking for nothing but someone dumb enough to come and wash your dishes. You go home and play your radio."

A sink full of dirty dishes. And laundry. There are aspects of living alone that can be defined as going out to the J. C. Penney store and buying $33 worth of new shorts and socks and t-shirts because everything you own is stacked up raunchy and stinking on the far side of the bed. And going out and buying paper plates at K-mart because you're tired of eating your meals crouched over the kitchen sink. You finally learn about dirty dishes. They stay dirty. And those girls, like my skinny friend, have learned a thing or two. There are genuine offers of solace and companionship, and there are dirty dishes and nursing. And then a trailer house, and three babies in three years, diapers, and he's gone to Alaska for the money. So back to barmaiding, this time with kids to support, babysitters.

Go home and play your radio.

THERE IS, of course, another Montana. Consider these remarks from the journals of James and Granville Stewart, 1862:

JANUARY 1, 1862. Snowed in the forenoon. Very cold in the afternoon. Raw east wind. Everybody went to grand ball given by John Grant at Grantsville and a severe blizzard blew up and raged all night. We danced all night, no outside storm could dampen the festivities.

JANUARY 2. Still blowing a gale this morning. Forty below zero and the air is filled with driving, drifting snow. After breakfast we laid down on the floor of the several rooms, on buffalo robes that Johnny furnished, all dressed as we were and slept until about two-o'clock in the afternoon, when we arose, ate a fine dinner, then resumed dancing which we kept up with unabated pleasure . . . danced until sunrise.

JANUARY 3. The blizzard ceased about daylight, but it was very cold with about fourteen inches of snow badly drifted in places and the ground bare in spots. We estimated the cold at about thirty-five below, but fortunately there was but little wind. After breakfast all of the visitors left for home, men, women, and children, all on horseback. Everyone got home without frost bites.

Sounds pretty good. But Granville Stewart got his. In the great and deadly winter of 1886–1887, before they learned the need of stacking hay for winter, when more than one million head of cattle ran the Montana ranges, he lost two-thirds of his cow herd. Carcasses piled in the coulees and fence corners come springtime, flowers growing up between the ribs of dead longhorn cattle, and the mild breezes reeking with decay. A one-time partner of Stewart's, Conrad Kohrs, salvaged 3,000 head out of 35,000. Reports vary, but you get the sense of it.

Over across the Continental Divide to where the plains begin on the east side of the Crazy Mountains, in the Two Dot country, on bright mornings you can gaze across the enormous swale of the Musselshell, north and east to the Snowy Mountains, 50 miles distant and distinct and clear in the air as the one mountain bluebell you picked when you came out from breakfast.

But we are not talking spring, we are talking winter and haystacks. A man we know, let's call him Davis Patten, is feeding cattle. It's February, and the snow is drifting three feet deep along the fence lines, and the wind is carrying the chill factor down to about 30 below. Davis Patten is pulling his feed sled with a team of yellow

Belgian geldings. For this job, it's either horses or a track-layer, like a Caterpillar D-6. The Belgians are cheaper and easier to start.

Davis kicks the last remnant of meadow hay, still greenish and smelling of dry summer, off the sled to the trailing cattle. It's three o'clock in the afternoon and already the day is settling toward dark. Sled runners creak on the frozen snow. The gray light is murky in the wind, as though inhabited, but no birds are flying anywhere. Davis Patten is sweating under his insulated coveralls, but his beard is frozen around his mouth. He heads the team toward the barns, over under the cottonwood by the creek. Light from the kitchen windows shows through the bare limbs. After he has fed the team a bait of oats, then Davis and his wife Loretta will drink coffee laced with bourbon.

Later they watch television, people laughing and joking in bright Sony color. In his bones Davis recognizes, as most of us do, that the principal supporting business of television is lies, truths that are twisted about a quarter turn. Truths that were never truths. Davis drifts off to sleep in his Barca-Lounger. He will wake to the white noise from a gray screen.

It is important to have a sense of all this. There are many other lives, this is just one, but none are the lives we imagine when we think of running away to Territory.

Tomorrow Davis Patten will begin his day chopping ice along the creek with a splitting maul. Stock water, a daily chore. Another day with ice in his beard, sustained by memories of making slow love to Loretta under down comforters in their cold bedroom. Love, and then quickfooting it to the bathroom on the cold floors, a steaming shower. Memories of a bed that reeks a little of child making.

The rewards of the life, it is said, are spiritual, and often they are. Just standing on land you own, where you can dig any sort of hole you like, can be considered a spiritual reward, a reason for not selling out and hitting the Bahamas. But on his winter afternoons Davis Patten remembers another life. For ten years, after he broke away from Montana to the Marines, Davis hung out at the dragster tracks in the San Joaquin Valley, rebuilding engines for great, roaring, ass-busting machines. These days he sees their stripped red-and-white dragchutes flowering only on Sunday afternoons. The "Wide World of Sports." Lost horizons. The intricate precision of cam shaft adjustments.

In the meantime, another load of hay.

UP IN TOWNS along the highline, Browning and Harlem and Malta, people are continually dying from another kind of possibility. Another shot of Beam on the rocks and Annie Greensprings out back after the bars are closed. In Montana they used to erect little crosses along the highways wherever a fatality occurred. A while back, outside Browning, they got a dandy. Eleven deaths in a single car accident. *Guinness Book of World Records*. Verities. The highway department has given up the practice of erecting crosses: too many of them are dedicated to the disenfranchised.

Out south of Billings the great coal fields are being strip-mined. Possibilities. The history of Montana and the West, from the fur trade to tomorrow, is a history of colonialism, both material and cultural. Is it any wonder we are so deeply xenophobic, and regard anything east of us as suspect? The money and the power always came from the east, took what it wanted, and left us, white or Indian, with our traditions dismantled and our territory filled with holes in the ground. Ever been to Butte? About half the old town was sucked into a vast open-pit mine.

Verities. The lasting thing we have learned here, if we ever learn, is to resist the beguilements of power and money. Hang on to your land. There won't be any more. Be superstitious as a Borneo tribesman. Do not let them photograph our shy, bare-breasted beauties as they wash clothes along the stream bank. Do not let them steal your soul away in pictures, because they will if they get a chance, just as Beadle's Nickel-Dime Library westerns and Gene Autry B-movies gnawed at the soul of this country where we live. Verities have to be earned, and they take time in the earning—time spent gazing out over your personal wind-glazed fields of snow. Once earned, they inhabit you in complex ways you cannot name, and they cannot be given away. They can only be transmogrified—transformed into something surreal or fantastic, unreal. And ours have been, and always for the same reason: primarily the titillation of those who used to be Easterners, who are everywhere now.

These are common sentiments here in the mountain West. In 1923 Charlie Russell agreed to speak before the Great Falls Booster Club. After listening to six or seven booster speeches, he tore up his own talk and spoke. This is what he said:

> "In my book a pioneer is a man who turned all the
> grass upside down, strung bob-wire over the dust that

201

was left, poisoned the water and cut down the trees, killed the Indian who owned the land, and called it progress. If I had my way, the land here would be like God made it, and none of you sons of bitches would be here at all."

So what are we left with? There was a great dream about a just and stable society, which was to be America. And there was another great dream about wilderness individuals, mountain men we have called them, who would be the natural defenders of that society. But our society is hugely corrupt, rich and impossibly complex, and our great simple individuals can define nothing to defend, nothing to reap but the isolation implicit in their stance, nothing to gain for their strength but loneliness. The vast, sad, recurrent story which is so centrally American. Western Rednecks cherish secret remnants of those dreams, and still try to live within them. No doubt a foolish enterprise.

But that's why, full of anger and a kind of releasing joy, they plunge their Snowcats around frozen lakes at 90 miles an hour, coming in for a whiskey stop with eyes glittering and icicles bright in their whiskers, and why on any summer day you can look into the sky over Missoula and see the hang-gliding daredevils circling higher than the mountains. That's why you see grown men climbing frozen waterfalls with pretty colored ropes.

And then there seems to be a shooting a week in the doublewide village. Spastic violence. You know, the husband wakes up from his drunk, lying on the kitchen floor with the light still burning, gets himself an Alka-Seltzer, stumbles into the living room, and there is Mother on the couch with half her side blown away. The 12-gauge is carefully placed back where it belongs on the rack over the breakfront. Can't tell what happened. Must have been an intruder.

Yeah, the crazy man inside us. Our friends wear Caterpillar D-9 caps when they've never pulled a friction in their lives, and Buck knives in little leather holsters on their belts, as if they might be called upon to pelt out a beaver at any moment. Or maybe just stab an empty beer can. Ah, wilderness, and suicidal nostalgia.

Which gets us to another kind of pioneer we see these days, people who come to the country with what seems to be an idea that connection with simplicities will save their lives. Which simplicities are those? The condescension implicit in the program is staggering.

If you want to feel you are being taken lightly, try sitting around while someone tells you how he envies the simplicity of your life. What about Davis Patten? He says he is staying in Montana, and calling it home. So am I.

Despite the old Huckleberry Finn-mountain man notion of striking out for the territory, I am going to hang on here, best I can, and nourish my own self. I know a lovely woman who lives up the road in a log house, on what is left of a hard-earned farmstead. I'm going to call and see if she's home. Maybe she'll smile and come have a glass of beer with me and my cronies.

1988

ATLAS OF CIVILIZATION

by SEAMUS HEANEY

from PARNASSUS: POETRY IN REVIEW

A T THE VERY END of his life, Socrates' response to his recurring dream, which had instructed him to "practice the art," was to begin to put the fables of Aesop into verse. It was, of course, entirely in character for the philosopher to be attracted to fictions whose *a priori* function was to expose the true shape of things, and it was proper that even this slight brush with the art of poetry should involve an element of didacticism. But imagine what the poems of Socrates would have been like if, instead of doing adaptations, he had composed original work during those hours before he took the poison. It is unlikely that he would have broken up his lines to weep; indeed, it is likely that he would not only have obeyed Yeats's injunction on this score, but that he would have produced an oeuvre sufficient to confound the master's claim that "The intellect of man is forced to choose/ Perfection of the life or of the work."

It would be an exaggeration to say that the work of the Polish poet Zbigniew Herbert could pass as a substitute for such an ideal poetry of reality. Yet in the exactions of its logic, the temperance of its tone, and the extremity and equanimity of its recognitions, it does resemble what a twentieth-century poetic version of the examined life might be. Admittedly, in all that follows here, it is

BOOKS CONSIDERED IN THIS ESSAY:

Zbigniew Herbert. *Barbarian in the Garden.* Translated by Michael Marsh & Jaroslaw Anders. Carcanet 1986. 180 pp. $14.95

Zbigniew Herbert. *Selected Poems.* Translated by Czeslaw Milosz and Peter Dale Scott, with an Introduction by A. Alvarez. The Ecco Press 1986. 138 pp. $7.50 (paper)

Zbigniew Herbert. *Report from the Besieged City and Other Poems.* Translated, with an Introduction and Notes by John Carpenter and Bogdana Carpenter. The Ecco Press 1986. 82 pp. $12.50 $8.50 (paper)

an English translation rather than the Polish originals which is being praised or pondered, but what convinces one of the universal resource of Herbert's writing is just this ability which it possesses to lean, without toppling, well beyond the plumb of its native language.

Herbert himself, however, is deeply attracted to that which does not lean but which "trusts geometry, simple numerical rule, the wisdom of the square, balance and weight." He rejoices in the discovery that "Greek architecture originated in the sun" and that "Greek architects knew the art of measuring with shadows. The north-south axis was marked by the shortest shadow cast by the sun's zenith. The problem was to trace the perpendicular, the holy east-west direction." Hence the splendid utility of Pythagoras' theorem, and the justice of Herbert's observation that "the architects of the Doric temples were less concerned with beauty than with the chiselling of the world's order into stone."

These quotations come from the second essay in *Barbarian in the Garden,* a collection of ten meditations on art and history which masquerade as "travel writings" insofar as nine of them are occasioned by visits to specific places, including Lascaux, Sicily, Arles, Orvieto, Siena, Chartres, and the various resting places of the paintings of Piero della Francesca. A tenth one also begins and ends at a single pungent site, the scorched earth of an island in the Seine where on March 18, 1314, Jacques de Molay, Grand Master of the Order of the Templars, burned at the stake along with Geoffroi de Charney and another thirty-six brothers of their order. Yet this section of the book also travels to another domain where Herbert operates with fastidious professional skills: the domain of tyranny, with its police precision, mass arrests, tortures, self-inculpations, purges, and eradications, all those methods which already in the fourteenth century had begun to "enrich the repertoire of power."

Luckily, the poet's capacity for admiration is more than equal to his perception of the atrocious, and *Barbarian in the Garden* is an ironical title. This "barbarian" who makes his pilgrimage to the sacred places is steeped in the culture and history of classical and medieval Europe, and even though there is situated at the center of his consciousness a large burnt-out zone inscribed "what we have learned in modern times and must never forget even though we need hardly dwell upon it," this very consciousness can still muster a sustaining half-trust in man as a civilizer and keeper of civilizations. The book is full of lines which sing out in the highest registers of intellectual rapture. In Paestum, "Greek temples live under the golden sun of geometry." In Orvieto, to enter the cathedral is a surprise, "so much does the facade differ from the interior—as though the gate of life full of birds and colours led into a cold, austere eternity." In the presence of a Piero della Francesca: "He is . . . like a figurative painter who has passed through a cubist phase." In the presence of Piero's *Death of Adam* in Arezzo: "The entire scene appears Hellenic, as though the Old Testament were composed by Aeschylus."

But Herbert never gets too carried away. The ground-hugging sturdiness which he recognizes and cherishes in archaic buildings has its analogue in his own down-to-earthness. His love of "the quiet chanting of the air and the immense planes" does not extend so far as to constitute a betrayal of the human subject, in thrall to gravity and history. His imagination is slightly less skyworthy than that of his great compatriot Czeslaw Milosz, who has nevertheless recognized in the younger poet a kindred spirit and as long ago as 1968 translated, with Peter Dale Scott, the now reissued *Selected Poems*. Deliciously susceptible as he is to the *"lucidus ordo*—an eternal order of light and balance" in the work of Piero, Herbert is still greatly pleasured by the density and miscellany of what he finds in a book by Piero's contemporary, the architect and humanist Leon Battista Alberti:

> Despite its classical structure, technical subjects are mixed with anecdotes and trivia. We may read about foundations, building-sites, bricklaying, doorknobs, wheels, axes, levers, hacks, and how to 'exterminate and destroy snakes, mosquitoes, bed-bugs, fleas, mice, moths and other importunate night creatures.'

Clearly, although he quotes Berenson elsewhere, Herbert would be equally at home with a builder. He is very much the poet of a workers' republic insofar as he possesses a natural affinity with those whose eyes narrow in order to effect an operation or a calculation rather than to study a refinement. Discussing the self-portrait of Luca Signorelli which that painter entered in *The Coming of the Anti-Christ* (in the duomo at Orvieto) alongside a portrait of his master, Fra Angelico, Herbert makes a distinction between the two men. He discerns how Signorelli's eyes "are fixed upon reality . . . Beside him, Fra Angelico dressed in a cassock gazes inwards. Two glances: one visionary, the other observant." It is a distinction which suggests an equivalent division within the poet, deriving from the co-existence within his own deepest self of two conflicting strains. These were identified by A. Alvarez in his introduction to the original 1968 volume as the tender-minded and the tough-minded, and it is some such crossing of a natural readiness to consent upon an instinctive suspicion which constitutes the peculiar fiber of Herbert's mind and art.

There is candor and there is concentration. His vigilance never seems to let up and we feel sure that if he is enjoying himself in print (which is memory), then the original experience was also enjoyed in similar propitious conditions. All through *Barbarian in the Garden,* the tender-minded, desiring side of his nature is limpidly, felicitously engaged. In a church in a Tuscan village where "there is hardly room enough for a coffin," he encounters a Madonna. "She wears a simple, high-waisted dress open from breast to knees. Her left hand rests on a hip, a country bridesmaid's gesture; her right hand touches her belly but without a trace of licentiousness." In a similar fashion, as he reports his ascent of the tower of Senlis Cathedral, the writing unreels like a skein long stored in the cupboard of the senses. "Patches of lichen, grass between the stones, and bright yellow flowers"; then, high up on a gallery, an "especially beautiful Eve. Coarse-grained, big-eyed and plump. A heavy plait of hair falls on her wide, warm back."

Writing of this sort which ensures, in Neruda's words, that "the reality of the world should not be underprized," is valuable in itself, but what reinforces Herbert's contribution and takes it far beyond being just another accomplished print-out of a cultivated man's impressions is his skeptical historical sense of the world's unreliability. He is thus as appreciative of the unfinished part of Siena Cathedral and as unastonished by it as he is entranced by what is exquisitely finished: "The majestic plan remained unfulfilled, interrupted by the Black Death and errors in construction." The elegance of that particular zeugma should not blind us to its outrage; the point is that Herbert is constantly wincing in the jaws of a pincer created by the mutually indifferent intersection of art and suffering. Long habituation to this crux has bred in him a tone which is neither vindictive against art nor occluded to pain. It predisposes him to quote Cicero on the colonies of Sicily as "an ornamental band sown onto the rough cloth of barbarian lands, a golden band that was frequently stained with blood." And it enables him to strike out his own jocund, unnerving sentences, like this one about the Baglioni family of Perugia: "They were vengeful and cruel, though refined enough to slaughter their enemies on beautiful summer evenings."

Once more, this comes from his essay on Piero della Francesca, and it is in writing about this beloved painter that Herbert articulates most clearly the things we would want to say about himself as an artist: "The harmonized background and the principle of tranquillity," "the rule of the demon of perspective," the viewing of the world as "through a pane of ice," an "epic impassiveness," a quality which is "impersonal, supra-individual." All these phrases apply, at one time or another, to Herbert's poetry and adumbrate a little more the shapes of his "tough-mindedness." Yet they should not be taken to suggest any culpable detachment or abstraction. The impassiveness, the perspective, the impersonality, the tranquillity, all derive from his unblindable stare at the facts of pain, the recurrence of injustice and catastrophe; but they derive also from a deep love for the whole Western tradition of religion, literature, and art, which have remained open to him as a spiritual resource, helping him to stand his ground. Herbert is as familiar as any twentieth-century writer with the hollow men and has seen more broken columns with his eyes than most literary people have seen in their imaginations, but this does not end up in a collapse of his trust in the humanist endeavor. On the contrary, it summons back to mind the whole dimensions of that endeavor and enforces it once more upon our awareness for the great boon which it is (not *was*), something we may have thought of as vestigial before we began reading these books but which, by the time we have finished, stands before our understanding once again like "a cathedral in the wilderness."

Barbarian in the Garden was first published in Polish in 1962 and is consequently the work of a much younger man (Herbert was born in 1924) than the one who wrote the poems of *Report from the Besieged City*. But the grave, laconic, instructive prose, translated with such fine regard for cadence and concision by Michael Marsh and Jaroslaw Anders, is recognizably the work of the same writer. It would be wrong to say that in the meantime Herbert has matured, since from the beginning the look he turned upon experience was penetrating, judicial, and absolutely in earnest; but it could be said that he has grown even more secure in his self-possession and now begins to resemble an old judge who has developed the benevolent aspect of a daydreamer while retaining all the readiness and spring of a crouched lion. Where the poems of the reissued *Selected Poems* carry within themselves the battened-down energy and enforced caution of the situation from which they arose in Poland in the 1950s, the poems of the latest volume allow themselves a much greater latitude of voice. They are physically longer, less impacted, more social and genial in tone. They occur within a certain spaciousness, under a vault of winnowed comprehension. One thinks again of the *lucidus ordo,* of that "golden sun of geometry"; yet because of the body heat of the new poetry, its warm breath which keeps stirring the feather of our instinctive nature, one thinks also of Herbert's eloquent valediction to the prehistoric caves of the Dordogne:

> I returned from Lascaux by the same road I arrived. Though I had stared into the 'abyss' of history, I did not emerge from an alien world. Never before had I felt a stronger or more reassuring conviction; I am a citizen of the earth, an inheritor not only of the Greeks and Romans but of almost the whole of infinity. . . .
> The road opened to the Greek temples and the Gothic cathedrals. I walked towards them feeling the warm touch of the Lascaux painter on my palm.

It is no wonder, therefore, that Mr. Cogito, the poet's alibi/alias/persona/ventriloquist's doll/permissive correlative, should be so stubbornly attached to the senses of sight and touch. In the second section of "Eschatological Forebodings of Mr. Cogito," after Herbert's several musings about his ultimate fate—"probably he will sweep/ the great square of Purgatory"—he imagines him taking courses in the eradication of earthly habits. And yet, in spite of these angelic debriefing sessions, Mr. Cogito

> continues to see
> a pine on a mountain slope
> dawn's seven candlesticks
> a blue-veined stone
>
> he will yield to all tortures
> gentle persuasions

but to the end he will defend
the magnificent sensation of pain

and a few weathered images
on the bottom of the burned-out eye

3

who knows
perhaps he will manage
to convince the angels
he is incapable
of heavenly
service

and they will permit him to return
by an overgrown path
at the shore of a white sea
to the cave of the beginning

The poles of the beginning and the end are crossing and at the very moment when he strains to imagine himself at the shimmering circumference of the imaginable, Mr. Cogito finds himself collapsing back into the palpable center. Yet all this is lightened of its possible portentousness because it is happening not to "humanity" or "mankind" but to Mr. Cogito. Mr. Cogito operates sometimes like a cartoon character, a cosmic Don Quixote or matchstick Sisyphus; sometimes like a discreet convention whereby the full frontal of the autobiographical "I" is veiled. It is in this latter role that he is responsible for one of the book's most unforgettable poems, "Mr. Cogito—The Return," which, along with "The Abandoned," "Mr. Cogito's Soul," and the title poem, strikes an unusually intimate and elegiac note.

Mostly, however, Mr. Cogito figures as a stand-in for experimental, undaunted *Homo sapiens*, or, to be more exact, as a representative of the most courageous, well-disposed, and unremittingly intelligent members of the species. The poems where he fulfills this function are no less truly pitched and sure of their step than the ones I have just mentioned; in fact, they are more brilliant as intellectual reconnaissance and more deadly as political resistance; they are on the offensive, and to read them is to put oneself through the mill of Herbert's own personal selection process, to be tested for one's comprehension of the necessity of refusal, one's ultimate gumption and awareness. This poetry is far more than "dissident"; it gives no consolation to papmongers or propagandists of whatever stripe. Its whole intent is to devastate those arrangements which are offered as truth by power's window dressers everywhere. It can hear the screech of the fighter bomber behind the righteous huffing of the official spokesman, yet it is not content with just an exposé or an indictment. Herbert always wants to probe past official versions of collective experience into the final ring of the individual's perception and endurance. He does so in order to discover whether that inner citadel of human being is a selfish bolt hole or an attentive listening post. To put it another way, he would not be all that interested in discovering the black box after the crash, since he would far prefer to be able to monitor the courage and conscience of each passenger during the minutes before it. Thus, in their introduction, John and Bogdana Carpenter quote him as follows:

> You understand I had words in abundance to express my rebellion and protest. I might have written something of this sort: 'O you cursed, damned people, so and sos, you kill innocent people, wait and a just punishment will fall on you.' I didn't say this because I wanted to bestow a broader dimension on the specific, individual, experienced situation, or rather, to show its deeper, general human perspectives.

This was always his impulse, and it is a pleasure to watch his strategies for showing "deeper, general human perspectives" develop. In the *Selected Poems,* dramatic monologues and adaptations of Greek myth were among his preferred approaches. There can be no more beautiful expression of necessity simultaneously recognized and lamented than the early "Elegy of Fortinbras," just as there can be no poem more aghast at those who have power to hurt and who then do hurt than "Apollo and Marsyas." Both works deserve to be quoted in full, but here is the latter one, in the translation of Czeslaw Milosz:

> The real duel of Apollo
> with Marsyas

(absolute ear
versus immense range)
takes place in the evening
when as we already know
the judges
have awarded victory to the god

bound tight to a tree
meticulously stripped of his skin
Marsyas
howls
before the howl reaches his tall ears
he reposes in the shadow of that howl
shaken by a shudder of disgust
Apollo is cleaning his instrument

only seemingly
is the voice of Marsyas
monotonous
and composed of a single vowel
Aaa

in reality
Marsyas relates
the inexhaustible wealth
of his body

bald mountains of liver
white ravines of aliment
rustling forests of lung
sweet hillocks of muscle
joints bile blood and shudders
the wintry wind of bone
over the salt of memory
shaken by a shudder of disgust
Apollo is cleaning his instrument

now to the chorus
is joined the backbone of Marsyas
in principle the same A
only deeper with the addition of rust

this is already beyond the endurance
of the god with nerves of artificial fibre

along a gravel path
hedged with box
the victor departs
wondering
whether out of Marsyas' howling
there will not some day arise
a new kind
of art—let us say—concrete

suddenly
at his feet
falls a petrified nightingale
he looks back
and sees
that the hair of the tree to which Marsyas was fastened
is white
completely

About suffering he was never wrong, this young master. The Polish
experience of cruelty lies behind the poem, and when it first appeared it would have had the extra jangle of anti-poetry about it.
There is the affront of the subject matter, the flirtation with horror-
movie violence, and the conscious avoidance of anything "tender-
minded." Yet the triumph of the thing is that while it remains set
upon an emotional collision course, it still manages to keep faith
with "whatever shares / The eternal reciprocity of tears." Indeed,
this is just the poetry which Yeats would have needed to convince
him of the complacency of his objection to Wilfred Owen's work
(passive suffering is not a subject for poetry), although, in fact, it is
probably only Wilfred Owen (tender-minded) and Yeats (tough-
minded) who brought into poetry in English a "vision of reality" as
adequate to our times as this one.

"Apollo and Marsyas" is a poem, not a diagram. By now, the
anti-poetry element has evaporated or been inhaled so that in spite
of that devastating A note, the poem's overall music dwells in the
sorrowing registers of cello or pibroch. The petrified nightingale,
the tree with white hair, the monotonous Aaa of the new art, each
of these inventions is as terrible as it is artful, each is uttered from

the dry well of an objective voice. The demon of perspective rules while the supra-individual principle reads history through a pane of Francescan ice, tranquilly, impassively, as if the story were chiseled into stone.

The most celebrated instance of Herbert's capacity to outface what the stone ordains occurs in his poem "Pebble." Once again, this is an *ars poetica*, but the world implied by the poem would exclude any discourse that was so fancied-up as to admit a term like *ars poetica* in the first place. Yet "Pebble" is several steps ahead of satire and even one or two steps beyond the tragic gesture. It is written by a poet who grew up, as it were, under the white-haired tree but who possessed no sense either of the oddity or the election of his birthright. Insofar as it accepts the universe with a sort of disappointed relief—as though at the last minute faith were to re-nege on its boast that it could move mountains and settle back into stoicism—it demonstrates the truth of Patrick Kavanagh's contention that tragedy is half-born comedy. The poem's force certainly resides in its impersonality, yet its tone is almost ready to play itself on through into the altogether more lenient weather of personality itself.

> The pebble
> is a perfect creature
>
> equal to itself
> mindful of its limits
>
> filled exactly
> with pebbly meaning
>
> with a scent which does not remind one of anything
> does not frighten anything away does not arouse desire
>
> its ardour and coldness
> are just and full of dignity
>
> I feel a heavy remorse
> when I hold it in my hand
> and its noble body
> is permeated by false warmth

—Pebbles cannot be tamed
to the end they will look at us
with a calm and very clear eye

This has about it all the triumph and completion of the "finished man among his enemies." You wonder where else an art that is so contained and self-verifying can possibly go—until you open *Report from the Besieged City.* There you discover that the perfect moral health of the earlier poetry was like the hard pure green of the ripening apple: now the core of the thing is less packed with tartness and the whole oeuvre seems to mellow and sway on the bough of some tree of unforbidden knowledge.

There remain, however, traces of the acerbic observer; this, for example, in the poem where Damastes (also known as Procrustes) speaks:

I invented a bed with the measurements of a perfect man
I compared the travelers I caught with this bed
it was hard to avoid—I admit—stretching limbs cutting legs
the patients died but the more there were who perished
the more I was certain my research was right
the goal was noble progress demands victims

This voice is stereophonic in that we are listening to it through two speakers, one from the setup Damastes, the other from the privileged poet, and we always know whose side we are on. We are meant to read the thing exactly as it is laid out for us. We stand with Signorelli at the side of the picture, observantly. We are still, in other words, in the late spring of impersonality. But when we come to the poem on the Emperor Claudius, we are in the summer of fullest personality. It is not that Herbert has grown lax or that any phony tolerance—understanding all and therefore forgiving all—has infected his attitude. It is more that he has eased up on his own grimness, as if realizing that the stern brows he turns upon the world merely contribute to the weight of the world's anxiety instead of lightening it; therefore, he can afford to become more genial personally without becoming one whit less impersonal in his judgments and perceptions. So, in his treatment of "The Divine Clau-

215

dius," the blood and the executions and the infernal whimsicality are not passed over, yet Herbert ends up speaking for his villain with a less than usually forked tongue:

I expanded the frontiers of the empire
by Brittany Mauretania
and if I recall correctly Thrace

my death was caused by my wife Agrippina
and an uncontrollable passion for boletus
mushrooms—the essence of the forest—
became the essence of death

descendants—remember with proper respect and honor
at least one merit of the divine Claudius
I added new signs and sounds to our alphabet
expanded the limits of speech that is the limits of freedom

the letters I discovered—beloved daughters—
Digamma and Antisigma
led my shadow
as I pursued the path with tottering steps
to the dark land of Orkus

There is more of the inward gaze of Fra Angelico here, and indeed, all through the new book, Herbert's mind is fixed constantly on last things. Classical and Christian visions of the afterlife are drawn upon time and again, and in "Mr. Cogito—Notes from the House of the Dead," we have an opportunity of hearing how the terrible cry of Marsyas sounds in the new acoustic of the later work. Mr. Cogito, who lies with his fellows "in the depths of the temple of the absurd," hears there, at ten o'clock in the evening, "a voice // masculine / slow / commanding / the rising / of the dead." The second section of the poem proceeds:

we called him Adam
meaning taken from the earth

at ten in the evening
when the lights were switched off
Adam would begin his concert

216

to the ears of the profane
it sounded
like the howl of a person in fetters

for us
an epiphany

he was
anointed
the sacrificial animal
author of psalms

he sang
the inconceivable desert
the call of the abyss
the noose on the heights

Adam's cry
was made
of two or three vowels
stretched out like ribs on the horizon

This new Adam has brought us as far as the old Marsyas took us, but
now the older Herbert takes up the burden and, in a third section,
brings the poem further still:

after a few concerts
he fell silent

the illumination of his voice
lasted a brief time

he didn't redeem
his followers

they took Adam away
or he retreated
into eternity

the source
of the rebellion
was extinguished

and perhaps
only I

still hear
the echo
of his voice

more and more slender
quieter
further and further away

like music of the spheres
the harmony of the universe

so perfect
it is inaudible.

Mr. Cogito's being depends upon such cogitations (one remembers
his defense of "the magnificent sensation of pain"), though unlike
Hamlet, in Fortinbras's elegy, who "crunched the air only to vomit,"
Mr. Cogito's digestion of the empty spaces is curiously salutary.
Reading these poems is a beneficent experience: they amplify immensely Thomas Hardy's assertion that "if a way to the Better there
be, it exacts a full look at the Worst." By the end of the book, after
such undaunted poems as "the Power of Taste"—"Yes taste / in
which there are fibers of soul the cartilage of conscience"—and such
tender ones as "Lament," to the memory of his mother—"she sails
on the bottom of a boat through foamy nebulas,"—after these and
the other poems I have mentioned, and many more which I have
not, the reader feels the kind of gratitude the gods of Troy must
have felt when they saw Aeneas creep from the lurid fires, bearing
ancestry on his shoulders and the sacred objects in his hands.

The book's true subject is survival of the valid self, of the city, of
the good and the beautiful; or rather, the subject is the responsibility
of each person to ensure that survival. So it is possible in the end to
think that a poet who writes so ethically about the *res publica* might
even be admitted by Plato as first laureate of the ideal republic;
though it is also necessary to think that through to the point where
this particular poet would be sure to decline the office as a dangerous compromise:

now as I write these words the advocates of conciliation
have won the upper hand over the party of inflexibles
a normal hesitation of moods fate still hangs in the balance

218

cemeteries grow larger the number of the defenders is smaller
yet the defense continues it will continue to the end
and if the City falls but a single man escapes
he will carry the City within himself on the roads of exile
he will be the City

we look in the face of hunger the face of fire face of death
worst of all—the face of betrayal

and only our dreams have not been humiliated

(1982)

The title poem, to which these lines form the conclusion, is pivoted
at the moment of martial law and will always belong in the annals of
patriotic Polish verse. It witnesses new developments and makes old
connections within the native story and is only one of several poems
throughout the volume which sweeps the string of Polish national
memory. If I have been less attentive to this indigenous witnessing
function of the book than I might have been, it is not because I
undervalue that function of Herbert's poetry. On the contrary, it is
precisely because I am convinced of its obdurate worth on the home
front that I feel free to elaborate in the luxurious margin. Anyhow,
John and Bogdana Carpenter have annotated the relevant dates and
names so that the reader is kept alert to the allusions and connections which provide the book's oblique discharge of political energy.
As well as providing this editorial service, they seem to have managed the task of translating well; I had no sense of their coming
between me and the poem's first life, no sense of their having
interfered.

Zbigniew Herbert is a poet with all the strengths of an Antaeus,
yet he finally emerges more like the figure of an Atlas. Refreshed
time and again by being thrown back upon his native earth, standing his ground determinedly in the local plight, he nevertheless
shoulders the whole sky and scope of human dignity and responsibility. These various translations provide a clear view of the power
and beauty of the profile which he has established, and leave no
doubt about the essential function which his work performs, that of
keeping a trustworthy poetic canopy, if not a perfect heaven, above
our vulnerable heads.

1988

A SNAPPING TURTLE IN JUNE

by FRANKLIN BURROUGHS

from THE GEORGIA REVIEW

ALL THAT CAN usefully be said about New England weather has been said. It is arbitrary, precipitate, and emphatic, less certain than a baby's bottom. Like the mind, it isn't necessarily bound by chronology. April can suddenly hearken back to February; a few hours in January will be as balmy as a May afternoon—that is, as one of those rare May afternoons that aren't recollecting March or day-dreaming about September. Here on an overcast Tuesday morning late in June, it is summer sure enough, yet we must depend more upon the floral calendar than the thermometer for corroboration. We've had one spell of hot weather—temperature into the 90's, high humidity, bread going moldy in a day, crackers limp as old lettuce— but that was two weeks ago, and it has been cool since then, either rainy and chill or bright and breezy and autumnal.

But the flowers keep their seasons. Our fields, especially the poorer one that lies between the house and the river, are rich in buttercup and vetch, lesser stitchwort, fragrant bedstraw, and blue-eyed grass. From the standpoint of agriculture, these plants are weeds, and therefore absolutely reliable. Cold, wet, and drought do not deter them; the only way to thwart them is by herbicide or fertilizer. The buttercups are long-stemmed and grow in all but the lushest pastures. Vetch (called partridge-pea in South Carolina) grows in little tangles of vine, like untrellised morning glories, as do stitchwort and bedstraw, and so they fare best in a thin, ledgy, or sandy soil, where the grass is meager. On a moist, unsummery summer morning, these flowers make soft clots and smears of color throughout the watery green of the pasture grasses. Thriving amid the adversities of soil and climate, their inconspicuous beauty seems reflective of rural New England, and it is pleasing to learn that people here once found more than aesthetic solace in them. Stitchwort was so named because it was thought to cure "stitches"—pains in the side, of the sort that runners get—while bedstraw was used to lie upon, back when a bed was a board, covered with straw, covered with a sheet. Fragrant bedstraw is quite odorless in life, but reputedly grows savory in death, when sufficiently dried.

Except for the vetch, we had nothing in South Carolina like these field flowers or the daisies and hawkweed that populate the road shoulders at this season of the year, and there is not a great deal in the Maine summer that particularly recalls the summers of my Southern boyhood. But that strange Wordsworthian hunger for landscape, growing out of an individual and cultural maturity, is complexly regressive and involves much attempted calling back of things that probably exist only in the echo of the caller's voice. Fewer and fewer of us have Wordsworth's privilege of inhabiting as adults the landscape we inhabited as children—and of learning to recognize in it what he called "the language of my former heart." Even if luck and resolution enable us eventually to live in places of great beauty and interest, there is some quality of internal exile that shadows our relation to them.

This is a particular problem if you are a non-New Englander who comes to live in New England. New England is an image ready-made for you, no matter where you come from. It has so defined the American conception of landscape, and of the ideal human response to landscape, that it is not easy to arrive at a direct relation to it. It's rather like being married to a celebrity—your own response responds to a simplified and magnified public perception, as well as to the thing itself. Or, as a friend of mine, a tough-minded New Yorker, observed to me one November day, while we sat in a skiff in Broad Cove, looking across blue water that glinted and sparkled as though it were already full of ice shards, through crystal air and toward the shore with its patchwork of fields, woodlots, and bleak, bone-white houses gleaming in the sun: "Who are they trying to kid? This is the most *derivative* goddamned landscape I've ever seen in my life."

221

Boyhood was once almost as distinct a part of the American terrain as New England is, and, like New England, it had its heyday in the nineteenth century, and continued to be valued because, until fairly recently, it went on evoking the life of that century. There is the image of a sandy or a dusty road, the feel of the road under the feet, the cane pole carried over the shoulder, the drone of cicadas, the hair warm from the sun: the barefoot boy with cheeks of tan, the etchings and engravings of Winslow Homer, and supremely and inevitably, *Tom Sawyer* and *Huckleberry Finn*. In contrast, *girlhood* does not seem to generate this mirage. It doesn't evoke the same semitribal life, the living in a world rather closer to the wordless world of smells, itches, and yapping contentions of the unregulated dogs of small-town America than to the world of adults, or even to the world of the sort of regimented, housebroken, neurotic, pedigreed canines that one finds in the houses of one's friends.

There is of course much compensatory distortion in this image of boyhood, but I do not think it is altogether false. The boredom was as thick as the heat in Conway, South Carolina, and one learned to relish both in the summers. In our neighborhood, which is now an attractive suburban network of streets overhung with water oaks and sycamores, the streets were not yet paved—there was still a lot of unpaved road in the South at that time—and that gave, in a small way, texture and variety to life. In rainy seasons, the roads were slick and the puddles would turn to bogs, rutted out and mucky; occasionally a car, ineptly driven by one of the ladies of the neighborhood, would get stuck. But by summer the sun would have baked the roads hard beneath the dust that powdered them, and boys wore shoes only under compulsion. That is not possible where the streets are asphalt, and the tar sticks to your feet like napalm. I think girls wore shoes more regularly, in the fashion of their sisters in cities, but many of my impressions of girlhood must have been taken from my own sister, who was four years older and that much more aware of the world beyond the doorstep. In any event, I tended to associate femininity with paved streets, and knew for a fact that it was the ladies of the neighborhood, my own mother not excepted, who were most insistent that the roads be paved, so that they would not get stuck in the rainy weather, or have their children tracking mud into the house or getting their feet full of ringworm. From listening to them, you would have thought that they were the Victorian wives of British colonials, suddenly finding themselves in the Burmese or Australian outback, amid conditions of an appalling primitiveness.

At that time, the paved road stopped at the railroad tracks, about a quarter mile from our house. Then one day my great friend Ricky McIver and I walked down to the railroad tracks, preparing to follow them (which we were forbidden to do) along the causeway that ran through the swamps and eventually reached the trestle over Kingston Lake. But there, where the pavement ended, was a roadblock and a detour sign, apologizing for the inconvenience and announcing that this section of the road was to be surfaced. It was the beginning of a lifetime of symbolic Luddite resistance. We pushed over the roadblock, which was no more than a sawhorse, and threw the sign into the ditch beside the road. To no avail, needless to say: the road got paved anyway. History does not leave the backwaters of boyhood alone, and Ricky would soon enough find himself personifying it to barefoot villagers, who liked it no better than he had, in dusty hamlets full of yapping dogs outside Da Nang.

We were not, of course, thinking of pavement in terms of abstractions like History or Progress. It might have crossed our minds that its coming would mean that we had to wear shoes—or that more dogs would be run over, because cars would travel so much faster on the asphalt, and the dogs, like the children, thought of the streets as places of concourse and recreation. But probably nothing even that theoretical occurred to us. I think it was that we were mostly considering the snapping turtles that would, some time in the middle of every summer, appear in the road—sturdy little fellows, their shells not much bigger than a silver dollar. Paving the road would be the end of them.

All these things came to mind on this Tuesday morning in Maine, with the fields full of flowers and late June imitating early May, because, as I started out down the gravel road that connects our house to the highway, and drew abreast of the little quarter-acre pond that sits to the left of the road, here was, large as life and squarely in my way, a big mama snapping turtle, excavating herself a hole to lay her eggs in. I was in no particular hurry, and so I stopped and got out to investigate. Snappers are the most widely distributed of North American turtles, and they are by no means uncommon in Maine, but they are normally reclusive, and when one makes a public appearance it is not an event to be passed over lightly. This particular one certainly had no intention of being passed over lightly: if she had intended to blockade the road, she couldn't have chosen a better spot.

Several things distinguish them from other freshwater turtles, most obviously their size. The one at my feet was about two feet long, from the tip of her snout to the tip of her tail. When I eventually picked her up by the tail (and that is another distinguishing feature of snapping turtles—you pick up an ordinary turtle by the rim of its shell, but a snapper's neck is remarkably long and flexible, so you grab the creature by the tail and hold it well out from your body), I guessed she weighed a good twenty pounds.

The general proportions of a snapping turtle are wrong. The head is far too big; the shell is too little. The plastron, or undershell, is ridiculously skimpy—it seems barely adequate for the purposes of decency, and as useless as a bikini would be as far as anatomical protection is concerned. Consequently a snapper cannot withdraw into itself as other turtles do. It retracts the head enough to shield its neck and doesn't even attempt to pull in its legs and feet. The legs and tail are large in relation to the body: when a snapper decides to walk it really *walks;* the bottom of the shell is a couple of inches off the ground, and, with its dorsally tuberculate tail, long claws, and wickedly hooked beak, it looks like a scaled-down stegosaur.

A snapper compensates for its inadequate armor in a variety of ways, the most immediately apparent of which is athletic ability combined with a very bad temper. It can whirl and lunge ferociously, and, if turned over on its back, can, with a thrust and twist of its mighty neck, be upright and ready for mayhem. If you approach one out of water, it opens its mouth and hisses; if you get closer, it lurches at you with such vehemence that it lifts itself off the ground, its jaws snapping savagely at empty air. Archie Carr, whose venerable *Handbook to Turtles* (1952) is the only authority on these matters I possess, states that the disposition to strike is innate, and has been observed in hatchlings "not yet altogether free of their eggshells." An adult can strike, he reports, "with the speed and power of a big rattlesnake." Although Carr does not explicitly say so, the snapper appears to be one of those animals, like the hognose snake, that makes the most of its resemblance to a poisonous snake. Its pale mouth gapes open like a moccasin's, and its aggressiveness involves a certain exaggerated and theatrical posturing. Its official name

224

specifically and subspecifically suggests the highly unturtlelike impression that this creates: *Chelydra serpentina serpentina.* But the snapper, unlike the hognose, can back up its bluff. Its first-strike capability isn't lethal, but it isn't trivial either. According to boyhood folklore, a snapper can bite a broomstick in two, but I have seen the experiment conducted. It took a great deal of goading to persuade the turtle to seize the broomstick at all—it plainly would have preferred the hand that held it—but it finally took it, held it, and crushed and pulped it. Mama's broom handle came out looking like a piece of chewed-over sugarcane. Putting your hand in range of a big snapper would not be like putting it under a guillotine or axe; it would be more like putting it under a bulldozer: a slow, complete crunching.

The shell and skin are a muddy gray; the eye, too, is of a murky mud color. The pupil is black and shaped like a star or a spoked wheel. Within the eye there is a strange yellowish glint, as though you were looking down into turbid water and seeing, in the depths of the water, light from a smoldering fire. It is one of Nature's more nightmarish eyes. The eyes of dragonflies are also nightmarish, but in a different way—they look inhuman, like something out of science fiction. The same is true of the eyes of sharks. The snapper's eye is dull, like a pig's, but inside it there is this savage malevolence, something suggesting not only an evil intention toward the world, but the torment of an inner affliction. Had Milton seen one, he would have associated it with the baleful eye of Satan, an eye reflecting some internal hell of liquid fire—whether in Paradise or here on a soft June day, with the bobolinks fluttering aloft and singing in the fields. Snapping turtles did in fact once inhabit Europe, but they died out by the end of the Pleistocene, and so were unknown to what we think of as European history. But they look, nevertheless, like something that Europeans had half-imagined or dimly remembered even before they came to the New World and saw them for the first time: a snapper would do for a gargoyle, or a grotesque parody of a knight on his horse, a thing of armored evil.

Snappers feed on about anything, dead or alive: fish, flesh, or fowl. The fish they catch by luring them into range with their vermiform tongues, which may have something to do with the role of trickster that they assume in the mythology of North American Indians. But they can also be caught in a trap baited with bananas. They are not fastidious: "Schmidt and Inger (1957) tell the gruesome story of an elderly man who used a tethered snapping turtle to recover the bodies of people who had drowned."* We do not learn what this sinister gentleman fed his useful pet to encourage its predilection for waterlogged cadavers. I know on my own authority that snappers are death on ducks, and will rise like a shadow from the oozy muck of the bottom, under the jocund and unsuspecting drake as it briskly preens and putters on the surface of the pond, lock sudden jaws around one suspended leg, one webbed foot, and sink quietly back to the depths, their weight too much for the duck to resist, their jaws a functional illustration of necessity's sharp pinch. There in the darkness the duck is ponderously mauled, mutilated, and eaten, right down to the toenails. We watched a hen mallard and a brood of ducklings disappear from the little pond beside the road one summer—two or three inexplicable deductions per week—until at last only the very nervous hen and one trusting little duckling remained. Then there was only the duckling. It peeped and chirped and swam distractedly around the pond in a most heart-rending fashion. I tried to trap it so we could rear it in confinement and safety, but there was no catching it, and the next day it was gone too.

The law of tooth and nail is all right with me when it involves hawks and mice, or foxes and geese, or even sharks and swimmers—there is a redeeming elegance in most predators, a breathtaking speed and agility. If I thought I could tempt an eagle to stoop, I'd gladly stake my best laying hen in the yard to see it happen. But a snapper is an ugly proposition, more like cancer than a crab is. If one grabs your finger, you do not get the finger back— that too is boyhood folklore, but I have never tested it. Some propositions call for implicit faith, even in these post-theological and deconstructing days.

Unlike most of the other freshwater turtles, snappers never emerge to bask on rocks or logs. They come out in late spring or early summer; their emergence here coincides with the vetch, the stitchwort, bedstraw, and hawkweed. They need sandy soil to lay their eggs in, and such soil isn't always close to the sorts of boggy, miry waters they inhabit. They will often go overland a surprising distance before finally deciding on a spot to dig. Roadbeds and railway embankments can provide good sites that are reasonably

*Turtles: Perspectives and Research, ed. M. Harless and H. Morlock (New York: John Wiley and Sons, 1979), p. 289.

226

convenient to their usual habitats. Creatures of darkness, cursing the light, they lumber up from pond or river, and one morning you awake to the frantic yapping of dogs and go out, and there, foul and hissing, like some chieftain of the underworld at last summoned to justice and surrounded by reporters and cameras, stands a great gravid snapper. The flesh of her neck, legs, and tail—all the parts that ought to fit inside the shell but don't—has, on the underside, a grimy yellowish cast to it, is podgy, lewd, wrinkled, and soft. In Maine there will normally be one or two big leeches hanging onto the nether parts. These portions of the animal seem to have no proper covering—no scales, feathers, hair, or taut, smooth epidermis. It looks as though the internal anatomy had been extruded, or the whole animal plucked or flayed.

I'm not sure how much of this natural history Ricky McIver and I understood when we were nine or ten; we only knew that, trekking down a sandy road in midsummer, we would suddenly come upon a baby snapper, bustling along with remarkable purpose, as though on its way to catch a train. Of course we would catch the turtle, and one of us would take it home and put it in a dishpan with a little water and keep it under the bed, where all night long there would be the tinny scraping of little claws, as the turtle went round and round inside the pan. Sometimes one would escape, instigating a general panicky search of the room and the house. It would turn up far back under a sofa or cabinet, covered with dust and weakened by dehydration, but still able to muster a parched snap and hiss. Finally we would let it go into a drainage ditch. We never came upon a mother laying her eggs—given the heat, perhaps they did that at night down south. Up here I seem to come across one or two of them every year, and have learned to look for them along road shoulders in late June.

I backed the car up to the house to get Susan and Hannah—the older girls were still asleep—and our old pointer Jacob roused himself and walked down with us, conferring by his stiff-jointed, wheezing Nestorian solemnity an air of officialdom upon the occasion, as though we were a commission sent out to investigate an unregistered alien that had showed up in Bowdoinham. Hannah went along grudgingly, with a five-year-old's saving sense that any time the parents promised to show you something interesting, they probably had concealed motives of one sort or another. When we got to the turtle, Jacob hoisted his hackles, clapped his tail between his legs, and circled her a few times, then sat down and barked once. The turtle raised herself on her forelegs, head up, mouth agape; her hostility did not focus on any one of us so much as on the whole situation in which she found herself. Hannah looked at all of this and pronounced it boring; could she have a friend over to play? The dog seemed to feel that he had discharged his obligations by barking, and shambled over to the edge of the field, pawed fretfully at the ground, then settled himself, curled up, sighed, and went to sleep. The whole thing was beginning to take on the unpromising aspect of Nature Study, an ersatz experience.

We walked around behind the turtle, and there did make a discovery of sorts. Through all of the commotion that surrounded her anterior end, her hind legs were methodically digging. Their motion was impressively regular and mechanical—first one leg thrust down into the hole, then the other, smooth and steady as pistons. Whatever the snapper felt or thought about her situation plainly did not concern the legs, which were wholly intent on procreation. It seemed an awkward way to dig, the hind foot being a clumsy and inflexible instrument anyway, and having to carry on its operations huggermugger like that, out of sight and out of mind too, if the turtle could be said to have a mind. We could not see down into the hole, only the legs alternately reaching down, and a rim of excavated sand that was slowly growing up behind the rim of the turtle's shell. I was later to learn that the digging action, once begun, is as involuntary as the contractions of a mammal giving birth, and even a turtle missing one hind leg will dig in the same fashion, thrusting down first with the good leg, then with the amputated stump, until the job is done.

Hannah, an aficionado of the sandbox, permitted herself a cautious interest in this end of the turtle's operations, and wanted to inspect her hole. I wasn't sure about the ethics of this. It is a general law that you don't disturb nesting creatures; it was, after all, no fault of the snapper's if she failed to excite in us the veneration that generally attaches to scenes of maternity and nativity. On the other hand, she had chosen a bad place. I could see where my neighbor Gene Hamrick had carefully driven around her, going well over onto the shoulder to do so. Other neighbors might be less considerate, and the nest itself would, in any event, be packed hard by the traffic in a few weeks, rendering the future of the eggs and hatchlings highly uncertain. So I grasped her tail and hoisted her up. Aloft, she held herself rigidly spread-eagle, her head and neck parallel to the earth, and hissed mightily as I took her over and put her in the little ditch that drains the pond. Because of the recent rain, the ditch was flowing, and as soon as her front feet touched the water, all of her aggression ceased, and she seemed bent on nothing but escape. She had surprising power as she scrabbled at the banks and bottom of the ditch; it was like holding onto a miniature bulldozer. I let her go and she surged off down the ditch, head submerged and carapace just awash. She stopped once and raised her head and fixed us with her evil eye; the mouth dropped open in a last defiance. Then she lowered her head again and waddled out of sight.

We examined the hole. It looked as though it had been dug with a tablespoon—shapely and neat, a little wider at the bottom than at the top. There were no eggs. Hannah set methodically about refilling the hole, out of an instinct that seemed as compelling as the one that dug it. As she disturbed the sand, I caught a strong musky scent where the turtle had lain. That scent, which was also on my hand, recalled something that the sight of the turtle had not recalled, and that was a peculiar memory connected to the biggest snapping turtle I ever saw, or ever intend to see.

In my high-school summers, I worked for the Burroughs Timber Company, which was owned by a group of my father's first cousins. My immediate boss was Mr. Henry Richards; the crew consisted of the two of us and two cousins, Billy and Wendell Watson. Mr. Richards was not an educated man, and had in his younger days been something of a drinker and a fighter, but he had straightened himself out and gotten some training in forestry. He was good at his job, as far as I could judge—his job largely consisting of cruising and marking timber, overseeing logging operations, and generally keeping track of the company's woodlands. These were mostly small tracts, seldom more than a few hundred acres, scattered from one end of Horry County to the other. Mr. Richards was handsome: lean and weathered, with dark wavy hair, sleepy eyes, and the sort of indolent rasping voice that conveyed the authority of someone who had not always been perfectly nice. He was in his forties. Billy and Wendell were younger by ten or fifteen years, and both were countrymen, from the vicinity of Crabtree Creek.

I am not sure what degree of cousinage joined Billy and Wendell. The Watsons, like the Burroughses and a great many other families in the county, were an extended and numerous clan, and such clans generally divided into what religion had taught us to regard as the children of promise and the children of perdition, or sheep and goats. The binary opposition would express itself in terms of whatever general station in life the family occupied. Thus my Burroughs cousins tended to be either sober, quietly respectable merchants and landowners concerned with tobacco and timber—or drunkards, wastrels, and womanizers, men notorious in Horry County for the frequency with which they married and divorced.

Wendell belonged to the reputable branch of the Watson family— small farmers who held onto their land and led hard, frugal lives. In town, such people were referred to, somewhat inscrutably, as the salt of the earth. Billy came from the other side—poachers, moonshiners, people likely to be handy with a straight razor, who kept six or eight gaunt and vicious hounds (half of them stolen and all of them wormy) chained in the yard, along with a few unfettered chickens and a ragged mule, but who could hardly be called farmers. Their style of life and economy had probably been formed by the county's long history as a demifrontier, and had changed only minimally to accommodate the twentieth century when it eventually arrived.

Wendell was one of those rare county people who, out of some reaction to the dirt and despair of agriculture, had a highly developed fastidiousness. His face was bony, angular, and prim around the mouth; he always wore a dapper straw hat instead of the usual cap, so that his brow was never browned or reddened by the sun. His work shirt and pants were neatly creased, and I never saw them stained with sweat. He would stop for a moment in the resinous, stifling heat of a pine wood, extract a red bandanna handkerchief from his pocket, unfold it, and delicately dab at his brow, removing his hat to do so. Then he would look at the moist handkerchief the way you might look at a small cut or blister, with a slight consternation and distaste, and then fold the handkerchief, first into halves, then into quarters, then into eighths, until it fit back into his hip pocket as neatly as a billfold.

He was lanky, with comically large feet and big, bony, lightly freckled hands and wrists, and you would have expected him to have no strength or stamina at all. But he could use any of the tools we used—bushaxe or machete or grubbing hoe—with no sign of strain or fatigue, all day long, holding the tool gingerly, so that you expected him to drop it at any moment, but keeping a pace that the rest of us could not sustain. He had a crooked, embarrassed grin and said little. In the midday heat, sometimes we would take our lunch to an abandoned tenant house, to eat on the porch and catch whatever breeze funneled through the doorway. Then three of us would stretch out on the warped floorboards, hats over our faces, and doze for half an hour. Wendell never did. He would sit with his back to one of the rough timbers that held up the porch, pull out his pocket knife, and set about pruning his fingernails; then he would stick the knife into a floorboard with an air of finality, lift his head and stare out over the fields with the intense, noncommittal scrutiny of a poker player examining his cards, or of what he was, a countryman watching the big banks of cumulus clouds pile up on a July afternoon. Or he might whittle himself a toothpick and ply it carefully between his teeth, or study a map of the tract we were to cruise in the afternoon. He always kept a watch over himself, as though he feared he might otherwise grow slack and slovenly. He did not own a car, and was permitted to use the company truck to go to and from his house, and to keep it over the weekend. On Monday mornings it would be all washed and cleaned; Mr. Richards would ask him whether he'd been courting in it or was he just planning to sell it. Wendell would only laugh awkwardly at himself, and at his inability to think of a smart retort.

Billy Watson, to hear him tell it, was chiefly proud of having spent six years in the fourth grade, at the end of which time he was sixteen and not legally obligated to go to school anymore. Mr. Richards could not get over it. "Damn, Billy," he said more than once, "don't seem like you're *that* stupid." He'd say it because he relished Billy's invariable answer, always delivered in the same tone of pious resignation, as though he were speaking of some cross that the Lord had, in His ungovernable wisdom, given him to bear: "Oh, I wa'n't stupid. Just ornery." He was a big man, about six foot three, with powerful, rounded shoulders. He had a peculiar sort of physical complacence with himself, was loose and supple as a cat, and could squat or hunker longer and more comfortably, it seemed, than the average man could sit in an armchair. His hair was lank and reddish brown, and was usually seconded by a four- or five-day growth of stubble beard, stained with tobacco juice at the lower right corner of the mouth. It was a big, misshapen mouth, distended by the pouch in one cheek that is the outcome of a lifetime of chewing tobacco—Day's Work or Sun Apple. His teeth were few and far between, worn and yellowed as an old mule's. He had certainly never been to a dentist in his life, and might have been surprised to learn that such a profession existed.

Billy was a river rat; if he could have, he would have lived by doing nothing but trapping and fishing. He sometimes fished for sport: he could handle his stubby casting rod as though he had a kind of intelligence in his hands, placing each cast, cast after cast, far back under overhanging trees, with no pause, no hesitation, no calculation of the risks of getting the plug hung on a branch or snag. There was so much rhythm in it that you'd find yourself patting your foot if you watched him long enough. But he wasn't particular about how he caught fish or what fish he caught: redbreast, bream, goggle-eye, stumpknocker, warmouth, bass, catfish, eel, mudfish, redfin pike, shad, Virginia perch—even the herring that ran upriver in the spring.

If early on a Saturday morning in the spring you happened to be down by Mishoe's Fish Market, a little frame building perched by the edge of Kingston Lake, you might see Billy slipping easily along the near bank of the lake, in a ridiculously undersized one-man paddling boat. He'd give you a look before he drew up to the landing, ask you if there was anybody there. You'd look around for only one thing, a yellow car with a long antenna, because that might be someone from the state fish and game department, which kept an eye on Mr. Mishoe. Not seeing it, you'd say no, nobody here but old man Mishoe. There was a strange, watery peace to it. All the drab, ordinary life of the town was just a few hundred feet away, but here was Billy gliding silently up to the landing, dropping the paddle with muffled reverberation into the boat bottom, then stepping out, shackling the little boat to a cypress, and bending over to lift from it two moist croker sacks, each squirming with his night's work. You'd want to follow him through the fish market to the back, where Mr. Mishoe and one or two helpers would be cleaning and filleting fish. They'd stop to watch Billy empty his sacks into a cleaning sink—the secret, active ingredients of river and river swamp, wriggling, flapping, and gasping there in the back room of a store. The catfish, mudfish, eels, and shad were classified as nongame species and could, within certain limits, be fished and marketed commercially. The rest were pure contraband, which presumably increased their market value. Whatever their cash value was, Billy would receive it in a few greasy bills, walk up to the drugstore on Main Street, and buy himself a cup of coffee and a

232

doughnut. Townspeople who did not know him would edge away from the counter: he was a dirty, rough-looking man, unlaced boots flapping open at his ankles. His eyes, which were small and deep-set, reflected light strangely; they were green, and, in the strict sense of the word, *crazed,* as though the surface of the eye were webbed with minute cracks. You could not tell where they focused.

But Billy wasn't crazy or violent either, as far as I ever heard. Education is liberating in ways it does not always intend, and, by keeping Billy in the fourth grade, surrounded, year after year, by an unaging cohort of ten-year-olds, it liberated him from most notions of responsibility, foresight, or ambition. He had successfully learned how to avoid promotion, a lesson that ought to be learned and taught more often than it is. He had worked out at the plywood mill, upriver from Conway, and told me he had also done some house painting. But working for Mr. Richards and Burroughs Timber suited him best, and he was a valuable employee. He probably knew more about the company land than the company did, having hunted, fished, or trapped on most of it. When we would cruise timber, one of us would set the compass course for him, and then he could follow it, keeping careful count of his paces, marking each of the stations where we would stop and inventory all the timber in a quarter-acre plot, while Billy went ahead to the next station and marked the next plot. Often we would end the day on the back line of a tract, a long way from the truck. The logical thing in thick woods was to plot a course back to the truck and follow the compass out, but Billy would drop the compass into his pocket and strike off through the woods as nonchalantly as a man going across a parking lot. We'd follow. He did everything in such a headlong, unconsidering way that those of us who had gotten beyond the fourth grade could never bring ourselves to trust him entirely, and sooner or later somebody would call out: "Billy, you *sure* this is the right way?" "Time'll tell, boys; time'll tell," he'd call back. Time always did, and we would suddenly emerge from the woods, and there would be the road, and there would be the truck. Townspeople who knew Billy lost no occasion to point him out to you: "That's Billy Watson. Ain't got a lick of sense, but you won't find a better fisherman in this county."

We were working down toward the Pee Dee River, on a low, sandy ridge at the edge of the river swamp. The company had cleared the ridge two or three years earlier and planted it in pine seedlings, but now the hardwoods, regenerating from the stump, threatened to reclaim it for themselves. The smaller hardwoods we chopped down with machete or bushaxe; the larger ones we girdled—gouged a ring around the trunk, half an inch deep, which cut off the tree's supply of food and water, and left it to die on its feet. For this we had a machine called the Little Beaver. It consisted of a four-cycle Briggs and Stratton engine mounted on a packframe, with a flexible hydraulic hose, at the end of which was a notched disk that did the girdling. The machine seemed to have no muffler at all—it was louder than a chainsaw, hot on the back, and the noise and vibration of it were stunning. It was late July, and that sandy patch of scrub oak and seedling pine afforded no protection from the sun. We would trade off the Little Beaver at thirty-minute intervals; not even Wendell volunteered to take any more of its hammering than that.

At noon, as was the custom, we knocked off. Mr. Richards drove out to the Georgetown highway. He knew of a country store across the river, over in Georgetown County, and proposed to take us there for lunch. It was owned by a man named Marlowe. I'd seen it often enough, the usual little mean, flat-topped cinder-block building, painted white, with a screened door for ventilation, within which you could expect to find the standard items: canned goods, bread, a bit of fishing tackle, and one or two coolers full of soft drinks and milk. As we drove, Mr. Richards talked about the Marlowes, and we learned that they were an infamous clan, divided into two subspecific groups which intermingled freely: the regular Marlowes and the murdering Marlowes. If you insulted a regular Marlowe—for example, by catching him stealing your boat—he would, within a week or ten days, set your woodlot on fire, slash your tires, or shoot your dog. But if you did the same thing to a murdering Marlowe, why then your troubles were over—instantly and permanently. That is what Mr. Richards said, but he was something of a talker and not above hyperbole. We didn't take it seriously and probably weren't meant to. Wendell didn't say much—he never did—but he had a tight little grin and plainly didn't believe what he was hearing. Billy was keeping his eye on the swamp and river as we crossed over them—the Pee Dee was outside his usual territory, and he'd been talking all morning about how he aimed to fish her this fall, from Gallivant's Ferry clear down to Yauhannah Bridge, where we were now. When we pulled off the highway and parked in the thin shade of an oak beside Marlowe's store, Mr. Richards said for us to remember to act polite; we didn't need any trouble with these folks, and neither did Burroughs Timber.

When you walk out of the dazzle of noon into a little roadside store like that, it is almost like walking into a movie theater, the darkness seems so great. By the door was a counter with a cash register on it and a man behind it, and there was a shadowy figure in the back of the store, who turned out to be a boy younger than myself, sweeping the single aisle between the shelves. And there was a figure seated to the left of the door as I came in, and on the floor, at my feet, there was a sudden lunging rush.

If you have gotten this far, you have the advantage of knowing that it was, of course, a snapping turtle, but I did not. In the South Carolina woods in the summertime, snakes are never far out of your mind, and, for the first hour of the day, you watch your step. Fatigue and distraction set in soon enough, and you forget about snakes, and you could easily go two weeks without having any particular reason to remember them. But sooner or later you would come upon one, usually a little copperhead, neatly coiled at your feet, and so perfectly merged with the shadow-dappled floor of the forest that you'd begin to worry about all the ones that you hadn't happened to see. So when I heard the hiss and the rush I jumped.

The man in the chair laughed: "Scared you, didden he? I be goddam if you didden *jump*, boy. Don't believe I ever knew a white boy to jump like that." By this time I could see what it was, a snapping turtle stretched out there on the cement floor. It was a huge one—the carapace was matted with dried algae; the head was about the size of a grapefruit. The whole creature could not have been fitted into a washtub. It looked, once I had calmed down enough to look at it, ancient and tired, as though oppressed by its own ponderous and ungainly bulk. The room was thick with a swampy, musky smell, which at the time I did not realize came from the turtle. When I smelled it again in Maine, it did not specifically recall the physical scene—the turtle, the Marlowes, the dark little store. Instead, it brought back directly a sensation of alarm, confusion, and disorientation, in about the same way that the smell of ether does not bring back the operating room so much as it brings back the vertiginous feeling of the self whirling away from itself.

235

The others came in right behind me. I was too mortified by my own embarrassment and disgrace to see how they reacted to the whole scene, but I think they must have enjoyed it. It had been a good joke, to place the turtle just inside the threshold like that; if it had been played on anyone else, I would have laughed myself. Billy looked down at the turtle and said he'd never seen one that big. In the corner of the evil mouth, which was gaping open, was a big hook, with a piece of heavy line attached to it. "Caught him on a trotline, I see," said Billy.

Trotlines—a short length of line tied to a branch that overhangs the water, so that the baited hook is just below the surface—were and are a common way of fishing, and they were perfectly legal for catching certain species of fish at certain times of year. But they were so widely used by poachers that to call a man a *trotliner* might, if the man were sufficiently thin-skinned, seem tantamount to an indictment. I don't know. I only know that when Billy said "trotline" the man in the chair gave him a sudden look and got up.

When he stood, he lurched and swayed, and we could see that he was ruinously drunk. He was wiry, short, and grizzled, wore knee-high rubber boots with the swamp mud still on them. He glared at Billy: "Your name ain't *McNair*, is it?" Billy said it wasn't and tried to ask the man if anything besides turtles had been biting that morning, but the man kept on: "You sure it ain't *McNair?* You sure you ain't some of them wildlife boys come down here? What you got that aerial on your truck for if you ain't?" He was right about at least that much. The company truck did have a two-way radio, and it was painted yellow, which gave it an official look, but it seemed not simply ridiculous but perverse for the man to take the four of us— hot, dirty, and dressed in ordinary work clothes—for some kind of undercover squad from the Department of Fish and Wildlife.

The man behind the counter told him to shut up and sit down, but he spoke in a half-hearted way, as though he knew it were useless. The boy in the back of the store, where I'd gone to get some crackers, had stopped sweeping and gone up to the front to watch the fun. The drunk man was telling Billy exactly what he'd do to McNair if McNair ever stuck his nose in here; he got louder and louder, and seemed to be working himself into the conviction that Billy really was McNair. I got my crackers and came up to the counter. It did not occur to me that anything serious was going on, and even if it was, there was no reason to worry. The drunk man's head scarcely came to Billy's shoulder. It seemed that all of this might in some way still be part of the joke; if not, it would make a good joke to tell, how Billy Watson, of all people, had been mistaken for a game warden.

I was paying for my crackers when the man said: "Let McNair come in here and I'll show him *this*," and I looked up and he had a pistol in his hand. It came from under the counter, as I later learned—the drunk man had reached over and grabbed it when the man behind the counter had turned to the cash register.

It changed everything; the world began to slip away. I had no impulse to act, and did not exactly feel fear. It was more an instinct to call out to everybody, to say *wait a minute; how did we get here? what's going on? let's talk this over and see if we can't make sense of it*. Billy's back was to me. The pistol was a snub-nosed revolver—a heavy, ugly, blunt thing. It was as though I could see through Billy's eyes the rounded noses of the cartridges in the open ends of the cylinders. Everything was utterly distinct and utterly unreal: we were under water, or had fallen asleep and were dreaming and were struggling mightily to waken ourselves from the dream before it reached the point it was meant to reach. Nobody moved to interfere. The thing was going to take its course.

The drunk man had the pistol right in Billy's face, shaking it. His own face was white with rage. "I'd show him *this*," he said, "and *this* is what I'd do with it." He reached down so abruptly and savagely that I winced, and he snatched the turtle by the tail and dragged it out the door, onto the concrete pad beside the gas pumps. The weight of the turtle was great; the man straightened himself slowly, as though only his wrath had enabled him to haul it this far. The turtle seemed weary, deflated, too long out of water. The man nudged its head with his boot, and the turtle hissed and struck feebly toward him. The man glared down at it, letting his rage recover and build back in him. He looked like a diver, gathering to plunge. The turtle's mouth hung open; when it hissed again the man's arm suddenly jerked down with the pistol and he shot it, shattering the turtle's head. "That's what I'd do to that goddamned McNair."

The man came back in and sat down heavily, spent, and the world returned to its ordinary focus. Blood had spattered onto the man's boot and pant leg. By the time we finished buying lunch and were ready to leave, he was snoring easily. The man behind the cash register told the boy to tote that thing off into the bushes, and the boy did, dragging the turtle by the tail, the blood still welling from the smashed head. When we got back to the truck I glanced over there, not wanting to, and could see the head swarming with flies, the big feet limp in the sand.

As we were getting into the truck, Wendell (who seldom said anything) said, "Well." We looked at him. He elaborated, his face perfectly deadpan: "Well. Good thing none of them *bad* Marlowes happened to be in today."

Hannah finished filling the hole, tamped the sand smooth, and brushed her palms briskly against each other, signifying that the job was done. The dog roused himself and we all walked back up toward the house. A yellow warbler flew across in front of us—a quick flash of color—perched on a willow branch, sang its hurried, wheezy song, and dropped from sight. Birdsong lasts longer into the morning on these cool, overcast days. The bobolinks were still busy about it, a song that sounds something like an audiotape being rewound at high speed. A robin in a clump of sumacs sang its careful phrase, as though for the edification of less gifted birds, then listened to itself a moment, head cocked appreciatively, then sang the phrase again. A meadowlark whistled from a fencepost. New England seemed, as it often does, more perfect in the intensity of its seasonal moment, and in the whole seasonal cycle that can be felt within the moment, than any place has a right to be. I felt the fatal parental urge, wanting to point out to Hannah all the richness that surrounded her. But to Hannah such familiar sights and sounds were equivalent to presuppositions, invisible until disturbed.

Animals fit themselves enigmatically into the secondary ecology of human thinking. "They are all beasts of burden, in a sense," says Thoreau, "made to carry some portion of our thoughts." Turtles are especially burdened. In Hindu myth, Vishnu, floating on the cosmic sea, takes the form of a tortoise and sustains the world on his back. North American Indians, unacquainted with any sizeable tortoises, nevertheless had the same myth of turtle as Atlas. The Senecans told how the first people lived in the sky, until a woman, whose transgression involved a tree, was thrown out. Below her—very far below—there was only water. A few water birds were there, and these, seeing her descending, hurried to prepare a place for her. They dived to the bottom, found mud and a turtle, and persuaded the turtle to let them place mud on its back, and make a dry spot for her to land on. The woman landed; vegetation grew up out of the mud; and the familiar world we know came into being.

But the Indians weren't through with the turtle, or vice versa. Turtle turns trickster and, disguised as a young brave, seduces the daughter of the first woman. When the daughter realizes what her lover is, she dies, and from her body, as she prophesies in dying, grow the first stalks of corn and the equivocal blessings of agriculture. Among other tribes, in other myths, Turtle continues his depredations. Many tribes tell of his going on the warpath against the first people, who at last catch him and prepare his death. They threaten him with fire; he tells them that he loves fire. They threaten him with boiling water; he begs to be put immediately into the kettle, because he so relishes being boiled. They threaten to throw him into the river. "Anything but that," says Turtle, and so they throw him in. He sticks out his snout and laughs; they curse him and throw sticks, but he easily avoids them. And so Turtle takes up, one would surmise, the life of a snapper, coming ashore only briefly each year, seeming about as old as the earth, and spreading consternation. God knows what burden of thought the big snapper had borne for the drunk man at Yauhannah Bridge—he symbolized, I believe, a good deal more than the man's adversary, McNair.

I found myself wishing that Hannah had stumbled upon this morning's turtle herself and had confronted the potent oddity of the beast without having it all explained away for her. It might have stood a better chance then than it did now of becoming a fact in her imagination: something she would eventually remember and think about and think with from her days as a country girl. But what any child will think or remember is beyond anybody's knowing, including its own. The turtle had disappeared down the ditch; its hole had been filled. Meanwhile, Hannah let us know that we had on our hands a Tuesday morning in June, which was, with kindergarten over, a problem to be solved. Could she have a friend over? Could we go to town?

1989

ANONYMITY

by SUSAN BERGMAN

from THE NORTH AMERICAN REVIEW

> Turandot—*Gli enigmi sono tre, la morte una!*
> Caleph—*No, no! Gli inigmi sono tre, una la vita!*
> —Puccini

1. WITHOUT THE REAL NAME OF THE AUTHOR

THE SUMMER OF 1977, after my sophomore year in college, I took a job lifeguarding at a rooftop hotel swimming pool eight stories above the Boardwalk in Atlantic City. It was the summer gambling muscled in, and the sleepy ghetto town was intoxicated with the crisp new bills casino lords waved under every soon to be displaced nose. July, the Marlborough-Blenheim Hotel still lent the ramshackle grandeur of its lobby to deals deals deals, regardless of the wrecker ball that within weeks would polish off what explosives hadn't collapsed. Crime's entourage the white haired ladies stood in town meetings to decry had assembled. What I hadn't seen before that summer in the way of off-center sex and other permutations of greed, I learned breathing salt air in the company of transients and gamblers, and those who serviced them. Joe tended poolside bar on weekends when the mostly foreign tourists drank blender mixups that made them sink when I tried to teach them to swim. "Mickey Finns," Joe scraped his voice into my ear with a laugh. "It'll put'em on the bottom every time." On steamy afternoons before the blackjack tables' first cards had been dealt, to the carnival rantings of the penny arcade below, I stayed sober on the virgin mint nostalgia coolers Joe concocted in honor of the ferris wheel, or the green and white striped trolley, or the faded beach umbrellas. "Here's to you, Sappho (he kept an eye on me), to saving lives. Do it while there's still time!"

Joe first started calling me Sappho on one of the few rainy Saturdays that summer. *He pulled it like a paisley handkerchief from his hat*, or out of the overcast air, I guessed. At the time the name stood for the whole secret world to which he alluded and belonged—Mafia dandies, union men, the multicolored women who came and went for free drinks and a couple of laughs. I held my image of his image of me like a pose hardly apropos for an out-of-her-element Ohio girl taking in, for the first time, an Atlantic seaboard town. Sappho was a woman in a black bathing suit that buttoned down the front.

By the time Joe finished his crossword puzzle, the laundry crew sent up the day's hot from the dryer towels which were my living: a dollar tip per towel draped over the gentleman's arm, a two-dollar tip to show the lady to her chaise. There were the man and woman who pulled up a chair for me between them and spoke in slurred voices about many-partner sex. How it worked, how it would feel. My experiments toward physical intimacy had been modeled on Western Literary Romance as commonly available in the *Poetry of Love Anthology*, historical novels, or the comic books in my grandparents' Backwater Grocery store, which as a child I snuck under my skirt to read in the garage. One male and one female, a gradual crescendo in the same covered wagon train, glances, "Shall I compare thee to a summer's day?" a mountain pass, soda shop, the top down, taken by storm, "There be none of Beauty's daughters / With a magic like thee"; marriage. With nothing in my life up to that point to help translate what the couple were asking me to do, I can't remember much of what they described except that as I got up to go the gray-skinned man rolled his head on his shoulder and said, "Think about it, Pussy Pussy?" Arm's length and refusal, yet I had participated, listening, my awkwardness a hitch of conscience even as she began to coax, my fear the green trapeze I swung on over their heads. They seemed lonely to me, so I went with them for a lobster dinner after work and rode my bicycle down the Boardwalk home.

There was the flawless, smooth-skinned girl exactly my age, who Joe said Mr. Koroner kept, and whose red toenails he would rub as he walked by her chair. She simply sat, without a book, in

241

the sun, and never went near the water. If the general questions I posed could be met with one-word answers, she would say yes or no; if not she looked at the door, or petted the subtle incline under her ribs with her long spread fingers until I went away. Some days it was just the two of us for hours. I wanted to know where she'd found her scanty armor, and the way it worked.

The queens who snuck in in pods of three despised me for my breasts. They giggled in vigorous falsettos and spat directly at my feet, rubbing themselves against the pool lights, or the wooden slats of the chairs, or the deck rails. Masquerading as girls, they played out their episodes of how girls must behave, naming a hair out of place deshabille, trading an orange bracelet for a purple fringed scarf. My thighs were not right, the way they didn't rub together at the top like theirs. I could see why they preferred men. They leaned way out over the Boardwalk, all calling at once. They primped and rehearsed, the artifice of gendered accoutrement cubed. At first they came to swim, and chide, but as summer wore on and the crowds thinned, so did their act. My part in their carnival was cut to stage-hand, towel bearer. They had gotten to me and found the target wanting, or too easy.

For the photographer, who milled around the sun deck in plaid trunks with cameras hanging off his back, I was a sunny prop. In the back of my disorderly cupboards I still find the inch-by-inch blue plastic key-chain peek portraits of the French/Canadian duo with their arms around Sappho, smiling; the Hollywood mogul with his black bikini and me; Ed, the other lifeguard, who loved the racetrack, and me. It was part of the resort appeal of souvenirs and sideshows that went with the job. And there were two identical twin would-be gynecologist pool managers, whom we could not tell apart and who liked it that way. They were my boss and would jump in the water after me when I was swimming and try to pull me under. I slicked on suntan lotion before diving in, and one or the other of them would wrestle the great oily half-fish Sappho till she nearly drowned.

The hotel manager who gave me the job was what I called then a bachelor friend of my father's. Fortyish, masterfully handsome, the rumor was that he had fathered the child the owner's wife was about to have. But the owner wasn't worried. "It's his own rumor," Joe confided to me. "The fellow likes it behind closed doors." *Queen* was the "bachelor's" term for men who frolicked in the open. He owed my father a favor was how I heard it, so my friend got a job in the office answering phones for the summer and I got to work at the pool. I heard my father arguing with him past midnight some nights on the telephone. He would wrap and unwrap himself in the rubber cord. That summer I knew nothing of being kept, or of my father and his friends, or of the other Sappho, but I liked that name better than my old one. Joe made it sound learned and notorious, and when he introduced me, no one mixed me up with anyone else.

2. OF UNKNOWN NAME

August in Ohio emptied out horses and baseball, marigold gardens and salamander streams. We toted books and coins to the tree house and traded stories for silver dollars. I'd turned twelve in May. If a boy loved me he could hold me out over the edge of the wood plank platform in the air for an hour without letting go. If a boy loved you he would tie your wrists to a high branch with a thousand knots.

My first poems I didn't sign. They fit on 3-by-5 cards the exact size of what I thought and felt, which was the perfect size to report on Hopi Indians, or The Declaration of Independence, or nightingales and their nests. No name—that way Jackie, the neighbor's German cousin visiting for the summer, would be overcome with a pure, undesignated passion when he discovered them rolled up and tied with ribbons, tucked under his pillow, or in his shoes.

The beloved turns the handwritten page over to look for a name, any name. Who could have sent me this? It means what I mean. I will never have to speak again. It is what my life has meant all along to discover. Finding no name, he turns back to the words which burn behind his eyes, it is the words of the one whom he has loved forever—THE WORDS. I will go to her she is here with me. We will take us in our arms.

I pictured that if I left off my name, the words would loosen from me and the page so they could float out toward a cosmic, amorphous love-at-large that would somehow settle on Jackie as he slept. Isn't that what potions do? I would happen along, the poem's remedies cast over him. He would declare his mutual absorption in the nameless vocabulary of hearts and moons. We would wander in the fields and woods, or sit on the roof of the house being built down the road. He would hold out his hand in a fist in front of me and ask me to pull up on his thumb, which he liked me to do so that he could fart. Then he would kiss me. He was bodily and courageous enough to do such things even in front of parents. He was seventeen. He had an accent.

What happened was, my great grandmother had died and left me all her books. My family had driven to her house in Indiana and told me that I could take as many as would fit into one cardboard box, which I filled and emptied and rearranged until I could fit all of James Whitcomb Riley Hoosier Poet, Byron, Keats and Shelley, some sheet music with Art Nouveau ladies in flowing dresses, a few bound copies of an early women's magazine, and her notebooks and genealogies. What her dying did was to start me thinking about death and poems. So I promptly requested baptism into my parents' separatist Baptist church of 16 or so parishioners—to give up my life and replace it with the Word, to die as the pastor laid me back in the water, and to resurrect. And I began to transform lines from Byron's poems into facsimiles of my own, layering grace over ardor.

As though no one would notice—who had ever read George Gordon, Lord Byron but my great grandmother?—I borrowed liberally. Revision meant a shift of focus from description of the beloved, to being the beloved. I was the *thee* of the lines, I the beauty, the one waiting, the betrayer, no credit to the original. There were places I could go in the poems that I could not trespass in the everyday. Things to be. I was in the air of the poems, I the articulating will that compelled the circle of desire to turn around me, and to return. There were ladders and hallways, chandeliers, forbidden keys, long golden hair, a wand, a mountain I moved or moved through. I would read Byron's poems, then open to the front of the volume and carefully lift the yellow tissue back from the poet's portrait etched on the flyleaf, for inspiration. He was my first and last muse (a concept I have since understood to be a corruption of female-as-inspiration). But he worked for me. Every other line rhymed without fail or slant.

In Ohio, no one did notice they were Byron writ adolescent. But the pastor who had baptized me, the uncle of my love, either found one of the poems in its hiding place and demanded to have the complete work, or, as I suspect happened, was presented with the series, ribbons and all, as a great, hilarious betrayal of me by the villain Jackie. He knew. The poems would be burned ceremonially in the incinerator the two families shared. How did he know? Our lives leave clues. Passion and words are neither pure nor undesignated. Their spells wear off. You wake up to find you have adored an ass.

A sort of tribunal of spiritual discipline took place that evening, structured like the trial of Hester Prynne. I remember the "logical conclusions," prostitution and fornication, as they rhymed. My mother left the room. My father spoke to me in a rushed voice about how inappropriate such lustful poems were coming from a member of the Bride of Christ. I was part of them, he said, an ambassador, the old man of me put away, the new man wearing a white wedding dress. I don't say this to mock him now, and less to mock my own sincere participation in the outward acts of faith. He was both terrified and compelled by my imagination, and his own, which could only have its roots, he feared, in the wicked practices of the World from which he had withdrawn.

I'm not sure which was worse in his mind, the poems or the illustrations. My father handled them like snakes. You cannot fix snakes with poke root or goat's milk, though a shovel will do. There are so many of them. They multiply before your eyes. They look like your worst image of you, crawling on your lascivious belly. They get into the garden; every row of dirt you turn, you find them. They say those things. Plagued House of Pharaoh, the locust, blood, scabie, first-born Uh, uhhoww, even in the water. Is there no one to deliver us of this . . . ? That which I would not, that I do. If you stand in the center of the room cringing to have granted birth, if you shame the snake and revoke its entire permission, then.

What more graphic way for a child to learn the attachment of words to their source, than for her own—borrowed as they were from a passionate poet—to be read aloud in front of a roomful of people, to convict her, and to horrify them. You write the words: you will carry their praise or blame. These things didn't really happen, I told them. This isn't me, it's someone else. But to my interrogators, words equaled acts; concepts (in the hands of the unsympathetic) crime. I am still torn, actual Reader, between wanting to address you sincerely (as if it were possible), without the interference of art, and wanting the art to show between the two of us. As I listened to my harm it sounded rhythmic and eloquent, and though they stumbled over the loopy cursive, someone in the poems spoke exactly what I meant.

It had failed to work in a mighty way, the anonymity: the words claimed me whether or not I called them by my name. Not only the words but their content. I stopped crying when I slept. They taught me well, whatever else they meant for me to learn, that to write something down is to admit the secret, which will always give you away.

My books were forbidden, as was my writing of poems. For a rare, indecisive moment, my parents and the pastor (who to this day harrows a band of the adamant) discussed whether I should submit to the discipline of excommunication or receive a spank. How old is a twelve year old girl? The pastor sat me on his lap and recited parts of verses I wish I could remember: *the pure of heart, the good the better the best, think on these things,* no doubt. He said I would be watched—vigilance, penitence, abstinence. Didn't I like to play with girls my age? Couldn't I learn to sew? I was not allowed to say goodbye to Jackie, whose eighteenth birthday I also missed. I had wanted it to go: "When we two parted / In silence and tears, / Half broken hearted / To sever for years, / Pale grew thy cheek and cold, / Colder thy kiss; / Truly that hour foretold / Sorrow to this."

3. LACKING A NAME: *as one not assigned to any species*

On the thrust stage of the Guthrie Theater, in slow motion as the house lights dim, a mass of figures in the heat of an Algerian midday advances and recedes to the accompaniment of the Electric Arab Orchestra's whiny short-winded repetitions. Philip Glass has written the music for Jean Genet's "The Screens." The drum beat and the human commotion reduce to the twitch of a shoulder here, the face's tic against flies, a slow hand rising to sweep the forehead there. A shudder, a spasm, the bodies' feel perpetual and chronic.

The whole momentum of the six-hour event—90 characters, the golden skirts of the whore (dinner break of beef with currant and pine nuts, tabouli, eggplant salad), red flames in the orange grove, red umbrellas of the mourners—flushes toward oblivion. "I worked so hard to erase myself," Said, the central character says to his wife, Leila, who is so ugly he keeps her in a full-body veil. And in the end, as Genet tells the story, this is what his character achieves—not a better life, or an afterlife, but nothing.

The play's last three scenes take place overhead in the land of the dead. Heavy netting strung between the ceiling and the audience groans with the weight of its ever-replenished cache. The newly deceased crash one after the other through the paper portals and exclaim, "Oh, this is not what I'd expected!" After the third or fourth time the audience mouths the words with the actors. Said is not well after years in prison, years as society's kicking boy. They expect him any moment now, the dead, who roll, clumped in the net in their white robes like wetted cotton wads, humming. But Said makes it, somehow, outside the realm of people in the net. He escapes both life and afterlife: that one alleviation Genet could conceive for the self from the vantage of his life as orphan, thief, inmate, prostitute, writer. "Said is like me," Leila says, "he wants everything to fuck up as fast as it can."

So did my father, who was not nearly so clever as Genet at aesthetic consolations. Refusing to distinguish between the stage and himself, what oblivion he enacted played in the cramped theater of his body to stiff consequence. He died one stranger at a time until he finally caught it, and could pass it along.

"O you must have a Bluebeard closet!" says Richard Howard, who is not afraid of his. "Everybody does." His seductive poems flaunt in passage after passage what I imagine my father would have liked not to hide. The dead's secrets are tough to urge. A private room in an indigent ward, the name of an Episcopal minister to gay men, phone calls charged to my account that I can trace. I go back over the veiled signals: "Family man," he kept insisting, "Family man—I adore my perfect, model, church-going wife and—what a Family man resists makes him a square in the round world. You know this new scene of mine, Andy Warhol, von Furstenberg, people whisk me around town in their limousines. Clients of mine. I was supposed to meet them at this bar where the Most Gorgeous tall blackhaired woman can't take her eyes off me. She led me toward the back stairs and I tell her Family Man Happily Married, four beautiful children. Upstairs she's a man. Freak of Nature! The entire floor is pulsing with small colonies of partners in the dark. Men more beautiful than the next, with muscle and fiery loins. The pattern breaks—no, more fluid—it absorbs color and momentum, stalk in, stalk out, breath of a single beast, heave, stroke, as if it would dissolve me inside its scales. I didn't belong there, Sweetheart, and knew it as soon as . . . Clients take me there. You would like them. They wouldn't believe I have a daughter your age. Their barbers come to their apartments to shave them."

This is the part of the story he told me, his confidante, better not mention this to your mother. What he told my sister when she walked in on him in the bathroom fumbling with her mascara was that from so far away—a poorly lit room, the raised piano top casting a steep shadow—it would be hard for people to see who he was.

It started as a mystery of masks, whereof
You were the master, charagus, maze: amazing
Trollops, old men, lovers, you transformed them all,
Green-and-white Brighella, Polidoro, motley
Harlequin, the passionate Spaniard, and Elles . . .
("The Comedy of Art")

What kept my father's existence privy was less the lack of evidence, I suppose, than his meticulous track covering and refutation. And, no doubt, there was some confusion on his part *being* the most well-wrought mask he wore. Bluebeard, your family is right here with you. We are the part of the persona most put on and taken off. It is getting stuffy, all these dicks and our mother. The more I write about him, the more I feel like Noah's son, who finding his father drunk and without clothes held back the flaps of his tent and laughed. I am not uncovering my father's nakedness, I am getting some air.

Until the *NY Times Sunday Magazine* put it on the cover, hardly anyone said AIDS. The small-print names of my father's miscellany of diseases I'd been hearing from the Bellevue doctors were euphemisms. Cancer, we told our friends, a mild case of skin cancer and pneumonia. The early cases caught in the most promiscuous. Estimates of 1100 partners average, per life. Within a year, 8 of the 11 cases studied died. To New York and back on business, to San Francisco, the ship coming in, could I lend him air fare he would stay with friends. Could I just read him the numbers on my credit card over the phone, please sorry, he got there but he couldn't get back.

I walked up to the roof of our building and watched a tug-boat on the Hudson haul a rusty barge under the George Washington Bridge. Back downstairs I read the article again. He wasn't Haitian. He didn't use drugs. Maybe he used drugs, I'd look for needle marks. I read it again. Sanctimony is the child of imposture: I was the daughter of a cocksucker.

Just nod, I would say to them at the hospital. I'm not asking for a sentence, just a confirmation.

"You'll have to talk with your father."

In his delirium my father thinks I'm the Union Guard. He hardly breathes, Doctor Dansus, you would think he would want someone he loves to know something about him.

"The prognostic groups he falls into are not good. Anything we know is so inconclusive at this point that . . . "

Anything we ever know, fine, of course it's AIDS or you would tell me. What are you protecting, who . . . ? The cold March sun threaded the eye of the bridge over the East River. Tubes and incisions. The bridge laced all the way over, its neatness tiresome. If not for the random colors of cars outside his window, each with its passengers trying to talk, if not for the low boats, fly at the window. "You nurses are so lazy," my father said from his bed, mistaking me. "I will not let you destroy my life." Along the hospital parking lot they'd planted Acanthus trees that stank like wanton boys. The smell wiped out the disinfectant and his blue gown tied once in the back.

They called me one day that week sorry, wondering if I would release the body to science. There were three dimes, some small tins of hard imported candy, and a jar of bronzing cream in his bedside table drawer. I said no, we would ship the body whole to his mother and sister. They could dress him up.

Your father dies: you wish you didn't think good riddance. Every curse falls flat. What are we celebrating celebrities? What serial killers do we approve? How many patches for the quilt now, O ye who stitch in sympathy? How black is the day of pictures to the gallery wall? I have been waiting to say this. My sisters and I are calmer now. My mother holds a job and calls us.

We are calm. We watch it on television, the parade of VICTIMS. We are calm. We are not men. The men have written poems and empathetic screen jigs for each other, having undergone society's inflictions. Their versions master the neat shift from rage to tenderness, loose ends to closure: they make lousy art out of their losses, hurrying, before the subject is passé. I'm waving my arms now. Courage, dignity, a forced bloom of humor, elevation of *his* suffering, *his* point of view. National Public Radio chronicles the lover's last days. I hurry out to buy the last dress Perry Ellis designed. The men are dead.

After seven years the dreams have stopped. I would dig my fingers into his eye sockets and pull with my thumbs under his chin to try and tear the mask away. He would come into my house and rearrange the furniture, pasting layers of grass cloth on the walls. No one else in the dream recognized him. When I screamed he flinched and blinked, sometimes cowering behind the couch. My father played keyboard instruments, mostly church organs and dinner club grands. He did what he chose to do—I am my father's daughter: so do I.

The homosexual father prays before dinner and compares his calamity to Job's. The homosexual father sits in group therapy with his confused children and unsuspecting wife and discusses phantom trouble. The homosexual father is so frightened of his daughter's ordinary development that he finds a way to torment her for menstruating. The homosexual father contracts hepatitis and insists it was the seafood he ate that the rest of the family swallowed and survived. He is sick and yellow when his children meet the bill collectors at the door. The homosexual father disapproves as his daughters seek substitutes for him. The homosexual father lives as though the only life were his, or for him. "Were they not, devil-fish, angel fish and all the rest, the contents of one infinite, eternal body—his?" ("With the Remover to Remove"). "They will assume another life—their make-up will, by transforming them into 'others,' enable them to try any and every audacity: as they will be unencumbered by any social responsibility," wrote Genet in his rehearsal notes to Roger Blin.

That life, a lack, gaping, insatiable, cast out onto the waters, will come back to your children whom I intend to tell. I will say, you do not belong to the family you believe you do and it is not your fault for thinking the collar and tie before your eyes, the toupee, the poppers he does before he has sex with your mother, just to survive what his father did to him, are safe.

The year before he died—the days he felt back to normal—I would run into him on the street and we would have lunch I would pay for, all right. He would taste his food, lick his fingers and then tear off a piece of meat or cheese he would put in my baby's mouth. Go to HELL, DADDY. Go to Hell, every single fucking jack he ever fucked or was fucked by, the zillion Grand Central Station Royalty men's room flight attendant Times Square fucks. I don't mean it. I mean it but I could never say it to your face. I was holding the baby. You said "I don't think I want him to call me Granddad, please. Teach him to call me, oh, I don't know, SKIPPER."

We would walk back to Peter Stuyvesant's former gracious quarters now owned by Norman Vincent Peale's Church, and chat with the man who kept my father the months after the family was locked out of the beach house for not paying the rent. The man talked about his ministry to the gay community. He was trying to let me in on my father's condition without saying it. He felt around conversationally to see if he could pass the burden of my father's care along. My father was proud of the enormous room and pointed to the oil portraits, stumbling over the names. He looked to Mr. Tweed for correction. His skin was "rowdy," pea, onion peel yellow—it was my father's skin, I cannot get it right. His tongue as he tried to moisten his lips was white with fungus. Take some grapes with you, he offered, for the ride home.

1991

251

MAINTENANCE

by NAOMI SHIHAB NYE

from THE GEORGIA REVIEW

THE ONLY MAID I ever had left messages throughout our house: *Lady as I was cleaning your room I heard a mouse and all the clothes in your closet fell down to the floor there is too many dresses in there take a few off. Your friend Marta Alejandro.* Sometimes I'd find notes stuck into the couch with straight pins. *I cannot do this room today bec. St. Jude came to me in a dream and say it is not safe.* Our darkroom was never safe because the devil liked dark places and also the enlarger had an eye that picked up light and threw it on Marta. She got sick and had to go to a doctor who gave her green medicine that tasted like leaves.

Sometimes I'd come home to find her lounging in the bamboo chair on the back porch, eating melon, or lying on the couch with a bowl of half-melted ice cream balanced on her chest. She seemed depressed by my house. She didn't like the noise the vacuum made. Once she waxed the bathtub with floor wax. I think she was experimenting.

Each Wednesday I paid Marta ten dollars—that's what she asked for. When I raised it to eleven, then thirteen, she held the single dollars away from the ten as if they might contaminate it. She did not seem happy to get raises, and my friends (who paid her ten dollars each for the other days of the week) were clearly unhappy to hear about it. After a while I had less work of my own and less need for help, so I found her a position with two gay men who lived in the neighborhood. She called once to say she liked them very much because mostly what they wanted her to do was shine. Shine?

"You know, silver. They have a lot of bowls. They have real beautiful spoons not like your spoons. They have a big circle tray that shines like the moon."

My friend Kathy had no maid and wanted none. She ran ten miles a day and lived an organized life. Once I brought her a gift—a blue weaving from Guatemala, diagonal patterns of thread on sticks—and she looked at it dubiously. "Give it to someone else," she said. "I really appreciate your thinking of me, but I try not to keep things around here." Then I realized how bare her mantel was. Who among us would fail to place *something* on a mantel? A few shelves in her kitchen also stood empty, and not the highest ones either.

Kathy had very definite methods of housekeeping. When we'd eat dinner with her she'd rise quickly, before dessert, to scrape each plate and place it in one side of her sink to soak. She had Tupperware containers already lined up for leftovers and a soup pan with suds ready for the silverware. If I tried to help she'd slap my hand. "Take care of your own kitchen," she'd say, not at all harshly. After dessert she'd fold up the card table we'd just eaten on and place it against the wall. Dining rooms needed to be swept after meals, and a stationary table just made sweeping more difficult.

Kathy could listen to any conversation and ask meaningful questions. She always seemed to remember what anybody said—maybe because she'd left space for it. One day she described having grown up in west Texas in a house of twelve children, the air jammed with voices, crosscurrents, the floors piled with grocery bags, mountains of tossed-off clothes, toys, blankets, the clutter of her sisters' shoes. That's when she decided to have only one pair of shoes at any time, running shoes, though she later revised this to include a pair of sandals.

Somehow I understood her better then, her tank tops and wiry arms . . . She ran to shake off dust. She ran to leave it all behind.

Another friend, Barbara, lived in an apartment but wanted to live in a house. Secretly I loved her spacious domain, perched high above the city with a wide sweep of view, but I could understand the wish to plant one's feet more firmly on the ground. Barbara has the best taste of any person I've ever known—the best khaki-colored linen clothing, the best books, the name of the best masseuse. When I'm with her I feel uplifted, excited by life; there's so much to know about that I haven't heard of yet, and Barbara probably has. So I agreed to help her look.

We saw one house where walls and windows had been sheathed in various patterns of gloomy brocade. We visited another where the kitchen had been removed because the owners only ate in restaurants. They had a tiny office refrigerator next to their bed which I peeked into after they'd left the room: orange juice in a carton, coffee beans. A Krups coffee maker on the sink in their bathroom. They seemed unashamed, shrugging, "You could put a new kitchen wherever you like."

Then we entered a house that felt unusually vivid, airy, and hard-to-define until the realtor mentioned, "Have you noticed there's not a stick of wood anywhere in this place? No wood furniture, not even a wooden salad bowl, I'd bet. These people, very hip, you'd like them, want wood to stay in forests. The man says wood makes him feel heavy."

Barbara and her husband bought that house—complete with pear-shaped swimming pool, terraces of pansies, plum trees, white limestone rock gardens lush with succulents—but they brought wood into it. Never before had I been so conscious of things like wooden cutting boards. I helped them unpack and stroked the sanded ebony backs of African animals.

Then, after about a year and a half, Barbara called to tell me they were selling the house. "You won't believe this," she said, "but we've decided. It's the maintenance—the yardmen, little things always breaking—I'm so busy assigning chores I hardly have time for my own work anymore. A house really seems ridiculous to me now. If I want earth I can go walk in a park."

I had a new baby at the time and everything surprised me. My mouth dropped open, oh yes. I was living between a mound of fresh cloth diapers and a bucket of soiled ones, but I agreed to participate in the huge garage sale Barbara was having.

"That day," Barbara said later, "humanity sank to a new lowest level." We had made signs declaring the sale would start at nine A.M.—but by eight, middle-aged women and men were already ripping our boxes open, lunging into the back of my loaded pickup to see what I had. Two women argued in front of me over

254

my stained dishdrainer. I sold a kerosene heater which we'd never lit and a stack of my great-uncle's rumpled tablecloths, so large they completely engulfed an ironing board. One woman flashed a charm with my initial on it under my nose, saying, "I'd think twice about selling this, sweetheart—don't you realize it's ten carat?"

Afterwards we counted our wads of small bills and felt drained, diluted. We had spent the whole day bartering in a driveway, releasing ourselves from the burden of things we did not need. We even felt disgusted by the thought of eating—yet another means of accumulation—and would derive no pleasure from shopping, or catalogs, for at least a month.

While their new apartment was being refurbished, Barbara and her husband lived in a grand hotel downtown. She said it felt marvelous to use all the towels and have fresh ones appear on the racks within hours. Life seemed to regain its old recklessness. Soon they moved back to the same wind-swept apartment building they'd left, but to a higher floor. Sometimes I stood in their living room staring out at the horizon, which always seemed flawlessly clean.

My mother liked to sing along to records while she did housework—Mahalia Jackson, the Hallelujah Chorus. Sometimes we would sing duets, "Tell Me Why" and "Nobody Knows the Trouble I've Seen." I felt lucky my mother was such a clear soprano. We also sang while preparing for the big dinners my parents often gave, while folding the napkins or decorating little plates of hummus with olives and radishes.

I hungrily savored the tales told by the guests, the wild immigrant fables and metaphysical links. My mother's favorite friend, a rail-thin vegetarian who had once been secretary to Aldous Huxley, conversed passionately with a Syrian who was translating the Bible from Aramaic, then scolded me for leaving a mound of carrots on my plate.

"I'm not going to waste them!" I said. "I always save carrots for last because I love them best."

I thought this would please her, but she frowned. "Never save what you love, dear. You know what might happen? You may lose it while you are waiting."

255

It was difficult to imagine losing the carrots—what were they going to do, leap off my plate?—but she continued.

"Long ago I loved a man very much. He had gone on a far journey—our relationship had been delicate—and I waited anxiously for word from him. Finally a letter arrived and I stuffed it into my bag, trembling, thinking I would read it later on the train. Would rejoice in every word, was what I thought, but you know what happened? My purse was snatched away from me—stolen!—before I boarded the train. Things like that didn't even happen much in those days. I never saw the letter again—and I never saw my friend again either."

A pause swallowed the room. My mother rose to clear the dishes. Meaningful glances passed. I knew this woman had never married. When I asked why she hadn't written him to say she lost the letter, she said, "Don't you see, I also lost the only address I had for him."

I thought about this for days. Couldn't she have tracked him down? Didn't she know anyone else who might have known him and forwarded a message? I asked my mother, who replied that love was not easy.

Later my mother told me about a man who had carried a briefcase of important papers on a hike because he was afraid they might get stolen from the car. The trail wove high up the side of a mountain, between stands of majestic piñon. As he leaned over a rocky gorge to breathe the fragrant air, his fingers slipped and the briefcase dropped down into a narrow crevasse. They heard it far below, clunking into a deep underground pool. My mother said the man fell to the ground and sobbed.

The forest ranger whistled when they brought him up to the spot. "Hell of an aim!" He said there were some lost things you just had to say goodbye to, "like a wedding ring down a commode." My parents took the man to Western Union so he could telegraph about the lost papers, and the clerk said, "Don't feel bad, every woman drops an earring down a drain once in her life." The man glared. "This was not an earring—I AM NOT A WOMAN."

I thought of the carrots, and the letter, when I heard his story. And of my American grandmother's vintage furniture, sold to indifferent buyers when I was still a child, too young even to think of antique wardrobes or bed frames. And I also thought of another friend of my parents, Peace Pilgrim, who walked across America for years, lecturing about inner peace and world peace. A single, broad pocket in her tunic contained all her worldly possessions: a toothbrush, a few postage stamps, a ballpoint pen. She had no bank account behind her and nothing in storage. Her motto was, "I walk till given shelter, I fast till given food." My father used to call her a freeloader behind her back, but my mother recognized a prophet when she saw one. I grappled with the details. How would it help humanity if I slept in a cardboard box under a bridge?

Peace Pilgrim told a story about a woman who worked hard so she could afford a certain style of furniture—French Provincial, I think. She struggled to pay for insurance to protect it and rooms large enough to house it. She worked so much she hardly ever got to sit on it. "Then her life was over. And what kind of a life was that?"

Peace Pilgrim lived so deliberately she didn't even have colds. Shortly before her death in a car accident—for years she hadn't even ridden in cars—she sat on the fold-out bed in our living room, hugging her knees. I was grown by then, but all our furniture was still from thrift stores. She invited me to play the piano and sing for her, which I did, as she stared calmly around the room. "I loved to sing as a child," she said. "It is nice to have a piano."

In my grandmother's Palestinian village, the family has accumulated vast mounds and heaps of woolly comforters, stacking them in great wooden cupboards along the walls. The blankets smell pleasantly like sheep and wear coverings of cheerful gingham, but no family—not even our huge one on the coldest night—could possibly use that many blankets. My grandmother smiled when I asked her about them. She said people should have many blankets and head scarves to feel secure.

I took a photograph of her modern refrigerator, bought by one of the emigrant sons on a visit home from America, unplugged in a corner and stuffed with extra yardages of cloth and old magazines. I felt like one of those governmental watchdogs who asks how do you feel knowing your money is being used this way? My

257

grandmother seemed nervous whenever we sat near the refrigerator, as if a stranger who refused to say his name had entered the room.

I never felt women were more doomed to housework than men; I thought women were lucky. Men had to maintain questionably pleasurable associations with less tangible elements—mortgage payments, fan belts and alternators, the IRS. I preferred sinks, and the way people who washed dishes immediately became exempt from after-dinner conversation. I loved to plunge my hands into tubs of scalding bubbles. Once my father reached in to retrieve something and reeled back, yelling, "Do you always make it this hot?" My parents got a dishwasher as soon as they could, but luckily I was out of college by then and never had to touch it. To me it only seemed to extend the task. You rinse, you bend and arrange, you measure soap—and it hasn't even started yet. How many other gratifications were as instant as the old method of washing dishes?

But it's hard to determine how much pleasure someone else gets from an addiction to a task. The neighbor woman who spends hours pinching off dead roses and browned lilies, wearing her housecoat and dragging a hose, may be as close as she comes to bliss, or she may be feeling utterly miserable. I weigh her sighs, her monosyllables about weather. Endlessly I compliment her yard. She shakes her head—"It's a lot of work." For more than a year she tries to get her husband to dig out an old stump at one corner but finally gives up and plants bougainvillea in it. The vibrant splash of pink seems to make her happier than anything else has in a long time.

Certain bylaws: If you have it, you will have to clean it. Nothing stays clean long. No one else notices your messy house as much as you do; they don't know where things are supposed to go anyway. It takes much longer to clean a house than to mess it up. Be suspicious of any cleaning agent (often designated with a single alphabetical letter, like C or M) that claims to clean everything from floors to dogs. Never install white floor tiles in the bathroom if your family members have brown hair. Cloth diapers eventually make the best rags—another reason beyond ecology. Other people's homes have charisma, charm, because you don't have to know them inside out. If you want high ceilings you may have to give up closets. (Still, as a neighbor once insisted to me, "high ceilings make you a better person.") Be wary of vacuums with headlights; they burn out in a month. A broom, as one of my starry-eyed newlywed sisters-in-law once said, *does a lot*. So does a dustpan. Whatever you haven't touched, worn, or eaten off of in a year should be passed on; something will pop up immediately to take its place.

I can't help thinking about these things—I live in the same town where Heloise lives. And down the street, in a shed behind his house, a man produces orange-scented wood moisturizer containing beeswax. You rub it on three times, let it sit, then buff it off. Your house smells like a hive in an orchard for twenty-four hours.

I'd like to say a word, just a short one, for the background hum of lesser, unexpected maintenances that can devour a day or days—or a life, if one is not careful. The scrubbing of the little ledge above the doorway belongs in this category, along with the thin lines of dust that quietly gather on bookshelves in front of the books. It took me an hour working with a bent wire to unplug the birdfeeder, which had become clogged with fuzzy damp seed—no dove could get a beak in. And who would ever notice? The doves would notice. I am reminded of Buddhism whenever I undertake one of these invisible tasks: one acts, without any thought of reward or foolish notion of glory.

Perhaps all cleaning products should be labeled with additional warnings, as some natural-soap companies have taken to philosophizing right above the price tag. Bottles of guitar polish might read: "If you polish your guitar, it will not play any better. People who close their eyes to listen to your song will not see the gleaming wood. But you may feel more intimate with the instrument you are holding."

Sometimes I like the preparation for maintenance, the motions of preface, better than the developed story. I like to move all the chairs off the back porch many hours before I sweep it. I drag the mop and bucket into the house in the morning even if I don't intend to mop until dusk. This is related to addressing envelopes months before I write the letters to go inside.

Such extended prefacing drives my husband wild. He comes home and can read the house like a mystery story—small half-baked clues in every room. I get out the bowl for the birthday cake two days early. I like the sense of house as still life, on the road to becoming. Why rush to finish? You will only have to do it over again, sooner. I keep a proverb from Thailand above my towel rack: *"Life is so short / we must move very slowly."* I believe what it says.

My Palestinian father was furious with me when, as a teenager, I impulsively answered a newspaper ad and took a job as a maid. A woman, bedfast with a difficult pregnancy, ordered me to scrub, rearrange, and cook—for a dollar an hour. She sat propped on pillows, clicking her remote control, glaring suspiciously whenever I passed her doorway. She said her husband liked green jello with fresh fruit. I was slicing peaches when the oven next to me exploded, filling the house with heavy black smoke. My meat loaf was only half baked. She shrieked and cried, blaming it on me, but how was I responsible for her oven?

It took me a long time to get over my negative feelings about pregnant women. I found a job scooping ice cream and had to wrap my swollen wrists in heavy elastic bands because they hurt so much. I had never considered what ice cream servers went through.

These days I wake up with good intentions. I pretend to be my own maid. I know the secret of travelers: each time you leave your home with a few suitcases, books, and note pads, your maintenance shrinks to a lovely tiny size. All you need to take care of is your own body and a few changes of clothes. Now and then, if you're driving, you brush the pistachio shells off the seat. I love ice chests and miniature bottles of shampoo. Note the expansive breath veteran travelers take when they feel the road spinning open beneath them again.

Somewhere close behind me the outline of Thoreau's small cabin plods along, a ghost set on haunting. It even has the same rueful eyes Henry David had in the portrait in his book. A wealthy woman with a floral breakfast nook once told me I would "get over him" but I have not—documented here, I have not.

Marta Alejandro, my former maid, now lives in a green outbuilding at the corner of Beauregard and Madison. I saw her recently, walking a skinny wisp of dog, and wearing a bandanna twisted and tied around her waist. I called to her from my car. Maybe I only imagined she approached me reluctantly. Maybe she couldn't see who I was.

But then she started talking as if we had paused only a second ago. "Oh hi I was very sick were you? The doctor said it has to come to everybody. Don't think you can escape! Is your house still as big as it used to be?"

1991

MINE OWN JOHN BERRYMAN

by PHILIP LEVINE

from THE GETTYSBURG REVIEW

I CAN'T SAY IF all poets have had mentors, actual living, breathing masters who stood or sat before them making the demands that true mentors must make if the fledgling is ever to fly. Some poets seem to have been totally self-starting, like the cars they used to build in Detroit; I'm thinking of such extraordinary examples as Emily Dickinson and Walt Whitman, who over a hundred years ago created not only their own gigantic works but the beginnings of something worthy enough to be American poetry, and they did it out of their imaginations and their private studies and nothing more. But then they had the advantage of being geniuses. And neither was from Detroit. I think also of those poets who *had* to be poets, whom no one or nothing short of death could have derailed from their courses—John Keats, Dylan Thomas, Arthur Rimbaud—and who outstripped their mentors before they even got into second gear. There are those who were lucky enough to find among their peers people of equal talent and insight to help them on their way—poets like Williams and Pound, who for the crucial early years of their writing careers ignited each other. Though, of course, Williams tells us in the "Prologue" to *Kora in Hell* that Ezra benefited also from the scathing criticism of Williams's father William George. Williams tells us that his father "had been holding forth in downright sentences upon my own 'idle nonsense' when he turned and became

262

equally vehement concerning something Ezra had written: what in heaven's name Ezra meant by 'jewels' in a verse that had come between them. These jewels,—rubies, sapphires, amethysts and whatnot, Pound went on to explain with great determination and care, were the backs of books as they stood on a man's shelf. 'But why in heaven's name don't you say so then?' was my father's triumphant and crushing rejoinder." Pound himself showed Ford Madox Ford some early verse, serious stuff, and Fordie laughed so hard upon reading the work he actually fell on the floor and "rolled around on it squealing with hilarity at the poems." Pound said that Ford's laughter saved him two years of work in the wrong direction. Terrible conditions have driven others to take up the pen in an effort to write their way out of the deepest nightmares imaginable—Wilfred Owen in the trenches, Edward Thomas in his melancholia, Hart Crane in the slough of Cleveland. In some cases it worked.

As for those of us here in the United States of America in the second half of the twentieth century, we have developed something called Creative Writing, a discipline that not only flourishes on hundreds of campuses but has even begun to invade the public schools. It has produced most of the poets—for better or worse—now writing in the country. One can only regard it as one of the most amazing growth industries we have. Thus, at the same time as we've made our society more racist, more scornful of the rights of the poor, more imperialist, more elitist, more tawdry, money-driven, selfish, and less accepting of minority opinions, we have democratized poetry. Today anyone can become a poet: all he or she need do is travel to the nearest college and enroll in Beginning Poetry Writing and then journey through the dozen stages of purgatory properly titled Intermediate Poetry Writing and Semi-Advanced Poetry Writing, all the way to Masterwork Poetry Writing, in which course one completes her epic on the sacking of Yale or his sonnet cycle on the paintings of Edward Hopper, or their elegies in a city dumpster, and thus earns not only an MFA but a crown of plastic laurel leaves. Do I sound skeptical? Let me sound skeptical.

But I also must in fairness add that it is impossible for me to imagine myself as the particular poet I have become—again for better or for worse—without the influence of a single teacher, my one great personal mentor, and amazingly enough I found him at the head of a graduate class at that most unfashionable of writing industries, the much-maligned Iowa Writers' Workshop. He was, of course, John Berryman, not yet forty years old but soon to be so, with one book of poems to his credit and stuck with the job of teaching poetry writing—for the first time in his life and for the last.

I did not go to the University of Iowa to study with John Berryman; in 1953 his reputation was based on *The Dispossessed*, that first book, and it was no larger than it should have been. The poem "Homage to Mistress Bradstreet" had not yet appeared in *The Partisan Review*, though it soon would and would create shock waves through the then-tiny world of American poetry. The attraction at Iowa was Robert Lowell, whose second book, *Lord Weary's Castle*, had received the Pulitzer Prize, and whose singular voice had excited young poets as far away as Michigan. I among them journeyed to Iowa and enrolled in Lowell's writing workshop and audited his seminar in modern poetry; this was the fall of '53, America under Eisenhower ("Wide empty grin that never lost a vote," Berryman would later write) transforming itself into America under Joe McCarthy.

To say I was disappointed in Lowell as a teacher is an understatement, although never having taken a poetry workshop I had no idea what to expect. But a teacher who is visibly bored by his students and their poems is hard to admire. The students were a marvel: we were two future Pulitzer Prize winners, one Yale winner, one National Book Critics Circle Award winner, three Lamont Prize winners, one American Book Award winner. Some names: Donald Justice, W. D. Snodgrass, Jane Cooper, William Dickey, Robert Dana, Paul Petrie, Melvin Walker LaFollette, Henri Coulette, Donald Petersen, and an extraordinarily gifted woman named Shirley Eliason, who soon turned to the visual arts and became a master. And your present speaker. I am sure there were others among the thirteen who were excited by Lowell as teacher, for Lowell was one to play favorites. No matter how much they wrote like Lowell, some of the poets could do no wrong; in all fairness to Lowell, he praised them even when they wrote like Jarrell. Needless to say, I could write nothing that pleased Lowell, and when at the end of the semester he awarded me a B, I was not surprised. Along with the B he handed me a little card with scribbled notes regarding my poems and then told me I had made more progress than anyone else in the class. "You have come the farthest," he drawled, which no doubt meant I had started from nowhere. "Then why the B?" I asked. "I've already given the A's out," he said. This was at our second and last fifteen-minute conference—which did not irritate me nearly as much as our first, when he accused me of stealing my Freudian insights and vocabulary from Auden. "Mr. Lowell," I had responded (I never got more intimate than Mister and he never encouraged me to do so), "I'm Jewish. I steal Freud directly from Freud; he was one of ours." Mr. Lowell merely sighed.

Lowell was, if anything, considerably worse in the seminar; we expected him to misread our poems—after all, most of them were confused and, with very few exceptions, only partly realized, but to see him bumbling in the face of "real poetry" was discouraging. The day he assured the class that Housman's "Lovliest of Trees, the Cherry Now" was about suicide, Melvin LaFollette leaned over and whispered in my ear, "We know what he's thinking about." His fierce competitiveness was also not pleasant to behold: with the exceptions of Bishop and Jarrell he seemed to have little use for any practicing American poet, and he once labelled Roethke "more of an old woman than Marianne Moore." He was eager to ridicule many of our recent heroes, poets I for one would have thought him enamored of: Hart Crane and Dylan Thomas. Still, he was Robert Lowell, master of a powerful and fierce voice that all of us respected, and though many of us were disappointed, none of us turned against the man or his poetry. As Don Petersen once put it, "Can you imagine how hard it is to live as Robert Lowell, with that inner life?"

During the final workshop meeting he came very close to doing the unforgivable: he tried to overwhelm us with one of his own poems, an early draft of "The Banker's Daughter," which appeared in a much shorter though still hideous version six years later in *Life Studies*. Someone, certainly not Lowell, had typed up three-and-a-half single-spaced pages of heroic couplets on ditto masters so that each of us could hold his or her own smeared purple copy of his masterpiece. He intoned the poem in that enervated voice we'd all become used to, a genteel Southern accent that suggested the least display of emotion was déclassé. I sat stunned by the performance, but my horror swelled when several of my classmates leaped to praise every forced rhyme and

265

obscure reference. (The subject was Marie de Medici, about whom I knew nothing and could care less.) No one suggested a single cut, not even when Lowell asked if the piece might be a trifle too extended, a bit soft in places. Perish the thought; it was a masterpiece! And thus the final class meeting passed with accolades for the one person present who scarcely needed praise and who certainly had the intelligence and insight to know it for what it was: bootlicking.

His parting words were unqualified praise of his successor, John Berryman, not as poet but as one of the great Shakespearean scholars of the age. And then he added that if we perused the latest issue of the *Partisan* we would discover the Mistress Bradstreet poem, clear evidence that Berryman was coming "into the height of his powers," a favorite phrase of Lowell's and one he rarely employed when speaking of the living. In fairness to Lowell, he was teetering on the brink of the massive nervous breakdown that occurred soon after he left for Cincinnati to occupy the Elliston Chair of Poetry. Rumors of his hospitalization drifted back to Iowa City, and many of us felt guilty for damning him as a total loss.

How long Berryman was in town before he broke his wrist I no longer recall, but I do remember that the first time I saw him he was dressed in his customary blue blazer, the arm encased in a black sling, the effect quite dramatic. As person and teacher, John was an extraordinary contrast to Lowell. To begin with, he did not play favorites: everyone who dared hand him a poem burdened with second-rate writing tasted his wrath, and that meant all of us. He never appeared bored in the writing class; to the contrary, he seemed more nervous in our presence than we in his. Whereas Lowell always sprawled in a chair as though visibly troubled by his height, John almost always stood and often paced as he delivered what sounded like memorized encomiums on the nature of poetry and life. Lowell's voice was never more than faintly audible and always encased in his curiously slothful accent, while Berryman articulated very precisely, in what appeared to be an actor's notion of Hotspur's accent. His voice would rise in pitch with his growing excitement until it seemed that soon only dogs would be able to hear him. He tipped slightly forward as though about to lose his balance, and conducted his performance with the forefinger of his right hand. The key word here is performance, for these were memorable meetings in which the class soon caught his excitement. All of us sensed that something significant was taking place.

Beyond the difference of personal preferences and presentation was a more significant one. Lowell had pushed us toward a poetry written in formal meters, rhymed, and hopefully involved with the griefs of great families, either current suburban ones or those out of the great storehouse of America's or Europe's past. We got thundering dramatic monologues from Savanarola and John Brown that semester. For Berryman it was open house. He found exciting a poem about a particular drinking fountain in a bus station in Toledo, Ohio. Lowell certainly would have preferred a miraculous spring in that other Toledo—though now that he was no longer a practicing Catholic, sainthood seemed also to bore him. Berryman was delighted with our curious efforts in the direction of free verse, on which he had some complex notions concerning structure and prosody. He even had the boldness to suggest that contemporary voices could achieve themselves in so unfashionable and dated a form as the Petrarchan sonnet. To put it simply, he was all over the place and seemed delighted with the variety we represented.

Their contrasting styles became more evident during the second meeting of the class. Lowell had welcomed a contingent of hangers-on, several of whom were wealthy townspeople dressed to the nines and hugging their copies of *Lord Weary's Castle*. Now and then one would submit a poem; Lowell would say something innocuous about it, let the discussion hang in mid-air for a moment, then move on to something else. Berryman immediately demanded a poem from one of this tribe. The poem expressed conventional distaste for the medical profession by dealing with the clichés of greed and indifference to suffering. (We later learned it was written by a doctor's wife.) John shook his head violently. "No, no," he said, "it's not that it's not poetry. I wasn't expecting poetry. It's that it's not true, absolutely untrue, unobserved, the cheapest twaddle." Then he began a long monologue in which he described the efforts of a team of doctors to save the life of a friend of his, how they had struggled through a long night, working feverishly. "They did not work for money. There was no money in it. They worked to save a human life because it was a human life and thus precious. They did not know who the man was, that he was a remarkable spirit. They knew only that he was too young to die, and so they worked to save him, and failing, wept." (It turned out the man was Dylan Thomas, but Berryman did not mention this at the time.) A decent poet did not play fast and loose with the facts of this world, he or she did not accept television's notion of reality. I had never before observed such enormous cannons fired upon such a tiny target. The writer left the room in shock, and those of us who had doubts about our work—I would guess all of us—left the room shaken.

We returned the next Monday to discover that Berryman had moved the class to a smaller and more intimate room containing one large seminar table around which we all sat. He was in an antic mood, bubbling with enthusiasm and delighted with our presence. He knew something we did not know: all but the hardcore masochists had dropped, leaving him with only the lucky thirteen. "We are down to the serious ones," he announced, and seemed pleased with the situation; he never again turned his powerful weapons on such tiny life rafts. In truth, once we'd discovered what he'd accomplished, we too were pleased not to have to share his attention with writers we knew were only horsing around.

Now came the hard task for him of determining what we knew and what we didn't know. At least half of us were trying to write in rhyme and meter, and a few of us were doing it with remarkable skill. It was at this meeting that he asked each of us to turn in a Petrarchan sonnet so that he might have some idea how far we'd come on the road to grace and mastery in the old forms. (The logistics were simple: we turned in our work on the Friday before our Monday meeting, and John selected the work to be dittoed and discussed in class.) He presented us with two models, both recited from memory.

THE SIRENS *by John Manifold*

Odysseus heard the sirens; they were singing
Music by Wolf and Weinberger and Morley

268

About a region where the swans go winging,
Vines are in color, girls are growing surely

Into nubility, and pylons bringing
Leisure and power to farms that live securely
Without the landlord. Still, his eyes were stinging
With salt and seablink, and the ropes hurt sorely.

Odysseus saw the sirens; they were charming,
Blonde, with snub breasts and little neat posteriors,
But could not take his mind off the alarming
Weather report, his mutineers in irons,
The radio failing; it was bloody serious.
In twenty minutes he forgot the sirens.

Recited in Berryman's breathless style, it sounded like something
he might have written; he had an uncanny knack of making
a great deal of poetry sound like something he might have written. And who was John Manifold? An obscure Australian poet
who fought in WW II, someone we should discover if we were
serious, as he was, about poetry. The second sonnet was Robinson's "Many Are Called?" which begins "The Lord Apollo, who
has never died. . . . " After reciting it John went back to a passage in the octave:

And though melodious multitudes have tried,
In ecstasy, in anguish, and in vain,
With invocation sacred and profane
To lure him, even the loudest are outside.

"Who are those multitudes?" he almost shouted. Petrie, a great
lover of Robinson, answered, "The poets." "Exactly, Mr. Petrie,
the poets. Certainly the poets in this room." It was perfectly
clear he did not exclude himself.

Much to my horror my Petrarchan sonnet was selected for discussion on that third meeting. (I believe the poem no longer exists; I had the good luck never to have had it accepted for
publication.) Actually, it was not that bad: it was about food,
which had been an obsession of mine for several months; I was
running out of money and so ate very little and very badly. To be
more precise, the poem was about my mother's last Thanksgiving

feast, which I had returned home to participate in; since my mother was a first-rate office manager and a tenth-rate cook, the event had been a disaster. John discussed four poems that day. The first was not a Petrarchan sonnet, and as far as he could determine had no subject nor any phrasing worth remembering. The second did have a subject, but John went to the board to scan its meter. "This is NOT iambic," he said. After getting through four lines, he turned and headed directly toward the cowering poet, suspended the page over his head, and finally let it fall. "This is metrical chaos. Pray you avoid it, sir." I was next. Much to my relief, John affirmed that, yes, this was a Petrarchan sonnet; it was iambic and it did possess a fine subject—the hideous nature of the American ritual meal become a farce. He paused. "But, Levine, it is not up to its most inspired moments—it has accepted three mediocre rhymes, it is padded where the imagination fails. If it is to become a poem, the author must attack again and bring the entirety up to the level of its few fine moments." In effect John was giving us a lesson in how poems are revised: one listened to one's own voice when it was "hot" (a word he liked) and let that "hot" writing redirect one toward a radical revision. "No hanging back," he once said. "One must be ruthless with one's own writing or someone else will be." (I tried but failed to improve the poem. Even at twenty-six, I had not learned to trust the imagination.)

It was clear that among those poems considered, mine had finished second best, and for this I was enormously relieved. What follows is the best, exactly in the form we saw it on that late February Monday in 1953:

SONNET *by Donald Justice*

The wall surrounding them they never saw;
The angels, often. Angels were as common
As birds or butterflies, but looked more human.
As long as the wings were furled, they felt no awe.
Beasts, too, were friendly. They could find no flaw
In all of Eden: this was the first omen.
The second was the dream which woke the woman:
She dreamed she saw the lion sharpen his claw.

270

As for the fruit, it had no taste at all.
They had been warned of what was bound to happen;
They had been told of something called the world;
They had been told and told about the wall.
They saw it now; the gate was standing open.
As they advanced, the giant wings unfurled.

After reading the poem aloud, John returned to one line: "As for the fruit, it had no taste at all." "Say that better in a thousand words," he said, "and you're a genius." He went on: "One makes an assignment like this partly in jest, partly in utter seriousness, to bring out the metal in some of you and to demonstrate to others how much you still need to learn. No matter what one's motives are, no teacher has the right to expect to receive something like this: a true poem." Class dismissed.

A week later a telling incident occurred. The class considered a sonnet by one of its more gifted members, a rather confused and confusing poem which Berryman thrashed even though one member of the class found it the equal of the Justice poem from the previous week. The tortured syntax suggested Berryman's own "Nervous Songs," but he saw little virtue in the poem and felt it was more in the tradition of Swinburne than any contemporary poem should be, writing that tried to bully its readers with rhetoric rather than move them with the living language of the imagination. "Write good prose diction in a usual prose order," he said, "unless you've got a damn good reason for doing otherwise." (It was clear he must have felt he had a damn good reason for doing otherwise when he wrote "Bradstreet.") After class, as we ambled back to the student union for coffee and more poetry talk, the same student who had defended the poem informed Berryman that the author had recently had a sheaf of poems accepted by *Bottege Oscura,* then the best-paying and most prestigious literary magazine in the world. Berryman froze on the sidewalk and then turned angrily on the student and shouted, "Utterly irrelevant, old sport, utterly irrelevant!" He assured the man that absolute "shit" appeared in the so-called "best" publications, while much of the finest poetry being written went begging. (No doubt his own difficult early career had taught him that.) "You're stupid to have raised the subject, stupid or jejune." He paused a moment. "I'll give you the benefit of the doubt: jejune." John smiled, and the incident passed. He was incredibly serious about poetry, and one of us had learned that the hard way. In her gossipy *Poets in Their Youth*, Eileen Simpson would have us believe that all the poets in "the Berryman circle" ached to be the elected legislators of the world and suffered deeply because they were not among the famous and powerful. Everything I saw during the semester contradicted that view: the reward for writing a true poem was the reward of writing a true poem, and there was none higher.

In spite of his extraordinary sense of humor, the key to Berryman's success as a teacher was his seriousness. This was the spring of the Army-McCarthy hearings, the greatest television soap-opera before the discovery of Watergate. John, as an addicted reader of *The New York Times*, once began a class by holding up the front page so the class might see the latest revelation in the ongoing drama. "These fools will rule for a while and be replaced by other fools and crooks. This," and he opened a volume of Keats to the "Ode to a Nightingale," "will be with us for as long as our language endures." These were among the darkest days of the Cold War, and yet John was able to convince us—merely because he believed it so deeply—that nothing could be more important for us, for the nation, for humankind, than our becoming the finest poets we could become. And there was no doubt as to how we must begin to accomplish the task; we must become familiar with the best that had been written, we must feel it in our pulse.

"Levine, you're a scholar," he once roared out at me in class. "Tell us how you would go about assembling a bibliography on the poetry of Charles Churchill." A scholar I was not, and John knew it, but he had a point: that poets had to know these things. The ignorant but inspired poet was a total fiction, a cousin to Hollywood's notion of the genius painter who boozes, chases girls, and eventually kills himself by falling off a scaffold in the Sistine Chapel. "Friends," John was saying, "it's hard work, and the hard work will test the sincerity of your desire to be poets." He rarely mentioned inspiration, perhaps because he assumed that most of us had been writing long enough to have learned that it came to those who worked as best they could through the barren periods, and this was—he once told me—a barren period for him. So we knew how to begin the task of becoming a poet: study and work. And how did it end? Here John was just as clear: it never ended. Speaking of the final poems of Dylan Thomas, he made it clear they were merely imitations of the great work of his early and middle period. "You should always be trying to write a poem you are unable to write, a poem you lack the technique, the language, the courage to achieve. Otherwise you're merely imitating yourself, going nowhere because that's always easiest." And suddenly he burst into a recitation of "The Refusal to Mourn the Death by Fire of a Child in London," ending:

> Deep with the first dead lies London's daughter,
> Robed in the long friends,
> The grains beyond age, the dark veins of her mother,
> Secret by the unmourning water
> Of the riding Thames.
> After the first death, there is no other.

"Can you imagine possessing that power and then squandering it?" he asked. "During our lifetime that man wrote a poem that will never be bettered."

No doubt his amazing gift for ribaldry allowed him to devastate our poems without crushing our spirits, that and the recognition on his part that he too could write very badly at times. He made it clear to us from the outset that he had often failed as a poet and for a variety of reasons: lack of talent, pure laziness ("Let's face it," he once said to me, "life is mainly wasted time"), and stupid choices. "There are so many ways to ruin a poem," he said, "it's quite amazing good ones ever get written." On certain days he loved playing the clown. One Monday he looked up from the class list sent to him by the registrar and asked Paul Petrie why he was getting twice as much credit for the course as anyone else. Paul said he wasn't sure. "Perhaps," said John, "you're getting the extra units in Physical Education and Home Economics. I'd like you to arrive twenty minutes early and do fifty laps around the room and then erase the blackboard. You might also do a few push-ups or work on your technique of mixing drinks." He then discovered my name was not on the roll. (The truth was, lacking sufficient funds, I had not registered.) He asked me if I thought the registrar was anti-Semitic. No, I said, just sloppy.

"You realize," he said, "that until your name appears on this list you do not exist. Tell me," he added, "does anyone else see this Levine fellow? Sometimes I have delusions." As the weeks passed my name continued not to appear on the roster, and John continued to make a joke out of it. "Levine, should I go see the registrar and remedy this hideous state of affairs?" I assured him it was unnecessary, that it was just a meaningless slip-up, and I wasn't taking it personally. "You're quite sure it's not anti-Semitism, Levine? These are dark times." Indeed they were for many Americans, but for the young poets in this workshop they were nothing if not glory days.

"Levine," he said on another day, "when was the last time you read your Shakespeare?" "Last week," I said. "And what?" "*Measure for Measure*." "Fine. I've noticed you consistently complain about the quantity of adjectives in the poems of your classmates." This was true. "Is it the number that matters or the quality?" I failed to answer. "Remember your Blake: 'Bring out number, weight, & measure in a year of dearth.'" I nodded. "'Thy turfy mountains where live nibbling sheep.' Two nouns, two adjectives. Any complaints, Levine?" I had none. "Who wrote the line?" "Shakespeare," I said, "What play?" Again I was silent. His long face darkened with sadness. LaFollette answered, "*The Tempest*." "Levine, do not return to this class until you have reread *The Tempest*. I assume you've read it at least once." I had. "'Fresher than May, sweeter / Than her gold buttons on the boughs . . . ' Recognize it?" I did not. "There is great poetry hiding where you least suspect it, there for example, buried in that hideous speech from *The Two Noble Kinsmen*, Act III, Scene I." Much scratching of pens as the class bowed to their notebooks. "We must find our touchstones where we can."

Knowing I had gone to Wayne University in Detroit where John had once taught, he asked me if I'd studied with the resident Shakespeare scholar, Leo Kirschbaum, whom I had found a brilliant teacher. "Amazing fellow, Dr. Kirschbaum; singlehandedly he set back Lear scholarship two decades." Little wonder I'd failed to recognize the line from *The Tempest*. While he was on the subject of Shakespeare, he required the entire class to reread *Macbeth* by the next meeting. "'And yet dark night strangles the travelling lamp.' Hear how the line first strangles and then releases itself. Read the play carefully, every line, let it heighten your awareness of the extraordinary possibilities for dense imagery. You should know that Shakespeare had less than two weeks to complete the play. Why was that, Mr. Justice?" Don, well on his way to his doctorate, explained that the ascendancy to the English throne of James VI of Scotland called for a play in praise of James's Scotch ancestry. Berryman nodded. "Took him no time at all to write it, and yet it would take half the computers in the world a year to trace the development of the imagery that a single human imagination created and displayed in a play of unrivalled power." So much for the school of Engineering. We were never to forget that men and women of the greatest intellect and imagination had for centuries turned toward poetry to fulfill their private and civic needs.

Certain classes were devoted to special subjects relating to poetic practices, prosody for example. For two hours John lectured on the development of this study and how amazingly fragmented and useless the literature was. People of great learning and sensitivity had come to preposterous conclusions, and nothing in print was reliable. It was our duty to master this literature and discover what was useful and what was nonsense. "A man as learned as George Saintsbury, a man who had read and absorbed so much that in old age he took to studying doctoral dissertations from American universities just to keep busy, a man of that breadth of knowledge, gave us a three-volume study of prosodic practices in British and American poetry, and on almost every significant point he is wrong." Still, he urged us to read the work, for if nothing else it was a brilliant anthology of the diversity and richness of poetry in English. We, the hungry students, demanded to know to whom he went for "the scoop," another of his expressions. He laughed and pointed to his ear. There was no such book, and as in everything else we were thrown on our own. We would develop a prosody that would allow us to write the poetry we needed to write, or we wouldn't, in which case that poetry would never be written. And in order to do it right, we had to learn from those poets who had already done it—for as John made clear, those who best understood prosody— Shakespeare, Milton, Keats, Blake, Hopkins, Frost, Roethke— had better things to do than write handbooks for our guidance.

"Let us say you are appalled by the society in which you live— God knows it is appalling—and you want to create a poetry that speaks to the disgusting human conditions around you. You want to mount a powerful assault, you want to be the prophet Amos of the present age. To which poet would you turn for aid?" Silence from the class. "You want to evoke your rage, your righteous indignation, in numbers that will express the depthless power of your convictions. To whom do you turn?" A voice from the class: "Robert Lowell." "Good choice, but there is a danger here, correct?" The voice: "Yes, I already sound too much like Lowell. I'm doing my best to avoid him." Berryman: "Indeed you are. When I first saw your poems I thought you'd borrowed Cal's old portable Smith-Corona. Why not go to Cal's source, the poet upon whom he based the movement and the syntax of his own work? And who would that be?" Another voice from the class: "Pope." "No, no, you're blinded by his use of the couplet. Milton, our great Milton." Affirmative nods from the class; how could we not know something so obvious. John quoted "On the Late Massacre in Piedmont," using his forefinger to mark the ends of the lines so we heard how powerful the enjambment was. "Bring the diction three hundred years toward this moment and you have one of Cal's early sonnets." More nodding of heads. "And the key to such rhythmic power is . . . ?" Silence. "Speed, achieved by means of a complex syntax and radical enjambment. Speed translates always into rhythmic power, and speed is unobtainable in a heavily end-stopped line."

Then he turned to me. "For the power you so dearly aspire to, Levine, you must turn to the master, Milton, the most powerful poet in the language, though you might do well to avoid the Latinate vocabulary. Have you studied Latin?" Levine: "No." "You might consider doing so; that way you'll know what to avoid when you're stealing from Milton. Do you have another favorite among your contemporaries?" Levine: "Dylan Thomas." Berryman: "It doesn't show, Levine, it doesn't show; you've done a superb job of masking that particular debt. How have you managed that?" Levine: "I didn't. I wrote through my Dylan Thomas phase and quit. It was impossible for me to write under his influence and not sound exactly like him except terrible." Berryman: "Levine, you've hit upon a truth. Certain poets are so much themselves they should not be imitated; they leave you no room to be yourself, and Thomas was surely one of them, as was Hart Crane, who probably ruined the careers of more young poets than anything except booze. Levine, you might go to the source of Dylan's own lyrical mysticism, and who would that be?" Silence. "Mr. Justice?" Justice: "Blake." "Exactly, you might go to Blake, who is so impossibly lyrical and inventive no one in the world has the talent to sound like him." In an unusually hushed voice he recited all of Blake's early "Mad Song," ending:

> I turn my back to the east,
> From whence comforts have increased;
> For light doth seize my brain
> With frantic pain.

"Better to learn from a poet who does not intoxicate you," said Berryman, "better to immerse yourself in Hardy, whom no American wants now to sound like. A great poet seldom read." After class Henri Coulette said to me that he'd passed over Blake's "Mad Song" a dozen times and never heard it until John incanted it.

No one escaped unscathed. John advised Petrie to set aside his Shelley and Elinor Wylie and leap into modernism. Coulette was told to loosen up his strict iambics, to try to capture the quality of living speech. Strangely, he under-appreciated the formal elegance of William Dickey's work. Neither Petersen nor Jane Cooper was productive that semester; Jane later said she was put off by John's sarcasm. Shirley Eliason's work he found wonderfully dense and mysterious; he wanted more. "Write everything that occurs to you," he told us all; "you're young enough to still be searching for your voice. You certainly don't want to find it before you find your subject, and you're still young enough to accept failure." LaFollette seemed the greatest enigma to him. "Yes, yes, you have a genuine lyrical gift," he said one day in class, "but who encouraged you never to make sense, always to be opaque?" LaFollette eagerly revealed that he'd just finished a year's work with Roethke. "Yes," said John, "I can see the influence of Roethke, but Ted's best early work is remarkably straightforward on one level. Of course there is always the shadow of something more formidable, darker. Did Cal encourage this sort of obscurity?" LaFollette revealed he had also studied with Richard Eberhardt. John's mouth fell open as he stood speechless for several seconds. "You let Dick Eberhardt read your poems, and you are here to tell the tale. Amazing!"

He always wanted more work from Robert Dana, though when Dana finally gave him a poem of ninety-eight lines, he mused over it for a time and finally noted two good images. His parting words were, "If you're going to write something this long why don't you try making it poetry?" Meeting after meeting produced the same advice: "Write everything that occurs to you; it's the only way to discover where your voice will come from. And never be in a hurry. Writing poetry is not like running the four hundred meters. Coulette, do you remember what Archie Williams said his strategy was for running the four hundred meters?" (Coulette, the resident sports maven, did not know. Williams had won the gold at the '36 Berlin Olympics.) John went on: "Archie said, 'My strategy is simple; I run the first two hundred meters as fast as I can to get ahead of everyone, and I run the second two hundred meters as fast as I can to stay there.' Now that is NOT the way we write poetry, we are not in a race with anyone, but all of us are getting on in years and we'd better get moving." In other words, go as fast as you can but don't be in a hurry; we had a lifetime to master this thing, and with our gifts it would take a lifetime.

Even Justice got mauled. John found his "Beyond the Hunting Woods" a bit too refined, a bit too professionally Southern. Those dogs at the end of the poem, Belle and Ginger, all they needed were a few mint juleps. And Levine? Levine got his. According to John, Levine's best poem that semester was "Friday Night in the Delicatessen," in which a Jewish mother laments the fact that her sons are growing away from her, becoming Americans, becoming—you should forgive the expression—*goyim*. At one point she describes them with "hands for fights and alcohol." "Hands for fights, yes," said John, "but hands for alcohol? No. We drink alcohol, Levine, as I know you've learned—we absorb it through the digestive system. The fact we hold a glass of whiskey in our hands is not enough. The parallel structure is false, but this is an amazingly ambitious poem." (I lived on that word, "ambitious," for weeks, even after a friend said, "He forgot to add, 'Ambition should be made of sterner stuff.' ") Again I had finished second best. This poem was written to fulfill John's

278

assignment for an ode, the clear winner was "A Flat One," by De Snodgrass, a poem of enormous power that depicted the slow and agonizing death of a WW I veteran, and the vet's relationship with a hospital orderly who must kill to keep him alive. Even in this earlier "static semi-Symboliste version" (Snodgrass's description), it was a startling poem. (Although Lowell is generally credited for being the mentor behind the poems of *Heart's Needle* ["A Flat One" actually appears in De's second book, *After Experience*], De now claims that Lowell discouraged the writing of those poems, and quite forcefully. "Snodgrass, you have a mind," he'd said to him. "You mustn't write this kind of tear-jerking stuff." Berryman never found the poems sentimental; he tried to move De's writing further from traditional metrics toward something—as De put it—"more like his own experiments at the time . . . more like regular speech . . . less like the poetry being written at the time.")

A later class also began with a demonstration from the front page of *The New York Times*. "Allow me to demonstrate a fundamental principle of the use of language, which is simply this: if you do not master it, it will master you. Allow me to quote Senator McCarthy speaking of his two cronies, Cohen and Shine." Roy Cohen and David Shine were two assistants—investigators, he called them—of the Senator for whom he had gained extraordinary privileges which allowed Shine, for example, an ordinary enlisted man in the army, to avoid any of the more onerous or dangerous work of a soldier. "The Senator said the following: 'I stand behind them to the hilt.' We now know what Mr. McCarthy thinks we do not know, that he is about to stab them in the back, abandon them both as political liabilities." John was of course correct; within a few days the deed was done. "Because he is an habitual liar, Mr. McCarthy has blinded himself to the ability of language to reveal us even when we're taking pains not to be revealed. Exactly the same thing holds true with poetic form; if we do not control it, it will control us." He went on: "I do not mean to suggest that each time we enter the arena of the poem we must know exactly where we're headed. We have all learned that that is preposterous, for the imagination leads us where it will, and we must be prepared to follow, but—and this is the crucial point—should we lack the ability to command the poetic form, even if that form is formlessness, toward which our writing travels, we shall be mastered by that form and what we shall reveal is our ineptitude." He then turned to a student poem in formal meters and rhymed couplets and painstakingly analyzed it from the point of view of how the need to rhyme and to keep the meter had produced odd and unconvincing movements in the poem's narrative, as well as needless prepositional phrases and awkward enjambments. "A poem of real fiber, a rhymed poem, will find its rhymes on subjects, objects, and especially verbs, the key words of its content." He then quoted a poem of Hardy's which ended:

> So, they are not underground,
> But as nerves and veins abound
> In the growth of upper air,
> And they feel the sun and rain,
> And the energy again
> That made them what they were!

Again with his forefinger he scored the key words, and finally repeated that final line, " 'That made them what they were!'—my friends, what they were! That is the artist in command, that is triumph!"

Once again he seemed a walking anthology of poetic jewels, and once again we learned how exacting this thing with the poetry was. Later in Kenny's tavern, where many of us assembled after class, one poet recalled that Ignacio Sanchez Mejias, the matador elegized in Garcia Lorca's great poem, had once remarked, "This thing with the bulls is serious," and thus we produced a catch phrase for John's class: "This thing with the poems is serious."

What became increasingly clear as the weeks passed was that while John was willing on occasion to socialize with us, he was not one of us; he was the teacher, and we were the students. He had not the least doubt about his identity, and he was always willing to take the heat, to be disliked if need be. In private he once remarked to me that teaching something as difficult as poetry writing was not a popularity contest. "Even a class as remarkable as this one," he said, "will produce terrible poems, and I am the one who is obliged to say so." He sensed that the students had themselves developed a wonderful fellowship and took joy when any one of them produced something fine. Whether or not he took credit for any of this I do not know. To this day I can recall Bill Dickey studying a Justice poem almost with awe. "Do you see those rhymes?" he said to me. "I'll bet this is the first time they've been used in all our poetry!" I shall never forget Don Petersen's welcoming me up the mountain of poetry—at that time Don seemed to believe he was the guardian of the mountain. He told me in his curiously gruff and tender voice that a particular poem of mine was in fact a poem, and though the class—including John—had not taken to it, it was evidence that I had become a poet. His words were welcomed and genuine. I can recall my own thrill on seeing a particular poem by Jane Cooper in which her portrayal of a nocturnal hedgehog came so vividly to life I shuddered. I expressed my wonder openly and knew she heard it. One day both Henri Coulette and Robert Dana took me aside to tell me they could scarcely believe how far I'd come in a single year. We were all taking pride and joy in each other's accomplishments.

This fellowship was a delicate and lovely thing, a quality that always distinguishes the best creative writing classes. We were learning how much farther we could go together than we could singly, alone, unknown, unread in an America that never much cared for poetry. I don't honestly know how large a role John played in the creation of this atmosphere, but I do know it had not existed during Lowell's tenure; his favoritism, his intimacy with some students and visible boredom with others, tended to divide us into two hostile factions, the ins and the outs. In John's class we were all in and we were all out, we were equals, and instead of sinking we swam together. In spite of John's willingness to be disliked, he clearly was not disliked. Of course he was a marvelous companion, and on those evenings he sought company we were all eager to supply it, but we never forgot that come Monday afternoon the camaraderie would be forgotten and he would get to the serious business of evaluating and if need be decimating poems.

Sometimes his seriousness could be more than a little intimidating. On one occasion over drinks, before going to dinner with a group of student writers and faculty, John began to muse over a remarkable poem by the Welshman Alun Lewis, "Song: On seeing dead bodies floating off the Cape." Berryman believed that

Lewis was one of the great undiscovered talents of the era. He quoted a portion of the poem, an interior monologue by a woman who has had a vision of her lover's death at sea; then his memory failed him, and he apologized to the group. It so happened one of the poets present knew the poem and took up the recitation:

> The flying fish like kingfishers
> Skim the sea's bewildered crests,
> The whales blow steaming fountains,
> The seagulls have no nests
> Where my lover sways and rests.

His memory primed, John completed the poem, which ends with the woman lamenting the "nearness that is waiting in" her bed, "the gradual self-effacement of the dead." After a moment's silence John remarked, "The dead do not efface themselves; we, the living, betray their memories." John seemed lost in his reverie on the life and early death in war of the poet when another poet present, an enormous man who worked in town as a bartender and bouncer, began to praise one of John's own war poems which had appeared in *The Dispossessed*. Suddenly awakened, John shouted in the man's face, "We are talking about great poetry, do you get it, old sport, great poetry, and not the twaddle you have in mind. I do not appreciate bootlicking." A silence followed, and the moment passed. This thing with the poetry was indeed serious.

That semester Berryman conducted the most extraordinary seminar on other writers I've ever been a part of; again, for lack of funds, I was not registered, but I missed only a single class and that when the obligation to make some money took me elsewhere. The students were assigned a single long paper of considerable scope, the subject agreed upon by teacher and poet—for all the registered students were from the workshop. The papers themselves were never presented in class, but not because Berryman found them inadequate. Indeed he raved about their quality. The reason was simply that John felt he had news to bring us on the subject of poetry in English from Whitman to the present. The highlight of the semester was his presentation of the whole of "Song of Myself," which included the most memorable and impassioned reading of a poem I have ever in my life heard, along with the most complex and rewarding analysis of Whitman's design, prosody, and imagery ever presented. When he'd finished the reading, he stood in silence a moment and then from memory presented the final section again, concluding:

I bequeath myself to the dirt to grow from the grass I love,
If you want me again look for me under your boot-soles.

You will hardly know who I am or what I mean,
But I shall be good health to you nevertheless,
And filter and fibre your blood.

Failing to fetch me at first keep encouraged,
Missing me one place search another,
I stop somewhere waiting for you.

He stood for a moment in silence, the book trembling in his hand, and then in a quiet voice said, "Do you know what that proves? That proves that most people can't write poetry!"

When the semester began I was the only non-enrolled student attending, but so extraordinary were his performances that the news spread, and by the time he gave his final Whitman lecture the room was jammed to the bursting point. Crane, Stevens, Bishop, Roethke, Eliot, Auden, Dylan Thomas, and Hardy were also subjects of his lectures. These were not talks he gave off the top of his head. Far from it. He entered the room each night shaking with anticipation and armed with a pack of note cards, which he rarely consulted. In private he confessed to me that he prepared for days for these sessions. He went away from them in a state bordering on total collapse. It would be impossible to overestimate the effect on us of these lectures, for this was an era during which Whitman was out, removed adroitly by Eliot and Pound, and kept there by the Ironists and the New Critics who were then the makers of poetic taste. In 1954 in Iowa no one dreamed that within a few years Williams would be rescued from hell, the Beats would surface, and Whitman would become the good gray father of us all. (John himself later claimed the Beats didn't know how to read Whitman and mistook his brilliant rhythmic effects for prose. "They don't write poems," is the way he put it.) I cannot speak for the entire class, but I know that Petrie, Jane Cooper, Dana, Coulette, Justice, Snodgrass, and I were convinced that "Song of Myself" was the most powerful and visionary poetic statement ever made in this country. Those lectures not only changed our poetry, they changed our entire vision of what it meant to write poetry in America, what it meant to be American, to be human. "There is that lot of me and all so luscious," I suddenly sang to myself, and believed it, and thanks to John and father Walt I still believe it. Whitman had laid out the plan for what our poetry would do, and so large was the plan there was room for all of us to take our part, as for example, Roethke was doing, that poet who according to John "thought like a flower."

Unlikely it seems now that Berryman should have performed that task, for was he not an Eastern intellectual poet and part-time New Critic himself, a protégé of Mark Van Doren and R. P. Blackmur? Like so much that concerns Berryman, the answer is ambiguous. His reviews often sounded very much like what the New Critics were turning out, except they were far wittier and often more savage; in savagery only Yvor Winters could measure up to him. Who else would be bold enough to invent a poem that a poet might have written, nay should have written, as John did in a review of Patchen, and then define Patchen's weaknesses on the basis of the poem Berryman and not Patchen had written? But unlike Winters and the rest of the New Critics, he was unashamedly Romantic at the same time as he was distrustful of the "cult of sincerity." He was, as in so many things, his own man and in a very real sense a loner.

Before we parted that semester he performed two more services for me. The day before he left for New York City—he was going East to teach at Harvard that summer—we had a long conversation on what a poet should look like. The Oscar Williams anthology, one of the most popular of that day, included photographs of most of the poets at the back of the book; John and A. E. Housman were the only exceptions—they were represented by drawings. John's was very amateurish and looked nothing like him. I asked him why he'd used it instead of a photograph. He claimed he wanted neither but Oscar had insisted, and he'd taken the lesser of the two evils. He thought either was a distraction, though the drawing did make it clear he was ugly enough to be a poet. I didn't catch his meaning and asked him to explain. "No poet worth his salt is going to be handsome; if he or she is beautiful there's no need to create the beautiful. Beautiful people are special; they don't experience life like the rest of us." He was obviously dead serious, and then he added, "Don't worry about it, Levine, you're ugly enough to be a great poet."

The next day at the airport he was in an unusually manic mood. "Think of it, Levine, in a few hours I shall be mine own John Poins." Not knowing Wyatt's poem written from exile in rural England to Poins in London, I asked him what he meant.

> I am not he, such eloquence to boast
> To make the crow in singing as the swan,
> Nor call the lion of coward beasts the most,
> That cannot take a mouse as the cat can . . .

He quoted from memory. "Wyatt, Levine, Wyatt, his rough numbers would be perfect for your verse, you crude bastard." ("Crude bastard" was his highest form of compliment.) Before boarding he invited me to send him four or five poems in a year or so, and he'd be sure to get back to me to tell me how I was doing. Having seen an enormous carton of unopened mail in his apartment, I doubted he'd ever answer, but nonetheless a year-and-a-half later I sent him four poems. His response was prompt and to the point; with xs to mark the lines and passages he thought a disaster and checks where he found me "hot," along with specific suggestions for revision; there was not a single line unremarked upon. There was also a brief letter telling me things were going well in Minneapolis and that he was delighted to know I was fooling editors with my "lousy poems." He looked forward to seeing me one day. There was not the least doubt about what he was in fact saying: our days as student and teacher had come to an end. We could not exchange poems as equals in poetry because we were not equals and might never be, and yet I had come too far to require a teacher. I felt the same way. I'd had one great poetry writing teacher, I had studied with him diligently for fifteen weeks. From now on I had to travel the road to poetry alone or with my peers. This was his final lesson, and it may have been the most important in my development.

As the years pass his voice remains with me, its haunting and unique cadences sounding in my ear, most often when I reread my own work. I can still hear him saying, "Levine, this will never do," as he rouses me again and again from my self-satisfaction and lethargy to attack a poem and attack again until I make it the best poem I am capable of. His voice is there too when I teach, urging me to say the truth no matter how painful a situation I may create, to say it with precision and in good spirits, never in rancor, and always to remember Blake's words (a couplet John loved to quote): "A truth that's told with bad intent / Beats all the Lies you can invent." For all my teaching years, now over thirty, he has been a model for me. No matter what you hear or read about his drinking, his madness, his unreliability as a person, I am here to tell you that in the winter and spring of 1954, living in isolation and loneliness in one of the bleakest towns of our difficult Midwest, John Berryman never failed his obligations as a teacher. I don't mean merely that he met every class and stayed awake, I mean that he brought to our writing and the writing of the past such a sense of dedication and wonder that he wakened a dozen rising poets from their winter slumbers so that they might themselves dedicate their lives to poetry. He was the most brilliant, intense, articulate man I've ever met, at times even the kindest and most gentle, and for some reason he brought to our writing a depth of insight and care we did not know existed. At a time when he was struggling with his own self-doubts and failings, he awakened us to our singular gifts as people and writers. He gave all he had to us and asked no special thanks. He did it for the love of poetry.

1992

ON DUMPSTER DIVING

by LARS EIGHNER

from THE THREEPENNY REVIEW

Long before I began Dumpster diving I was impressed with Dumpsters, enough so that I wrote the Merriam-Webster research service to discover what I could about the word "Dumpster." I learned from them that "Dumpster" is a proprietary word belonging to the Dempsey Dumpster company.

Since then I have dutifully capitalized the word although it was lowercased in almost all of the citations Merriam-Webster photocopied for me. Dempsey's word is too apt. I have never heard these things called anything but Dumpsters. I do not know anyone who knows the generic name for these objects. From time to time, however, I hear a wino or hobo give some corrupted credit to the original and call them Dipsy Dumpsters.

I began Dumpster diving about a year before I became homeless.

I prefer the term "scavenging" and use the word "scrounging" when I mean to be obscure. I have heard people, evidently meaning to be polite, use the word "foraging," but I prefer to reserve that word for gathering nuts and berries and such which I do also according to the season and the opportunity. "Dumpster diving" seems to me to be a little too cute and, in my case, inaccurate because I lack the athletic ability to lower myself into the Dumpsters as true divers do, much to their increased profit.

I like the frankness of the word "scavenging," which I can hardly think of without picturing a big black snail on an aquarium wall. I live from the refuse of others. I am a scavenger. I think it a sound and honorable niche, although if I could I would naturally prefer to live the comfortable consumer life, perhaps—and only perhaps— as a slightly less wasteful consumer owing to what I have learned as a scavenger.

While my dog Lizbeth and I were still living in the house on Avenue B in Austin, as my savings ran out, I put almost all my sporadic income into rent. The necessities of daily life I began to extract from Dumpsters. Yes, we ate from Dumpsters. Except for jeans, all my clothes came from Dumpsters. Boom boxes, candles, bedding, toilet paper, medicine, books, a typewriter, a virgin male love doll, change sometimes amounting to many dollars: I acquired many things from Dumpsters.

I have learned much as a scavenger. I mean to put some of what I have learned down here, beginning with the practical art of Dumpster diving and proceeding to the abstract.

What is safe to eat?

After all, the finding of objects is becoming something of an urban art. Even respectable employed people will sometimes find something tempting sticking out of a Dumpster or standing beside one. Quite a number of people, not all of them of the bohemian type, are willing to brag that they found this or that piece in the trash. But eating from Dumpsters is the thing that separates the dilettanti from the professionals.

Eating safely from the Dumpsters involves three principles: using the senses and common sense to evaluate the condition of the found materials, knowing the Dumpsters of a given area and checking them regularly, and seeking always to answer the question "Why was this discarded?"

Perhaps everyone who has a kitchen and a regular supply of groceries has, at one time or another, made a sandwich and eaten half of it before discovering mold on the bread or got a mouthful of milk before realizing the milk had turned. Nothing of the sort is likely to happen to a Dumpster diver because he is constantly reminded that most food is discarded for a reason. Yet a lot of perfectly good food can be found in Dumpsters.

Canned goods, for example, turn up fairly often in the Dumpsters I frequent. All except the most phobic people would be willing to eat from a can even if it came from a Dumpster.

Canned goods are among the safest of foods to be found in Dumpsters, but are not utterly foolproof.

Although very rare with modern canning methods, botulism is a possibility. Most other forms of food poisoning seldom do lasting harm to a healthy person. But botulism is almost certainly fatal and often the first symptom is death. Except for carbonated beverages, all canned goods should contain a slight vacuum and suck air when first punctured. Bulging, rusty, dented cans and cans that spew when punctured should be avoided, especially when the contents are not very acidic or syrupy.

Heat can break down the botulin, but this requires much more cooking than most people do to canned goods. To the extent that botulism occurs at all, of course, it can occur in cans on pantry shelves as well as in cans from Dumpsters. Need I say that home-canned goods found in Dumpsters are simply too risky to be recommended.

From time to time one of my companions, aware of the source of my provisions, will ask, "Do you think these crackers are really safe to eat?" For some reason it is most often the crackers they ask about.

This question always makes me angry. Of course I would not offer my companion anything I had doubts about. But more than that I wonder why he cannot evaluate the condition of the crackers for himself. I have no special knowledge and I have been wrong before. Since he knows where the food comes from, it seems to me he ought to assume some of the responsibility for deciding what he will put in his mouth.

For myself I have few qualms about dry foods such as crackers, cookies, cereal, chips, and pasta if they are free of visible contaminates and still dry and crisp. Most often such things are found in the original packaging, which is not so much a positive sign as it is the absence of a negative one.

Raw fruits and vegetables with intact skins seem perfectly safe to me, excluding of course the obviously rotten. Many are discarded for minor imperfections which can be pared away. Leafy vegetables, grapes, cauliflower, broccoli, and similar things may be contaminated by liquids and may be impractical to wash.

Candy, especially hard candy, is usually safe if it has not drawn ants. Chocolate is often discarded only because it has become discolored as the cocoa butter de-emulsified. Candying after all is one method of food preservation because pathogens do not like very sugary substances.

All of these foods might be found in any Dumpster and can be evaluated with some confidence largely on the basis of appearance. Beyond these are foods which cannot be correctly evaluated without additional information.

I began scavenging by pulling pizzas out of the Dumpster behind a pizza delivery shop. In general prepared food requires caution, but in this case I knew when the shop closed and went to the Dumpster as soon as the last of the help left.

Such shops often get prank orders, called "bogus." Because help seldom stays long at these places pizzas are often made with the wrong topping, refused on delivery for being cold, or baked incorrectly. The products to be discarded are boxed up because inventory is kept by counting boxes: a boxed pizza can be written off; an unboxed pizza does not exist.

I never placed a bogus order to increase the supply of pizzas and I believe no one else was scavenging in this Dumpster. But the people in the shop became suspicious and began to retain their garbage in the shop overnight.

While it lasted I had a steady supply of fresh, sometimes warm pizza. Because I knew the Dumpster I knew the source of the pizza, and because I visited the Dumpster regularly I knew what was fresh and what was yesterday's.

The area I frequent is inhabited by many affluent college students. I am not here by chance; the Dumpsters in this area are very rich. Students throw out many good things, including food. In particular they tend to throw everything out when they move at the end of a semester, before and after breaks, and around midterm when many of them despair of college. So I find it advantageous to keep an eye on the academic calendar.

The students throw food away around the breaks because they do not know whether it has spoiled or will spoil before they return. A typical discard is a half jar of peanut butter. In fact nonorganic peanut butter does not require refrigeration and is unlikely to spoil in any reasonable time. The student does not know that, and since it is Daddy's money, the student decides not to take a chance.

Opened containers require caution and some attention to the question "Why was this discarded?" But in the case of discards from student apartments, the answer may be that the item was discarded through carelessness, ignorance, or wastefulness. This can sometimes be deduced when the item is found with many others, including some that are obviously perfectly good.

Some students, and others, approach defrosting a freezer by chucking out the whole lot. Not only do the circumstances of such a find tell the story, but also the mass of frozen goods stays cold for a long time and items may be found still frozen or freshly thawed.

Yogurt, cheese, and sour cream are items that are often thrown out while they are still good. Occasionally I find a cheese with a spot of mold, which of course I just pare off, and because it is obvious why such a cheese was discarded, I treat it with less suspicion than an apparently perfect cheese found in similar circumstances. Yogurt is often discarded, still sealed, only because the expiration date on the carton had passed. This is one of my favorite finds because yogurt will keep for several days, even in warm weather.

Students throw out canned goods and staples at the end of semesters and when they give up college at midterm. Drugs, pornography, spirits, and the like are often discarded when parents are expected—Dad's day, for example. And spirits also turn up after big party weekends, presumably discarded by the newly reformed. Wine and spirits, of course, keep perfectly well even once opened.

My test for carbonated soft drinks is whether they still fizz vigorously. Many juices or other beverages are too acid or too syrupy to cause much concern provided they are not visibly contaminated. Liquids, however, require some care.

One hot day I found a large jug of Pat O'Brien's Hurricane mix. The jug had been opened, but it was still ice cold. I drank three large glasses before it became apparent to me that someone had added the rum to the mix, and not a little rum. I never tasted the rum and by the time I began to feel the effects I had already ingested a very large quantity of the beverage. Some divers would have considered this is a boon, but being suddenly and thoroughly intoxicated in a public place in the early afternoon is not my idea of a good time.

I have heard of people maliciously contaminating discarded food and even handouts, but mostly I have heard of this from

291

people with vivid imaginations who have had no experience with the Dumpsters themselves. Just before the pizza shop stopped discarding its garbage at night, jalapeños began showing up on most of the discarded pizzas. If indeed this was meant to discourage me it was a wasted effort because I am a native Texan.

For myself, I avoid game, poultry, pork, and egg-based foods whether I find them raw or cooked. I seldom have the means to cook what I find, but when I do I avail myself of plentiful supplies of beef which is often in very good condition. I suppose fish becomes disagreeable before it becomes dangerous. The dog is happy to have any such thing that is past its prime and, in fact, does not recognize fish as food until it is quite strong.

Home leftovers, as opposed to surpluses from restaurants, are very often bad. Evidently, especially among students, there is a common type of personality that carefully wraps up even the smallest leftover and shoves it into the back of the refrigerator for six months or so before discarding it. Characteristic of this type are the reused jars and margarine tubs which house the remains.

I avoid ethnic foods I am unfamiliar with. If I do not know what it is supposed to look like when it is good, I cannot be certain I will be able to tell if it is bad.

No matter how careful I am I still get dysentery at least once a month, oftener in warm weather. I do not want to paint too romantic a picture. Dumpster diving has serious drawbacks as a way of life.

I learned to scavenge gradually, on my own. Since then I have initiated several companions into the trade. I have learned that there is a predictable series of stages a person goes through in learning to scavenge.

At first the new scavenger is filled with disgust and self-loathing. He is ashamed of being seen and may lurk around, trying to duck behind things, or he may try to dive at night.

(In fact, most people instinctively look away from a scavenger. By skulking around, the novice calls attention to himself and arouses suspicion. Diving at night is ineffective and needlessly messy.)

Every grain of rice seems to be a maggot. Everything seems to stink. He can wipe the egg yolk off the found can, but he cannot erase the stigma of eating garbage out of his mind.

That stage passes with experience. The scavenger finds a pair of running shoes that fit and look and smell brand new. He finds a pocket calculator in perfect working order. He finds pristine ice cream, still frozen, more than he can eat or keep. He begins to understand: people do throw away perfectly good stuff, a lot of perfectly good stuff.

At this stage, Dumpster shyness begins to dissipate. The diver, after all, has the last laugh. He is finding all manner of good things which are his for the taking. Those who disparage his profession are the fools, not he.

He may begin to hang onto some perfectly good things for which he has neither a use nor a market. Then he begins to take note of the things which are not perfectly good but are nearly so. He mates a Walkman with broken earphones and one that is missing a battery cover. He picks up things which he can repair.

At this stage he may become lost and never recover. Dumpsters are full of things of some potential value to someone and also of things which never have much intrinsic value but are interesting. All the Dumpster divers I have known come to the point of trying to acquire everything they touch. Why not take it, they reason, since it is all free.

This is, of course, hopeless. Most divers comes to realize that they must restrict themselves to items of relatively immediate utility. But in some cases the diver simply cannot control himself. I have met several of these pack-rat types. Their ideas of the values of various pieces of junk verge on the psychotic. Every bit of glass may be a diamond, they think, and all that glistens, gold.

I tend to gain weight when I am scavenging. Partly this is because I always find far more pizza and doughnuts than water-packed tuna, nonfat yogurt, and fresh vegetables. Also I have not developed much faith in the reliability of Dumpsters as a food source, although it has been proven to me many times. I tend to eat as if I have no idea where my next meal is coming from. But mostly I just hate to see food go to waste and so I eat much more than I should. Something like this drives the obsession to collect junk.

As for collecting objects, I usually restrict myself to collecting one kind of small object at a time, such as pocket calculators, sunglasses, or campaign buttons. To live on the street I must anticipate my needs to a certain extent: I must pick up and save warm bedding I find in August because it will not be found in Dumpsters in November. But even if I had a home with extensive storage space I could not save everything that might be valuable in some contingency.

I have proprietary feelings about my Dumpsters. As I have suggested, it is no accident that I scavenge from Dumpsters where good finds are common. But my limited experience with Dumpsters in other areas suggests to me that it is the population of competitors rather than the affluence of the dumpers that most affects the feasibility of survival by scavenging. The large number of competitors is what puts me off the idea of trying to scavenge in places like Los Angeles.

Curiously, I do not mind my direct competition, other scavengers, so much as I hate the can scroungers.

People scrounge cans because they have to have a little cash. I have tried scrounging cans with an able-bodied companion. Afoot a can scrounger simply cannot make more than a few dollars a day. One can extract the necessities of life from the Dumpsters directly with far less effort than would be required to accumulate the equivalent value in cans.

Can scroungers, then, are people who *must* have small amounts of cash. These are drug addicts and winos, mostly the latter because the amounts of cash are so small.

Spirits and drugs do, like all other commodities, turn up in Dumpsters and the scavenger will from time to time have a half bottle of a rather good wine with his dinner. But the wino cannot survive on these occasional finds; he must have his daily dose to stave off the DTs. All the cans he can carry will buy about three bottles of Wild Irish Rose.

I do not begrudge them the cans, but can scroungers tend to tear up the Dumpsters, mixing the contents and littering the area. They become so specialized that they can see only cans. They earn my contempt by passing up change, canned goods, and readily hockable items.

There are precious few courtesies among scavengers. But it is a common practice to set aside surplus items; pairs of shoes, clothing, canned goods, and such. A true scavenger hates to see good stuff go to waste and what he cannot use he leaves in good condition in plain sight.

Can scroungers lay waste to everything in their path and will stir one of a pair of good shoes to the bottom of a Dumpster, to be lost or ruined in the muck. Can scroungers will even go through individual garbage cans, something I have never seen a scavenger do.

Individual garbage cans are set out on the public easement only on garbage days. On other days going through them requires trespassing close to a dwelling. Going through individual garbage cans without scattering litter is almost impossible. Litter is likely to reduce the public's tolerance of scavenging. Individual garbage cans are simply not as productive as Dumpsters; people in houses and duplexes do not move as often and for some reason do not tend to discard as much useful material. Moreover, the time required to go through one garbage can that serves one household is not much less than the time required to go through a Dumpster that contains the refuse of twenty apartments.

But my strongest reservation about going through individual garbage cans is that this seems to me a very personal kind of invasion to which I would object if I were a householder. Although many things in Dumpsters are obviously meant never to come to light, a Dumpster is somehow less personal.

I avoid trying to draw conclusions about the people who dump in the Dumpsters I frequent. I think it would be unethical to do so, although I know many people will find the idea of scavenger ethics too funny for words.

Dumpsters contain bank statements, bills, correspondence, and other documents, just as anyone might expect. But there are also less obvious sources of information. Pill bottles, for example. The labels on pill bottles contain the name of the patient, the name of the doctor, and the name of the drug. AIDS drugs and anti-psychotic medicines, to name but two groups, are specific and are seldom prescribed for any other disorders. The plastic compacts for birth control pills usually have complete label information.

Despite all of this sensitive information, I have had only one apartment resident object to my going through the Dumpster. In that case it turned out the resident was a University athlete who was taking bets and who was afraid I would turn up his wager slips.

Occasionally a find tells a story. I once found a small paper bag containing some unused condoms, several partial tubes of flavored sexual lubricant, a partially used compact of birth control pills, and the torn pieces of a picture of a young man. Clearly she was through with him and planning to give up sex altogether.

Dumpster things are often sad—abandoned teddy bears, shredded wedding books, despaired-of sales kits. I find many pets lying in state in Dumpsters. Although I hope to get off the streets so that Lizbeth can have a long and comfortable old age, I know this hope is not very realistic. So I suppose when her time comes she too will go into a Dumpster. I will have no better place for her. And after all, for most of her life her livelihood has come from the Dumpster. When she finds something I think is safe that has been spilled from the Dumpster I let her have it. She already knows the route around the best Dumpsters. I like to think that if she survives me she will have a chance of evading the dog catcher and of finding her sustenance on the route.

Silly vanities also come to rest in the Dumpsters. I am a rather accomplished needleworker. I get a lot of materials from the Dumpsters. Evidently sorority girls, hoping to impress someone, perhaps themselves, with their mastery of a womanly art, buy a lot of embroider-by-number kits, work a few stitches horribly, and eventually discard the whole mess. I pull out their stitches, turn the canvas over, and work an original design. Do not think I refrain from chuckling as I make original gifts from these kits.

I find diaries and journals. I have often thought of compiling a book of literary found objects. And perhaps I will one day. But what I find is hopelessly commonplace and bad without being, even unconsciously, camp. College students also discard their papers. I am horrified to discover the kind of paper which now merits an A in an undergraduate course. I am grateful, however, for the number of good books and magazines the students throw out.

In the area I know best I have never discovered vermin in the Dumpsters, but there are two kinds of kitty surprise. One is alley cats which I meet as they leap, claws first, out of Dumpsters. This is especially thrilling when I have Lizbeth in tow. The other kind of kitty surprise is a plastic garbage bag filled with some ponderous, amorphous mass. This always proves to be used cat litter.

City bees harvest doughnut glaze and this makes the Dumpster at the doughnut shop more interesting. My faith in the instinctive wisdom of animals is always shaken whenever I see Lizbeth attempt to catch a bee in her mouth, which she does whenever bees are present. Evidently some birds find Dumpsters profitable, for birdie surprise is almost as common as kitty surprise of the first kind. In hunting season all kinds of small game turn up in Dumpsters, some of it, sadly, not entirely dead. Curiously, summer and winter, maggots are uncommon.

The worst of the living and near-living hazards of the Dumpsters are the fire ants. The food that they claim is not much of a loss, but they are vicious and aggressive. It is very easy to brush against some surface of the Dumpster and pick up half a dozen or more fire ants, usually in some sensitive area such as the underarm. One advantage of bringing Lizbeth along as I make Dumpster rounds is that, for obvious reasons, she is very alert to ground-based fire ants. When Lizbeth recognizes the signs of fire ant infestation around our feet she does the Dance of the Zillion Fire Ants. I have learned not to ignore this warning from Lizbeth, whether I perceive the tiny ants or not, but to remove ourselves at Lizbeth's first pas de bourrée. All the more so because the ants are the worst in the months I wear flip-flops, if I have them.

(Perhaps someone will misunderstand the above. Lizbeth does the Dance of the Zillion Fire Ants when she recognizes more fire ants than she cares to eat, not when she is being bitten. Since I have learned to react promptly, she does not get bitten at all. It is the isolated patrol of fire ants that falls in Lizbeth's range that deserves pity. Lizbeth finds them quite tasty.)

By far the best way to go through a Dumpster is to lower yourself into it. Most of the good stuff tends to settle at the bottom because it is usually weightier than the rubbish. My more athletic companions have often demonstrated to me that they can extract much good material from a Dumpster I have already been over.

To those psychologically or physically unprepared to enter a Dumpster, I recommend a stout stick, preferably with some barb or hook at one end. The hook can be used to grab plastic garbage bags. When I find canned goods or other objects loose at the bottom of a Dumpster I usually can roll them into a small bag that I can then hoist up. Much Dumpster diving is a matter of experience for which nothing will do except practice.

Dumpster diving is outdoor work, often surprisingly pleasant. It is not entirely predictable; things of interest turn up every day and some days there are finds of great value. I am always very pleased when I can turn up exactly the thing I most wanted to find. Yet in spite of the element of chance, scavenging more than most other pursuits tends to yield returns in some proportion to the effort and intelligence brought to bear. It is very sweet to turn up a few dollars in change from a Dumpster that has just been gone over by a wino.

The land is now covered with cities. The cities are full of Dumpsters. I think of scavenging as a modern form of self-reliance. In any event, after ten years of government service, where everything is geared to the lowest common denominator, I find work that rewards initiative and effort refreshing. Certainly I would be happy to have a sinecure again, but I am not heartbroken not to have one anymore.

I find from the experience of scavenging two rather deep lessons. The first is to take what I can use and let the rest go by. I have come to think that there is no value in the abstract. A thing I cannot use or make useful, perhaps by trading, has no value however fine or rare it may be. I mean useful in a broad sense— so, for example, some art I would think useful and valuable, but other art might be otherwise for me.

I was shocked to realize that some things are not worth acquiring, but now I think it is so. Some material things are white elephants that eat up the possessor's substance.

The second lesson is of the transience of material being. This has not quite converted me to a dualist, but it has made some headway in that direction. I do not suppose that ideas are immortal, but certainly mental things are longer-lived than other material things.

Once I was the sort of person who invests material objects with sentimental value. Now I no longer have those things, but I have the sentiments yet.

Many times in my travels I have lost everything but the clothes I was wearing and Lizbeth. The things I find in Dumpsters, the love letters and ragdolls of so many lives, remind me of this lesson. Now I hardly pick up a thing without envisioning a time I will cast it away. This I think is a healthy state of mind. Almost everything I have now has already been cast out at least once, proving that what I own is valueless to someone.

Anyway, I find my desire to grab for the gaudy bauble has been largely sated. I think this is an attitude I share with the very wealthy—we both know there is plenty more where what we have came from. Between us are the rat-race millions who have confounded their selves with the objects they grasp and who nightly scavenge the cable channels looking for they know not what.

I am sorry for them.

1992

A DAY AT THE ST. REGIS WITH DAME EDITH

by PERDITA SCHAFFNER

from AMERICAN SCHOLAR

A FAMILY FRIEND, a personage, visits your city for the first time. You send flowers and enclose a note. "Do let me know if there is anything I can do." You may get taken up on the offer.

My telephone rang very early one Monday morning.

"This is Edith. Osbert has been convocated. We are alone, we are desperate."

The royal We, voice in anguish.

Edith and Osbert, the Sitwells, had been lionized from the moment they stepped down the gangplank, were installed in a luxury suite at the St. Regis, and booked for lectures and readings across the United States.

Osbert had gone away for the weekend and hadn't returned, leaving not a penny in his sister's purse. There was a bank account, but she had to go in person and sign things. Where was Wall Street, she wanted to know. And shoes, she needed shoes, her favorite pair had got mislaid. Left on the ship? Or not even packed? Unclear. Her lecture shoes—she didn't know what to do. Then we would have lunch. Afterwards we would go to the Museum of Modern Art to see Tchelitchew's *Hide and Seek*, a painting she adored.

"Oh, my dear, I realize I'm battening on you, but if you could and would come to the rescue. . . . "

Of course I could and would, without delay.

300

It was mid-October, a steamy Indian summer day. Edith was already in the lobby, wearing voluminous robes, a scarlet turban, a heavy fur cape—her usual array of outsize sparkling jewelry.

"So good of you, dear. Now how do we get to Wall Street—the very fastest way?"

I didn't quite see Edith on the subway. The doorman hailed a cab and helped her in, an unwieldy production in itself. The traffic was fierce, the heat unbearable. Tight squeeze in back. She sat ramrod straight, obviously ill at ease, and pulled the fur cape tighter around her.

"Driver, please, I feel a terrible draught, would you be so good as to close your window."

Nonplussed, he complied.

We picked up speed on the East River Drive.

"New York—Osbert's been here before and loves it. I'm absolutely terrified, yet it's so beautiful. Oh my passport, they said I had to bring it for official identity or something absurd—don't say I forgot."

She delved into a large drab satchel—the kind old ladies used to call "my knitting bag"—extricating cosmetics, notebooks, scrib- bled poems, and jewels. At the very bottom she found the comforting navy blue square British passport.

The window jolted open a mere crack, bringing a blessed waft of fresh air.

"Oh driver, Sir, I know I'm a frightful nuisance, but . . . "

"Very happy to meet you, Miss Sitwell," said the bank manager.

The Plantagenet Queen drew herself to full height, towering over him.

"*Doctor* Sitwell."

The poor man was crushed. Edith was funny that way, obsessed with titles and rank, ever desperate for recognition. She had, some years ago, received two honorary doctorates, one from the University of Leeds and one from the University of Sheffield. She clung to them. D.Litt., D.Litt. after her name, on all her correspondence, let no one forget.

The manager was subsequently forgiven for his faux pas. She thanked him quite obsequiously, stuffed the new checkbook and a thick wad of cash into the "knitting bag."

301

We found a bigger cab this time. Another terrible draught assailed us through one of the back windows—jammed an inch open; nothing to be done about it.

Next on the agenda, shoes. The bane of her existence, Edith could never find any to fit. Suitable shoes were not comfortable, comfortable shoes were not suitable. These, she pointed to the clodhoppers on her feet, were the only ones she could bear, other than the mislaid pair handmade by a little man in Rome. I directed the cab to I. Miller.

Difficult feet: narrow, long, and very bony in odd places. Boxes came out by the dozen and piled up all around. This one twisted her arches, that one pinched her big toe most excruciatingly. Another was too wide at the heel, would slip and send her pitching head-first into the audience. Edith was extravagantly gracious and apologetic as she dispatched the salesman off on yet another foray. He tried so hard, to no avail.

Defeated, we walked a few blocks and came to a store with a glitzy window display where everything was on sale.

"Let's try here," she said.

Edith immediately spied a bin full of fake brocade bedroom slippers marked down to $3.99. Perfect fit on the first try.

"Do you think I can possibly get away with it?"

The robes would conceal them, I assured her. Anyway, with the spotlight on her face and her voice enthralling the audience, nobody would even notice her feet. She bought them.

Room service back at the St. Regis: a double martini for Edith, the size of a birdbath, she specified. She was quiet during lunch, withdrawn. Our expedition had taken a lot out of her. She was uneasy over Osbert's absence, and apprehensive about the weeks ahead. The Grand Tour: the Middle West, back through Boston, then Yale University, ending up with two major appearances in New York. Scary unknown territories, new audiences. How would they react, she wondered, would anyone even bother to come? I realized how intensely vulnerable she was, underneath the flamboyance, beyond her spectacular façade.

"We will now have a rest," she announced as the dishes were cleared away. "Make yourself comfortable."

She retired to her bedroom.

The Sitwells, the three of them—Edith, Osbert, and Sacheverell, known as Sashie—and my mother, the poet H. D., and her life-long companion Bryher had all known each other over the years, as cordial acquaintances. The war brought about the true meeting of minds. Restless travelers grounded on our small beleaguered island. Ardent creative spirits determined to rise above the dreariness and weariness and intermittent terrors of those times. Sashie was no longer an immediate member of the triumverate. He had a life of his own, as country squire with his beautiful wife Georgia and their two sons.

"Like the uncle of a king," is how Gertrude Stein described Osbert. Patrician, infinitely kind, courteous, elegantly understated. "Very tiresome" was his only comment on a night of bombing that had nearly blown him from his home. He and Bryher became the very closest of friends. They met every morning for a walk in Hyde Park. They exchanged long letters when separated, even wrote to each other when both were in town—afterthoughts on their earlier conversation.

Edith was anything but understated. She never faced the world until late afternoon, yet she seemed ever present through telephone calls and letters. She'd finished a poem or couldn't finish it. Her throat had flared up again, her lumbago was killing her, insomnia was driving her to the brink of madness. My mother retreated from these little dramas. Bryher loved them and would go rushing off bearing cough syrup, liniment, reference books from the London Library.

If she felt up to it, Edith would come to tea—"as strong as lye," her standard order. She always descended in full regalia, turning the most informal visit into a pageant.

She thrived on vendettas. Enemies were everywhere: stupid critics, obtuse editors, importunate neophytes who thrust manuscripts at her for a first reading, coughers and sneezers who sprayed her with deadly infections. The lunatics, she called them, one and all; she lived perpetually on their fringe. Inanimate objects joined the conspiracy: a loose carpet whipping round her ankle like a dragon's tail, collapsing beds, crashing cupboards. Her imagery was vivid, highly diverting, even if one never quite knew what to believe. Some of her complaints were mostly for show, an everlasting reaction from early life. Some scars would not heal. She was an unwanted girl, followed by two desired brothers; a strange gawky child sequestered in that somber pile, Renishaw Hall. "I have a feeling we forgot something," said her father, Sir George, as they set out on a journey. "Yes, Sir," the butler replied. "We forgot Miss Edith."

Edith was always nice to me. In turn, I was careful not to sneeze. Or to submit manuscripts—heaven forfend. She could be extraordinarily kind. She genuinely cared about people, especially about young people whose work she respected. She also burdened herself with an endless gaggle of lame ducks, most of whom sounded indistinguishable from the lunatics.

She resided at the Sesame Pioneer and Imperial Club, a Victorian enclave typical of its kind: genteel, short on capital, badly in need of repair. It offered no private bathrooms—join the queue down the hall. Frayed wicker chairs lined the lobby. The furniture in the lounge was oversized and upholstered in dark brown velvet. An unlikely venue, Edith had chosen it because she wished to be anonymous. To a degree she was. Heads turned as she passed, then the well-bred conversations continued. She took no notice of her fellow members, nor of the shabby furniture and peeling paint. The Sesame—for short—solved the housekeeping problem and lent itself to her routine. She took early morning tea at bedside, and there she remained for most of the day, surrounded by books, notebooks, pens, and pencils. A sacroiliac condition made it painful for her to sit up at a desk; bed was always her working area. She also suffered from chronic insomnia and often woke long before the tea tray arrived, working compulsively for hours.

Sometimes she dressed and emerged for lunch, depending on her mood and the day's schedule. When work was done she liked to entertain. A very clever chef performed wonders on the dull wartime fare, the staff was amiable and willing. Edith could lay things on; she arranged lunch and dinner parties for such guests as Evelyn Waugh, T. S. Eliot, E. M. Forster, and the Nicolsons, Harold and Vita.

And she did teas—little teas, big teas. I was on the tea list. The little teas were a fearful strain. Disparate groups with nothing in common, tongue-tied; each guest was expected to take the floor and shine solo.

The big teas were great fun. Edith commandeered the brown velvet lounge. Room enough to accommodate groups and subgroups, space to move around and move on. There would be a cross section of the famous, the near famous, and those who could have been either—if only we could figure out who they were. Stephen Spender showed up in a fire fighter's uniform. Lieutenant Alec Guinness, an actor beyond spear-carrying parts, was not yet *the* actor he would become, his career postponed for a while. Edith claimed him and his wife Merula as cousins, dating her lineage from Hereward and the Wake. Osbert was invariably the co-host; sometimes Sashie, too, who was similar in appearance and manner; and occasionally Georgia, of whom it was rumored she never read a book, but was so refreshing in that galère, so beautiful, that who cared. Along with other minor acolytes, I passed plates of yellow cake and played guessing games. That peppery lady over there in animated discourse with a couple of GI's. She looked like Ivy Compton-Burnett, was she, wasn't she . . . ? Circle closer, one's instincts instructed, eavesdrop.

On one of the morning walks, Osbert told Bryher of his plan, a poetry reading to benefit the Free French in England. The Queen had agreed to be a patroness, and to attend with her then young daughters, Elizabeth and Margaret. He hoped my mother, H. D., would participate. Bryher rallied his poets. For the next few weeks no one talked of anything else. Rehearsals, tea parties, endless telephone calls. The ladies practiced their curtsies and discussed what to wear. Clothes were rationed, a new dress would use up a whole year's coupons. No problem for Edith, who would wear what she always wore. The others hunted through cupboards, mended, and made do.

Beatrice Lillie was the program seller. "When is she going to sing?" Princess Margaret piped up. The poets read in alphabetical order, H. D. followed by T. S. Eliot—she tremulous, he composed but dry. The first part of the program ended with John Masefield, poet laureate. Then they filed off to an anteroom to be presented to the royal party.

So far everything was very decorous, according to plan. The unforeseen would occur, however. Lady Dorothy Wellesley—former protégée of W. B. Yeats—had fortified herself with a couple of drams. She mistook Harold Nicolson for Osbert, and attacked him with an umbrella. Beatrice Lillie broke up the fight.

Vita Sackville-West, Sitwell and Sitwell, Stephen Spender, professionals all, delivered with panache. Further down the alphabet the elderly poet W. J. Turner mumbled and bumbled inaudibly, interminably, crowding scholarly Arthur Waley's slot. He had to be stopped. Lady Dorothy Wellesley had a hard time getting started. All in all a most memorable event, a lovely splash in the dark bog of 1943, when it seemed the war would go on forever.

June 6, 1944, D day at last, still a hellish long way to go. In London the worst of times since the blitz, with its abominable robots, V's 1 and 2, flying bombs and rockets, falling indiscriminately where they would, twenty-four hours a day. The V 1's sounded variously like helicopters, lawn mowers, revved-up motorboats. The V 2's were far more destructive, but descended without warning; at least we didn't have to monitor their progress across the sky. A disrupted city, inhabitants burrowing in like hysterical rabbits—just what Hitler had in mind. We went about our business as usual.

They were assembled all three, Edith, Osbert, and Sashie, at the Churchill Club, a social and cultural center for Allied officers. Osbert had read and talked of a work in progress. Edith was on stage, reading a poem inspired by the 1940 bombings, "Still Falls the Rain." We heard *it* coming, the lawn mower variety, lower and lower and louder and louder, about to tear off the roof and chop down the staircase. Nobody flinched. Edith read on, raising her voice over the racket, modulating it as the thing continued on its way. That moment, and the applause that followed, has remained one of my personal highlights of the war.

From shoes on Fifth Avenue to the firing line—quite a stretch.

Edith emerged from her room at three o'clock on the dot, rested, purposeful. We set off for the Museum of Modern Art.

We contemplated *Hide and Seek* close up, stepped back a way, and sat down, all in total silence. A disturbing picture, I thought, but I was not the one to say so. A little girl chasing a butterfly through a thicket, strange surrealist vegetation, disembodied heads.

Pavel Tchelitchew, Pavlik, was the love of Edith's life. He reciprocated, called her his muse, his sibyl, his inspiration, glass flower under glass. Separated by the war, he in America, she in England, they wrote to each other constantly. The greatest love letters of all time, it has been said, they recently have been assembled and immured in a vault at Yale University, sealed until the year 2000. He was a homosexual, however. "That of which they speak," she would lament—meaning physical passion—"I was made for it, I have never known it, I never will."

We sat for another half hour, Edith lost and gone, looking desolate.

"Nobody paints dandelion fluff like Pavlik," she finally remarked.

I didn't know the whole story. I heard it later from other sources. Their momentous reunion had taken place at dockside. Pavlik gave a big party that night. He invited her to a private viewing early the next morning before the museum opened to the public. She was shaky from a stormy passage, disoriented; longed to see his picture, but please could she wait a day or two.

Tchelitchew was offended, grudgingly agreed to a later date. Confronted by the masterpiece, volatile master at her side, she couldn't think of anything to say. He waited for her ecstatic reaction. She remained silent. He sulked and smoldered. They parted company on the sidewalk.

Edith wrote him a long letter, no doubt the most eloquent of the lot. She pleaded humility. She had been overwhelmed by an experience too great for mere words, she could never do it justice. He never forgave her, a major rift set in.

So she returned with an unbiased and uninformed companion, me. Maybe she swept in there daily. Anyway, whether on the sixth or the second viewing, her only comment was on the dandelion fluff. We walked back to the hotel.

"Dr. Sitwell," the receptionist was well trained. "Sir Osbert has just returned."

I was graciously dismissed.

"Oh, my dear, I've battened on you, taken up your whole day, but really, I don't what I would have done."

A pleasure, I assured her, an *honor*.

Dame Edith, Dame of the British Empire—with that ultimate accolade, the Doctor business went right out the window. It's now twenty-five years since her death, twenty since Osbert's. And quite recently, Sashie died at the age of ninety.

The year 2000 is no longer an abstraction out of science fiction. I hope I live to see it. Not for the date, per se, nor the new century, which will be as awful and marvellous as all the others, but I do want to read those love letters. Will they be the sensation of that new year, or will they be published quietly by some university press and soon forgotten? I ponder literary immortality. Many people have never even heard of the Sitwells. I remember their unremitting dedication, their high standards. I look at the long row of books on my shelf. Surely it must all count for something.

1992

WALLACE STEVENS

by ROBERT HASS

from THE THREEPENNY REVIEW

MY NINETEENTH birthday was also the birthday of one of my college friends. I went to an early class in logic that morning. I think we were reading Aristotle's *Posterior Analytics*, because when I got back to my room a group of my friends was there with several bottles of champagne and I remember that inthe ensuing hilarity there was much speculation about the comic possibilities in the title of that treatise. My friend Tom had been to a class (it was a Catholic men's college, St. Mary's) which somehow involved the Latin names for various illicit sexual positions—*coitus reservatus, coitus interruptus, coitus inter femores,* and so on—and this was also the source of a lot of buffoonery that blent nicely into the subject of posterior analytics, and at some point in the proceedings one of the more advanced of us got out the volume of Wallace Stevens' *Collected Poems* in its handsome soft blue dust jacket and read "The Emperor of Ice Cream." I had never heard the poem before and it seemed to me supremely pleasing. It was March in California, high spring, the hills still green, with grazing cattle in them, plum trees in blossom, the olive trees around the campus whitening whenever a breeze shook them, and at some point a group of us were marching through the field full of mustard flowers and wild radish in the back of the dormitory, banging on pans with spoons and strumming tennis rackets and chanting out the poem, or at least the first stanza of it which I find now is what I still have in memory:

Call the roller of big cigars,
The muscular one, and bid him whip
In kitchen cups concupiscent curds.
Let the wenches dawdle in such dress
As they are used to wear, and let the boys
Bring flowers in last month's newspapers.
Let be be the finale of seem.
The only emperor is the emperor of ice cream.

It is probably significant that I don't have the second stanza by heart. I don't know if I took in the fact that the poem was a proposition about behavior at a funeral. If I did, it could only have seemed to me that morning and afternoon immensely droll. I was a sophomore. I read it as a sophomore poem. The year before in my freshman year—I make this confession publicly—I had taped above my desk along with other immortal lines a little poem by Edna St. Vincent Millay that went something like this:

My candle burns at both its ends.
It will not last the night.
But ah my foes and oh my friends,
It gives a proper light.

I had by the following year understood that it was deeply uncool to have lines of Millay adorning one's room, and had replaced them with something appropriately gloomy by Jean-Paul Sartre, but at that time I took the Stevens line in more or less the same spirit as Millay's, as permission to have fun, to live in the spirit of comedy. I see now that they were in fact probably written out of the same anti-Victorian spirit in the 1920s; they may even have been written in the same year. And Stevens' poem is more or less permanently associated for me with that bibulous and raucous first experience of it. I don't remember for sure what if anything I knew about Wallace Stevens except that he was a modern poet.

I want to come back to "The Emperor of Ice Cream," but let me say a word about coming across a couple of other Stevens poems which complicated my understanding of it. In the fall after the spring I have been describing, a group of us—eight, I think—quadruple-dating—were on our way to dinner and a movie and couldn't decide where we wanted to go or what we wanted to see, and the driver, in a moment of inspiration, said, "Oh, the hell with it, let's go to Carmel and run on the beach." It was a three-hour drive then from Berkeley to Carmel. We stopped for sandwiches and wine, we had very little money, so there was no question of staying in a motel, which meant sleeping on the beach if we didn't drive back in the middle of the night; people had people to notify if they were going to stay out all night. One woman who had a father whom we all hated—an amazingly unpleasant man who actually made his living by running a lab that tested for venereal disease and who insisted on testing his daughters regularly—was quite worried, which made the rest of us feel appealingly reckless. I don't remember exactly who was there. The driver was a year ahead of me in school, famously smart, a philosophy major who at the end of his senior year read a French novel about Dien Bien Phu and, quoting Nietzsche on the true aristocrat, enlisted in a branch of the service I'd never heard of called Special Forces, where he claimed he would learn to parachute, ski cross-country, and fight bare-handed in jungles in places like Annam and Cochin China, which was now called Vietnam. His girlfriend was Philippine, extremely beautiful, the daughter of some kind of politician, we understood, and a French major. It was she who produced the white Vintage paperback volume of Wallace Stevens at some point in the drive and suggested that we take turns reading the stanzas of "Sea Surface Full of Clouds."

I was stunned by the poem. I am still stunned by the poem. After we had read around and gotten over the shock and novelty of the way the adjectives play over and transform the surface of the poem, and had read a few others, and other books were produced and other poems read, the conversation moved on, but I got my hands on Marie's Stevens, and after we had arrived in Carmel and got some more wine and watched the sun set over Carmel Bay in a light rain, I suggested we read the poem again, which we did—to humor me, I think, while the last light smoldered on the horizon. Then we tried to build a fire on the beach, but the rain turned into a lashing Pacific storm and we spent the night quite wet, eight of us crammed into the car in the parking lot, laughing a lot—it was very sexy, as I remember—and making jokes about cars and autoeroticism. I will start to feel like Kinebote, the lunatic annotator of other people's poems with incidents

311

from his own life in Nabokov's *Pale Fire,* if I tell you the story of the lives of each of the people in the car: Marie who returned to the Philippines and who I know had two children and whose spine was badly injured when she was struck by a car, Killpack who did go to Vietnam and then Army Intelligence toward the end of the war and after that seemed to disappear from sight, another friend who was a classics major and later managed a café and wrote poems and died of cancer a couple of years ago. But I will resist, except to say that the poem stays with me in the way that songs you fall in love to stay with you as a kind of figure for that time and those people, and their different lives will always feel to me as if they are playing out in time the way the adjectives of experience play over the adamant nouns in Stevens' poem: rosy chocolate and chophouse chocolate and musky chocolate, perplexed and tense and tranced machine.

And there was the incident of "The Snow Man." It was at a wedding at the end of my sophomore year, of a woman we all liked, large, placid, Irish, a drama major, and the daughter of the man who conducted the last big band in the last seedy, once glamorous dance hall in San Francisco in the 1950s, when dancing to Maury Monohan's orchestra was a city-wide trope for absurdly retro behavior. She was marrying a guy we only grudgingly liked—perhaps we were jealous—but we all showed up for the wedding. And at the reception in one of the rooms of a house that sat over a steep hillside cliff, one of my classmates announced that he was going to kill himself. I came onto this drama late and it's still not clear to me how it began, but when I came into the room, there was a small knot of people standing around one of my friends—his name was Zack and he was an acting student—who was standing by an open window. He looked wild-eyed and he was talking to his friend Tony, with whom I knew he had been in the Navy. They were inseparable friends and they cultivated a certain cool bleakness that was stylish then, so that someone of our group had called them the Laurel and Hardy of tragedy. At that moment it looked to me distinctly as if Tony was goading Zack. They had apparently been talking about "the void," the term for nothingness we all used, and Zack must have spoken of his despair, because Tony was telling him with pure scorn that he didn't feel despair because he didn't feel anything. He was always acting, always a fake, generating histrionics to make himself feel real, feel anything at all. Look, jump, if you want, Tony was saying, Who do you think cares? And you know, he said, you might just have to do it because you've talked yourself into it. It was at that point that Zack said, "I feel it." Hitting his stomach: "I feel it. You know the 'nothing that is not there and the nothing that is'? Well, this is the nothing that fucking is, baby." I thought later that there was something like sexual tension between them, and at that moment I thought that Zack really might jump and that Tony was clearly trying to cut off his avenues of escape, but the truth is I was so besotted with literature at the time that I remember mainly being impressed that someone could quote Wallace Stevens at a moment like that.

As it happened, Zack did not jump. The bride, Agnes, came into the room after Zack had climbed out the window and onto the balcony, and she began talking to him and then suggested we all leave, which we did, and after a while they came downstairs together and danced to her father's orchestra. If I were Nabokov, I could leave them dancing to "Have You Ever Seen a Dream Walking," which I have recently read was one of Wallace Stevens' favorite songs and was the kind of song Agnes' father was apt to play, but I'm not and I have some sense of shame. As for the nothing that is, I was soon enough in graduate school, where the discussion of the poem focused on whether or not it was in favor of a pathetic fallacy, which was another matter; and not long after that I had begun to read around in Buddhism and to see that there were other ways of thinking about the void and that what I loved in the cleanness of the writing of that poem might be connected to those other ways. And sometime in that period I came to see that "the nothing that was," was connected to the way the adjectives in "Sea Surface Full of Clouds" played over the nouns, the way that it seemed the quality of things, the accidents (as someone might say who had been dipped in Aristotle) but not their essence, could be known. And I suppose I must have connected that floating thought to the comedy of "The Emperor of Ice Cream," though I don't exactly remember doing so.

When I was an undergraduate, poetry was much more for me a matter of poems than of poets. But in graduate school I began to acquire some sense of Wallace Stevens. I was never very interested in the Keatsian side of his writing, the wedding cake ba-

313

roque of "The Comedian as the Letter C." What I loved in him was the clarity. I wasn't against the other so much as I just didn't take it in, and I certainly didn't understand the issues implicit in the two sides of his style. I knew a few poems, and almost as soon as I began to acquire an attitude toward Stevens, various things intervened to qualify my first hypnotic attraction to him. A couple of things that can stand for this change are the civil rights movement and my discovery in my senior year of the essays of James Baldwin, and through him the essays of Albert Camus, which began to awaken a different political and moral sense in me. And also the assassination of John Kennedy in 1963 and the ensuing escalation of the war in Vietnam. I was in a lecture course on poetry given by Yvor Winters when I heard the news of Kennedy's assassination; it was the fall of my first year of graduate study. By then I had some idea of who Stevens was and I had read Winters' essay which, though it's clear Winters thought Stevens was a great poet, nevertheless indicts him for a kind of trivial hedonism at the core of his thought. I was disposed to argue with every word Winters spoke, and I thought he was wrong about Stevens, but not entirely wrong. For different reasons from Winters', of course. The country we were growing up into—its racism, the violence it was unleashing in Asia, what seemed in those early years the absolute acquiescence of our elders in that violence—changed the tenor of my thinking about literature, and made Wallace Stevens seem much less attractive as a model.

Arguments about him raged in my group of friends. We knew by then that Stevens had been an executive of the Hartford Insurance Company, that he was making good money during the Depression, and lived well. One of my closest friends among the graduate students was Jiri Wyatt, and he was particularly skeptical of Stevens. Jiri had spent his early childhood hidden with his Jewish parents from the Nazis in the attic of a Slovakian farmhouse. He was much more politically sophisticated than the rest of us, and he was very funny and very bright. I remember specifically arguing with him. I was inclined to take Stevens' side. Jiri had gone to school in Boston. He could be scathing on the subject of what he called Harvard aestheticism, a new category to me, and enraged by the idea of a whole generation of English professors and graduate students fawning over the novels of Virginia Woolf and Henry James and poems of T. S. Eliot as a cover

314

for indulging in their fantasies of belonging to a social class that answered to their aesthetic refinement. "They're cripples," he'd say. "Laughable. I mean, my God, look at this century." At Tressider Union under the oak trees in the spring sun. The war was escalating rapidly. We were all listening to Bob Dylan and the Beatles. "But Stevens' subject," I'd argue, "is epistemology." And Jiri, I think it was Jiri, impatiently: "Oh, come on. At some point epistemology is a bourgeois defense against actually knowing anything."

We did know or had heard that Stevens had written a letter to a friend who was buying tea for him in Ceylon, in which he said that he didn't care what kind of tea he was sent, as long as it couldn't be had in the United States; and I took that story to be, classically, an emblem of our relation to South Asia, and thought that its attitude was connected to what I had learned from Winters and Jiri to think of as Stevens' Harvard aesthete 1910 dandyism—not morally repellent, especially because it was so unconscious and so much of its time, but unsatisfactory, not useful. I also knew (it was widely quoted among us) Stevens' reaction to Mussolini's invasion of Ethiopia: that, if the coons had taken it from the monkeys, the Italians might as well take it from the coons. That too seemed provincial blindness, but less forgivable. I also knew—or sensed, it hadn't quite happened yet—that Stevens was in the process of becoming what I think he was not then thought to be, one of the central modern poets.

It was in this context that I began to replay in my mind the lines from "The Emperor of Ice Cream." The first thing that struck me was its lordliness. Part of our pleasure in chanting it several years before had been its imperiousness. Call the roller of big cigars, no doubt a Cuban or a Puerto Rican, and set him to work in the kitchen, where, in some fantasy out of Henry James or Charles Laughton's *Henry VIII*, "wenches" were employed. In 1963 (my students now don't quite believe this), white men of the older generation in the United States still commonly called the black men who worked in airports handling luggage, "Boy." I listened again to the line that commanded "boys to bring flowers in last month's newspapers." And while I was at it, I noticed that "last month's newspapers" was a figure for history, one I feel the sweetness of now. Who cares about history? Let the boys use it to wrap flowers in when they come courting. But at the time—or

315

was it at that age? I was twenty-two; Stevens was forty-three, twice my age, when he wrote the poem—taking history seriously seemed a central task of poetry.

When I tried myself to write poems about history and politics, I had in mind writing a poem about the California landscape and the United States seizure of California after the Mexican-American War, and about the Dow Chemical plant in the southern part of San Francisco Bay that was manufacturing napalm for the Asian War. And I thought vaguely that I would focus that poem on the person of a woman, the daughter of the first harbor-master of Yerba Buena, as San Francisco was then called. Her fiancé had been murdered by Kit Carson in the skirmishes that occurred when the old Californian families resisted the United States expeditionary force. It was a way of writing about the violence in American history; and when I sat down to the poem—which is published in my first book, *Field Guide*, and is called "Palo Alto: The Marshes"—the first line I wrote was, "She dreamed along the beaches of this coast." It was a couple of days before it occurred to me that I had lifted and transposed the first line of "The Idea of Order at Key West," and when I did, I remembered that the name of the fiancé whom Kit Carson killed was Ramon, and it gave me a place for writing the poem. My consciousness of Stevens' poem fell away as I worked, but its starting point is an instance of how polemical my relation to him felt to me in those years. He felt to me as if he needed to be resisted, as if he were a luxury, like ice cream, that I couldn't indulge.

Years later, though, when I looked at "The Emperor of Ice Cream" again, I felt much more forgiving of the tone of the poem. I said to myself, this isn't Babbitt fantasizing himself a houseful of servants in Hartford, it is Prospero speaking, as I had read, to his daughter, and speaking in the subjunctive at that. But saying it one also had to say that in Shakespeare, and throughout English literature, royalty expressed as power over others is a central figure for the power of imagination. And somewhere in those years it occurred to me that the poem is about death, which I thought made it a more wonderful and darker joke than I had understood. And at some still later stage—I think it must have been after reading Helen Vendler on the use of subjunctive

316

in Stevens, but also after I had had enough experience of failure and disappointment in my own life to get it—I felt the pathos of the wishing in the poem and of the grammar that expresses it, so that by the time I was the age of Stevens when he wrote the poem, the three words "let be be. . ." struck me as a brilliant and sad figure for the fundamental human wish that seems so often impossible for us, and that Stevens had taken for one of his central themes.

And on another occasion—I can remember the shower in which the thought occurred to me, aquamarine tile, the house of a lover—thinking about what I then conceived to be the sadness of the poem, I was wondering about its fundamental gaiety and how it was achieved, and I thought about that delicious phrase that transforms itself from assonance into alliteration, "and bid him whip in kitchen cups concupiscent curds," and lets you know that, at least in language, magic can happen. It struck me suddenly that "bid him whip in kit/chen cups" contained the longest sequence (five in a row) of consecutively assonantal syllables I could think of in a poem. Toweling off, I must have been mumbling the lines to myself. "What are you thinking about," she said. She was wearing a pale, sea-green towel. "I was thinking: Bid him whip in kitchen cups concupiscent curds." "Concupiscent what?" she asked. "Curds," I said, looking her in the eye, trying out an imitation of W. C. Fields, "concupiscent curds."

As I was rereading the poem in the last few weeks, thinking about this essay, I made another discovery. I decided that the crucial thing about it in the end is the rhythm of the first six lines of the second stanza, that stanza I had neglected to take in twenty-five years ago when I was not interested in hearing about death:

> Take from the dresser of deal
> Lacking the three glass knobs, that sheet
> On which she embroidered fantails once
> And spread it so as to cover her face.
> If her horny feet protrude, they come
> To show how cold she is, and dumb.

This is as pitiless as any verse in Stevens, I think. That enjambment at the end of the fifth line and the stutter of a stop in the sixth deliver the last two syllables as baldly as anyone could contrive, and the rhyme—bum, bum—could not be more hollow. It is writing that returns the word "mordant" to its etymological root. And though I still think it is funny, it seems to me now to be, and to be intended to be, point-blank and very dark. And there are other things to notice. I think my disgust with the class-ridden drollery of the first stanza was not altogether misplaced, but it is certainly undercut by that shabby or melancholy or funny, in any case accurate, domestic touch—the glass knobs missing from the deal dresser. And there is a kind of *memento mori* in the peacock tail that had been—"once," he writes, to suggest the pathos of all our efforts at decor—embroidered on the sheet. And there is also something plain-dealing and very like Robert Frost in the diction: "so as to cover"; and if her horny feet protrude, "they come to show. . ." Every detail of the writing is meant to make this death as homely and actual as, what?, not Guatemala certainly. As any death in Emily Dickinson.

The second-to-last line of the poem—"Let the lamp affix its beam"—was for a while the only line in the poem that I thought was pure padding. He needed a rhyme for "cream" and a final flourish, hence a spotlight, hence "beam" and the otherwise meaningless lamp. But once you sense how dark, mordant, sardonic, pitiless a reading this poem can sustain, the lamp becomes an interesting figure for the focus of consciousness. It would seem that the beam is affixed on the stage where the final, now supremely ambiguous refrain is going to occur: "The only emperor. . ." One paraphrase might be: turn your attention to living, seize the day. If it says that, it also says: by all means turn your attention away from those horny toes. A sort of *memento non mori*. Or, to borrow a phrase from Eliot, human-kind cannot bear very much reality. It is also possible to read it to mean the opposite: that one should affix the beam on the horny toes, so that one understands from a clear look at the reality of death that there can be no emperor but ice cream, no real alternative to death but dessert while you can get it. Which is, I suppose, nearer to my first reading of the poem and to what Winters meant by Stevens' hedonism. I think the issue may be undecidable, finally, since both readings are grammatically permissible and both in their way in character. And perhaps the point lies in the poem's seeming poised on the knife edge between these two

318

attitudes. But however one reads these penultimate lines, they carry their darkness into the last line. Which makes for a very different poem from the one those college boys thought they were chanting thirty years ago as they waded through wet hillside grass in the early spring, and brings it nearer to the nothingness spoken of by Zack, whom I see now and then on late night TV playing a psychotic killer or a gaunt, hunted drug dealer in reruns of *Cagney and Lacey* or *Hill Street Blues*.

It may not be completely accidental that while I was puzzling over the ending of "The Emperor of Ice Cream," a photograph appeared in the newspaper of a pair of stolid Dutch workmen removing a statue of Mikhail Gorbachev (who was briefly and quite literally an emperor) from its stand and carrying it rigidly horizontal, immobilized in a gesture of seigneurial self-assurance, from Madame Tussaud's Wax Museum in Amsterdam. It made me think also that the poem, if it has anything to say about political power, does so by talking about politics and pleasure and death. And it may not be wrong, in its merciless way, about where power usually resides in the world.

I imagine I am not through thinking about this poem, or about "Sunday Morning" or "The Snow Man" or "Thirteen Ways of Looking at a Blackbird" or "The Idea of Order at Key West" or "Of Mere Being" or "The World as Meditation," which are other poems I have been brooding over and arguing with myself about for much of my adult life. But I heard it early and I've lived with it for some time, and I thought that it would serve for one image of the way poems happen in your life when they are lived with, rather than systematically studied. Which I understand is how Stevens, though he was certainly not against the systematic study of anything, thought poetry mainly lived.

1993

HOMAGE TO THE RUNNER: BLOODY BRAIN WORK

by MARVIN BELL

from AMERICAN POETRY REVIEW

WRITING POETRY is a way of life, not a career.

Ray Mullen, potter and painter, on his retirement from teaching: "No matter what you make, you can't buy a day of your life."

Word comes from eastern Long Island that another of my favorite former teachers has died.

Mike, and Mike's brother, Perry, whose card identifies him as "the P-Man," have come to haul away some bedsprings, the heavy bank teller's machine that Jason and friends pushed up the driveway into the carport a decade ago, and some metal storage shelves from Sears that were our first bookcases. Perry spots my wooden wagon and wants to buy it to fix it up. The sides are missing, but ok. Dorothy tells him the story of how I got the wagon, how I fell as a small child and split open my head and had to go to the doctor for stitches and how after that I wouldn't get a haircut because all I knew is that someone in a white coat wanted to do something to my head. So my father gave Johnny-the-Barber a red wagon with which to tempt me on my way home from school. Dorothy tells Perry the story in the hope that the story will go with the wagon, and of course she's right: material things are not a life but evidence of a life.

And Mike's brother says, "Every kid ought to have a wagon that has a story attached to it. When I was a kid, I had a disease that was dissolving my hip joint. I had to be in a body cast for thirteen months. So my father bought me a little metal wagon and my sister used to pull me around the trailer park. One day we got too wild and I fell out and broke the body cast, so they had to take me back to the hospital and I had to have it done all over again."

Mike will have to come back to take away my radio equipment, from the days when I was W2IDK. Amateur radio was a way of life, not a career. This was before transistors replaced tubes and technology made single sideband sound normal. Before that, a voice on single sideband (which takes half as much room on the dial as a normal modulated voice signal), sounded like Donald Duck. On Field Day, we'd put up tents, string antennas and mount beams, fix up places to sleep and to cook, start up the generators and stay on the air for two days to test our ability in emergencies. "Hams" were strange people then, oddballs who knew something and who shared their information generously but who didn't care if others heard about them or not. The "shack" (an attic) where I first heard the mysteries of short wave and code belonged to W2EBT. "Two Eggs, Bacon & Toast," he called himself, and "Elderly, Bald & Toothless." The shack in the woods where I built my first transmitter, a twenty-watt piezoelectric crystal-controlled oscillator, and power supply belonged to the reclusive W2OQI ("Two Ossified Queer Indians"), who showed me how, and I caught a ride to radio club meetings with W2FCH (Herbert Snell, who called himself "Two Females Chasing Herbie").

Now I sometimes wander out to the cliffs at Fort Worden, outside Port Townsend, Washington, where in June the local hams still set up for Field Day. But now they use TV and fax machines, their transmitters are tiny, their beam antennas don't have to go up on trees to fall over, and they eat and sleep in campers and trailers. When Mike wants to, he can take away my Lysco 600-watt transmitter, my HQ129X receiver, which came from the radio room of a Coast Guard boat, my Vibroflex key with its repeating dot mechanism, and the rest of it. I see the c.w. operators at Field Day using their monokeys, which have repeating dot and dash mechanisms both, with the result that their "fists" have no personalities. I learned plenty from my time as a ham radio operator, but I'm glad I didn't stay to be overcome by technical gee-whiz and the comforts of home.

And Mike can take away my photo enlarger and the rest of the darkroom equipment. Those were great days, the days of Aaron Siskind and Harry Callahan and Ansel Adams and Robert Heinecken and Nathan Lyons and Walter Chappell and Henry Holmes Smith and Van Deren Coke and the young Jerry Uelsmann and Clarence John Laughlin and Art Sinsabaugh and Minor White and a whole generation of hot young photographers gathered around Minor at the Rochester Institute of Technology and around Siskind and Callahan at the Institute of Design in Chicago. I met some of these photographers while attending Alfred University, and others when I lived in Syracuse and Rochester and still others when I lived in Chicago. This, too, was a community, and creative photography was a way of life, not a career. Nowadays photography is taught in most art departments. For a while, even after I stopped photographing, I'd be asked to visit photography classes. But the students wanted to talk about photography, while I thought we should talk about pictures, and then when they put up their pictures most of the things they hung were related to photographs as rendering is to drawing. These weren't art, they were technique. These weren't compositions, they were symbolic records. The students would resist whenever I suggested they put aside their 35-mm. direct viewfinder cameras and start using cameras with ground glass viewfinders so that they could learn about light and composition. They took photographs that were literary illustrations. They were earnest students on a career track, and they didn't, wouldn't, and couldn't understand. There continued to be many good photographer-artists at work in this country, but their images soon floated in a sea of images while viewers paused only for the sensationalistic.

As for my own photos, I let them go to seed. I was all set to print a portfolio of nudes—pieces of the body sculpted by light—for Margaret Randall's bilingual magazine out of Mexico, *El Corno Emplumado*, when I stopped photographing and printing. I had learned to see as a photographer, which was of more moment to me than producing pictures to frame. It was a way of life, not a career. All that remains on our walls from that time are three images I made without the camera by printing paper "negatives" torn from the funnies: both sides of the page can be seen along with the dots (holes) in the screens then used to print newspaper graphics.

I haven't yet decided if I'm going to give away my cornet and trumpet. The cornet is a Bach handmade job, built before the Bach factory sold out to Conn, a horn which used to belong to Ned Mahoney, who sat second chair to James Burke, the virtuoso soloist with the Edwin Franko Goldman Band. Many a time my friend Roger and I sat in the front row at the Goldman Band concerts in New York City's Central Park with the score to that night's solo spread out on our laps. And the trumpet is an Olds Mendez with two triggers (to flatten the normally sharp tones when the first or third valves are pressed, though one can do this by lip). I used that horn to play Jeremiah Clarke's "Trumpet Voluntary" with Dan Clayton in black robes from the pulpit on Easter. Music was my introduction to artists and nighthawks. I don't think I have ever lost the feeling that late hours and creative expression go together. (I began this essay after midnight. It is now 3:30 a.m. What time will I quit to sleep?—About 6 a.m.) We horn players were a community. We tried to make money, but there wasn't much to be made, so it had to be a way of life for most of us, not a career. Yes, my music teacher hoped I'd go to music school, but the idea was to become a teacher. The idea then was always first to earn a living and then to take private time for art.

I've seen Carl Fracassini recently, in New Mexico where he is retired. Frac was my pottery and drawing teacher, and he doesn't expect to live much longer. He asked me to pick some of his drawings to take home. He was a great teacher and a wonderful artist who lacked the pretensions of his colleagues—he preferred to cook and build and hunt and fish and make pots and drawings and create a community among his students—and so he never received the full measure of respect he deserved at the university. No matter to those of us who learned quality and community from him. Mike won't have to take away any pots. Except for a couple that Dorothy rescued, I broke them all when I gave up potting.

I visit a sophomore "core literature" class to observe one of my advisees. The teacher does her job well, and the class is alert, but these are students from "ordinary" backgrounds like mine— not the children of professionals but of workers and small business owners, probably raised largely without the benefits of special classes, private schools, foreign travel, or substantial home libraries. They lack the courage to be articulate, so they speak in an all-purpose colloquial flow designed to show how well they fit in rather than how they stand out: plenty of "you know's" and "I mean's" and "kind of's," lots of "like's" but no "as if's," all of their speech having a general quality of imprecision that nonetheless communicates what they wish to express so long as things remain simple. They seem to understand what they mean, but they never quite say it. Ultimately, as with imprecision in poetry, when the conversation grows more complex, they will be able to say neither what they understand nor what they do not understand. Most of the time, however, it won't make any difference.

In the poetry seminar, we have been reading Bishop and O'Hara, with Dugan and Jarrell on tap. Bishop comes up first. What a pleasure to read poetry bearing such precise powers of observation, such precision of language, and such careful and effective rhetorical emphasis, with the courage of open-faced and even-handed syntax, the courage of accessibility, the courage not to overwrite, the courage to have a viewpoint without faking a vision. The whole group feels it. This is one of those seminars in which, if the members of the class want to absorb new influences, I'm game. Bell's rules: (1) No one has to write a "good" poem; and (2) Teacher has to do the assignment too. The first time, we write poems after the fashion of Bishop or O'Hara. In fact, we write our own poems but under the flag of surrender to some aspect of another's poem. In a later meeting, I hand out a few poems by Neruda from an early book, *Residence on Earth*. Let's see if we can combine Bishop's reticence and observation with Neruda's abandon, Bishop's vertical thrust with Neruda's horizontal speed. What I don't say is that it doesn't matter whether or not one can actually do it, but only that the assigned influences and the deadline take the writer away from his or her self-absorption and self-importance, including *a priori* themes and agendas. Also, that the students give themselves permission to fail. And that they learn, eventually, the value of the arbitrary when it receives sufficient attention—but that is more complicated than needs be said.

A little Neruda goes a long way. I make a crack to the effect that our lives are filled with passion and physical detail, while in American poetry hysteria and anxiety often pass for passion, and filler takes the place of observation. I think to myself, but don't say aloud, that we have a band of poetry critics whose own prose styles naturally lead them to prefer overwriting of all kinds, which they may perhaps think is a signal of literary ambition.

During the core literature class, I wrote down, "Literature is for beginners." I was thinking about thinking. Because, for the poet, after all, poetry is the result, not the intention. Poetry is the residue of bloody brain work, the signal that a process has taken place that creates an emotional approach to thinking. All technique is subsumed in what we later call the "poetic" quality of the text. All the fame in the world is secondary to the epiphanic moment when the poem began to cohere. For the poet, the true consequence is the next poem: hence, a way of life, not a career.

Deby Groover, a potter and printmaker from Athens, Georgia, tells me over coffee that her first pottery teacher said to the class, "If you have any attachment to anything you make, then you better go ahead and break it now."

I don't have any heavy poetry equipment for Mike to haul away. I do plan to sell my papers and many of my books soon. I need to clear some space. Poetry has accumulated around me. I didn't set out to teach where I teach. I set out to earn a living, figuring I could write no matter what. I had a wonderful son at an early age and, when the marriage ended, I kept him with me. I had to make a living. I wouldn't have had it any other way. Still, when I was asked to return to the Writers' Workshop, I hesitated before saying yes. It was still a community then, a smaller community, finding its direction inside the community. Today, like other writing programs, it's heavy on visitors and events, with a decided emphasis on official reputations, and it thus takes its instructions from outside. Like other universities, mine now constantly measures its standing and judges its faculty in ways that

325

damage the community. In this dog-eat-dog economy, education, too, has become more of a career than a way of life.

My seminar students had dropped off but one poem to be xeroxed for class. I had mine: that made two. I was downhearted: hadn't they been able to become selfless enough, to improvise, to swing, to play, to relax, to get down, couldn't those who were wearing the emperor's new clothing shed it to believe in the referential possibilities of words, hadn't they seen the lesson of Bishop's poems and O'Hara's and Neruda's, absent the fawning criticism and the literary fighting for position that follows them, hadn't they understood that those three poets were finally just like them?

And then they came to class, which is held at our home, and Dorothy put out things to eat and drink, and we let some Tom Waits play as we gathered, and they had all written their poems after all and xeroxed them in time, and the freshness of their words and the emotional weight of their pretend-abandon made our group of poems written to deadline a better worksheet than they could expect in any of the sections of the graduate poetry workshop where their more "important" and "original" poems were to be discussed—the ones they made up from ambition and order and fancy talk—and some of them were saying that they were planning to put these poems on the worksheets for the other classes, and we said ok, next week it's all O'Hara and the week after that it will be all Bishop and then it will be Dugan, and once again the world was all right if it could provide this sort of opportunity for community and thought and high spirits with writing at the core.

Poetry is a way of life, not a career. A career means you solicit the powerful and the famous. A way of life means you live where you are with the people around you. A career means you become an authority. A way of life means you stay a student, even if you teach for a living. A career means your life increasingly comes from your art. A way of life means your art continues to arise from your life. Careerism feeds off of the theoretical, the fancified, the complicated, the coded, and the overwrought: all forms of psychological cowardice. A way of life is nourished by the practical, the unadorned, the complex, and a direct approach to the mysterious. Obscurity is a celebrated path to nowhere, an affliction. For poetry to be a way of life in a referential world, it requires of us the courage of clarity—linear, syntactical and referential—which in no way compromises the great wildness of experience and imagination (think of Bishop, O'Hara, Neruda, Dugan, Jarrell . . .). The rewards for this courage and this surrender to influence (a form of community) and clarity are beyond career.

Which are you pursuing: a way of life or a career? The scent of literary careerism has never been stronger. Conversely, the need for each of us to find a way of life—to quote a Dugan poem, "personal life wrung from mass issues in a bloody time and lived out hiddenly"—has never been of more moment.

To most of my current and past students, thank you, wherever you are. To W2EBT and W2OQI and W2FCH, to my dead teachers and friends, to the last few who remember how it was in the arts, to those who still practice in secret or solitude, to Robert Heinecken on his impending retirement, to the sound of Miles Davis playing standards through a straight mute, to all those in my life with pizazz and humility whose lingo had the snap of reality and the metabolic shiver of deep feeling and who did not judge and compete but laughed a lot—my mortal indebtedness.

1993

A THOUSAND BUDDHAS

by BRENDA MILLER

from THE GEORGIA REVIEW

My hand's the universe,
it can do anything. —Shinkichi Takahashi

I

I HAVE NEVER been touched by someone blind, but I can imagine what it would be like. She would read me like Braille, her fingertips hovering on the raised points of my flesh, then peel back the sheets of my skin, lay one finger on my quivering heart. We could beat like that, two hummingbirds, and become very still. Her hands might move across my abdomen, flick the scar below my belly button. My eyelids would flutter at her touch, and my skin dissolve into hot streams of tears.

I have never been touched by a blind person, but I have given whole massages with my eyes halfway closed, and the bodies I touched became something else. Their boundaries disappeared, and they spread out on the table—masses of flesh, all the borders gone. I touched them in tender places: between the toes, under the cheekbones, along the high-arching curves of their feet. When I opened my eyes they coalesced into something human, but I walked outside and slipped into the pool, feeling like a primordial fish, all my substance gone. I'd see them afterward, and they leaned toward me, their mouths open, but they hardly spoke. My arms opened and they fell against me; I held my hands on the middle of their backs, holding their hearts in place.

Sometimes they cried. I was too professional, then, to cry, knew that I had to keep some distance in order to make this re-

328

lationship work. If I had cried, then we might have been lovers, and that would make it wrong somehow when they handed me the check for thirty dollars. Sometimes they pressed the payment into my hands and looked away, and said *I can't even tell you.* I nudged them in the direction of the baths, and they went like obedient children, their naked bodies swaying under their towels as they shuffled across the old, wooden bridge.

II

I have a picture from that time—of myself in the hot tub at Orr Hot Springs. At least, some people claim it is me, pointing out the slope of my breasts, the flare of my hips, the unique circumference of my thighs. Positive identification is impossible since the woman in the picture cradles her face in her hands.

Light streams through a low doorway into the gazebo, and this young woman leans her back against the deck. The sunlight zeroes into a circle on her belly. Jasmine bush and bamboo are reflected in the glass. The woman bends her head and covers her eyes as if she were about to weep. Steam rises and beads on the glass, obscuring detail and memory.

The woman is not weeping. She is scooping up the water from the tub and splashing it to her face. If this woman is me, she is mumbling some kind of grateful prayer, alchemizing the water into a potion that will heal.

It's easy to know what we're doing, once we're not doing it anymore.

III

Before I lived at Orr Hot Springs, I spent a summer baking bread for fifty children on a farm outside Willits. I didn't know I was in practice for becoming a massage therapist, but I knew I mended wounds buried deep inside me as I handled the huge mounds of dough. ("Talking things out" carves paths around and in-between the issues, but the body knows things the mind could never face.) The repetitive motions of grasping and pushing, the bend of my waist, the slow ache in my shoulder—before long, I became automatic and blank. I kept my hands covered in flour and thought continually of food, of what is nourishing. I dreamed of my mouth always open and filled.

Children clustered around me, tugged at my apron, took little balls of dough and rolled them lightly between their teeth. The bread rose and came out of the oven, broke into tender crumbs, tasted good. I watched the children and gave them small lumps of dough to press. I touched their miniature shoulders and smiled, but I said very little. At the midsummer dance, they braided flowers into my hair and held my hands, as if I were an old person convalescing from a long, wasting illness.

IV

Today I look at my hands. I remember the bodies I've touched, the lives that came through them. Sometimes I trace the edges of my fingers, as children in kindergarten do on newsprint with green tempera paint. Hands become what they have held; our hands shape themselves around what they hold most dear, or what has made an impression, or what we press on others.

My friend Dana once grabbed my hand off the stick shift as I drove through L.A. "These," he said running a fingertip around my palm, "are healing hands."

I drove with my left hand on the wheel, while he examined every finger of my right. I swerved to avoid a dog.

"They're like a sculptor's hands," he said dreamily, dropping my hand and gripping his own.

Dana is a sculptor with a propensity for twisted nude forms, estranged limbs, fingers in a bowl. Once, before he left for Peru, he painted all his walls, the appliances, even his books, a startling white: a "blank canvas," he said, for his friends to spill upon. And we did, troweling up purples and reds, oranges and blues, a cacophony of personalities rolling across his walls.

I pressed my hands in blue paint and hand-walked an awkward bridge along the wall above his couch.

V

What follows may, or may not, be true:
"It's been too long," the man said.

330

My old lover Jon stepped inside, closed the door, and settled himself carefully on the edge of my massage table. "I just came to soak in the baths, decided to get a massage on the spur of the moment," he said. "I didn't know it was you."

We stared at each other. I don't know what he saw in my face—a barrier, perhaps, a careful retreat—but in his face I saw a deep sorrow. My eyes involuntarily shifted into professional gear, scanning his body and making notes: a slump in the left shoulder, a grim tightness in the left arm and fist, chest slightly concave, breathing shallow.

In massage school, before we were lovers, Jon and I had been partners. The teacher insisted on partner rotation, but somehow Jon and I ended up together more times than not. We learned well on each other. We breathed freely; we allowed each other's hands to cup the muscles and slide, so slowly, down the length of connecting fibers and tissue; we allowed thumbs to probe deep into unyielding spots. It was like a dance—the way our teacher said it always should be: an effortless give and take, back and forth, with the breath as well as the body. Communication—transcendent and absolute.

"Listen," Jon was saying. "I understand if you don't want to do this." His body leaned toward me, and my spine tipped forward in response. A massage room is a very close environment. Intimacy is immediate; truth prevails.

I glanced away and gazed at the far wall, at the painting called *A Thousand Buddhas* he had given me as a graduation present. For the last year, I had looked at that picture every day, and every day it reminded me of Jon less and less. A process of pain, moving ahead on its own momentum. The primary Buddha sat in the center, immovable, surrounded by a helix of buddhas that spun around and around.

My palms relaxed—a good sign. "It might be awkward," I said, "but I'll try." I took a deep breath, and whatever had been prickling at my throat subsided.

What did my body feel when I placed my hands on Jon's back? My palms curved instinctively to the crook of his shoulders; my own shoulders softened when I asked Jon to breathe, and I inhaled with him, stretching my lungs, and on the exhale my hands slid down his back, kneading the muscles on the downward slide, pulling up along the lats, crossing over his spine, and again and again, until he seemed to flatten and there was no distinction between the flesh of his back or the bones in his arms or the curve of his buttocks—no distinction, in fact, between his breath and mine. I felt a small opening in my heart, a valve releasing, and an old love—a love aged and smooth as wine—flowed down my arms and sparked on Jon's skin. I knew, then, that sometime in the night I would remember this gushing, and I would be shattered by a sense of tremendous loss, a grasping ache in my palms, and I would cry, but even this certainty could not stop my hands in their circular route through Jon's familiar and beautiful body. He inhaled and began to sob. The tears shuddered through his back, his arms, his legs, and I felt them empty from him in one bountiful wave. My right hand floated to rest on his sacrum. My left hand brushed the air above his head in long, sweeping arcs.

There is a powder that covers the heart, a sifting of particles fine as talc. It is protection—gauzy and insubstantial, but protection nonetheless. Occasionally, a hand rubs against you and wipes a patch clear. That's when the heart bulges, beating with a raw and healthy ferocity.

VI

I keep another picture hidden in a drawer: me before I moved to Orr Springs—before I even knew such places existed. I am young, young, young.

I am standing barefoot on the porch of a cabin within Prairie Creek State Park on the north coast of California. It is late summer. I am wearing a purple tank top, tight Levis, and a forest ranger's hat. The morning sun is full in my face, and I am smiling a goofy, lopsided grin, my hands at my sides, my feet planted solidly on the wooden planks.

·I am pregnant—about three weeks along—and the embryo is curled tightly in a fallopian tube. The pregnancy will end one week later in a long, terrifying miscarriage, but in the picture I do not know this. I don't even know I am pregnant. I am twenty-one years old and healthy from a long summer in Wyoming. It is a beautiful morning, and I am happy to be back in California. My world has not yet shifted to include the indifferent hands of nurses, the blind lights of an operating dome, the smell of bandages steeped in antiseptics and blood.

If you look carefully at the belly for some sign of the child, at the face for some indication of motherhood, there is none. The snapshot is flat and ordinary: a young woman on vacation, nothing more. But I look at this photo and sense a swelling in my pelvis, a fullness in my breasts. I feel my skin inviolate and smooth, the substance of everything I've lost and meant to regain.

VII

Someone called them midwife's hands. A midwife's hands cradle and protect, hold a life between them. Recall the classic posture for the hands in photographs: one hand cupped under the baby's emerging head, the other lightly curled on the baby's crown.

There is a polarity position like this: at the client's head, cradling, not pulling but imparting the sense of emergence just the same. If you stay long enough—motionless, breathing little sips out of the air—the head appears to become larger, grows and trembles. The eyelids flutter. Sometimes I have touched the top of my head to the top of my client's head, and we were plugged in; we took deep breaths, heaved long important signs.

VIII

Sean was born. Not from my body. From Rhea's. I held the mirror at an angle so she could see the crown of his head as it split her body in two.

The midwife placed one hand on the skull and rotated it so the face pointed toward heaven. The eyes were open, glazed with an unearthly shine.

Rhea screamed. The world paused and listened. The body followed, sheathed in cream and wax.

IX

What does the body contain? And how do the hands release it? In the late seventies, "hug clinics" opened on college campuses

333

in California. Distraught people were invited to drop in if they needed to be secured for a moment by a pair of strong, encircling arms.

One of the most powerful massage holds I've used has the client on his side, curled into a fetal position. I cupped one hand to the base of the spine, laid the other on the back between the shoulder blades. These are the two places our mother's hands fell when holding us as babies.

Some people cried with little shoulder-shaking sobs. Others fell promptly asleep. Most of them believed my hands were still on them long after I'd walk away.

X

In the hospital, the nurse stuck an IV needle into the back of my hand, over and over. I squinted and clenched my teeth.

"Does that hurt?" the nurse said, looking up, scowling.

I nodded.

"It's not supposed to hurt," she said, setting the needle aside and trying again.

When she was done, I lay on top of the covers, shivering, my eyes halfway closed, my palm flat on the bed. The IV fluid ticked into my blood. Already, I could feel myself forgetting everything.

My body was a container of pain. And then it contained nothing—an absence so absolute I couldn't even cry.

XI

The hand is shaped to touch the different parts of the world. We hurt, and the hand reaches to the chest. A newborn's head fits snugly into the center of a palm. Fertile soil runs through our fingers, or we mold our hands into a cup sealed for a drink of water. We can use our hands like primeval jaws to pluck whatever is ripe.

The midwife had fingers so long I almost asked her if she played the piano. The words were nearly out of my mouth, but then she handed Sean to me, and I forgot about pianos, about that kind of music.

334

I held him while the midwife and Rhea struggled with the afterbirth. I held him against my shoulder. His eyes were open; he blinked slowly and rarely, like a baby owl. The light in the room was gold, the color of honey. I thought I saw something in his eyes, but I can't be sure. I thought I saw a nod of acceptance, a little man bowing to me, his hands pressed together in an attitude of prayer.

XII

They came to me hot and pink from the baths, most of my work already done. They came naked and slick and gorgeous.

What did I give them? Nothing but myself—and not even that, but rather the benefit of my whole attention, the focus of my hands on them, the focus of my heart. I don't know how long the change lasted. They left the room and lingered in the baths, got out, got dressed, and drove home. I waved goodbye and walked up the steps to my cabin, looked out my window to the luscious woods, and thought about these people more than I probably should have. When the time approached for me to leave Orr Springs, I thought about them with a frantic longing for a life that could be balanced and whole.

I wanted to massage myself before I left. I wanted to send myself off with a stroke of my fingers and a hand along my spine: an affirmation for abundance, a momentary release from every memory that weighed me down. I thought it might help, if only for the drive out on the rutted and dusty road.

XIII

Years after I left Orr Springs, I worked for the Human Resource Council in Missoula, Montana. I didn't massage people anymore. I tried, but I zipped through the parts of the body as if I were taking inventory. I chattered like a barber giving a haircut. I thought about dinner, gas mileage, bills to be paid.

In my job, I interviewed clients and determined their eligibility for a heating-assistance program. Many of the people I saw were elderly and disabled; all of them had stories to tell, stories that could take a lifetime. I had only twenty minutes to spend with each one. I found that when I gave them my whole and complete attention for even five minutes, that was enough. I looked them in the eyes and smiled, laughed with them, murmured consolations. They looked back and told me what they knew. My hands kept very still on my desk.

One seventy-six-year-old woman spoke to me in short, disjointed sentences, her head nodding emphatically with each word, spittle forming at the corners of her mouth. She smelled of cigarettes and bitter lemons. As I walked her to the door of my office, she swirled about and grabbed me around the waist. She was only as tall as my chest, and I settled my arms onto her shoulders. We stood like that for a few seconds under the fluorescent lights, the computers humming around us. Then I slid one hand down her back and held her there; my hand quivered, near as it was to her old and fragile heart.

XIV

I'm lying on my massage table. It's for sale. I'm lying on it, and I feel utterly relaxed. My breath swirls through my body in a contented daze.

I'm lying on my back. I open my eyes, and I see my face. I see me leaning over the table. My right hand comes to rest on my womb; my left hand hovers over my throat.

Forgive Me. Those are the words that pass between us.

1994

SKUNK DREAMS

by LOUISE ERDRICH

from THE GEORGIA REVIEW

W<small>HEN</small> I was fourteen, I slept alone on a North Dakota football field under the cold stars on an early spring night. May is unpredictable in the Red River Valley, and I happened to hit a night when frost formed in the grass. A skunk trailed a plume of steam across the forty-yard line near moonrise. I tucked the top of my sleeping bag over my head and was just dozing off when the skunk walked onto me with simple authority.

Its ripe odor must have dissipated in the frozen earth of its winterlong hibernation, because it didn't smell all that bad, or perhaps it was just that I took shallow breaths in numb surprise. I felt him—her, whatever—pause on the side of my hip and turn around twice before evidently deciding I was a good place to sleep. At the back of my knees, on the quilting of my sleeping bag, it trod out a spot for itself and then, with a serene little groan, curled up and lay perfectly still. That made two of us. I was wildly awake, trying to forget the sharpness and number of skunk teeth, trying not to think of the high percentage of skunks with rabies, or the reason that on camping trips my father always kept a hatchet underneath his pillow.

Inside the bag, I felt as if I might smother. Carefully, making only the slightest of rustles, I drew the bag away from my face and took a deep breath of the night air, enriched with skunk, but clear and watery and cold. It wasn't so bad, and the skunk didn't stir at all, so I watched the moon—caught that night in an envelope of silk, a mist—pass over my sleeping field of teenage guts

337

and glory. The grass in spring that has lain beneath the snow harbors a sere dust both old and fresh. I smelled that newness beneath the rank tone of my bag-mate—the stiff fragrance of damp earth and the thick pungency of newly manured fields a mile or two away—along with my sleeping bag's smell, slightly mildewed, forever smoky. The skunk settled even closer and began to breathe rapidly; its feet jerked a little like a dog's. I sank against the earth, and fell asleep too.

Of what easily tipped cans, what molten sludge, what dogs in yards on chains, what leftover macaroni casseroles, what cellar holes, crawl spaces, burrows taken from meek woodchucks, of what miracles of garbage did my skunk dream? Or did it, since we can't be sure, dream the plot of *Moby-Dick,* how to properly age parmesan, or how to restore the brick-walled, tumbledown creamery that was its home? We don't know about the dreams of any other biota, and even much about our own. If dreams are an actual dimension, as some assert, then the usual rules of life by which we abide do not apply. In that place, skunks may certainly dream themselves into the vests of stockbrokers. Perhaps that night the skunk and I dreamed each other's thoughts or are still dreaming them. To paraphrase the problem of the Chinese sage, I may be a woman who has dreamed herself a skunk, or a skunk still dreaming that she is a woman.

In a book called *Death and Consciousness,* David H. Lund—who wants very much to believe in life after death—describes human dream-life as a possible model for a disembodied existence:

> Many of one's dreams are such that they involve the activities of an apparently embodied person whom one takes to be oneself as long as one dreams. . . . Whatever is the source of the imagery . . . apparently has the capacity to bring about images of a human body and to impart the feeling that the body is mine. It is, of course, just an image body, but it serves as a perfectly good body for the dream experience. I regard it as mine, I act on the dream environment by means of it, and it constitutes the center of the perceptual world of my dream.

Over the years I have acquired and reshuffled my beliefs and doubts about whether we live on after death—in any shape or form, that is, besides the molecular level at which I am to be absorbed by the taproots of cemetery pines and the tangled mats of fearfully poisoned, too-green lawn grass. I want something of the self on whom I have worked so hard to survive the loss of the body (which, incidentally, the self has done a fairly decent job of looking after, excepting spells of too much cabernet and a few idiotic years of rolling my own cigarettes out of Virginia Blond tobacco). I am put out with the marvelous discoveries of the intricate biochemical configuration of our brains, though I realize that the processes themselves are quite miraculous. I understand that I should be self-proud, content to gee-whiz at the fact that I am the world's only mechanism that can admire itself. I should be grateful that life is here today, though gone tomorrow, but I can't help it. I want more.

Skunks don't mind each other's vile perfume. Obviously, they find each other more than tolerable. And even I, who have been in the presence of a direct skunk hit, wouldn't classify their weapon as mere smell. It is more on the order of a reality-enhancing experience. It's not so pleasant as standing in a grove of old-growth red cedars, or on a lyrical moonshed plain, or watching trout rise to the shadow of your hand on the placid surface of an Alpine lake. When the skunk lets go, you're surrounded by skunk presence: inhabited, owned, involved with something you can only describe as powerfully *there*.

I woke at dawn, stunned into that sprayed state of being. The dog that had approached me was rolling in the grass, half-addled, sprayed too. The skunk was gone. I abandoned my sleeping bag and started home. Up Eighth Street, past the tiny blue and pink houses, past my grade school, past all the addresses where I had baby-sat, I walked in my own strange wind. The streets were wide and empty; I met no one—not a dog, not a squirrel, not even an early robin. Perhaps they had all scattered before me, blocks away. I had gone out to sleep on the football field because I was afflicted with a sadness I had to dramatize. Mood swings had begun, hormones, feverish and brutal. They were nothing to me now. My emotions had seemed vast, dark, and sickeningly private. But they were minor, mere wisps, compared to skunk.

I have found that my best dreams come to me in cheap motels. One such dream about an especially haunting place occurred in a rattling room in Valley City, North Dakota. There, in the home of the Winter Show, in the Rudolph Hotel I was to spend a week-long residency as a poet-in-the-schools. I was supporting myself, at the time, by teaching poetry to children, convicts, rehabilitation patients, high-school hoods, and recovering alcoholics. What a marvelous job it was, and what opportunities I had to dream, since I paid my own lodging and lived low, sometimes taking rooms for less than ten dollars a night in motels that had already been closed by local health departments.

The images that assailed me in Valley City came about because the bedspread was so thin and worn—a mere brown tissuey curtain—that I had to sleep beneath my faux fur Salvation Army coat, wearing all of my clothing, even a scarf. Cold often brings on the most spectacular of my dreams, as if my brain has been incited to fevered activity. On that particular frigid fall night, the cold somehow seemed to snap boundaries, shift my time continuum, and perhaps even allow me to visit my own life in a future moment. After waking once, transferring the contents of my entire suitcase onto my person, and shivering to sleep again, I dreamed of a vast, dark, fenced place. The fencing was chain-link in places, chicken wire, sagging X wire, barbed wire on top, jerry-built with tipped-out poles and uncertain corners nailed to log posts and growing trees. And yet it was quite impermeable and solid, as time-tested, broken-looking things so often are.

Behind it, trees ran for miles—large trees, grown trees, big pines the likes of which do not exist in the Great Plains. In my dream I walked up to the fence, looked within, and saw tawny, humpbacked elk move among the great trunks and slashing green arms. Suave, imponderable, magnificently dumb, they lurched and floated through the dim-complexioned air. One turned, how-ever, before they all vanished, and from either side of that flimsy-looking barrier there passed between us a look, a communion, a long and measureless regard that left me, on waking, with a sen-sation of penetrating sorrow.

I didn't think about my dream for many years, until after I moved to New Hampshire. I had become urbanized and seden-tary since the days when I slept with skunks, and I had turned inward. For several years I spent my days leaning above a strange desk, a green door on stilts, which was so high that to sit at it I

340

bought a barstool upholstered in brown leatherette. Besides, the entire Northeast seemed like the inside of a house to me, the sky small and oddly lit, as if by an electric bulb. The sun did not pop over the great trees for hours—and then went down so soon. I was suspicious of Eastern land: the undramatic loveliness, the small scale, the lack of sky to watch, the way the weather sneaked up without enough warning.

The woods themselves seemed bogus at first—every inch of the ground turned over more than once, and even in the second growth of old pines so much human evidence. Rock walls ran everywhere, grown through and tumbled, as if the dead still had claims they imposed. The unkillable and fiercely contorted trees of old orchards, those revenants, spooked me when I walked in the woods. The blasted limbs spread a white lace cold as fire in the spring, and the odor of the blossoms was furiously spectral, sweet. When I stood beneath the canopies that hummed and shook with bees, I heard voices, other voices, and I did not understand what they were saying, where they had come from, what drove them into this earth.

Then, as often happens to sparring adversaries in 1940's movies, I fell in love.

After a few years of living in the country, the impulse to simply *get outside* hit me, strengthened, and became again a habit of thought, a reason for storytelling, an uneasy impatience with walls and roads. At first, when I had that urge, I had to get into a car and drive fifteen hundred miles before I was back in a place that I defined as *out*. The West, or the edge of it anyway, the great level patchwork of chemically treated fields and tortured grazing land, was the outside I had internalized. In the rich Red River Valley, where the valuable cropland is practically measured in inches, environmental areas are defined and proudly pointed out as stretches of roadway where the ditches are not mowed. Deer and pheasants survive in shelter belts—rows of Russian olive, plum, sometimes evergreen—planted at the edges of fields. The former tall-grass prairie has now become a collection of mechanized gardens tended by an array of air-conditioned farm implements and bearing an increasing amount of pesticide and herbicide in each black teaspoon of dirt. Nevertheless, no amount of reality changed the fact that I still *thought* of eastern North Dakota as wild.

341

In time, though, *out* became outside my door in New England. By walking across the road and sitting in my little writing house—a place surrounded by trees, thick plumes of grass, jets of ferns, and banks of touch-me-not—or just by looking out a screen door or window, I started to notice what there was to see. In time, the smothering woods that had always seemed part of Northeastern civilization—more an inside than an outside, more like a friendly garden—revealed themselves as forceful and complex. The growth of plants, the lush celebratory springs made a grasslands person drunk. The world turned dazzling green, the hills rode like comfortable and flowing animals. Everywhere there was the sound of water moving.

And yet, even though I finally grew closer to these woods, on some days I still wanted to tear them from before my eyes.

I wanted to *see*. Where I grew up, our house looked out on the western horizon. I could see horizon when I played. I could see it when I walked to school. It was always there, a line beyond everything, a simple line of changing shades and colors that ringed the town, a vast place. That was it. Down at the end of every grid of streets: vastness. Out the windows of the high school: vastness. From the drive-in theater where I went parking in a purple Duster: vast distance. That is why, on lovely New England days when everything should have been all right—a spring day, for instance, when the earth had risen through the air in patches and the sky lowered, dim and warm—I fell sick with longing for the horizon. I wanted the clean line, the simple line, the clouds marching over it in feathered masses. I suffered from horizon sickness. But it sounds crazy for a grown woman to throw herself at the sky, and the thing is, I wanted to get well. And so to compensate for horizon sickness, for the great longing that seemed both romantically German and pragmatically Chippewa in origin, I found solace in trees.

Trees are a changing landscape of sound—and the sound I grew attached to, possible only near large deciduous forests, was the great hushed roar of thousands and millions of leaves brushing and touching one another. Windy days were like sitting just out of sight of an ocean, the great magnetic ocean of wind. All around me, I watched the trees tossing, their heads bending. At times the movement seemed passionate, as though they were flung together in an eager embrace, caressing each other, branch to branch. If there is a vegetative soul, an animating power that all things share, there must be great rejoicing out there on windy days, ecstasy, for trees move so slowly on calm days. At least it seems that way to us. On days of high wind they move so freely it must give them a cellular pleasure close to terror.

Unused to walking in the woods, I did not realize that trees dropped branches—often large ones—or that there was any possible danger in going out on windy days, drawn by the natural drama. There was a white pine I loved, a tree of the size foresters call *overgrown,* a waste, a thing made of long-since harvestable material. The tree was so big that three people couldn't reach around it. Standing at the bottom, craning back, fingers clenched in grooves of bark, I held on as the crown of the tree roared and beat the air a hundred feet above. The movement was frantic, the soft-needled branches long and supple. I thought of a woman tossing, anchored in passion: calm one instant, full-throated the next, hair vast and dark, shedding the piercing, fresh oil of broken needles. I went to visit her often, and walked onward, farther, though it was not so far at all, and then one day I reached the fence.

Chain-link in places, chicken wire, sagging X wire, barbed wire on top, jerry-built with tipped-out poles and uncertain corners nailed to log posts and growing trees, still it seemed impermeable and solid. Behind it, there were trees for miles: large trees, grown trees, big pines. I walked up to the fence, looked within, and could see elk moving. Suave, imponderable, magnificently dumb, they lurched and floated through the dim air.

I was on the edge of a game park, a rich man's huge wilderness, probably the largest parcel of protected land in western New Hampshire, certainly the largest privately owned piece I knew about. At forty square miles—25,000 acres—it was bigger than my mother's home reservation. And it had the oddest fence around it that I'd ever seen, the longest and the tackiest. Though partially electrified, the side closest to our house was so piddling that an elk could easily have tossed it apart. Certainly a half-ton wild boar, the condensed and living version of a tank, could have strolled right through. But then animals, much like most humans, don't charge through fences unless they have sound reasons. As I soon found out, because I naturally grew fascinated with the place, there were many more animals trying to get into the park than out, and they couldn't have cared less about ending up in a hunter's stew pot.

These were not wild animals, the elk—since they were grained at feeding stations, how could they be? They were not domesticated either, however, for beyond the no-hunt boundaries they fled and vanished. They were game. Since there is no sport in shooting feedlot steers, these animals—still harboring wild traits and therefore more challenging to kill—were maintained to provide blood pleasure for the members of the Blue Mountain Forest Association.

As I walked away from the fence that day, I was of two minds about the place—and I am still. Shooting animals inside fences, no matter how big the area they have to hide in, seems abominable and silly. And yet, I was glad for that wilderness. Though secretly managed and off limits to me, it was the source of flocks of evening grosbeaks and pine siskins, of wild turkey, ravens, and grouse, of Eastern coyote, oxygen-rich air, foxes, goldfinches, skunk, and bears that tunneled in and out.

I had dreamed of this place in St. Thomas, or it had dreamed me. There was affinity here, beyond any explanation I could offer, so I didn't try. I continued to visit the tracts of big trees, and on deep nights—windy nights, especially when it stormed—I liked to fall asleep imagining details. I saw the great crowns touching, heard the raving sound of wind and thriving, knocking cries as the blackest of ravens flung themselves across acres upon indifferent acres of tossing, old-growth pine. I could fall asleep picturing how, below that dark air, taproots thrust into a deeper blankness, drinking the powerful rain.

Or was it so only in my dreams? The park, known locally as Corbin's Park, after its founder Austin Corbin, is knit together of land and farmsteads he bought in the late nineteenth century from 275 individuals. Among the first animals released there, before the place became a hunting club, were thirty buffalo, remnants of the vast Western herds. Their presence piqued the interest of Ernest Harold Bayne, a conservation-minded local journalist, who attempted to break a pair of buffalo calves to the yoke. He exhibited them at county fairs and even knit mittens out of buffalo wool, hoping to convince the skeptical of their use-

344

fulness. His work inspired sympathy, if not a trend for buffalo yarn, and collective zeal for the salvation of the buffalo grew until by 1915 the American Bison Society, of which Bayne was secretary, helped form government reserves that eventually more than doubled the herds that remained.

The buffalo dream seems to have been the park's most noble hour. Since that time it has been the haunt of wealthy hunting enthusiasts. The owner of Ruger Arms currently inhabits the stunning, butter-yellow original Corbin mansion and would like to buy the whole park for his exclusive use, or so local gossip has it.

For some months I walked the boundary admiring the tangled landscape, at least all I could see. After my first apprehension, I ignored the fence. I walked along it as if it simply did not exist, as if I really was part of that place which lay just beyond my reach. The British psychotherapist Adam Phillips has examined obstacles from several different angles, attempting to define their emotional use. "It is impossible to imagine desire without obstacles," he writes, "and wherever we find something to be an obstacle we are at the same time desiring something. It is part of the fascination of the Oedipus story in particular, and perhaps narrative in general, that we and the heroes and heroines of our fictions never know whether obstacles create desire or desire creates obstacles." He goes on to characterize the Unconscious, our dream world, as a place without obstacles: "A good question to ask of a dream is: What are the obstacles that have been removed to make this extraordinary scene possible?"

My dream, however, was about obstacles still in place. The fence was the main component, the defining characteristic of the forbidden territory that I watched but could not enter or experience. The obstacles that we overcome define us. We are composed of hurdles we set up to pace our headlong needs, to control our desires, or against which to measure our growth. "Without obstacles," Phillips writes, "the notion of development is inconceivable. There would be nothing to master."

Walking along the boundary of the park no longer satisfied me. The preciousness and deceptive stability of that fence began to rankle. Longing filled me. I wanted to brush against the old pine bark and pass beyond the ridge, to see specifically what was there: what Blue Mountain, what empty views, what lavender hillside, what old cellar holes, what unlikely animals. I was filled with poacher's lust, except I wanted only to smell the air. The linked web restraining me began to grate, and I started to look for weak spots, holes, places where the rough wire sagged. From the moment I began to see the fence as permeable, it became something to overcome. I returned time after time—partly to see if I could spot anyone on the other side, partly because I knew I must trespass.

Then, one clear, midwinter morning, in the middle of a half-hearted thaw, I walked along the fence until I came to a place that looked shaky—and was. I went through. There were no trails that I could see, and I knew I needed to stay away from any perimeter roads or snowmobile paths, as well as from the feeding stations where the animals congregated. I wanted to see the animals, but only from a distance. Of course, as I walked on, leaving a trail easily backtracked, I encountered no animals at all. Still, the terrain was beautiful, the columns of pine tall and satisfyingly heavy, the patches of oak and elderly maple from an occasional farmstead knotted and patient. I was satisfied and, sometime in the early afternoon, I decided to turn back and head toward the fence again. Skirting a low, boggy area that teemed with wild turkey tracks, I was just heading toward the edge of a deadfall of trashed dead branches and brush, when I stared too hard into the sun, and stumbled.

In a half crouch, I looked straight into the face of a boar, massive as a boulder. Cornfed, razor-tusked, alert, sensitive ears pricked, it edged slightly backward into the covering shadows. Two ice picks of light gleamed from its shrouded, tiny eyes, impossible to read. Beyond the rock of its shoulder, I saw more: a sow and three cinnamon-brown farrows crossing a small field of glare snow, lit by dazzling sun. The young skittered along, lumps of muscled fat on tiny hooves. They reminded me of snowsuited toddlers on new skates. When they were out of sight the boar melted through the brush after them, leaving not a snapped twig or crushed leaf in his wake.

I almost didn't breathe in the silence, letting the fact of that presence settle before I retraced my own tracks.

Since then, I've been to the game park via front gates, driven down the avenues of tough old trees, and seen herds of wild pigs and elk meandering past the residence of the gamekeeper. A no-hunting zone exists around the house, where the animals are almost tame. But I've been told by privileged hunters that just beyond that invisible boundary they vanish, becoming suddenly and preternaturally elusive.

There is something in me that resists the notion of fair use of this land if the only alternative is to have it cut up, sold off in lots, condominiumized. Yet the dumb fervor of the place depresses me—the wilderness locked up and managed but not for its sake; the animals imported and cultivated to give pleasure through their deaths. All animals, that is, except for skunks.

Not worth hunting, inedible except to old trappers like my great uncle Ben Gourneau, who boiled his skunk with onions in three changes of water, skunks pass in and out of Corbin's Park without hindrance, without concern. They live off the corn in the feeding cribs (or the mice it draws), off the garbage of my rural neighbors, off bugs and frogs and grubs. They nudge their way onto our back porch for catfood, and even when disturbed they do not, ever, hurry. It's easy to get near a skunk, even to capture one. When skunks become a nuisance, people either shoot them or catch them in crates, cardboard boxes, Hav-A-Hart traps, plastic garbage barrels.

Natives of the upper Connecticut River valley have neatly solved the problem of what to do with such catches. They hoist their trapped mustelid into the back of a pickup truck and cart the animal across the river to the neighboring state—New Hampshire to Vermont, Vermont to New Hampshire—before releasing it. The skunk population is estimated as about even on both sides.

We should take comfort from the skunk, an arrogant creature so pleased with its own devices that it never runs from harm, just turns its back in total confidence. If I were an animal, I'd choose to be a skunk: live fearlessly, eat anything, gestate my young in just two months, and fall into a state of dreaming torpor when the cold bit hard. Wherever I went, I'd leave my sloppy tracks. I wouldn't walk so much as putter, destinationless, in a serene belligerence—past hunters, past death overhead, past death all around.

1994

OYEZ À BEAUMONT

by VICKI HEARNE

from RARITAN

A STUDENT of mine called two days ago and asked, "What do the experts do when their dogs die?"

He developed a calcium deposit on his upper spine, did my good Airedale Gunner, and it would hurt him to track, so Gunner and I stopped tracking, stopped retrieving and jumping, not because he wouldn't have gone on if it were up to him, and awhile after that he was very ill with cancer, and after a time of that, too much of that, I had him killed. Gallant Gunner, brave Gunner, gay Gunner. Once, late one evening on a beach in Malibu, he took down a man who was attacking me with a knife. The vet had to patch Gunner up some, but he didn't turn tail the way my assailant did. Brave Gunner. Harken to Gunner. Twenty-four hours later, bandaged, he clowned and told jokes for the kids at Juvenile Hall, performing for the annual Orange Empire Dog Club Christmas party. Oh, rare and dauntless Gunner. Even his hip, broken when a prostate tumor grew right through the bone, did not stop the courage of his gaiety, but I did. My friend Dick Koehler said, "He is lucky to have a good friend like you," to encourage me, you see, to get on with it, kill him, and Dick was right, of course, right, because when there is nothing much left of a dog but his wounds you should bury those decently.

Until he died, he was immortal, and the death of an immortal is an event that changes the world. That is all for now about Gunner, because what it does to you when such a dog dies is not fit to print. "Der Tod ist groß," writes Rilke. "Death is huge." But various psychologists deny that it is as huge as all that when it is an animal that is mourned. I have read statistically studded reassurances that mourning for a cat lasts at most one month, for a dog three. I have read that when an animal dies there are no regrets, no rehearsal of the wail, "If only I had," and also that the splendid thing about animals, what is said to make them so convenient to our hearts, like antidepressants, is that when we mourn them, we are only mourning a personal loss and not "the loss of life and potential," according to Professors Beck and Katcher, authorities on all of this at the University of Pennsylvania.

That is the way psychological authorities talk—"Eventually an animal *can* be replaced," they write in their books, but this is not how the experts talk. (I realize that psychologists and such like are generally understood to be experts, but I have met none who were experts in the various ways my good Gunner's work with scent developed, especially when he started scenting out the human heart.) But I am just a dog trainer. My thinking, such as it is, I learned from the animals, for whom happiness is usually a matter of getting the job done. Clear that fence, fetch in those sheep, move those calves, win that race, find that guy, retrieve that bird. The happiness of animals is also ideologically unsound, as often as not, or at least it is frequently wanting in propriety, as when your dog rolls in something awful on his afternoon walk, or your cat turns off your answering machine.

In over a quarter of a century of training I have never met an animal who turned out to be replaceable, and Dick says, "Hell, even trees are irreplaceable, but we don't know that, and *that* is our loss." The loss the dog trainer has in mind is the loss of eternity, for, as Wittgenstein put it: "Denn lebt er ewig, der in der gegenwart lebt." "So he lives forever, who lives in the present," wrote the philosopher, and this is how the animals live, in the present, which is why the expert's difficult and apparently harsh advice, advice they occasionally take themselves, is: "Another dog. Same breed, as soon as possible." Not because another dog of the same breed will be the same, but because that way you can pick up somewhere near where you left off, say that you have it in you.

In a children's book called *Algonquin: The Story of a Great Dog*, there is a quarrel between two brothers, old men they were, grandfather and great-uncle to the boy who tells the story.

Grandsir is angry because Uncle Ovid is going to take on the training of the grand young Pointer named Algonquin; he is angry because he wants no more of the "grief and the rage and the ashes." He shouts at his brother, "Do you know what it does to you? Do you know what it does every time one of them dies?" but Uncle Ovid just says, "Don't tell me. I am an old man and it would not be good for me to know," and he trains that Pointer who turns out to be something else again at the field trials. Mr. Washington says, "I think sometimes that he would pity his bracemates, were he not enough of a gentleman to know that they would rather die than be pitied," and Algonquin wins and wins and wins and then Algonquin starts to get a lung disease and can't work well, is distressed therefore, because he is losing his work, his happiness, and Uncle Ovid sends him out on his last run and shoots him while he is on point, while there is still something more to him than his wounds.

At the end of that story, when Grandsir suggests that it is time for the boy who has been witness to all of this to get another dog, he says to his grandfather, "Irish Setters don't win field trials, do they? I mean, you are not in much danger of getting a great dog?" Grandsir purses his lips and agrees, "Not much." The boy says, "Then an Irish Setter would be nice."

There exist mighty dogs, the dangerous kind who take hold of your heart and do not let go. But avoiding the great ones does not get you out of it. If, like the boy in *Algonquin*, you already know what a great dog is, then the knowledge marks you. If you do not know, then you are still in danger, for if you give her a civilized upbringing, every collie is Lassie *in propria persona,* killing that snake in your heart, driving off the cougar that lurks there, sending for help. This is not because all dogs are great dogs but rather because all dogs are both irreplaceable and immortal and as Rilke says, "Der Tod ist groß."

One day I talked about death with my friend—my teacher and friend, for these are synonyms in the trainer's world—Dick Koehler. I had told him about the results obtained at the University of Pennsylvania. "Dick! The news is out! There are no regrets when a dog dies," and Dick said, "Oh, then my several thousand students who say to me, 'If only I had done what you said, Mr. Koehler,' or 'If only I had worked with her more,'—they're all hallucinating, right?"

"Must be," I reply, "for it says here that dogs are replaceable, and grief for them lasts no more than three months," and right before my eyes Dick Koehler starts looking a little funny; he startles me. He is thinking of Duke, dead several decades now. Hallucinating that Duke had been irreplaceable. Duke was a Great Dane, one of your great dogs, too. Duke was a movie dog; some of you may remember him from *The Swiss Family Robinson*.

"What was so irreplaceable about Duke?" I asked.

"Well, it's not every day you find a Great Dane who thinks a 255-pound tiger is a kitty cat. Not every day you find a Great Dane who will hit a sleeve and go through a second-story window, not just once, not just twice, but seven times and it was as good the last time as the first time."

Soon after Duke died, there was Topper, of *The Ugly Dachshund*, various TV series. "Topper paid the rent for about three years there," said Dick. "I mean, he did all the work on that series." Topper died like this: the great dog and his son were playing, horsing around after a day's work, and his son slammed into him and ruptured his spleen and Dick realized it too late for the vet to fix things up, and so had him put down. That was over two decades ago, Dick's most recent Great Dane.

Dick talks about Duke and Topper and the thing starts to happen to me again, the merging of all of the elegies, all of the great dogs. "There is nothing left but his name . . . but there never was a dog like Algonquin," or, "It's all regrets," or, "After he got in his car and drove away I dug a grave and lined it with the bright fallen leaves and there I buried all that could die of my good Fox," or "He was allus kind to the younguns and he kilt a rattlesnake onct," or one of my favorites, the passage in T. H. White's *The Sword in the Stone*. The great hound named Beaumont is on the ground, his back broken by the boar, and the expert, the Master of Hounds, William Twyti, has been hurt also. Twyti limps over to Beaumont and utters the eternal litany, "Hark to Beaumont. Softly, Beaumont, mon amy. Oyez à Beaumont the valiant. Swef, le douce Beaumont, swef, swef." Then he nods to Robin Wood, and holds the hound's eyes with his own, saying "Good dog, Beaumont the valiant, sleep now, old friend Beaumont, good old dog," while the huntsman kills the dog for him: "Then Robin's falchion let Beaumont out of this world, to run free with Orion and to roll among the stars."

What next, though? The narrator of *Algonquin* decides to go for an Irish Setter. But that is not what the experts say to do. They say, "Another dog, same breed, right away." It takes courage, courage that Master Twyti seems to have had, for he rose from beside Beaumont's wounds and "whipped the hounds off the corpse of the boar as he was accustomed to do. He put his horn to his lips and blew the four long notes of the Mort without a quaver." He called the other hounds to him.

Another dog, same breed, right away. Or a pack of them, and not because there were any replacements for Beaumont in that pack. The other hounds were all right, but there were no Beaumonts among them, and there is no point in saying otherwise. I don't mean by that that there are not plenty of great dogs around. "There are a lot of them," says Dick. Yeah. They're a dime a dozen. So are great human hearts; that's not the point. We are by way of being connoisseurs of dogs, some of us, but one falls into that, and a dog is not a collector's item, not for Dick Koehler, anyhow, whom I have seen risk himself in more ways than one, over and over, day in and day out, ever since I met him when I was nineteen and he straightened out Stevie, a German Shepherd cross I had then, who was charging children but was a nice dog after we took care of that, who lived for twelve years after Dick showed me how to train him, who shook the ground just as hard as Beaumont did when he died. My teacher and friend Dick Koehler is a maniac for training dogs instead of killing them. Deaf dogs, three-legged dogs, dogs with chartreuse spots on their heads. He hasn't gotten around to getting another Dane, though there have been other dogs, of course. *Of course.*

But "Master William Twyti startled The Wart, for he seemed to be crying," and this book, *The Sword in the Stone*, is about the education of great hounds and of a great king. King Arthur in fact. Immortal Beaumont, douce, swef, swef. And immortal Arthur—douce, douce, harken to Arthur, they would say in time about: *Regis quondam regisque futuri.* The once and future king. Which is to say, this is all of it about the education of any hound and any boy.

"But won't it hurt?" my student asked me recently when I gave that advice: *another dog, same breed, as soon as possible.* "Won't it hurt my daughter again?" Oh, it hurts, especially when, as is so often the case, you have a part in the dog's death.

Perhaps because you were careless and he got run over, or because, like Master Twyti, you gave the nod to the vet or to the huntsman with his falchion.

There is the falchion, and then sometimes you must speak abruptly into the face of grief, for grief gives bad advice. Grief will tell you to throw your heart into the grave with the dog's corpse, and this is ecologically unsound. The ants will take care of the corpse in a few weeks, but a discarded heart stinks for quite some time. Two days ago that student of mine called, a woman in her late thirties. She had gotten a new pup for her eight-year-old daughter, and at a few months of age the pup had died because left in her crate with her collar on, and the collar got caught on the handle of the crate. "My daughter is so upset, my husband says it would be too bad to get another dog and have something else happen. What do the experts do?"

I said in tones of vibrant command, "Another dog, same breed, right away." Nothing else, for wordiness is not in order when you are discussing, as we so often are, the education of a queen.

A decade went by between the death of Gunner and the purchase of the new Airedale pup. That was as soon as I could get to it, what with one thing and another.

1994

SEX

by IRMA WALLEM

from ZYZZYVA

IT WAS SUNDAY afternoon, the loveliest time of the week, and I had just come out of the reading room when Melvin asked me if I wanted a ride to my room. I decided I would rather go out into the yard for some fresh air, which was O.K. with Melvin. He is a blond man with a slight build, but he was strong enough to hold open the heavy outer door and push my wheelchair through at the same time.

We went along the walks and I admired the flowers with absolutely no idea of what was about to happen, when suddenly he said, "I'm going to put it right on the line. What I'm interested in is sex. I haven't had any since a year before my wife died, seven years ago, and that makes eight years."

Nothing in my past had quite prepared me for Melvin's problem. The men in my life had done a lot of stuff before they asked me. Or they hadn't asked. "Where do you plan to do this?" I managed to reply.

"My roommate is gone for the day," he told me. "We can go to my room."

We went in the big door and past the nurses' station. No one was around to stop us from doing what we were apparently planning to do. We headed straight for Aisle C, Room Six. He opened the door and we went in. On Melvin's side of the room there was a bed, an overstuffed chair and a big oak dresser. Since there was nothing pretty anywhere, not even so much as a plastic rose stuck in a coffee mug, I could tell it was the sort of room no woman had anything to do with.

"Do you want to sit in the chair?" he asked.

I explained that the chair was too low for me. I had to stay in my wheelchair. We sat facing each other. "What if a nurse comes to check on you?" I asked.

"They always knock." He seemed to have an answer for everything.

"Where have you been the last eight years?" I asked.

"I've been living with my daughter, helping her husband on their farm."

"So you didn't know many women down there? There are lots of women here, how did you happen to choose me?"

"I don't know," he said. "I just thought you'd been around the block."

"It isn't that I don't want to help you," I told him. "It's my arthritis. It takes me five minutes to lay flat in bed."

Then he truly surprised me. He stood up and leaned over my wheelchair and gave me a kiss on the lips.

"That's the way to start," I told him. "Next time you find somebody, you don't ask. You have to do a lot of stuff first, but asking isn't one of them."

"Maybe I should take you to your room," he said, looking like he'd been swatted with a newspaper. We went out the door and nobody noticed.

Before Samuel first moved in, a woman at our table acted a little doubtful when she heard that he was coming. "He's quite a ladykiller," she told us, "and he has only one hand."

I wrote a letter to my daughter, Marsha, and told her we were about to get a ladykiller in our midst. It was a pleasant thing to anticipate. Soon after, I saw a new man at the snack bar with a stub where his left hand should have been. I said, "Hello, Samuel." He looked surprised and pleased.

Next day I said, "Hello, Samuel," again, and then I asked him about his life since supper wasn't ready yet. "It'll take a while," he said. It did.

Because Samuel turned out to be hard of hearing, a two-sided conversation wasn't easy, but I soon learned that if you asked him almost any question he'd get going so fast that it wasn't easy to stop him and not too necessary to ask any more questions. I soon wished I was younger, with enough time to write his story in a novel.

Samuel's grandparents had moved to the Ukraine at the invitation of the queen, to have free land and teach the peasants how to farm, Mennonites, he told me, practically have topsoil in their blood. Then

355

the Communists took over. They had entered Samuel's home one night, told everyone to leave, and killed the oldest son to show they weren't kidding around. Samuel's family left with all nine children, taking only what they could carry. Samuel said they "lived like dogs" for two years, until they got to Turkey, where the Mennonites were building a school. The church people contacted other Mennonites in Pennsylvania who sent $750 for boat tickets. When they got to America they found a foreclosed farm ready and waiting for them, with a pantry full of food. The Mennonites had even butchered a hog. Everything was perfect, except that two of Samuel's little sisters had died on the way.

When Samuel was 20, his father decided he needed a wife. He knew of a family of Mennonites in Canada who had four marriageable daughters. He got in touch and sort of ordered up one of them. Then Samuel went to Canada and returned with his bride. She turned out perfect in every way. They bought a farm. She saved her egg money, and he grew tobacco, and they paid off their mortgage in three years. He told me there was a write-up in the paper that had a headline reading, "Russian Farmer Shows Americans How to Farm." Nobody burned down their house, so I guess nobody got riled.

Working in the fields the day after their first baby was born, Samuel got his hand caught in the cultivator. The doctor happened to be visiting at the time, so he cut off the smashed hand and sewed up the stub. The hardest part for Samuel was that it spoiled his wife's joy in the new baby.

It all sounded romantic and wonderful, but it isn't always enjoyable to listen to men brag on their dead wives, especially if the wives were just too perfect and the men are still attractive.

One day my roommate at the time, Mamie, and I were given the job of making a big thank-you card for the free pizza served us at an outdoor lunch. I painted flowers in the corner and printed a big THANK YOU across the top. Mamie's job was to take the card around to all the residents to sign. When she came back after taking a look into every room, she told me, "Samuel has the most beautiful furniture of any room and his place is as neat as a pin."

The next time Samuel started to push me home from the snack bar, I asked if I could see his room. He hesitated a minute and then turned and headed back to C wing and pushed me inside his room, leaving the door ajar in a sort of disappointing way. There was a huge wall cabinet with mirror and shelves filled with china and figurines. It covered half the wall space. "These all belonged to my wife," he said. "She liked beautiful things."

I exclaimed over the carved bed and dresser and he said, "My wife liked beautiful furniture."

He then showed me a picture of his wife and himself standing together, looking calm and happy. She had long hair, brown, parted in the middle and drawn back from a face that was neither beautiful nor homely. She was wearing a long-sleeved, blue polka-dotted dress, very plain. So this was the woman, I thought to myself, who was perfect in every way and who would come to his bed naked, Samuel told me, and slide in beside him. She had been his beloved for 59 years and he still had love left over. Gently he touched the head of a beautiful, brown-eyed German doll with a brown velvet dress. He said it was on his wife's pillow the night she died, five years before.

Feeling it was time for a change of subject, I asked him how he had happened to become a carpenter and then a contractor who had built 104 houses, all with one hand.

"My wife wanted a house," he said, and I thought to myself, "Oh dear, of course." He went to where some men were putting up a house and he stood around until they offered him a job. Then he built a house on his own and somebody liked it so well that he sold it and built his wife another house. He did that six times, until she said finally that she'd had enough of moving and wasn't going to pack everything up ever again. So Samuel built her a house with windows that looked out over the valley and there she stayed until she died.

My favorite Samuel story is the one he told about making babies. He said, "She wanted a little girl so I worked and worked and got her one. Then she wanted a boy, so I worked and got one of those for her, too. Then she wanted another boy and so I worked until she had one. Then I told her, 'You don't have to make babies when you make love.' I was afraid we wouldn't be able to send them all to college."

Samuel didn't like the food when he first came because, he told me, they didn't cook like his wife had. Nobody could quilt the way she had, either, or can preserves. Nobody could do anything half as well as she could.

I decided it was time for me to return to my own room, with its yellow painted dresser and worn-out easy chair and nothing at all perfect in any way. Samuel bent down and gave me a good smacking kiss, the kind that makes you forget about a man's perfect wife and her Best-of-

357

Show piccalilli relish. "If you were a little bit younger, I'd ask you to marry me," he said.

The next time my roommate was at the doctor's office and he felt free to kiss me again, he said, "I'd ask you to marry me, but I guess I'm getting a little old. I'm afraid I couldn't handle you." What he said was true, except it still would've been nice to have been married to him for maybe a week or two, until we ran out of anything new to talk about. There was still a lot of life left in his kisses. He might constantly talk about his wife's virtues, but he still seemed to have a little love left for all the other women he knew—and they knew it.

I asked him, "Do you watch television?"

He said he owned one but never watched it.

"Then who taught you how to kiss like that?"

He took my question seriously. "Nobody taught me. This is all me."

Since I had written to my daughter that Samuel was coming, and that he was known as a ladykiller, I wrote her another letter explaining that, though I had been warned, I was his first victim.

One of Samuel's best moves is the face hug. He gave one to 94-year old Viola, and she said, "I guess I'm not as old as I thought I was." I told my daughter how he gave shoulder squeezes, a new thrill with his stub where his hand had been, and how different pressures with his strong good hand seem to mean different things. When someone else got hold of the handles of my wheelchair, there wasn't the same electricity.

My daughter wrote back and asked, "Aren't there other women there as beautiful and sexy as you are, so the boys won't have to fight over you?" I said of course there were, but they weren't in wheelchairs. Not long after that, Marsha called to wish me a happy birthday and I told her, "It's happened—a new woman and she's younger and more beautiful. I don't know about sexy," I told her, "but she's very thin and is in a wheelchair." She also had been moved to our table, I told Marsha, and that she was a once-blonde person who thinks she is on vacation. Plus, she got Samuel to play Bingo, which I never could.

"You just stay in there fighting," Marsha said. "There's probably some flaw in her character."

When I wrote my next letter to Marsha, I told her how right she had been. There was no need to worry about Hilda. She had definitely not "been around the block." She had been in Chicago and San Francisco all of her life, was well educated and had been a legal secretary. She didn't tell us anything about any man in her past, she only talked about her sister. She had never had a cherry coke at the corner drugstore, because she had gone to a private boarding school. She had never been bitten by a chigger or a wood tick. She had no respect for the black-eyed peas, which we know kept starvation away in Depression days, and she never heard of salt pork or huckleberry pie. She had never tasted fresh-butchered pork chops fried fast to keep the flavor. She would never think of listening to replays of the Lawrence Welk Show.

Now Jim, who was born in Oklahoma like I was, decided that we had to educate her since she'd missed out on most of the good things in life. This was an uphill battle. When Ray and I crumbled our biscuits into the white gravy, Hilda said it was gruesome. Though she is thin and has a citified sort of style, there was no standing in line to give her a push because she is a hard woman to please. Still, it was heartbreaking to hear her make plans for a future of travel and study. Samuel came over to our table, not too long after we'd heard they were "a couple," and gave her some arm squeezes, but they didn't seem to thrill her, which made up my mind right then that she was no competition. However, by then Jim was looking better and better to me and those arm squeezes had lost a little of their electricity.

Then Samuel left in order to make sure his daughter didn't run through all his money, and soon after Ted went, too, which made me sorry because he was a good conversation-starter. Plus he had the only mustache in the room. He had been to every place in the United States and told us at our table about every single one of them. Everybody else kept quiet and ate because they couldn't match his experiences. He only stayed a month, but during that time he took it as his duty to push my wheelchair whenever he could because, he said, his wife had been in a wheelchair for 15 years and he was used to them.

His place to my left was quickly taken by Frank, whose arthritis had bent him until he was hunchbacked. He was enduring great suffering, but he insisted on coming to the table and taking part in our conversation, which always is the liveliest in the dining room. We all talked about our lives and Frank said he'd been married 63 years to the same woman and had nine children. He had married when he was 18 and never had another woman.

I was the only person who answered him. "I've been married twice," I said. Then I felt a need to give him a small shock. "Twice, legal," I added.

That was the night he pushed me to my room, even though he had to use one of those four-cornered walkers. He could see, and so could

I, that Samuel—who was by now disappointed in Hilda's lack of romance—was heading our way from his table on the other side of the room, and that Jim also seemed inclined to give me a push, too.

Frank whispered to me, "You carry my cane and I'll push you." He grabbed the handles of my wheelchair, and I grasped his cane. The women at the other tables stared at us as we swept by. When we reached my room, Mamie, my roommate, was there ahead of us. She also stared. She had been expecting one of my usual pushers, not this man who was all bent over and panting as if we were an Olympic bobsled team.

Frank didn't make it to breakfast next morning. I felt to blame because, as it turned out, he was hardly able to walk. At noon the nurses brought him to our table in his wheelchair. He had been in lots of pain, but he managed one of his slow smiles. He could only eat a little bit of food, but he came again that night, still in a wheelchair. He was able to wheel himself out into the reading room after supper, and I followed him on my own steam this time. I parked beside him and tried to find something to say that would make him look more cheerful, but he was deep in gloom. "I'm ready to go home to be with Jesus," he said. "I hope he calls me soon to get me out of this misery."

I reached over and patted his hand. There was so little to say, and it seemed as if I had done enough damage without getting him all fired up again. "I'd like to ask you two things," he said. I expected a mighty serious question from a man about to meet his Maker. "Did a great big man ever get on top of you?"

"No, all the men who got on top of me were small," I answered.

He nodded, letting this sink in. "Which one was the best?"

"The one with the most experience," I told him.

That night he was found dead on the floor when the nurse went in to give him his nine o'clock pills.

Now our table was all filled with women, except for Jim. This kept him busy pouring our coffee and tea, because the coffee containers we have are heavy and their tops often stick and the milk cartons are difficult for us to open. Besides, it's nice having a man do these things and Jim, who is a manly sort of man, enjoys feeling needed.

1996

360

JESSICA, THE HOUND & THE CASKET TRADE

by THOMAS LYNCH

from WITNESS

> *She went to a long-established, "reputable" undertaker. Seeking to save the widow expense, she chose the cheapest redwood casket in the establishment and was quoted a low price. Later, the salesman called her back to say the brother-in-law was too tall to fit into this casket, she would have to take the one that cost $100 more. When my friend objected, the salesman said, "Oh, all right, we'll use the redwood one, but we'll have to cut off his feet."*
> —Jessica Mitford, The American Way of Death

THE SAME MORTICIAN who once said he'd rather give away caskets than take advantage of someone in grief later hung billboards out by the interstate—a bosomy teenager in a white bikini over which it read *Better Bodies by Bixby* (not the real name) and the phone numbers for his several metro locations.

I offer this in support of the claim that there are good days and there are bad days.

No less could be said for many of the greats.

I'm thinking of Hemingway's take on Pound when he said, "Ezra was right half the time, and when he was wrong, he was so wrong you were never in any doubt of it." But ought we be kept from "The River-Merchant's Wife" by his mistaken politics? Should outrage silence the sublime?

The same may be asked of Mr. Bixby's two memorable utterances.

Or, as a priest I've long admired once said, "Prophesy, like poetry, is a part-time job—the rest of the time they were only trying to keep their feet out of their mouths." I suppose he was trying to tell me something.

Indeed, mine is an occupation that requires two feet firmly on the ground, less for balance, I often think, than to keep one or the other from angling toward its true home in my craw.

I sell caskets and embalm bodies and direct funerals.

Pollsters find among the general public a huge ambivalence about funeral directors. "I hope you'll understand it if I never want to see you again," the most satisfied among my customers will say. I understand.

And most of the citizenry, stopped on the street, would agree that funeral directors are mainly crooks, "except for mine . . . " they just as predictably add. "The one who did my (insert primary relation) was really helpful, really cared, treated us like family."

This tendency to abhor the general class while approving of the particular member is among the great human prerogatives—as true of clergy and senators as it is of teachers and physicians. Much the same could be said of time: "Life sucks," we say, "but there was this moment . . . " Or of racial types: "Some of my best friends are (insert minority) . . . " Or of the other "(Insert sex)! You can't live with them and you can't live without them!"

Of course, there are certain members of the subspecies—I'm thinking lawyers, politicians, revenue agents—who are, in general and in particular, beyond redemption and we like it that way. "The devil you know's better than the one you don't . . . " is the best we can say about politicians. And who among us wants a "nice" divorce attorney or has even one fond memory involving a tax man? Really, now.

But back to caskets and bodies and funerals.

When it comes to caskets I'm very careful. I don't tell folks what they should or shouldn't do. It's bad form and worse for business. I tell them I don't have any that will get them into heaven or keep them out. There's none that turns a prince into a frog or, regrettably, vice-versa. There isn't a casket that compensates for neglect nor one that hides true love, honorable conduct or affection.

If worth can be measured by what they do, it might help to figure out what caskets "do" in the inanimate object sense of the verb.

How many here are thinking HANDLES? When someone dies, we try to get a handle on it. This is because dead folks don't move. I'm not making this part up. Next time someone in your house quits breathing, ask him to get up and answer the phone or maybe get you some ice water or let the cat out the back door. He won't budge. It's because he's dead.

There was a time when it was easier to change caves than to drag the dead guy out. Now it's not so easy. There's the post office, the utilities, the closing costs. Now we have to remove the dead. The sooner the better is the rule of thumb, though it's not the thumb that will make this known.

This was a dour and awful chore, moving the dead from place to place. And like most chores, it was left to women to do. Later, it was discovered to be a high honor—to bear the pall as a liturgical role required a special place in the procession, special conduct and often a really special outfit. When hauling the dead hither and yon became less the chore and more an honor, men took it over with enthusiasm.

In this it resembles the history of the universe. Much the same happened with protecting against the marauding hordes, the provision of meaty protein sources, and more recently, in certain highly specialized and intricate evolutions of food preparation and child care.

If you think women were at least participant and perhaps instrumental in the discovery of these honors, you might better keep such suspicions to yourself. These are not good days to think such thoughts.

But I stray again. Back to business.

Another thing you'll see most every casket doing is being horizontal. This is because folks that make them have taken seriously the demonstrated preference of our species to do it on the level. Oh, sure—it can be done standing up or in a car or even upside down. But most everyone goes looking for something flat. Probably this can be attributed to gravity or physics or fatigue.

So horizontal things that can be carried—to these basic properties, we could add a third: it should be sturdy enough for a few hundred pounds. I'm glad that it's not from personal experience that I say that nothing takes the steam out of a good funeral so much as the bottom falling out.

And how many of you haven't heard of this happening?

A word on the words we're most familiar with. *Coffins* are the narrow, octagonal fellows—mostly wooden, nicely corresponding to the shape of the human form before the advent of the junk food era. There are top and bottom, and the screws that fasten the one to the other are often ornamental. Some have handles, some do not, but all can be carried. The lids can be opened and closed at will.

Caskets are more rectangular and the lids are hinged and the body can be both carried and laid out in them. Other than shape, coffins and caskets are pretty much the same. They've been made of wood and metal and glass and ceramics and plastics and cement and the dear knows what else. Both are made in a range of prices.

But *casket* suggests something beyond basic utility, something about the contents of the box. The implication is that it contains something precious: heirlooms, jewels, old love letters, remnants and icons of something dear.

So casket is to coffin as tomb is to cave, grave is to hole in the ground, pyre is to bonfire. You get the drift? Or as, for example, eulogy is to speech, elegy to poem, or home is to house or husband to man. I love this part, I get carried away.

But the point is a *casket* presumes something about what goes in it. It presumes the dead body is important to someone. For some this will seem like stating the obvious. For others, I'm guessing, maybe not.

But when buildings are bombed or planes fall from the sky, or wars are won or lost, the bodies of the dead are really important. We want them back to let them go again—on our terms, at our pace, to say you may not leave without permission, forgiveness, our respects—to say we want our chance to say good-bye.

Both coffins and caskets are boxes for the dead. Both are utterly suitable to the task. Both cost more than most other boxes.

It's because of the bodies we put inside them. The bodies of mothers and fathers and sons, daughters and sisters and brothers and friends, the ones we knew and loved or knew and hated, or hardly knew at all, but know someone who knew them and who is left to grieve.

In 1906, John Hillenbrand, the son of a German immigrant, bought the failing Batesville Coffin Company in the southeastern Indiana town of the same name. Following the form of the transportation industry, he moved from a primarily wooden product to products of metal that would seal against the elements. *Permanence* and *protection* were concepts that Batesville marketed successfully during and after a pair of World Wars in which men were being sent home in government boxes. The same wars taught different lessons to the British for whom the sight of their burial grounds desecrated by bombs at intervals throughout the first half-century suggested permanence and protection were courtesies they could no longer guarantee to the dead. Hence the near total preference for cremation there.

Earth burial is practiced by "safe" societies and by settled ones. It presumes the dead will be left their little acre and that the living will be around to tend the graves. In such climates any fantasies of permanence and protection thrive. And the cremation rate in North America has risen in direct relation to the demographics and geographics of mobility and fear and the ever more efficient technologies of destruction.

The idea that a casket should be sealed against air and moisture is important to many families. To others it means nothing. They are both right. No one need explain why it doesn't matter. No one need explain why it does. But Batesville, thinking that it might, engineered the first "sealed" casket with a gasket in the 1940s and made it available in metal caskets in every price range from the .20 gauge steels to the coppers and bronzes. One of the things they learned is that ninety-six percent of the human race would fit in a casket with interior dimensions of twenty-five inches and exterior dimensions of six-foot, six-inches.

Once they had the size figured out and what it was that people wanted in a casket—protection and permanence—then the rest was more or less the history of how the Hillenbrand brothers managed to make more and sell more than any of their competition. And they have. You see them in the movies, on the evening news being carried in and out of churches, at gravesides, being taken from hearses. If someone's in a casket in North America chances are better than even it's a Batesville.

We show twenty-some caskets to pick from. They're samples only. There are plenty more we can get within a matter of hours. What I carry in blue, my brother Tim, in the next town, carries in pink. What I have tailored, Tim carries shirred. He carries one with *The Last Supper* on it. I've got one with the *Pietá*. One of his has roses on the handles. One of mine has sheaves of wheat.

You name it. We've got it. We aim to please.

We have a cardboard box (of a kind used for larger appliances) for seventy-nine dollars. We also have a mahogany box (of a kind used for Kennedy and Nixon and Onassis) for nearly eight grand. Both can be carried and buried and burned. Both will accommodate all but the tallest or widest citizens, for whom, alas, as in life, the selection narrows. And both are available to any customer who can pay the price.

Because a lot of us tend to avoid the extremes, regardless of how we elect to define them, we show a wide range of caskets in between and it would look on a chart like one of those bell curves: with the most in the middle and the least at either end. Thus, we show three oak caskets and only one mahogany, a bronze, a copper, a stainless steel, and six or seven regular steels of various gauges or thicknesses. We show a cherry, a maple, two poplars, an ash, a pine and a particle board and the cardboard box. The linings are velvet or crepe or linen or satin, in all different colors, tufted or ruffled or tailored plain. You get pretty much what you pay for here.

I should probably fess up that we buy these caskets for less than we sell them for—a fact uncovered by one of our local TV news personalities, who called himself the News Hound, and who was, apparently, untutored in the economic intrigues of wholesale and retail. It was this same News Hound who did an exposé on Girl Scout cookie sales— how some of the money doesn't go to the girls at all, but to the national office where it was used to pay the salaries of "staff."

It was a well-worn trail the News Hound was sniffing—a trail blazed most profitably by Jessica Mitford, who came to the best-selling if not exactly original conclusion that the bereaved customer is in a bad bargaining position. When you've got a dead body on your hands it's hard to shop around. It's hard to shop for lawyers when you're on the lam, or doctors when your appendix is inflamed. It's not the kind of thing you let out to bids.

Lately there has been a great push toward "pre-arrangement." Everyone who's anyone seems to approve. The funeral directors figure it's money in the bank. The insurance people love it since most of the funding is done through insurance. The late Jessica, the former News Hound, the anti-extravagance crowd—they all reckon it is all for the best, to make such decisions when heads are cool and hearts are unencumbered by grief and guilt. There's this hopeful fantasy that by pre-arranging the funeral, one might be able to pre-feel the feelings, you know, get a jump on the anger and the fear and the helplessness. It's as modern as planned parenthood and pre-nuptial agreements and as useless, however tidy it may be about the finances, when it comes to the feelings involved.

And we are uniformly advised "not to be a burden to our children." This is the other oft-cited *bonne raison* for making your final arrangements in advance—to spare them the horror and pain of having to do business with someone like me.

366

But if we are not to be a burden to our children, then to whom? The government? The church? The taxpayers? Whom? Were they not a burden to us—our children? And didn't the management of that burden make us feel alive and loved and helpless and capable?

And if the planning of a funeral is so horribly burdensome, so fraught with possible abuses and gloom, why should an arthritic septuagenarian with blurred vision and some hearing loss be sent to the front to do battle with the undertaker instead of the forty-something heirs-apparent with their power suits and web browsers and cellular phones? Are they not far better outfitted to the task? Is it not their inheritance we're spending here? Are these not decisions they will be living with?

Maybe their parents do not trust them to do the job properly.

Maybe they shouldn't.

Maybe they should.

The day I came to Milford, Russ Read started pre-arranging his funeral. I was getting my hair cut when I first met him. He was a massive man still, in his fifties, six-foot-something and four hundred pounds. He'd had, in his youth, a spectacular career playing college and professional football. His reputation had preceded him. He was a "character"—known in these parts for outrageous and libertine behavior. Like the Sunday he sold a Ford coupe off the used-car lot uptown, taking a cash deposit of a thousand dollars and telling the poor customer to "come by in the morning when the office is open" for the keys and paperwork. That Russ was not employed by the car dealer— a devout Methodist who kept holy his Sabbaths—did not come to light before the money had been spent on sirloins and cigars and round after round of drinks for the patrons of Ye Olde Hotel—visiting matrons from the Eastern Star, in town with their husbands for a regional confab. Or the time a neighbor's yelping poodle—a dog disliked by everyone in earshot—was found shot one afternoon during Russ' nap time. The neighbor started screaming at one of Russ' boys over the back fence, " . . . when I get my hands on your father!" Awakened by the fracas, Russ appeared at the upstairs window and calmly promised, "I'll be right down, Ben." He came down in his paisley dressing gown, decked the neighbor with a swift left hook, instructed his son to bury "that dead mutt" and went back upstairs to finish his nap. Halloween was Russ' favorite holiday which he celebrated in more or less pre-Christian fashion, dressing himself up like a Celtic warrior, with an antlered helmet and mighty sword which, along with his ponderous bulk and black beard and booming voice, would scare the bejaysus out of the wee trick-or-treaters who nonetheless were drawn to his porch by stories of full-sized candy bars sometimes wrapped in five-dollar bills. Russ Read was, in all ways, bigger than life so that the hyperbole that attended the gossip about him was like the talk of heroes in the ancient Hibernian epics—Cuchulainn and Deirdre and Queen Maeve, who were given to warp-spasms, wild couplings, and wondrous appetites.

When he first confronted me in the barber's chair, he all but blotted out the sun behind him.

"You're the new Digger O'Dell I take it."

It was the black suit, the wing tips, the gray striped tie.

"Well, you're never getting your mitts on my body!" he challenged.

The barber stepped back to busy himself among the talcums and clippers, uncertain of the direction the conversation might take.

I considered the size of the man before me—the ponderous bulk of him, the breathtaking mass of him—and tried to imagine him horizontal and uncooperative. A sympathetic pain ran down my back. I winced.

"What makes you think I'd want anything to do with your body?" I countered in a tone that emphasized my indignation.

Russ and I were always friends after that.

He told me he intended to have his body donated to "medical science." He wanted to be given to the anatomy department of his alma mater, so that fledgling doctors could practice on him.

"Won't cost my people a penny."

When I told him they probably wouldn't take him, on account of his size, he seemed utterly crestfallen. The supply of cadavers for medical and dental schools in this land of plenty was shamefully but abundantly provided for by the homeless and helpless who were, for the most part, more "fit" than Russ was.

"But I was an All-American there!" Russ pleaded.

"Don't take my word for it," I advised. "Go ask for yourself."

Months later I was watering impatiens around the funeral home when Russ screeched to a halt on Liberty Street.

"OK, listen. Just cremate me and have the ashes scattered over town from one of those hot-air balloons." I could see he had given this careful thought. "How much will it cost me, bottom line?"

I told him the fees for our minimum services—livery and paperwork and a box.

368

"I don't want a casket," he hollered from the front seat of his Cadillac idling at curbside now.

I explained we wouldn't be using a casket as such, still he would have to be *in* something. The crematory people wouldn't accept his body unless it was *in* something. They didn't *handle* dead bodies without some kind of handles. This made tolerable sense to Russ. In my mind I was thinking of a shipping case, a kind of covered pallet compatible with fork-lifts and freight handlers, that would be sufficient to the task.

"I can only guess at what the balloon ride will cost, Russ. It's likely to be the priciest part. And, of course, you'd have to figure on inflation. Are you planning to do this very soon?"

"Don't get cute with me, Digger," he shouted. "Whadasay? Can I count on you?"

I told him it wasn't me he'd have to count on. He'd have to convince his wife and kids—the nine of them. They were the ones I'd be working for.

"But it's *my* funeral! My money."

Here is where I explained to Russ the subtle but important difference between the "adjectival" and "possessive" applications of the first-person singular pronoun for ownership—a difference measured by one's last breath. I explained that it was really *theirs* to do—his survivors, his family. It was really, listen closely, "the heirs"—the money, the funeral, what was or wasn't done with his body.

"I'll pay you now," he protested. "In cash—I'll pre-arrange it. Put it in my Will. They'll have to do it the way I want it."

I encouraged Russ to ponder the worst-case scenario: his wife and his family take me to court. I come armed with his Last Will and Preneed documents insisting that his body get burned and tossed from a balloon hovering over the heart of town during Sidewalk Sale Days. His wife Mary, glistening with real tears, his seven beautiful daughters with hankies in hand, his two fine sons, bearing up manfully, petition the court for permission to lay him out, have the preacher in, bury him up on the hill where they can visit his grave whenever the spirit moves them to.

"Who do you think wins that one, Russ? Go home and make your case with them."

I don't know if he ever had that conversation with them all. Maybe he just gave up. Maybe it had all been for my consumption. I don't know. That was years ago.

When Russ died last year in his easy chair, a cigar smoldering in the ash tray, one of those evening game-shows flickering on the TV, his son came to my house to summon me. His wife and his daughters were weeping around him. His children's children watched and listened. We brought the hearse and waited while each of the women kissed him and left. We brought the stretcher in and, with his son's help, moved him from the chair, then out the door and to the funeral home where we embalmed him, gave him a clean shave, and laid him out, all of us amazed at how age and infirmity had reduced him so. He actually fit easily into a Batesville Casket—I think it was Cherry, I don't remember.

But I remember how his vast heroics continued to grow over two days of wake. The stories were told and told again. Folks wept and laughed out loud at his wild antics. And after the minister, a woman who'd known Russ all her life and had braved his stoop on Halloween, had had her say about God's mercy and the size of heaven, she invited some of us to share our stories about Russ and after that we followed a brass band to the grave, holding forth with "When the Saints Go Marching In." And after everything had been said that could be said, and done that could be done, Mary and her daughters went home to the embraces of neighbors and the casseroles and condolences and Russ' sons remained to bury him. They took off their jackets, undid their ties, broke out a bottle and dark cigars and buried their father's body in the ground that none of us thought it would ever fit into. I gave the permit to the sexton and left them to it.

And though I know his body is buried there, something of Russ remains among us now. Whenever I see hot-air balloons—fat flaming birds adrift in evening air—I sense his legendary excesses raining down on us, old friends and family—his blessed and elect—who duck our heads or raise our faces to the sky and laugh or catch our breath or cry.

In even the best of caskets, it never all fits—all that we'd like to bury in them: the hurt and forgiveness, the anger and pain, the praise and thanksgiving, the emptiness and exaltations, the untidy feelings when someone dies. So I conduct this business very carefully because in the years since I've been here, when someone dies, they never call Jessica or the News Hound.

They call me.

1998

NEW YORK DAYS, 1958–1964

by CHARLES SIMIC

from THE GETTYSBURG REVIEW

EVEN THE OLD ROMANS knew. To have a poet for a son is bad news. I took precautions. I left home when I was eighteen. For the next couple of years, I lived in a basement apartment next to a furnace that hissed and groaned as if it were about to explode any moment. I kept the windows open in all kinds of weather, figuring that then I'd be able to crawl out to the sidewalk in a hurry. All winter long I wrote bad poems and painted bad pictures wearing a heavy overcoat and gloves in that underground hole.

At the Chicago newspaper where I worked, I proofread obituaries and want ads. At night I dreamed of lost dogs and funerals. Every payday I put a little money aside. One day I had enough to quit my job and take a trip to Paris, but I treated my friends to a smorgasbord in a fancy Swedish restaurant instead. It wasn't what we expected: there was too much smoked fish and pickled herring. After I paid the bill, everybody was still hungry, so we went down the street for pizza.

My friends wanted to know: When are you going to Paris? "I've changed my mind," I announced, ordering another round of beers. "I'm moving to New York, since I no longer have the money for Paris." The women were disappointed, but the fellows applauded. It didn't make sense, me going back to Europe after being in the States for only four years. Plus, to whom in Paris would I show my poems written in English?

"Your poems are just crazy images strung arbitrarily together," my pals complained, and I'd argue back: "Haven't you heard about surrealism and free association?" Bob Burleigh, my best friend, had a degree in English from the University of Chicago and possessed all the critical tools to do a close analysis of any poem. His verdict was: "Your poems don't mean anything."

My official reply to him was: "As long as they sound good, I'll keep them." Still, in private, I worried. I knew my poems were about something, but what was it? I couldn't define that "something" no matter how hard I tried. Bob and I would often quarrel about literature till the sun came up. To show him I was capable of writing differently, I wrote a thirty-page poem about the Spanish Inquisition. In the manner of Pound in his *Cantos*, I generously quoted original descriptions of tortures and public burnings. It wasn't surrealism, everybody agreed, but you still couldn't make heads or tails of what was going on. In one section, I engaged Tomás de Torquemada in a philosophical discussion, just as Dostoyevsky's Ivan did with the Grand Inquisitor. I read the poem to a woman called Linda in a greasy spoon on Clark Street. When we ran to catch a bus, I left the poem behind. The next morning, the short-order cook and I tried to find it buried under the garbage out back. But it was a hot summer day, and the trash in the alley smelled bad and was thickly covered with flies. So we didn't look too closely.

Later, I stood at the corner where we caught the bus the night before. I smoked a lot of cigarettes. I scratched my head. Several buses stopped, but I didn't get on any of them. The drivers would wait for me to make up my mind, then give me a dirty look and drive off with a burst of speed and a parting cough of black smoke.

I LEFT CHICAGO in August 1958 and went to New York, wearing a tan summer suit and a blue Hawaiian shirt. The weather was hot and humid. The movie marquees on 42nd Street were lit up twenty-four hours a day. Sailors were everywhere, and a few mounted policemen. I bought a long cigar and lit it nonchalantly for the benefit of a couple of young girls who stood at the curb afraid to cross the busy avenue.

A wino staggered up to me in Bryant Park and said: "I bark back at the dogs." A male hooker pulled a small statue of Jesus out of his tight pants and showed it to me. In Chinatown I saw a white hen pick a card with my fortune while dancing on a hot grill. In Central Park the early morning grass was matted where unknown lovers lay. In my hotel room I kept the mirror busy by making stranger and stranger faces at myself.

"Sweetheart," a husky woman's voice said to me when I answered the phone at four in the morning. I hung up immediately.

It was incredibly hot, so I slept naked. My only window was open, but there was a brick wall a few feet outside of it and no draft. I suspected there were rats on that wall, but I had no choice.

Late mornings, I sat in a little luncheonette on 8th Street reading the sports pages or writing poems:

> In New York on 14th Street
> Where peddlers hawk their wares
> And cops look the other way,
> There you meet the eternal—
> Con-artists selling watches, silk ties, umbrellas,
> After nightfall
> When the crosstown wind blows cold
> And my landlady throws a skinny chicken
> In the pot to boil. Fumes rise.
> I can draw her ugly face on the kitchen window,
> Then take a quick peek at the street below.

It was still summer. On advice from my mother, I went to visit an old friend of hers. She served me tea and cucumber sandwiches and asked about my plans for the future. I replied that I had no idea. I could see that she was surprised. To encourage me, she told me about someone who knew at the age of ten that he wanted to be a doctor and was now studying at a prestigious medical school. I agreed to come to a dinner party where I would meet a number of brilliant young men and women my age and profit by their example. Of course, I failed to show up.

At the Phoenix Book Shop in the Village, I bought a book of French stories. It was on sale and very cheap, but even so I had only enough money left to buy a cup of coffee and a toasted English muffin. I took my time sipping the lukewarm coffee and nibbling my muffin as I read the book. It was a dark and rainy night. I walked the near-empty streets for hours in search of the only two people I knew in the city. Not finding them home, I returned to my room, crawled shivering under the covers, and read in the silence, interrupted only by the occasional wailing of an ambulance:

> Monsieur Lantin had met the girl at a party given one
> evening by his office superior and love had caught him in
> its net.

She was the daughter of a country tax-collector who had died a few years before. She had come to Paris then with her mother, who struck up acquaintance with a few middle-class families in her district in the hope of marrying her off. They were poor and decent, quiet and gentle. The girl seemed the perfect example of a virtuous woman to whom every sensible young man dreams of entrusting his life. Her simple beauty had a modest, angelic charm and the imperceptible smile which always hovered about her lips seemed to be a reflection of her heart.

After midnight my hotel was as quiet as a tomb. I had to play the radio real low with my ear brushing against it in the dark. "Clap your hands, here comes Charlie," some woman sang, a hot Dixieland band backing her up, but just then I didn't think it was very funny.

WHILE THE WEATHER was still good, I sat on benches in Washington Square Park or Central Park, watching people and inventing stories to go along with their faces. If I was wearing my only suit and it rained, I sat in the lobbies of big hotels smoking cigars. I went window-shopping almost every night. An attractive pair of shoes or a shirt would make me pay a return visit even after midnight. The movies consumed an immense amount of my time. I would emerge after seeing the double feature twice, dazed, disoriented, and hungry. I often had toothache and waited for days for it to go away. I typed with two fingers on an ancient Underwood typewriter, which woke my hotel neighbors. They'd knock on my walls until I stopped. On a Monday morning while everyone else was rushing off to work, I took a long subway ride to Far Rockaway. Whenever the subway came out of the ground, I would get a glimpse of people working in offices and factories. I could tell they were hot and perspiring. On the beach there were only a few bathers, seemingly miles apart. When I stretched out on the sand and looked up, the sky was empty and blue.

When I was on the way home late one night, a drunk came out of a dark doorway with a knife in hand. He swayed and couldn't say what he wanted. I ran. Even though I knew there was no chance he would catch up with me, I didn't stop for many blocks. When I finally did, I no longer knew where I was. Around that time, I wrote:

Purse snatchers
Keep away from poor old women
They yell the loudest.
Stick to young girls,
The dreamy newlyweds
Buying heart-shaped pillows for their beds.
Bump into a drunk instead,
Offer a pencil to sell.
When he pulls out a roll of bills,
Snatch all he's got and split.
Duck that nightstick
Or your ears will ring
Even in your coffin.

I AM NOT EXAGGERATING when I say that I couldn't take a piss without a book in my hand. I read to fall asleep and to wake up. I read at my various jobs, hiding the book among the papers on my desk or in the half-open drawer. I read everything from Plato to Mickey Spillane. Even in my open coffin, some day, I should be holding a book. *The Tibetan Book of the Dead* would be most appropriate, but I'd prefer a sex manual or the poems of Emily Dickinson.

The book that made all the difference to my idea of poetry was an anthology of contemporary Latin-American verse that I bought on 8th Street. Published by New Directions in 1942 and long out of print even then, it introduced me to Jorge Luis Borges, Pablo Neruda, Jorge Carrera Andrade, Drumond de Andrade, Nicholas Guillen, Vicente Huidobro, Jorge de Lima, César Vallejo, Octavio Paz, and so many others. After that anthology, the poetry I read in literary magazines struck me as pretty timid. Nowhere in *The Sewanee Review* or *The Hudson Review* could I find poems like "Biography for the use of the birds" or "Liturgy of my Legs" or this one, by the Haitian poet Emile Roumer, "The Peasant Declares His Love":

High-yellow of my heart, with breasts like tangerines,
you taste better to me than eggplant stuffed with crab,
you are the tripe in my pepper-pot,
the dumpling in my peas, my tea of aromatic herbs.
You're the corned beef whose customhouse is my heart,
my mush with syrup that trickles down the throat.
You're a steaming dish, mushroom cooked with rice,

crisp potato fried, and little fish fried brown . . .
My hankering for love follows you wherever you go.
Your bum is a gorgeous basket brimming with fruits and meat.

The folk surrealism, the mysticism, the eroticism, and the wild flights of romance and rhetoric in these poets were much more appealing to me than what I found among the French and German modernists that I already knew. Of course, I started imitating the South Americans immediately:

I'm the last offspring of the old raven
Who fed himself on the flesh of the hanged . . .
A dark nest full of old misfortunes,
The wind raging above the burning tree-tops,
A cold north wind looking for its bugle.

I WAS READING Jakob Boehme in the New York Public Library on 42nd Street on a hot, muggy morning when a woman arrived in what must've been last night's party dress. She was not much older than I, but the hour and the lack of sleep gave her a world-weary air. She consulted the catalog, filled out a slip, received her book, and sat down at a table across from mine. I craned my neck, I squinted in my nearsighted way, and I even brushed past her a couple of times, but I could not figure out what she was reading. The book had no pictures, and it wasn't poetry, but she was so absorbed that her hair fell into her eyes. Perhaps she was sleeping.

Then, all of a sudden, when I was absolutely sure she was snoozing away, she turned a page with a long, thin finger. Her fingers were too thin, in my opinion. Was the poor dear eating properly? Was she dying of consumption? Her breasts in her low-cut black dress, on the other hand, looked pretty healthy. I saw no problem there.

Did she notice me spying on her? Absolutely not, unless she was a consummate actress, a budding Gene Tierney.

Of all of the people I watched surreptitiously over the years, how many noticed me and still remember me the way I remember them? I just have to close my eyes, and there she is, still reading her mysterious book. I don't see myself and have no idea what I look like or what clothes I'm wearing. The same goes for everyone else in the large reading room. They have no faces; they do not exist. She's reading slowly and turning the pages carefully. The air is heavy and muggy and the ceiling fan doesn't help. It could be a Monday or a Thursday, July or August. I'm not even certain if it was 1958 or 1959.

I went to hear Allen Tate read his poems at New York University. There were no more than twenty of us all together: a few friends of the poet, a couple of English professors, a scattering of graduate students, and one or two oddballs like me seated way in the back. Tate was thin and dapper, polite, and read in what I suppose could be described as a cultivated Southern voice. I had already read some of his essays and liked them very much, but the poetry, because of its seriousness and literary sophistication, was tedious. You would have to be nuts to want to write like that, I thought, remembering Jorge de Lima's poem in which he describes God tattooing the virgin: "Come, let us read the virgin, let us learn the future . . . /O men of little sight." Not a spot on her skin without tattoos: "that is why the virgin is so beautiful," the Brazilian poet says.

ON A HOT NIGHT in a noisy, crowded, smoke-filled jazz club, whiskey and beer were flowing, everyone was reeling with drink. A fat woman laughed so hard, she fell off her chair. It was hard to hear the music. Someone took a muted trumpet solo I tried to follow with my left ear, while with my right I had to listen to two women talk about a fellow called Mike, who was a scream in his bathing suit.

It was better to go to clubs on weeknights, when the crowd was smaller and there were no tourists. Best of all was walking in after midnight, in time to catch the final set of the night. One night when I arrived, the bass and drums were already playing, but where was Sonny Rollins, whom I came to hear? Finally we heard a muffled saxophone: Sonny was in the men's room, blowing his head off. Everybody quieted down, and soon enough he came through the door, bobbing his shaved head, dark shades propped on a nose fit for an emperor. He was playing "Get Happy," twisting it inside out, reconstituting it completely, discovering its concealed rhythmic and melodic beauties, and we were right there with him, panting with happiness.

It was great. The lesson I learned was: cultivate controlled anarchy. I found Rollins, Charlie Parker, and Thelonious Monk far better models of what an artist could be than most poets. The same was true of the painters. Going to jazz clubs and galleries made me realize that there was a lot more poetry in America than one could find in the quarterlies.

AT ONE OF THE READINGS at NYU given by a now forgotten academic poet of the 1950s, just as the professional lovers of poetry in the audience were already closing their eyes blissfully in anticipation of the poet's familiar, soul-stirring clichés, there was the sound of paper being torn. We all turned around to look. A shabby old man was ripping newspapers into a brown shopping bag. He saw people glare at him and stopped. The moment we turned back to the poet who went on reading, oblivious of everything, in a slow monotone, the man resumed ripping, but now more cautiously, with long pauses between rips.

And so it went: the audience would turn around with angry faces, he'd stop for a while and then continue while the poet read on and on.

MY FIRST JOB in the city was selling dress shirts in Stern's Department Store on 42nd Street. I dressed well and learned how to flash a friendly smile. Even more importantly, I learned how to let myself be humiliated by the customers without putting up the slightest resistance.

My next job was in the Doubleday Bookstore on 5th Avenue. I would read on the sly while the manager was busy elsewhere. Eventually I could guess what most of the customers wanted even before they opened their mouths. There were the bestseller types and the self-help book types, the old ladies in love with mysteries, and the sensitive young women who were sure to ask for Khalil Gibran's *The Prophet*.

But I didn't like standing around all day, so I got a job typing address labels at New York University Press. After a while they hired another fellow to give me help. We sat in the back room playing chess for hours on end. Occasionally, one of the editors would come and ask us to pick up his dry cleaning, pay an electric bill, buy a sandwich or a watermelon.

Sal and I took our time. We sat in the park and watched the girl students go by. Sal was a few years older than I, and a veteran of the Air Force. When he was just a teenager, his parents died suddenly and he inherited the family bakery in Brooklyn. He got married and in two years had ruined the business.

How? I wanted to know. "I took my wife to the Latin Quarter and Copacabana every night," he told me with obvious satisfaction. He joined the Air Force to flee his creditors. Now he was a veteran and a homespun philosopher.

Sal agreed with H. L. Mencken that you are as likely to find an honest politician as you are an honest burglar. Only the church, in his view, was worse: "The priests are all perverts," he confided to me, "and the Pope is the biggest pervert of all."

"What about Billy Graham?" I asked, trying not to drop my watermelon.

"That's all he thinks about," Sal assured me with a wink.

The military was no better. All the officers he had met were itching to commit mass murder. Even Ike, in his opinion, had the mug of a killer.

Only women were good. "If you want to have a happy life," he told me every day, "learn to get along with the ladies."

AFTER SEVERAL FLEABAG HOTELS, I finally found a home at Hotel Albert on 10th Street and University Place. The room was small, and of course the window faced a brick wall, but the location was perfect, and the rent was not too high. From Friday noon to Sunday morning, I had plenty of money. The rest of the week, I scraped by on candy bars for lunch and hamburgers or cheap Chinese food for dinner. Later I would buy a glass of beer for fifteen cents and spend the rest of the night perfecting the art of making it last forever.

My first poems were published in the Winter 1959 issue of *The Chicago Review,* but other publications came slowly after that: the mail brought me rejection slips every day. One, I remember, had a personal note from the editor that said: "Dear Mr. Simic, you're obviously an intelligent young man, so why do you waste your time writing so much about pigs and cockroaches?"

To spit on guys like you, I wanted to write back.

AFTER WORK ON FRIDAYS, my friend Jim Brown and I would tour the bars. We'd start a few beers at the Cedar Tavern, near our rooms, then walk over to the San Remo on MacDougal Street, where Brown would have a martini and I would drink red wine. Afterwards, we would most likely go to the White Horse, where Brown had a tab, to drink whiskey. With some of the regulars, Brown would discuss everything from socialism to old movies; I didn't open my mouth much, for the moment I did and people heard my accent, I would have to explain where I came from, and how, and why. I thought of printing a card, the kind deaf panhandlers pass around, with my life story on it and an abbreviated account of the geography and history of the Balkans.

Around midnight Brown and I would walk back to the Cedar, which was packed by then, and have a nightcap. Over hamburgers, Brown would harangue me for not having read François Rabelais or Sir Thomas Browne yet. Later, lying in my bed, with drink and talk floating in my head and the sound of creaking beds, smokers' coughs, and love cries coming from the other rooms, I would not be able to sleep. I would go over the interesting and stupid things I had heard that night.

For instance, there were still true believers around in those days who idealized life in the Soviet Union and disparaged the United States. What upset me the most was when some nice-looking, young woman would nod in agreement. I reproached myself for not telling her how people over there were turned into angels at the point of a gun. My shyness and cowardice annoyed me no end. I couldn't fall asleep for hours and then, just as I was finally drifting off, one of my rotten teeth would begin a little chat with me.

WITH THE ARRIVAL of the Beats, both as a literary movement and as a commercial venture, the scene changed. Coffee shops sprang up everywhere in the Village. In addition to folk singing and comedy acts, they offered poetry readings. *Where the Beat Meet the Elite,* said a banner over a tourist trap. "Oh God, come down and fuck me!" some young woman prayed in her poem, to the horror of out-of-town customers.

But New York was also a great place for poetry: within the same week, one could also hear John Berryman and May Swenson, Allen Ginsberg and Denise Levertov, Frank O'Hara and LeRoi Jones. I went to readings for two reasons: to hear the poets and to meet people. I could always find, sitting grumpily in the corner, someone with whom it was worth striking up a conversation. The readings themselves left me with mixed feelings. One minute I would be dying of envy, and the next with boredom and contempt. It took me a few years to sort it all out. In the meantime, I sought other views. I'd spot someone thumbing an issue of *The Black Mountain Review* in The Eighth Street Bookstore and end up talking to them. Often that would lead to a cup of coffee or a beer. No matter how hip you think you are, someone always knows more. The literary scene had a greater number of true originals then than it has today—autodidacts, booze hounds, and near-derelicts who were walking encyclopedias—for example Tony, an unemployed bricklayer, who went around saying things like: *Even the mutes are unhappy since they've learned to read lips,* and *It took me sixty years to bend down to a flower.*

Then, there was the tall, skinny fellow with graying hair I talked to after hearing Richard Wilbur read at NYU. He told me that the reason contemporary poets were so bad is because they were lazy. I asked what he meant, and he explained: "They write a couple of hours per week, and the rest of the time they have a ball living in the lap of luxury with rich floozies hanging on their arms and paying their bills. You've got to write sixteen hours per day to be a great poet." I asked him what he did, and he muttered that he worked in the post office.

During one of my rare trips back to Chicago to visit my mother, Bob Burleigh told me about a terrific young poet I ought to meet. His name was Bill Knott. He worked nights in a hospital emptying bedpans and was usually at home during the day. He lived in a rooming house not too far away, so we went to see him.

An old woman answered the bell and said Bill was upstairs in his room. But when we knocked there was no answer. Bob shouted, "It's me, Bob." Just as we were about to leave, I heard a sound of hundreds of bottles clinking together, and the door opened slowly. Soon we saw what it was: we had to wade through an ankle-deep layer of empty Pepsi bottles to advance into the room. Bill was a large man in a dirty, white T-shirt; one lens of his glasses was wrapped with masking tape, presumably broken. The furnishings were a bed with a badly stained mattress, a large poster of Monica Vitti, a refrigerator with an old TV set on it, and a couple of chairs and a table with piles of books on them. Bob sat on the bed, and I was given a chair after Bill swept some books onto the floor. Bill, who hadn't sat down, asked us: "How about a Pepsi?" "Sure," we replied. "What the heck!" The fridge, it turned out, contained nothing but rows and rows of Pepsi bottles.

We sipped our sodas and talked poetry. Bill had read everything: we spoke of René Char, and Bill quoted Char from memory. Regarding contemporary American poetry, we were in complete agreement: except for Robert Bly, James Wright, Frank O'Hara, and a few others, the poets we read in the magazines were the most unimaginative, dull, pretentious, know-nothing bunch you were ever likely to encounter. As far as these poets were concerned, Arthur Rimbaud, Hart Crane, and Guillaume Apollinaire might never have existed. They knew nothing of modern art, cinema, jazz. We had total contempt for them. We bought magazines like *Poetry* in those days in order to nourish our rage: Bob and I regularly analyzed its poems so we could grasp the full range of their imbecility. I did not see any of Bill Knott's poems that day, but later he became one of my favorite poets.

BACK IN NEW YORK, I had a long talk with Robert Lowell about nineteenth-century French poetry. We were at a party following a reading at the Y. It was late, and most people had gone home. Lowell was seated in an armchair, two young women were sitting on the floor, one on each side of him, and I was on the floor facing him. Although he spoke interestingly about Charles Baudelaire, Tristan Corbiere, and Jules Laforgue, what had me totally captivated were not his words, but his hands. Early in our conversation, he massaged the women's necks; after a while he slid his hands down inside their dresses and worked their breasts. They didn't seem to mind, hanging on his every word. Why wasn't I a great poet? Instead of joining in, I started disagreeing with him, told him he was full of shit. True, I had flunked out of school in Paris, but when it came to the French vernacular, my ear could not be faulted. Lowell did not seem to notice my increasing nastiness, but his two groupies certainly did. Finally, I said good night and split. I walked from the upper West Side down to my room in the Village, fuming and muttering like an old drunk.

ANOTHER TIME I was drinking red wine, chain-smoking, and writing, long past midnight. Suddenly, the poem took off, the words just flowing, in my head a merry-go-round of the most brilliant similes and metaphors. *This is it!* I was convinced there had never been such a moment of inspiration in the whole history of literature. I reread what I'd written and had to quit my desk and walk around the room, I got so excited. No sooner was I finished with one poem than I started another even more incredible one. Toward daybreak, paying no attention to my neighbor's furious banging on the wall, I typed them out with my two fingers and finally passed out exhausted in the bed. In the morning, I dragged myself to work, dead tired but happy.

When evening came, I sat down to savor what I wrote the night before, a glass of wine in my hand. The poems were terrible! Incoherent babble, surrealist drivel! How could I have written such crap? I was stunned, depressed, and totally confused.

Still, it wasn't the first time this had happened: nights of creative bliss followed by days of gagging. With great clarity I could see every phony move I had made, every borrowing, every awkwardness. Then I found myself in a different kind of rush: I had only seconds left to rip up, burn, and flush down the toilet all these poems before the doctors and nurses rushed in and put me in a straightjacket. Of course, the next night, I was at it again, writing furiously and shaking my head in disbelief at the gorgeous images and metaphors flooding out of my pen.

I have thrown out hundreds of poems in my life, four chapters of a novel, the first act of a play, fifty or so pages of a book on Joseph

382

Cornell. Writing poetry is a supreme pleasure, and so is wiping the slate clean.

TODAY PEOPLE SOMETIMES ASK me when I decided to become a poet. I never did. The truth is, I had no plans: I was content merely to drift along. My immigrant experience protected me from any quick embrace of a literary or political outlook. Being a suspicious outsider was an asset, I realized at some point. Modernism, which is already a collage of various cultures and traditions, suited me well. The impulse of every young artist and writer to stake everything on a single view and develop a recognizable style was, of course, attractive, but at the same time I knew myself to be pulled in different directions. I loved Whitman, and I loved the Surrealists. The more widely I read, the less I wanted to restrict myself to a single aesthetic and literary position. I was already many things, so why shouldn't I be the same way in poetry?

One evening I would be in some Village coffee shop arguing about Charles Olson and Projective Verse, and the next evening I would be eating squid in a Greek restaurant, arguing in Serbian with my father or uncle Boris about Enrico Caruso and Beniamino Gigli, Mario Del Monaco, and Jussi Bjorling.

On one such evening, a nice, old, silver-haired lady, pointing to three other silver-haired ladies smiling at us from the next table, asked Boris and me: "Would you, please, tell us what language you are speaking?"

Boris, who never missed an opportunity to play a joke, made a long face, sighed once or twice, and—with moist eyes and a sob in his voice—informed her that, alas, we were the last two remaining members of a white African tribe speaking a now nearly extinct language.

That surprised the hell out of her! She didn't realize, she told us, now visibly confused, that there were native white African tribes.

"The best kept secret in the world," Boris whispered to her and nodded solemnly while she rushed back to tell her friends.

It was part of being an immigrant and living in many worlds at the same time, some of which were imaginary. After what we had been through, the wildest lies seemed plausible. The poems that I was going to write had to take that into account.

1998

383

TWO ACCIDENTS: REFLECTIONS ON CHANCE AND CREATIVITY

by LEWIS HYDE

from THE KENYON REVIEW

> Chance and chance alone has a message for us. Everything
> that occurs out of necessity, everything expected, repeated
> day in and day out, is mute. Only chance can speak to us.
> We read its messages much as gypsies read the images
> made by coffee grounds at the bottom of a cup.
>
> MILAN KUNDERA (48)

I.   The Lucky Find

OUTSIDE my study door a bird has built its nest with the usual twigs
and moss but also, in this case, with two strips of paper torn from the
sides of my computer printout. The bird did not set out in search of
those white strands, of course, but when it happened to find them it
knew how to weave a habitable home. "I do not seek, I find": this is Picasso's famous dictum, underlining the wandering portion of his artistic practice. In both cases, an intelligence makes itself at home in the
happening world, one not so attached to design or purpose as to
blinker out the daily wealth of accidents. "Chance itself pours in at
every avenue of sense: it is of all things most obtrusive" (Hacking 200).
I happened on that sentence from the philosopher C. S. Pierce late in
the day I was writing these paragraphs, as I happened on that bird

early in the morning. A friend was stuck writing her thesis when, wandering aimlessly through the library, she happened on a carrel where someone had spread out just the article she needed. Antonio Stradivari, wandering in Venice one day, came upon a pile of broken, waterlogged oars, out of which he made some of his most beautiful violins. A lucky find gave Picasso one of his famous sculptural creations:

> Guess how I made that head of a bull. One day, in a rubbish heap, I found an old bicycle seat, lying beside a rusted handlebar . . . and my mind instantly linked them together. The idea for this *Tête de Taureau* came to me before I had even realized it. I just soldered them together. . . . (Picasso 157)

In classical Greece the accidental find was called a *hermaion,* which means a "gift-of-Hermes," though it should be said that because Hermes was such a duplicitous god his "gifts" can entail both finding and loss. He is generous, but also a thief. In a journal entry Carl Kerényi records how a book of his disappeared on a boat trip: "Does Hermes wish to play . . . with me again? . . . I am left with the feeling of being stolen from, something uncanny, a vague sense of change of circumstances—truly something hermetic" (Kerényi, *Hermes* iv-v). Accidental loss, accidental gain—both flow from Hermes, the single constant being accident.

And yet that formulation doesn't quite catch the tone of things, for with the right kind of attention it is the *happy* accident, the creative accident, that Hermes engenders. Perhaps Kerényi's use of the word "uncanny" bears attention: In hermetic territory, who is to say what is loss and what is gain? It's hard to get your bearings. There's a "change of circumstance," that's all you know, for in uncanny space the terms themselves collapse, and a sudden loss (my computer crashes, my car keys disappear) can flip and become a sudden gain (I slow down, I go walking in the woods).

The idea of "finding" itself bespeaks this indeterminate space. There are many ways in this world to acquire things: you can make something with your labor, you can buy it, you can receive it as a gift, you can steal it, and so on. "Finding" occupies an odd position in any such list. If I pocket a five-dollar bill found in the trash at the edge of a deserted parking lot, am I a thief? How should we describe a farmer who bumps into buried treasure with his plow (this being Aristotle's old example of a chance event)? He gets the gold not by working for it, not as a present from friend or relation, not by stealing it, not by purchase. . . . We are in a shady area here, and shady language is in order. "It fell off the truck" is the American version of what the ancient Greeks meant by a *hermaion*.

To speak of happy accident is not to deny the negative side of chance; we all know that accident can bring great loss and grief, contingency can breed great tragedy. But for the tone that accompanies a "gift of Hermes" we might look at an example that features the god himself. In the *Homeric Hymn to Hermes* we hear how Hermes, newly born, stepped from his mother's cave and bumped into something unexpected—a wood turtle waddling past.

> Hermes picked up the turtle with both hands
> and carried his lovely toy into the house.
> He turned her over and with a scoop of grey iron
> scraped the marrow from her mountain shell.
> And, just as a swift thought can fly through the
> heart of a person haunted with care,
> just as bright glances spin from the eyes,
> so, in one instant, Hermes knew what to do and did it.
> He cuts stalks of reed to measure, fitted them through
> the shell and fastened their ends across the back.
> Skillfully, he tightened a piece of cowhide,
> set the arms in place, fixed a yoke across them,
> and stretched seven sheep-gut strings to sound in
> harmony[1]

In this way and in this slightly manic mood the young god made the first lyre. He is a little like Picasso with the bicycle parts in the rubbish heap; not everyone would have made something of that encounter ("What's out there?" "Just an old turtle."), but when Hermes is around, coincidence turns fertile.

The ingredients of such prolific moments—surprise, quick thinking, sudden gain, and so forth—suffuse them with humor, not tragedy. Hermes laughs when he happens upon the turtle. Picasso once described his amusement coming upon some sea urchins in a tidal pool: "The sense of sight enjoys being surprised. . . . It's the same law which governs humor. Only the unexpected sally makes you laugh" (Picasso 90). The agile mind is pleased to find what it was not looking for. Someone once said that Picasso painted to do a kind of "research"; the remark annoyed him, and prompted him to formulate his sense of "finding":

In my opinion to search means nothing in painting. To find, is the thing. Nobody is interested in following a man who, with his eyes fixed on the ground, spends his life looking for the pocketbook that fortune should put in his path. The one who finds something . . . , even if his intention were not to search for it, at least arouses our curiosity, if not our admiration. . . .

When I paint, my object is to show what I have found and not what I am looking for. (Picasso 71–72)

Whoever the gods of fortune are, they will drop things in your path, but if you search for those things you will not find them. Wandering is the trick, and giving up on "loss" or "gain," and then agility of mind.

*

What, if anything, does an accident, lucky find, or chance event reveal? For most ancient or believing peoples the answer is simple: accidents are no accident; they reveal the will of the gods. What happens on earth follows the designs of heaven, and if it appears to be random chance that is only because our sight is not capacious enough to see that apparent chance always follows grand design. An expert on Greek oracles tells us that in ancient Greece, ". . . the drawing of lots was governed, not by chance, but by the will of the gods" (Flaceliere 17). Such has also been the Christian understanding for centuries. In his *Anatomy of Melancholy*, Robert Burton writes that "Columbus did not find out America by chance, but God directed him. . . . It was contingent to him, but necessary to God" (OED *sv contingent*). Even today in the United States, Amish communities elect their bishops by a lottery, which they understand to reveal God's will in the matter.

In cases where a character like Hermes is taken to be the agent of chance it now becomes apparent why he is also thought of as a herald or messenger. With Hermes, contingency is prophecy, at least to those who have the ears to hear. Hermes gives his followers acute hearing; they call him "the god of the third ear," the one that can hear an essence buried in an accident. There is a form of divination associated with Hermes called *cledonomancy*, derived from *cledon*, which means an accidental but portentous remark, the language version of a lucky find. Long ago Pausanias described this oracle of "Hermes-of-the-

Marketplace": At dusk as the lamps are being lit the petitioner leaves a "coin of local money" at the image of Hermes, whispers the questions he hopes to have answered, puts his hands over his ears, and walks away. When he takes his hands from his ears, the first words he hears contain the oracle's reply. All the better if the words are uttered by a child or a fool, someone clearly incapable of calculating an effect (Flaceliere 9–10).

Hermes, then, is not only an agent of luck, he helps to draw heaven's hidden meanings out of luck's apparent nonsense. In the modern world we find a similar conjunction of accident and insight, only the discovered meanings now lie in the head rather than the heavens, for we have translated the ancient art of inquiring into the will of the gods into psychological terms. "Divination techniques . . . are techniques to catalyze one's own unconscious knowledge," says Marie Louise von Franz in a typical modern formulation (38). Von Franz was a student of Carl Jung's, and it was Jung in his preface to the *I Ching* who famously announced that when we find meaning in synchronous events (the uncanny encounter in a distant city, say, or the three of spades turned up on the third of May) we are getting insight into "the subjective . . . states of the observer or observers" (xxiv). Freud was less directly concerned with divination, but his understanding of chance was similar. All his lectures on "the psychology of errors" are addressed to an imagined doubter who would say that slips of the tongue "are not worth my explanation; they are little accidents" (27). On the contrary, Freud argues, what hides in the unconscious only "masquerades as a lucky chance," and we must learn to remove the mask (69). Slips of the tongue and other errors "are serious mental acts; they have their meanings"; they "are not accidents" (41). Seeming mistakes will appear "as omens" to all those who have hermeneutic "courage and resolution" (53).

I suppose we will have to say it is no accident how many artists in the twentieth century had a similar understanding at the same time. Picasso believed that no painting can be plotted out beforehand and yet nothing is an accident, a seeming contradiction unless we understand that Picasso believed in the deep self, a personality of which the artist is not necessarily aware. "I consider a work of art as the product of calculations," he once said, "calculations that are frequently unknown to the author himself. It is exactly like the carrier pigeon, calculating his return to the loft. The calculation that precedes intelligence" (Picasso 30). What leads this pigeon-like artist are his desires, his impulses. In a work of art, "what counts is what is spontaneous, impulsive" (21). "Art is not the application of a canon of beauty but what the instinct and the brain can conceive beyond any canon. When we love a woman we don't start measuring her limbs. We love with our desires . . ." (11).

One of Picasso's favorite assignments for a young artist was to have him or her try to draw a perfect circle. It can't be done; everyone draws a circle with some particular distortion, and that distorted circle is *your* circle, an insight into *your* style. "Try to make the circle as best you can. And since nobody before you has made a perfect circle, you can be sure that your circle will be completely your own. Only then will you have a chance to be original" (45). The deviations from the ideal give an insight into the style, and thus Picasso says, "from errors one gets to know the personality" (45).

This, then, is the sense in which an artist works with accidents, yet when he or she is done "there are no accidents. Accidents, try to change them—it's impossible. The accident reveals man" (91). With Picasso, as with Jung and Freud, accidents point to the concealed portion of the man or woman to whom they happened.

Ancient or modern, then, one continuing line of thought holds that accidents break the surface of our lives to reveal hidden purpose or design. The carefully interwoven structures of thought and social practice provide stability and structure, but they bring a kind of blindness and stupidity, too. Gifts of Hermes tear little holes in those fabrics to offer us brief intelligence of other realms.

*

That, at least, is one answer to the question of what a lucky find reveals. But here Hermes himself might come forward to complicate things. When he bumps into the tortoise, he seems to be giving a *hermaion* to himself, and what, we might ask, does *it* reveal? Who is sending a message to whom? In another story Hermes divides some sacrificial meat by lottery: in the Greek tradition a lottery is supposed to reveal the will of the gods, but when a god holds one, whose will is being revealed? The implication seems to be that heaven itself is not immune from chance. When a character like Hermes is around, the gods themselves suffer from uncertainty, and if that is the case an accidental find must sometimes reveal something other than heavenly will or hidden purpose. A remark by Carl Kerényi suggests what this might be: "Chance and accident," he says, "are an intrinsic part of primeval chaos [and] Hermes carries over this peculiarity of primeval chaos—accident—into the Olympian order" (Kerényi, "Primordial Child" 57).

In this conceit the cosmos is an orderly thing surrounded by chaos, confusion, muddle. "Opportunities are not plain, clean gifts," writes the psychoanalyst James Hillman; "they trail dark and chaotic attachments to their unknown backgrounds . . ." (154). It must be that sometimes our assertions about higher order and hidden design are fables we have made up to help us ignore our own contingency. Accidents tear little holes in the fabric of life to reveal, well, little holes. In one of the books he published under the general title *Hermès*, Michael Serres, a French philosopher of science, writes skeptically about our assumptions of underlying unity in things. "The real," Serres suggests, may be "sporadic," made of "fluctuating tatters." Perhaps "the state of things consists of islands sown in archipelagoes on the noisy, poorly-understood disorder of the sea . . ." (xiii). Perhaps accidents reveal, not hidden realms of greater order, but a world of shifting fragments, noise, and imperfection. Accident is the revelation of accident.

In all fairness to the nature of hermetic accidents, however, I must here double back on myself one last time and add that in the case of the tortoise-shell lyre and the lottery I mentioned, when Hermes works with chance he does more than upset the order of things. If Hermes is involved, after a touch of chaos comes another cosmos. Hermes is a god of luck, but more than that, he stands for what might be called "smart luck" rather than "dumb luck." These two kinds of luck figure in Latin mythology, where Mercurius stands for the smart and Hercules for the dumb. "Should a *stupid* fellow have good luck, he owes it to the witless Hercules . . . ," Kerényi writes, referring us to a story in Horace in which "Mercurius once let Hercules talk him into enriching a stupid man. Mercurius showed him a treasure which he could use to buy the piece of land he was working. He did so, but then proved himself unworthy of the Hermetic windfall by continuing to work the same piece of land!" (Kerényi, *Hermes* 24–25).

That is "dumb luck," the luck of all gamblers whose winnings never enrich them, the luck of the grocery store clerk who hits the lottery, quickly spends himself into bankruptcy, and returns to being a clerk. It is sterile luck, luck without change. "Smart luck," on the other hand, adds craft to accident—in both senses, technical skill and cunning. Hermes is a skillful maker of the lyre, and he is canny as well, leveraging the wealth his *hermaion* brings. Hermes "trades up" with his lyre; he doesn't become just a turtle farmer or a lyre maker with an unpaid small business loan. Late in the *Hymn* he sings a song with his new instrument, and the tune seduces his brother Apollo, from whom he has recently stolen a herd of cattle. After Hermes stops singing, the *Hymn* says, "Apollo was seized with a longing he could do nothing about; he opened his mouth and the words flew out: 'Butcher of cattle, trickster, busy boy, friend of merry-makers, the things you're interested in are worth fifty cows. Soon I believe we shall settle our quarrel in peace.' "

Hermes, at this point in the *Hymn,* is actually involved in negotiating for certain divine powers; Apollo not only knows that, he accepts the music of the lyre as a part of the exchange. Under the manic spell of this *hermaion,* Apollo cancels the debt that Hermes incurred by his theft. The point is simply that this lucky find does more than add chaos to Apollo's world. The lyre *is* disruptive, of course—with it Hermes gets the spellbound Apollo to abandon his sense of what should properly happen to a thief. So, on the one hand, a touch of chaos comes into the Olympian order; but, on the other hand, it doesn't endure because Hermes soon weaves his lucky find into the scene he has disturbed (forever after Apollo plays the lyre as part of his own repertoire). Thus does Hermes show us how "smart luck" responds to hermetic windfalls.

*

Perhaps, then, what a lucky find reveals first is neither cosmos nor chaos but the mind of the finder. It might even be better to drop "cosmos" and "chaos," and simply say that a chance event is a little bit of the world as it is—a world always larger and more complicated than our cosmologies—and that smart luck is a kind of responsive intelligence invoked by whatever happens.

A story of scientific discovery makes a good illustration. "Chance favors the prepared mind" is Louis Pasteur's famous aphorism, and his own career abundantly illustrates its meaning. The neurologist James Austin has described one famous case:

> Pasteur was studying chicken cholera when his work was interrupted for several weeks. During the delay, the infectious organisms in one of his cultures weakened. When

injected, these organisms no longer caused the disease. However, this same group of fowls survived when he later reinoculated them with a new batch of virulent organisms. Pasteur made a crucial distinction when he recognized that the first inoculation was not a "bad experiment" but that the weakened organisms had exerted a protective effect. (202)

For chance to "favor the prepared mind" means, first of all, that chance events need a context before they can amount to anything. In evolution, a chance mutation disappears immediately if there is no hospitable environment to receive it; more to the point here, in this example Pasteur had a set of ideas about disease and inoculation and was thereby more able to recuperate his botched experiment. But notice that in addition to having a ready structure of ideas, the prepared mind is ready for what happens. It has its theories, but it attends as well to the anomaly that does not fit them. We therefore get this paradox: with smart luck, the mind is prepared for what it isn't prepared for. It has a kind of openness, holding its ideas lightly and willing to have them exposed to impurity and the unintended.

In a 1920 letter to a friend, James Joyce made a wonderful, quick remark on Hermes that links the god to this receptive mind. Joyce is musing on the mysterious plant, the *moly*, that Hermes gives Odysseus on the road to Circe's house. Classicists aren't sure what the *moly* is in fact (the wild garlic?), but Joyce has a hunch as to what it is in spirit:

> Moly is a nut to crack. My latest is this. Moly is the gift of Hermes, god of public ways, and is the invisible influence (prayer, chance, agility, *presence of mind,* power of recuperation) which saves in case of accident. . . . Hermes is the god of signposts: i.e. he is, specially for a traveller like Ulysses, the point at which roads parallel merge and roads contrary also. He is an accident of providence. (272)

What I like best here is the phrase Joyce underlines: when Hermes is around, his gifts reveal the *presence of mind.* Not some hidden structure of mind, necessarily (not the Oedipus complex or an instinct for beauty), but more simply some wit that responds and shapes, the mind on-the-road, agile, shifty in a shifting world, capable of recuperation, and located especially at the spot where roads "parallel . . . and contrary" converge. Paul Valéry's enigmatic assertion, "the bottom of the mind is paved with crossroads," speaks to me here, for the mind that has smart luck makes meaning from unlikely coincidence and juxtaposition.

How do we come by this wandering, crossroad mind? We already have it, I suppose, but those who take it seriously keep it awake through ritual attention to its gods, something as simple as touching the statute of Hermes as one leaves the town gate or enters the marketplace. At the thresholds where one crosses into territories of increased contingency, such small ritual action brings to mind the mind contingency demands. To go on a journey (or enter the painting studio) without consulting the god of the roads is to invite dumb luck; to take the god into account is to summon the presence of mind that can work with whatever happens. The first lucky find (or unlucky loss!) will reveal whether or not anything has responded to the summons.

II.   A Net to Catch Contingency

In the late 1940s D. T. Suzuki, the Japanese Buddhist scholar, lectured at Columbia University, and one of these lectures gave the composer John Cage a key insight into what was already a part of his method. Suzuki drew a circle on the blackboard and sectioned off a bit of it with two parallel lines. The full circle stood for the possible range of mind, while the small part between the lines stood for the ego. Cage remembers Suzuki saying that "the ego can cut itself off from this big Mind, which passes through it, or it can open itself up" (52).[2]

It is especially by our "likes and dislikes," Cage says, that we cut ourselves off from the wider mind (and the wider world). Likes and dislikes are the lap dogs and guard dogs of the ego, busy all the time, panting and barking at the gates of attachment and aversion and thereby narrowing perception and experience. Furthermore, the ego itself cannot intentionally escape what the ego does—intention always operates in terms of desire or aversion—and we therefore need a practice or discipline of *non*intention, a way to make an end run around the ego's habitual operations. The Zen tradition, Cage says, suggests the practice of cross-legged meditation: "You go *in* through discipline, then you get free of the ego." Cage thought his own artistic practice moved in the other direction to the same end: "I decided to go *out*. That's why I decided to use the chance operations. I used them to free myself from the ego" (229).

What do you want for lunch, a hamburger or a hot dog? Flip a coin, and the decision will have nothing to do with your habitual tastes. Would you like silence here, a sustained flute tone, the noise of traffic, or the car alarm? You might hate car alarms, as I do, but with Cage's method "you" and "I" do not get to choose. Cage says:

> I have used chance operations . . . in a way involving a multiplicity of questions which I ask rather than choices that I make. . . . If I have the opportunity to continue working, I think the work will resemble more and more, not the work of a person, but something that might have happened, even if the person weren't there. (52–53)

"Something that might have happened," by haps, per chance. Cage's faith was that this method would, as meditation promises, "open the doors of the ego" so as to turn it "from a concentration on itself to a flow with all of creation" (20). Cage was fond of repeating Meister Eckehart's assertion that "we are made perfect by what happens to us rather than by what we do" (Cage, *Silence* 64); therefore Cage not only allowed things to happen, he developed a practice that encouraged them to do so.

Popular perceptions of Cage tend not to see that for Cage chance operations were a spiritual practice, a discipline. One kind of courting of chance is exactly the opposite of discipline, of course—the young person putting herself at risk, the gambler on a spree, the speculator playing with a relative's money. Cage was a playful man, but these are not his uses of chance, as he himself often struggled to make clear. In recommending nonintention he once explained, "I'm not saying, 'Do whatever you like,' and yet that's precisely what some people now think I'm saying. . . . The freedoms I've given [in a musical score] have not been given to permit just anything that one wants to do, but have been invitations for people to free themselves from their likes and dislikes, and to discipline themselves" (102).

In many ways the discipline Cage recommended was as stringent as that of any monk on a month-long meditation retreat. He asked that intention be thwarted rigorously, not occasionally or whimsically. He *worked hard* at chance. He would literally spend months tossing coins and working with the *I Ching* to construct a score. It took so much time he would toss coins as he rode the New York subway to see friends. One famous piece less than five minutes long took him four years to write. And when a piece was finished it was not meant to be an occasion for improvisation; it was meant to be played *within the constraints* chance had determined. "The highest discipline is the discipline of chance operations. . . . The person is being disciplined, not the work" (219). The person is being disciplined away from his or her "likes and dislikes," away from the ego's habitual attitudes and toward a fundamental change of consciousness.

An even fuller sense of the intentions of Cage's nonintention can be gleaned from the several places where he contrasts his own practice with the work of other artists who might seem, at first glance, to be engaged in a similar enterprise. Cage distanced himself from improvisation, from automatic art, and from methods of spontaneous composition, even though such things might initially seem related to his project. The score for Cage's *Concert for Piano and Orchestra,* for example, "frees" the orchestra at one point, and if you listen to the Town Hall recording of this piece you will hear one of the woodwinds improvise a bit of Stravinsky at that point. "You could look at the part I had given him," Cage later commented, "and you'd never find anything like that in it. He was just going wild—not playing what was in front of him, but rather whatever came into his head. I have tried in my work to free myself from my own head. I would hope that people would take that opportunity to do likewise" (68–69).

For the same reasons, Cage was not drawn to an art like that of Jackson Pollock. Pollock's working assumption was that the wildness of his paintings expressed his deep, primitive, and feeling self, and Cage would argue, I think, that no matter how "deep" the self is, it is still the self. "Automatic art . . . has never interested me, because it is a way of falling back, resting on one's memories and feelings subconsciously, is it not? And I have done my utmost to free people from that" (173). Cage much preferred the incidental drawings that are scattered throughout Thoreau's *Journals:* "The thing that is beautiful about the Thoreau drawings is that they're completely lacking in self-expression" (126).

*

The point of Cage's art, then, is not to entertain nor to enchant but to open its maker (and, perchance, its audience) to the world, to what is the case. In one of his oft-repeated stories, Cage tells of a time when he had just left an exhibit of paintings by his friend Mark Tobey: "I was standing at a corner of Madison Avenue waiting for a bus and I happened to look at the pavement, and I noticed the experience of looking at the pavement was the same as the experience of looking at the Tobey. Exactly the same. The aesthetic enjoyment was just as high" (175). Cage is praising Tobey here, not criticizing him, for Tobey's work had opened its viewer's eyes; he could *see* and enjoy what previously might have been the city's dull and unregarded asphalt skin. Such is one function of twentieth-century painting, says Cage, "to open our eyes," as its music should open our ears (174). As one of Cage's colleagues, the painter Jasper Johns, says: "Already it's a great deal to see anything clearly . . ." (Copeland 48).

I should add here that Cage's ideas have some authority for me because I have had the experience they describe. I first heard Cage himself in 1989 when he gave Harvard's Norton lectures, in his case, a collage of text fragments—drawn from Thoreau, Emerson, the *Wall Street Journal,* older Cage lectures—assembled and ordered through a series of chance operations. I found the lectures sometimes amusing but mostly boring; I walked out of the first one before it was over. But then a funny thing happened. I couldn't get the experience out of my head; the readings had cocked my ear, as it were, so that situation after situation recalled them to me. Nowadays in any city in the world one constantly hears a complicated sound collage—fragments of the radio, phrases coming out of shop doorways, the passing traffic, the honk of horns, the click of a door latch. From all around us, noises join coincidentally at the ear and, like it or not, this is the world we are given to hear. Having heard Cage I hear it more clearly.

Then I spent a summer some years later in Berkeley, California, writing an early draft of this essay and reading Cage's prose pieces and interviews. At the same time I was sitting zazen at the Berkeley Zen Center and often, as I sat, I was suddenly conscious of the sounds around me—of bird song punctuating the drone of a jet plane, for example, with a conversation from a nearby house as a sort of middle theme. These moments of hearing were *amusing,* and I have to wonder if my amusement wasn't the happiness of letting the world happen. I found I could briefly drop my unconscious, reflexive filtering, and when I did, it was as if I'd had water in one ear for years and suddenly it disappeared. In an interview Cage once described his own struggle with his *dislike* of the background drones of machines like refrigerator motors. "I spent my life thinking we should try to get rid of them. . . . What has happened is that I'm beginning to enjoy those sounds, I mean that I now actually listen to them with the kind of enjoyment with which I listen to the traffic. Now, the traffic is easy to recognize as beautiful, but those drones are more difficult and I didn't really set out to find them beautiful. . . . They are, so to speak, coming to me" (97). There is a state of mind that finds the sound of the refrigerator motor interesting, even at 3:00 A.M.

Cage readily admits that the change of mind that leads to this sort of interest is one of the purposes of his purposelessness. "I think that music has to do with self-alteration; it begins with the alteration of the composer and conceivably extends to the alteration of the listeners. It by no means secures that, but it does secure the alteration in the mind of the composer, changing the mind so that it is changed not just in the presence of music, but in other situations too" (99).

Chance operations can change the mind because they circumvent intention. "Everyday life is more interesting than forms of celebration," Cage once said, adding the proviso: "*when* we become aware of it. That *when*," he explained, "is when our intentions go down to zero. Then suddenly you notice that the world is magical" (208). The Tibetan Buddhist teacher, Chogyam Trungpa, once said that "magic is the total appreciation of chance." We are more likely to appreciate chance if we stop trying to control what happens, and one way to do that is to cultivate nonintention. To do it totally is to realize how fully the world is already happening inside us and around us, as if by magic.

In one sense, "art" itself disappears as a result of such a practice. In later years Cage felt that his own technique of composition had changed him, "and the change that has taken place is that . . . I find my greatest acoustic, esthetic pleasure in simply the sounds of the environment. So that I no longer have any need not only for other people's music but I have no need really for my own music" (99–100). An art produced in this spirit is hardly an art at all, at least not in the sense of leaving any durable object behind, any recognizable trace of the ego's intentions. In his book *For the Birds,* Cage tells of a party he once attended: "As I was coming into the house, I noticed that some very interesting music was being played. After one or two drinks, I asked my hostess what music it was. She said, 'You can't be serious?' " (22). It was a piece of his own, as it happens.

Such a piece differs markedly, I think, from the creations that an artist like Picasso makes when a lucky find surprises his eye, or at least the artists differ markedly. To articulate how they differ I want to borrow an idea from the theory of evolution. In his book *Chance and Ne-*

397

cessity, the French biologist Jacques Monod distinguishes between a creation and a revelation, between "absolute newness" and a newness that arises predictably from conditions already present. For example, Monod calls the sugar crystal formed in a cooling sugar solution a "revelation" because its appearance merely reveals a potential already present in the warm solution. It is a foreseeable event and not, therefore, a pure creation. On the other hand, a genetic mutation that survives to become the seed of a new species is a pure creation; nothing in the context out of which it came could have let us foresee what in fact appeared (Monod 87, 116).

In these terms, Picasso's *Tête de Taureau* is a revelation, not a creation. I am actually following Picasso himself when I say this: "The accident *reveals* man," he says (91). In the case of the *Tête de Taureau,* what we see, in case we had not seen it before, is that Picasso's "deep personality" is in love with the bulls and bullfighting. Some of his earliest images are of bullfights (John Richardson's biography reproduces two that Picasso drew when he was nine years old) (30). The bull's head is a part of his mental landscape so it is no surprise when his eye catches a familiar pattern in the handlebars and bicycle seat. It is an accidental find, to be sure, but it is a symptomatic accident. If there were bottle racks or a face of Christ in that rubbish heap, Picasso did not see them. Were Matisse to look over the same rubbish heap he might have found something much more colorful. If the mathematician Benoit Mandelbrot had cast his eye over that rubbish he might have seen a feathery rill of mud or a paisley oil slick. And John Cage? We could not predict what Cage would find, at least not if he came to the rubbish heap carrying the *I Ching* under his arm.

In Cage's terms, then, Picasso's attention to accident is a way of exploring the self, but not of leaving it, and it therefore runs the risk of indulgence and repetition. I am reminded of the theater director Peter Brook's critique of actors who try to get in touch with their "deep" selves: "The method actor . . . is reaching inside himself for an alphabet that is . . . fossilized, for the language of signs from life that he knows is the language not of invention but of his conditioning. . . . What he thinks to be spontaneous is filtered and monitored many times over. Were Pavlov's dog improvising, he would still salivate when the bell rang, but he would feel sure it was all his own doing: 'I'm dribbling,' he would say, proud of his daring" (Copeland 47).

The materials in Picasso's accidental find (the bicycle seat, for instance) are new, but the art he shapes from them returns us to a

Picasso we know very well. Picasso, of course, was quite happy to work with accident as a tool of revelation ("From errors one gets to know the personality!"), but Cage was not ("Personality is a flimsy thing on which to build an art."), for Cage was after what Monod would call the "absolute newness" of pure chance (Picasso 45; Cage, *Silence* 90). He was not out to discover any hidden self, nor did he think chance operations would reveal any hidden, already existing divine reality, as ancient diviners thought. "Composition is like writing a letter to a stranger," he once said. "I don't hear things in my head, nor do I have inspiration. Nor is it right, as some people have said, that because I use chance operations my music is written not by me, but by God. I doubt whether God, say he existed, would take the trouble to write my music" (74).

*

If the products of Cage's chance operations are not revelations, either of the self or of the divine, then what exactly are they? As I have said, in one sense they are "nothings," experiences whose lack of purpose has as their purpose the creation of a kind of awareness or attention ("Not things, but minds," was one of Cage's aphorisms [Cage, *Themes* 11]). Nonetheless, while Cage is clearly more interested in consciousness than in art objects, he does sometimes speak as if he were an object maker, describing his works as inventions or discoveries, and his process as a labor to "bring . . . new things into being" (207). This minor theme in his self-descriptions interests me because in it I hear echoes of Monod's idea that pure chance might lead to absolute newness, to creations that could not have been foreseen even if one knew the unrevealed contents of self or cosmos. Almost as a matter of definition, such absolute newness (in either evolution or art) can only arise if the process itself has no purpose, for where there is purpose, creations reveal it and are not, therefore, absolutely new.

Cage once said, for example, that a "happening" should create a thing wholly unforeseeable. In 1952 Cage and a group of friends at Black Mountain College produced one of the first happenings, a mixed theatrical performance whose shape was devised by chance operations (it included Cage reading one of his lectures from the top of a stepladder and the painter Robert Rauschenberg playing records on an old Victrola [Revill 161]). Much later Cage would say: "A Happening should be like a net to catch a fish the nature of which one does not know" (113), a remark that resonates nicely with Monod's sense of "absolute" creation, for in evolution, too, the addition of chance to necessity means that creation always "catches fish" the nature of which can never be predicted. Cases of convergent evolution (in which similar species evolve in similar but distant ecosystems) demonstrate the point nicely. In both Africa and South America, for example, fish that must navigate in muddy water have evolved a method of sensing what is around them that involves broadcasting a weak electric field. For such electrolocation to work, the body of the fish becomes a sort of receiving antenna and must therefore be held stiff, which means the fish cannot undulate to swim the way most fish do. Electric fish, therefore, propel themselves by means of a single large fin that runs the length of the body. In the African species, the fin runs along the fish's back, but in South America it runs along the belly (Dawkins 97–99). Such beings arise from the play of chance and necessity; the nature of electricity necessarily stiffens the body, but the propelling fin is located by haps. Because pure chance is involved, in the evolution of species and in a John Cage happening, "fish" appear, the nature of which no one could have predicted from the original circumstances.

To say this another way, in both cases whatever emerges—no matter how beautiful or useful—is not the fruit of any hidden purpose. Cage, like Picasso, might have been able to say "I do not seek, I find," but in Cage's case his lucky finds never reveal unconscious motives. One of Cage's early innovations was to stick all sorts of objects into the strings of a piano (screws, bolts, pieces of paper), producing unpredictable and novel noises. "I placed objects on the strings, deciding their position according to the sounds that resulted. So, it was as though I was walking along the beach finding shells. . . . I found melodies and combinations of sounds that worked with the given structure" (62–63). If Cage was looking for "what works," it might seem at first that he did have purposes here, and that he was allowing his taste to guide him. But if that is the case it is hard to explain why he never made use of his lucky finds. That is to say, when Cage happened upon a melody he liked he didn't then go on to build with it, repeat it, weave it into a climax, and so forth. To do so would be to promulgate his "likes and dislikes," and by that begin again to shape and solidify the ego. Just as the play of chance in evolution is not directed toward any end, even when durable beauty arises from it, so when chance handed Cage an interesting melody he never took it as a sign of his purposes (as Picasso might), nor did he allow it to arouse his intention. He moved on to let chance decide what happens next.[3]

Thus, and despite the fact that Cage sometimes spoke as if his art produced objects, this line of thought takes us back to his aphorism, "Not things, but minds." Cage was above all dedicated to creating a kind of awareness, believing that if we rigorously allow chance to indicate what happens next we will be led into a fuller apprehension of what the world happens to be. Take what is probably Cage's best known composition, a piece called *4' 33"*, four minutes and thirty-three seconds of silence broken into three movements (each indicated by the piano player lowering and raising the lid of the piano). The same year this piece was written, in 1952, Cage had a chance to visit an anechoic chamber at Harvard University, a room so fully padded that it was said to be absolutely silent. Alone in the room, Cage was surprised to hear two sounds, one high, one low; the technicians told him these were the sounds of his nervous system and his circulating blood. At that point he realized that there is no such thing as silence; there is only sound we intend and sound we do not intend (228–29; Revill 162–64). Thus *4' 33"* is not so much a "silence" piece as a structured opportunity to listen to unintended sound, to hear the plenitude of what happens. The audience at the premiere of *4' 33"* "missed the point," Cage once remarked. "What they thought was silence . . . was full of accidental sounds. You could hear the wind stirring outside during the first movement. During the second, raindrops began patterning the roof, and during the third the people themselves made all kinds of interesting sounds as they talked or walked out" (65).

Theories of evolution have shown us that, even though it is difficult at first to imagine how a process that depends on chance can be creative, nonetheless it is by such a process that creation itself has come to be. I have been interested in Jacques Monod's picture of the role of chance in the creation of the biosphere partly because his language resonates with Cage's in so many respects. On the one hand, Monod recognizes that there is a kind of self-protective egotism to all living things, which is to say, all living things perpetuate themselves through invariance (DNA is remarkably stable), and guard themselves against the "imperfections" that chance might visit upon them. On the other hand, invariance means that living things, by themselves, cannot adapt when the world around them changes, nor change to occupy empty niches of the biosphere. In nature, true change requires happy accidents. "The same source of fortuitous perturbations, of 'noise,' which

401

in a nonliving . . . system would lead little by little to the disintegration of all structure, is the progenitor of evolution in the biosphere and accounts for its unrestricted liberty of creation," Monod writes, calling DNA "[a] registry of chance, [a] tone-deaf conservatory where the noise is preserved along with the music" (116–17).

This echoes Cage's aesthetic quite precisely. He was not blind to the fact that cultures and selves guard and replicate their ideals, their beauties, their masterpieces, but he did not cast his lot with durable structures, he cast it with perturbation. He turned toward chance to relieve the mind of its protective garment of received ideas so that it might better attend to the quietly stirring wind or the rain patterning the roof. He made an art that was a sort of net to catch contingency. He cocked his ear for noise, not the old harmonies, sensing that noise can lead to something as remarkable as this world, and believing that, in a civilization as complex and shifting as ours has become, a readiness to let the mind change as contingency demands may be one prerequisite of a happy life.

Notes

[1]All citations to the *Homeric Hymn to Hermes* are from my own unpublished translation. For a good English version with the Greek original, see *Hesiod, the Homeric Hymns and Homerica,* translated by Hugh G. Evelyn-White (Cambridge: Harvard UP, 1914).

[2]Unless otherwise indicated, all of John Cage's remarks are taken from Richard Kostelanetz's wonderfully well-composed book of interviews, *Conversing with Cage.*

[3]Cage was rigorous in his devotion to chance, to the consternation even of his friends. The composer Earle Brown once argued for the mixture of chance and choice: "I feel you should be able to toss coins, and then decide to use a beautiful F sharp if you want to—be willing to chuck the system in other words. John won't do that" (Tomkins 74).
Mark Twain's witticism about Wagner—"His music is better than it sounds"—nicely catches the complexity of my own reaction to Cage (walking out on him and then being haunted). Like Earle Brown, I prefer the play of chance and intention to the purity of Cage's method. But I also realize that he cleared a field no one had entered, and set a marker there. Even those who do not follow him into his field benefit from the sight of that marker.

Works Cited

Austin, James H. *Chase, Chance, and Creativity.* New York: Columbia UP, 1978.
Cage, John. *For the Birds.* In conversation with Daniel Charles. Boston: Marion Boyars, 1981.

————. *Silence.* Middletown: Wesleyan UP, 1961.

————. *Themes & Variations.* Barrytown: Station Hill, 1982.

Copeland, Roger. "Against Instinct: The Denatured Dances of Merce Cunningham." *Working Papers* (Fall 1990): 41–57.

Dawkins, Richard. *The Blind Watchmaker.* New York: W. W. Norton, 1987.

Flaceliere, Robert. *Greek Oracles.* Trans. Douglas Garman. New York: W. W. Norton, 1965.

Freud, Sigmund. *A General Introduction to Psychoanalysis.* Garden City: Garden City Publishing, 1943.

Hacking, Ian. *The Taming of Chance.* Cambridge: Cambridge UP, 1990.

Hillman, James. *Puer Papers.* Dallas: Spring Publications, 1979.

Joyce, James. *Selected Letters of James Joyce.* Ed. Richard Ellmann. New York: Viking, 1975.

Jung, Carl G. Foreword. *The I Ching.* 3rd ed., Bollingen Series XIX. Princeton: Princeton UP, 1967. xxi–xxxix.

Kerényi, Carl. "The Primordial Child in Primordial Times." In C. G. Jung and C. Kerényi, *Essays on a Science of Mythology.* Princeton: Princeton UP, 1969. 25–69.

————. *Hermes, Guide of Souls.* Dallas: Spring Publications, 1986.

Kostelanetz, Richard. *Conversing with Cage.* New York: Limelight Editions, 1991.

Kundera, Milan. *The Unbearable Lightness of Being.* New York: Harper, 1984.

Monod, Jacques. *Chance and Necessity.* New York: Vintage, 1972.

The Oxford English Dictionary. 20 vols. Oxford: Clarendon Press, 1989.

Picasso, Pablo. *Picasso on Art.* Ed. Dore Ashton. New York: Da Capo, 1972.

Revill, David. *The Roaring Silence. John Cage: A Life.* New York: Arcade, 1992.

Richardson, John. *A Life of Picasso.* Vol. I: *1881–1906.* New York: Random House, 1991.

Serres, Michel. *Hermes: Literature, Science, Philosophy.* Baltimore: Johns Hopkins UP, 1983.

Tomkins, Calvin. *The Bride & The Bachelors.* New York: Viking, 1965.

Von Franz, Marie-Louise. *On Divination and Synchronicity, the Psychology of Meaningful Chance.* Toronto: Inner City Books, 1980.

1998

A HEMINGWAY STORY

by ANDRE DUBUS

from THE KENYON REVIEW

In my thirtieth summer, in 1966, I read many stories by John O'Hara and read Hemingway's stories again, and his "In Another Country" challenged me more than I could know then. That summer was my last at the University of Iowa; I had a master of fine arts degree and, beginning in the fall, a job as a teacher, in Massachusetts. My wife and four children and I would move there in August. Until then, we lived in Iowa City and I taught two freshman rhetoric classes four mornings a week, then came home to eat lunch and write. I wrote in my den at the front of the house, a small room with large windows, and I looked out across the lawn at an intersection of streets shaded by tall trees. I was trying to learn to write stories, and was reading O'Hara and Hemingway as a carpenter might look at an excellent house someone else has built.

That summer "In Another Country" became one of my favorite stories written by anyone, and it still is. But I could not fully understand the story. What's it *about?* I said to a friend as we drove in his car to the university track to run laps. He said: It's about the futility of cures. That nestled beneath my heart, and displaced my confusion. Yes. The futility of cures. Then everything connected and formed a whole, and in the car with my friend, then running with him around the track, I saw the story as you see a painting, and one of the central images was the black silk handkerchief covering the wound where the young man's nose had been.

Kurt Vonnegut was our neighbor. We had adjacent lawns; he lived behind us, at the top of the hill. One day that summer he was outside on his lawn or on his front porch four times when I was outside, and we waved and called to each other. The first time I was walking home from teaching, wearing slacks and a shirt; the next time I was wearing shorts and a T-shirt I had put on to write; then I wore gym shorts without a shirt and drove to the track; in late afternoon, wearing another pair of slacks and another shirt, I walked up to his house to drink. He was sitting on his front porch and, as I approached, he said: "Andre, you change clothes more than a Barbie doll."

Kurt did not have a telephone. That summer the English Department hosted a conference, and one afternoon a man from the department called me and asked me to ask Kurt to meet Ralph Ellison at the airport later in the day, then Mrs. Ellison at the train. She did not like to fly. I went up to Kurt's house, and he came to the back door. I said: "They want us to pick up Ellison at the airport. Then his wife at the train."

"Swell. I'll drive."

Later he came driving down the brick road from his house and I got in the car and saw a paperback of *Invisible Man* between us on the seat. The airport was in Cedar Rapids, a short drive. I said: "Are you going to leave the book there?"

"I'm teaching it. I thought it'd be phony to take it out of the car."

It was a hot afternoon. We left town and were on the highway, the corn was tall and green under the huge midwestern sky, and I said: "They didn't really ask for both of us to pick up Ellison. Just you."

"I knew that."

"Thanks. How are we going to recognize him? Do we just walk up to the only Negro who gets off the plane?"

Kurt looked at me and said: "Shit."

"We could just walk past him, pretend we couldn't see him."

"That's so good, we ought to do it."

The terminal was small and we stood outside and watched the plane land, and the people filing out of it, and there was one black man. We went to him and Kurt said: "Ralph Ellison?" and Ellison smiled and said: "Yes," and we shook his hand and got his things and went to the car. I sat in the back and watched Ellison. He saw *Invisible Man* at once but did not say anything. As we rode on the highway he looked at the cornfields and talked fondly of the times he had hunted pheasants here with Vance Bourjaily. Then he picked up his book and said: "It's still around."

Kurt told him he was teaching it, and I must have told him I loved it because I did and I do, but I only remember watching him and listening to him. Kurt asked him if he wanted a drink. He did. We went to a bar near the university, and sat in a booth, Ellison opposite Kurt and me, and ordered vodka martinis. We talked about jazz and books, and Ellison said that before starting *Invisible Man* he had read Malroux's *Man's Fate* forty times. He liked the combination of melodrama and philosophy, he said, and he liked those in Dostoyevski too. We ordered martinis again and I was no longer shy. I looked at Ellison's eyes and said: "I've been rereading Hemingway's stories this summer, and I think my favorite is 'In Another Country.' "

He looked moved by remembrance, as he had in the car, talking about hunting with Vance. Looking at us, he recited the story's first paragraph: " 'In the fall the war was always there, but we did not go to it any more. It was cold in the fall in Milan and the dark came very early. Then the electric lights came on, and it was pleasant along the streets looking in the windows. There was much game hanging outside the shops, and the snow powdered in the fur of the foxes and the wind blew their tails. The deer hung stiff and heavy and empty, and small birds blew in the wind and the wind turned their feathers. It was a cold fall and the wind came down from the mountains.' "

When we took Ellison to his room on the campus, it was time for us to go to the train and meet his wife. Kurt said to Ellison: "How will we recognize her?"

"She's wearing a gray dress and carrying a beige raincoat." He smiled. "And she's colored."

Wanting to know absolutely what a story is about, and to be able to say it in a few sentences, is dangerous: It can lead us to wanting to possess a story as we possess a cup. We know the function of a cup, and we drink from it, wash it, put it on a shelf, and it remains a thing we own and control, unless it slips from our hands into the control of gravity; or someone else breaks it, or uses it to give us poisoned tea. A story can always break into pieces while it sits inside a book on a shelf; and, decades after we have read it even twenty times, it can open us up, by cut or caress, to a new truth.

I taught at Bradford College in Massachusetts for eighteen years, and in my first year, and many times afterward, I assigned "In Another Country" to students. The first time I talked about it in a classroom I understood more of it, because of what the students said, and also because of what I said: words that I did not know I would say, giving voice to ideas I did not know I had, and to images I had not seen in my mind. I began by telling them the story was about the futility of cures; by the end of the class I knew it was not. Through my years of teaching I learned to walk into a classroom wondering what I would say, rather than knowing what I would say. Then I learned by hearing myself speak; the source of my speaking was our mysterious harmony with truths we know, though very often our knowledge of them is hidden from us. Now, as a retired teacher, I mistrust all prepared statements by anyone, and by me.

Still, after discussing "In Another Country" the first time with Bradford students, I did not go into the classroom in the years after that, knowing exactly what I would say about the story. Probably ten times in those eighteen years I assigned "In Another Country" and began our discussion by focusing on the images in the first two paragraphs, the narrator—who may be Nick Adams—bringing us to the hospital, and to the machines "that were to make so much difference," and I talked about the tone of that phrase, a tone achieved by the music of the two paragraphs, a tone that tells us the machines will make nothing different.

The story shifts then to the Italian major. He was a champion fencer before the war; now he is a wounded man whose right hand is shrunken; it is the size of a baby's hand, and he puts it into a machine which the doctor says will restore it to its normal size. Neither the major's hand nor the major will ever be normal. The narrator's knee is injured and the small proportion he gives it in the story lets us know that it will be healed. I told my students, when they were trying to understand a story that seemed difficult, to look at its proportion: the physical space a writer gives each element of the story. "In Another Country" moves swiftly from the futility of cures, to what it is that the physical curing cannot touch, and, yes, the young man who lost his nose and covered his face with a black silk handkerchief is a thematic image in the story, but it is not in the center of the picture, it is off to the side.

In the center of this canvas is death. That is why the narrator, though his knee will be normal again, will not himself be normal. Or perhaps not for a very long time. After the first hospital scene he tells of his other comrades, the Italian soldiers he walks home from the hospital with; all of them, in the war, have lived with death. Because of this, they feel detached, and they feel insulated from civilians and others who have not been in the war. The narrator is frightened, and at night moves from the light of one street lamp to another. He does not want to go to the war again. So the story now has moved from the futility of cures back to war, where it began with its opening line and the paragraph that shows the lovely pictures of Milan; while, beneath that tactile beauty, the music is the sound of something lost, and the loss of it has changed even the sound of the wind, and the sight of blowing snow on the fur of animals.

A war story, then; and while the major and narrator sit at their machines in the hospital, the major teaches Italian grammar to the narrator. I cannot know why Hemingway chose Italian grammar, but my deepest guess is that his choice was perfect: two wounded men, talking about language, rather than faith in the machines, hope for healing, or the horror of war. I am not saying they ought to be speaking about these things. There are times when it is best to be quiet, to endure, to wait. Hemingway may be our writer who has been the most badly read. His characters are as afraid of pain and death as anyone else. They feel it, they think about it, and they talk about it with people they love. With the Italian major, the narrator talks about grammar.

Then the story moves again, in the final scene. Until now, it has seemed to be a story about young men who have lost that joy in being alive which is normal for young and healthy people, who have not yet learned that within the hour they may be dead. The story has been about that spiritual aging that war can cause: in a few moments, a young soldier can see and hear enough, taste and touch and smell enough, to age his spirit by decades while his body has not aged at all. The quickness of this change, of the spirit's immersion in horror, may cause a state of detachment from people whose lives are still normal, and who receive mortality's potion, drop by tiny drop, not in a torrent.

But in the story's final scene, the major furiously and bitterly grieves, scolds the narrator, then apologizes, says that his wife has just died and, crying, leaves the room where the machines are. From their doctor the narrator learns that the major had waited to marry until he was out of the war. His wife contracted pneumonia and in three days she was dead, and now in the story death is no longer the haunting demon of soldiers who have looked into its eyes. It is what no one can escape. The major reasonably believed he was the one in danger, until he was home from the war. Then death attacked his exposed flank, and breathed pneumonia into his wife. The story has completed its movement. A few notes remain: softly, a piano and bass, and faint drums and cymbals; we cymbals; we see the major returning to put his hand in the machine. He keeps doing this.

Two years after I retired from teaching, and twenty years after that last summer in Iowa City, I was crippled in an instant when a car hit me, and I was in a hospital for nearly two months. I suffered with pain, and I thought very often of Ernest Hemingway, and how much physical pain he had suffered, and how well he had written about it. In the hospital I did not think about "In Another Country." I thought about "The Gambler, the Nun, and the Radio," and was both enlightened and amused, for always when I had talked about that story with students, I had moved quickly past the physical pain and focused on the metaphysical. Philosophy is abundant in that story; but I had to live in pain, on a hospital bed, before I could see that bodily pain deserved much more than I had given it. Always I had spent one fifty-minute class on the story. I should have used two class sessions; the first one would have been about pain.

A year after my injury, in a time of spiritual pain, I dreamed one night that I was standing on both my legs with other people in a brightly lit kitchen near the end of the day. I did not recognize any of the people, but in the dream they were my friends; one was a woman who was deeply hurting me. We were all standing, and I was pretending to be happy, and no one could see my pain. I stood near the stove. The kitchen door to the lawn was open, and there was a screen door and, from outside, Ernest Hemingway opened it and walked in, looking at me across the length of the room. He wore his fishing cap with a long visor He walked straight to me and said: "Let's go fishing," I walked with him, outside and down a sloping lawn to a wharf. We went to the end of the wharf where a large boat with an inboard motor was tied. Then we stood in the cabin, Hemingway at my right and holding the wheel with both hands; we moved on a calm bay and were going out to sea. It was dusk and I wondered if it was too late to go to sea, and I had not seen him carrying fishing rods, and I wondered if he had forgotten them. But I worried for only a moment. Then I looked up at his profile and knew that he knew what he was doing. He had a mustache but no beard and was about forty and still handsome.

The next night a writer's workshop I host gathered in my living room. When they left I sat in my wheelchair in the dining room and remembered my dream, and remarked for the first time that Hemingway had his head, and I had my missing leg, and the leg I do have was no longer damaged. Then I remembered reading something that John Cheever either wrote or said: During one long dark night of the soul, Ernest Hemingway spoke to him. Cheever said that he had never heard Hemingway's voice, but he knew that this was his voice, telling Cheever that his present pain was only the beginning. Then, sitting in my chair in the quiet night, I believed that Hemingway had come to me while I was suffering, and had taken me away from it, out to sea where we could fish.

A few months later, in winter, I wrote to Father Bruce Ritter at Covenant House in New York and told him that I was crippled and had not yet learned to drive with hand controls; that my young daughters were no longer living with me; that I hosted, without pay, a writers' workshop, but its members could afford to pay anyone for what I did, and they did not really need me; and I felt that when I was not with my children I was no longer a useful part of the world. Father Ritter wrote to me, suggesting that I tutor a couple of high school students. In Haverhill there is a home for girls between the ages of fourteen and eighteen. They are in protective custody of the state, because of what people have done to them. In summer I phoned the home, and asked if they wanted a volunteer. Someone drove me there to meet a man in charge of education. A light rain was falling. At the home I looked through the car window at a second-story window and saw an old and long-soiled toy, a stuffed dog. The man came out and stood in the rain and I asked him what I could do. He said: "Give them stories about real people. Give them words and images. They're afraid of those."

So that fall, in 1988, we began; and nearly eight years later, girls with a staff woman still come to my house on Monday nights, and we read. For the first seven years I read to them; then they told me they wanted to read, and now I simply choose a book, provide soft drinks and ash trays, and listen. One night in the fall of 1991, five years after my injury, I read "In Another Country" to a few girls and a staff woman. This was the first time I had read it since my crippling. I planned to read it to the girls, then say about it what I had said so many times to students at Bradford College. I stopped often while reading the story, to tell them about images and thematic shifts. When I finished reading it, I talked about each part of it again, building to my explanation of the story's closing lines: "The major did not come to the hospital for three days. Then he came at the usual hour, wearing a black band on the sleeve of his uniform. When he came back, there were large framed photographs around the wall, all sorts of wounds before and after they had been cured by the machines. In front of the machine the major used were three photographs of hands like his that were completely restored. I do not know where the doctor got them. I always understood we were the first to use the machines. The photographs did not make much difference to the major because he only looked out the window."

Then because of my own five years of agony, of sleeping at night and in my dreams walking on two legs, then waking each morning to being crippled, of praying and willing myself out of bed to confront the day, of having to learn a new way to live after living nearly fifty years with a whole body—then, because of all this, I saw something I had never seen in the story, and I do not know whether Hemingway saw it when he wrote it or later or never, but there it was, there it is, and with passion and joy I looked up from the book, looked at the girls' faces and said: "This story is about healing too. The major keeps going to the machines. And he doesn't believe in them. But he gets out of his bed in the morning. He brushes his teeth, He shaves. He combs his hair. He puts on his uniform. He leaves the place where he lives. He walks to the hospital, and sits at the machines. Every one of those actions is a movement away from suicide. Away from despair. Look at him. Three days after his wife has died, he is in motion. He is sad. He will not get over this. And he will get over this. His hand won't be cured but someday he will meet another woman. And he will love her. Because he is alive."

The girls watched me, nodding their heads, those girls who had suffered and still suffered. But for now, on this Monday night, they sat on my couch, and happily watched me discover a truth; or watched a truth discover me, when I was ready for it.

1999

411

A MURDER OF CROWS

by DANIEL HENRY

from NORTHERN LIGHTS

THE CROW'S writhing body throws diamonds in the rare rainforest sunlight. The bird flies crazily—twisting, twirling, hiccuping—as if warning us or clowning out a declaration of war. It careens to the buffer-forest's edge and clings to a treetop where it screeches for hours. As the summer dusk gathers at midnight, the bird suddenly ceases its racket, ushering an undertow that tugs at our dreams through the night. So ends the first day of a siege that offers new insight into the collective term for crows—murder.

False Island is forty miles north of Sitka, Alaska, as the crow flies. The camp was built at the toe of what local foresters claim was once the largest clearcut in the world. A battered swath two to ten miles wide persists across 60 miles of Chichigof Island, on the northwestern coasts of the Tongass National Forest, where towering spruce were clearcut and replaced by tightly woven thickets of devil's club and red alder. Before it became a Forest Service retreat for the young and restless in 1979, False Island was a logging camp made up of a dozen herky-jerky ATCO trailers connected by a mile of solder. Standing apart from these aluminum worm-casings were a little red schoolhouse, a generator shed, a log house sewage plant, and assorted second-thought outbuildings.

Served by a whopping roadbuilding budget, the Forest Service built a web of roads which allowed loggers living at False Island to haul out enough trees to supply a boggling number of upscale Japanese subdivisions. But because they still liked the sound of wind rushing through trees and the way moss-piled carpets grew deep in a mature forest, the boys kept 20 acres of old growth "buffer" adjacent to one side of camp and called it "the woods." The woods still shelter the mouth of Clear Creek into which hundreds of thousands of salmon replay their genetic destiny every summer.

This postage stamp forest hugs the pebbly shores of Jingleshell Cove on the Chichigof side of Peril Strait, a timid reminder of what was once an uninterrupted rainforest sprawling from northern California to the Alaska Peninsula. The squared-off patch of trees is a ghost of what struck naturalist John Muir as the "tropical luxuriance" he saw in the seamless woods. Nonetheless, its relative isolation and fecundity make the remnant grove a haven for animals. Shaggy brown bears still stroll and feed among fellow fauna in this hallowed space: mink, wolf, marten, deer, coyote, porcupine, birds, fish. Look. There, a dozen bald eagles glower over the broad tideflat from the mossy outstretched branches of the remaining 700 year-old Sitka spruce trees. There, four adult bears scoop humpies out of the creek while a sow leads a pair of cubs along a beach not sixty feet from employee quarters. Breathy explosions of killer whales prowling offshore ring among the surviving members of this token arboretum, still standing witness to the brief, reckless conquests exacted upon the neighborhood by itinerant humanity.

It is a dead calm midsummer's afternoon when a couple of pals and I watch the first crow barrel down Main Street, squawking out its primal alarm. Late lunch on a cable spool picnic table outside the cookshack. On this day most of the 80 workers in the Young Adult Conservation Corps camp are scattered throughout the Tongass on spike camps. Our ten-day missions are to build log picnic shelters and fish ladders, muck out the cross-Admiralty Island canoe trail, plant trees or survey the inventory trails in pristine stands being readied for harvest. In the end, we will return to False Island for a few days of showers, friends, and hot grub, then light out again for the backcountry. My official title is "Group Living Specialist," meaning that when the crews are in, I organize capture the flag, film fests, kayak trips, and community gardening; when they're out, I head up whoever's left to work on camp maintenance, hustle supplies off floatplanes and barges, stir sewage, and otherwise sustain camp survival on the island's remote shores. Crows are common visitors to camp, but not like the crazy one swooping by us, screeching its apocalyptic warning.

Two sounds of the second morning stand clear in my memory. The first is of the solitary crow perched in a treetop raucously cawing over

413

and over in a clipped, repetitive cadence that comes to resemble the safety beep of a commercial truck backing up. The second sound is the harsh scrape of coarse feathers raking the air to interrupt our morning coffee before we could even see the squadron of a hundred crows turn a corner onto Main Street and blow past us. They scatter when they hit the trees, then join the sentinel bird in its tightly paced call. But the birds cry in different rhythms, creating a demonic clatter that builds throughout the day.

By midnight, enough crows have arrived to put one or more birds on all spruce boughs outsweeping into the camp fringe and along the beach. I hunch around a driftwood fire with friends swatting no-see-ums and appraising the shadowed crow streaks over our heads. In an hour's time, the crows' congregation assumes evolving forms: flying monkeys from Wizard of Oz, jet fighter packs, insect swarms. Isabel pokes the coals with her stick. Weird, she says. A convention without joy, like a funeral. But why—who's it for? She jabs her sword in the glowing eye, then retreats into murky light and a mounting barrage.

The raucous symphony builds to a stadium roar on the third day when camp director Pete and I walk one end of the grove to the other. Tens of thousands of crows have transformed our solemn woodland asylum into a clamorous, stinking squalor. Shit flies everywhere, as do feathers, piss, and corvid epithets screamed at full volume. When we get back to camp, a visiting green-shirter from the Sitka district office asks Pete if he thinks that there's anything we should do. Pete snorts. What? Call the cavalry?

Others around camp are letting the birds get to them. Quinn takes half of her lunchbreak to caw loudly and throw beach pebbles at the blaring black mass in the trees. Jay Blazo (so named after he dowsed a cooking fire with a half-can of Blazo white gas, then rolled away while his co-workers beat the flames out of his clothing) reports that he's acquired a headache from the ruckus. His friend, Whitebird, vouches for him by grimacing on demand. Whitebird is in camp recovering from an injury sustained while lighting his farts in threadbare jeans. Blazo's crew sneaked out of camp without him. They are my camp crew assigned to erecting a cement incinerator not far from the woods, so close-up exposure to the birds has prompted paranoia of cinematic proportions. Big Jim overhears their complaints and beams his ample, mischievous grin. He turns to show the shit-streaked barcode on the back of his jacket.

We are not alone in our preoccupation with this screeching black tide. Lone ravens and eagles perch on the periphery. A marten makes its rare appearance one morning in a bristling patch of wild celery at the forest's edge. Red-tailed hawks ride updrafts a thousand feet over the trees. Dozens of Steller's jays sit watching from the smaller trees in camp, oddly silent.

The favorite subject for breakfast discussion on the fourth day is the effect the crows are having on our sleep. One of two cooks, Michael, is as grouchy and sullen as the bald eagle we watched swoop down on a beached salmon that morning and, missing it, slam into a rootwad. He says that the crows' commotion last night even drowned out a Grateful Dead jam he'd cranked up on his Walkman. Michael's scowl is a sou'easterly slamming up the ragged coast to rip away any memory of blue sky. He's drunk a gallon of coffee since getting up at 4:30; his harangue is especially honed as we trancewalk within earshot. The upshot of Michael's compulsions is that his bad days are the camp's best. Our reward from his anger is a sumptuous spread: French toast in teetering columns, troughs of steaming home fries, fruit salad, link and soy sausage, fresh-squeezed grapefruit juice. Michael leans over the food, mumbling about having to eat crow to win back sleep. We nod our tacit agreement, bleary and irritated at the rising ranks of crows in the woods. The food helps. What happens after breakfast helps even more.

Big Jim is the first to leave the mess hall to face the day's work. Moments later the door opens and his shaggy blond head reappears. There's that smile again. Check it out, he says.

The rest of us, including Michael, do.

Drizzle leaks from a pregnant cloudbank scraping the treetops. There is a faint drumming on the ATCO roofs. A raven lands nearby, chuckling softly. We are swallowed in a sudden hush. The crows have vanished.

Or so we think. Closer inspection reveals thousands of muted black birds filling in the spaces of the forest like notes in a manic symphony score. Songbirds pick at berries and bugs in the clearcut tangle, gulls mew and scream over fish left on the tideflats, but the crow-ladened trees remain reticent until a few minutes before lunch.

Whitebird's face is ashen under his black bristles when he comes in for the lunchbreak. It's evil, come words between waxen lips. Consciously or not, he imitates the askew glare that Hitchcock

415

commanded from Tippi Hedron's eyes in *The Birds,* pinned open in horror during a slashing winged attack. Evil, he repeats. Totally outta control. We listen. Pandemonium roars from the stand of old trees. We run into the woods for a closer look.

It is a hell-fight beyond our imagination.

Bodies rain from the trees. Dying birds hit the forest floor screaming like warriors startled by their final vulnerability. Their black breasts' normal gloss fades under blood and duff, pierced to the heart by beaks bearing ancient regards. We watch with grotesque fascination as silent cries issue from the twisting jaws of birds whose heads are attached to their bodies only by a strand of sinew. Many of the feathered shadows writhing on the ground are composed of two or three crows pinned to each other by their beaks and claws. Eyes hang by bloody bits of gristle. Some birds spin in silly circles as they attempt flight without one or both wings. Eviscera showers us with the life essence still wriggling out of it.

We carefully pick a route from treetrunk to treetrunk to avoid being hit by the shrieking black death clusters. Despite our caution, though, we can't escape splatters of blood flying everywhere, staining crimson Rorschachs into our clothing. It is the price for satisfying our morbid curiosity, to cloak ourselves in the blood of this killing place. When I realize that in my revulsion I've stopped breathing, I turn and beeline back to camp. Leave the birds to their own dark rituals.

The mad cacophony of bird battle continues in diminishing waves until late. After a while, we hear individual death cries over the white noise of war, punctuated by kamikaze bursts of discovery and destruction. Then, in the grey of Northern midnight, a feeble line of crows straggles out from the grove, crossing the Strait and away to other forests on other islands.

The victors leave us with death and ringing silence until a varied thrush breaks into burred fluting at the brightening dawn. The hush lulls me into the deepest sleep of the week, swaddled in a blanket of aural relief. Even Michael sleeps in, so breakfast comes late on the fifth day of this story. Whitebird refuses to work at the incinerator on account of vibes. I walk out with him to inspect the scene.

The few bent carcasses littering the worksite are clues which lead us into the big trees. A palpable stench punches us as we step into spruce cover. Usually viridescent, the mossy floor is heaped with black, broken bodies. In some places the dead are piled up nearly two feet deep. We daintily pick a route through the mounds until it is impossible to move without crushing carcasses underfoot. Before long, we're kicking them like autumn leaves, raising clouds of feeding insects in our wake. Two hawks swerve in from the beach to pick through the remains. We become aware of a bloody slick accumulating on our rubber boots. Whitebird pulls back, turns and heaves. We head back for breakfast.

Throughout the day, people sneak away to the woods to inspect the aftermath of the showdown. Isabel and Pete return with a story about a family of mink they had watched scampering among the bodies. The mother was dragging stiffened remains to her brood of youngsters who would emerge from under a deadfall to shred their gifts. Blazo claims to have watched a boar brown bear cuffing crow drifts like a novice golfer in a sand trap.

Big Jim nudges me awake on the morning of the sixth day. Michael is chopping onions to Creedence Clearwater in the kitchen, but no one else stirs. You gotta see this, Big Jim insists. What is it? He slits his eyes like a secret buddha and turns towards the woods. Gotta see it for yourself.

I've reflected on that morning many times over the years. It was a humbling glimpse into the tireless life force that binds us beyond species, habitat, motivation, or income. Epiphanies such as this one come in sudden, startling surprise packages; the shock of recognition lingers a lifetime. Whether I analyze or re-examine the event in the context of wildlife phenomenon, timber practices, life cycles, or cosmic connectedness, I keep coming back to this scene:

The site of a horrific massacre has been transformed into a verdant, glowing forest floor. Even the puddles of body fluids pumped out in the crows' last mortal moments have been sopped up by the deep moss. The occasional ink-hued feather scuttering in a whispered breeze contains the only clues to the week's carnage. Big Jim and I sit, mouths open, wordless.

2000

BORROWED FINERY

by PAULA FOX

from THE THREEPENNY REVIEW

A PUBLICITY STILL of the actress Zasu Pitts, crouching half-naked among heaps of gold coins, an expression of demented rapacity on her face—an advertisement for the movie *Greed,* made in 1923, the year I was born—epitomized my childhood view of American banking and American business. As I grew older, my attitude toward money changed, but not by much. In my mind's eye, Zasu Pitts still holds out handfuls of coins, but she is not offering them, she is gloating over her possession of them.

The minister who took care of me in my infancy and earliest years saw to it that I didn't look down and out. Twice a year, in spring and in fall, he bought a few things for me to wear, sparing whatever he could from his yearly salary. Other clothes came my way donated by mothers in his congregation whose own children had outgrown them. They were mended, washed and ironed before they were handed on.

In early April, before my fifth birthday, my father mailed the minister two five-dollar bills and a written note. I can see him reading the note as he holds it and the bills in one hand while with the index finger of the other, he presses the bridge of his eyeglasses against his nose because he has broken his left stem.

This particularity of memory can be partly attributed to the rarity of my father's notes—not to mention enclosures of money—or else to the new dress that part of the ten dollars paid for. Or so I imagine.

The next morning the minister drove me in his old Packard car from the Victorian house on the hill where we lived in Newburgh, a Hudson Valley town half an hour distant and a few miles north of the Storm King promontory, which sinks into the river like an elephant's brow.

418

We went to Schoonmaker's department store on Water Street. The minister took my hand as we walked down the aisle. It was the first time he'd taken me to a big store. When we emerged onto the sidewalk, he was carrying a box that contained a white dotted Swiss dress. It had a Peter Pan collar and fell straight to its hem from smocked shoulders. He had written a poem for me to recite at the Easter service in the Congregational church where he preached. I would have something new to wear, to stand before all the people and speak his words. I loved the minister and I loved the dotted Swiss dress.

Years later when I read through the few letters and notes my father had sent to the minister, and that he'd saved, I realized how he had played the coquette in his apologies for his remissness in supporting me. His excuses were made with a kind of fraudulent heartiness, as though he were boasting, not confessing.

Unlike the meaning that lurked in his words, his handwriting was beautiful, an orderly flight of birds across yellowing pages.

WHEN I was ten or so, living with my Spanish grandmother in a one-room apartment in Kew Gardens, Long Island, with a Murphy pull-down bed in which we both slept, and that emerged in the evenings like a mastodon from the closet where it lived, I was the recipient of a paper sack stuffed with discarded clothes from my cousin, Natalie. Stained slips, wool stocking worn thin at the heels, garter belts with flaccid suspenders, and ragged brassieres were all wound about each other like sleeping snakes. At the very bottom of the sack was a folded print dress made of slippery material, rayon perhaps. It had a rope-like belt with tasseled ends that looped twice around my waist. I wore it to the public school I attended, though it was far too big, and its pattern of large ugly green flowers made it, somehow, unseemly.

Natalie, several years older than I, lived in a railroad flat in a Spanish Harlem tenement with her parents, a grown-up sister, and a yellow mongrel that bit everyone—or threatened to—except her father, my uncle Fermin. My grandmother and I made periodic visits to the flat. It was a long subway journey from Kew Gardens, long enough for my apprehension to deepen as we neared the end of the trip. Would Uncle Fermin be at home wearing a hat that hid his eyes? His skin was so white, his nose so like the blade of a knife!

On the long-ago Saturdays when one of us managed to scrape up money for tickets, Natalie and I would spend afternoons at the Blue-bird movie house on Broadway and, I think, 158th Street. Cartoons

419

preceded the feature film and were greeted with patches of wild applause. Along with Olive Oyl and her long feet and tiny head, I especially recollect Mickey Mouse, thin and worried-looking in those days as though he'd just eluded a laboratory technician's grab, not as he looks today, plump, smug and bourgeois.

And what movies we saw! The radiance of the actors and actresses, their eyes, their faces, their voices and movements. Their clothes! Even in prison movies, the stars shone in their prison clothes as if tailors had accompanied them in their downfall.

In the Bluebird, it was as though a woman sang stories larger than lives, about fate and love and evil enacted in shadowed rooms I couldn't enter, only glimpse from where I sat, rapt.

Some Saturdays as we returned to the tenement where Natalie lived, we heard thumping and could feel through the soles of our feet the vibrations of sound from my uncle's radio, all the way down from the fifth floor to the sidewalk where we had halted. On Natalie's face would appear a distressed, complicit smile, as though she held herself responsible for the noise.

It was not an ordinary radio. My uncle had built a plywood screen that covered the two narrow windows of the tiny parlor and had nailed or glued to it all the radio components, added two loudspeakers and, whenever he was in the flat, would turn up the volume as high as it would go.

The room felt ominous, as though something lived in it that might bring down the whole building. In summer, what breezes made their way down the street were shut out by the plywood screen, and in winter wind and cold leaked around its edges. My uncle sat in his coat and hat in the only armchair in the room, submerged in the uproar as though stupefied, the yellow dog at his feet growling, no doubt in baffled protest.

Neighbors stopped by the local police precinct to complain—only a very few tenants had telephones in those days—but the police never came. My grandmother would retire to one of the cell-like bedrooms and lie on a cot, one arm flung across her eyes and brow.

My uncle's wife, Elpidia, was a peasant woman from a Cuban village, and he had married her, I was told by my grandmother, to protest his engagement to the daughter of a plantation owner, an arrangement made by his father when Fermin was only a bad-tempered boy. She had married him out of dazzlement and some kind of love, and had come with him to the United States.

420

To escape the awful radio racket in the parlor as best I could, I used to go to the kitchen to watch Elpidia iron on a spindly board that resembled a wooden grasshopper. Grimly, as thought she were trying to kill it, she struck at it with a small black iron she had heated on the stove. Whatever garments were spread on the board's surface frequently bore scorch marks.

On other days on our visits to the flat, I would find my aunt slumped on a stool drawn up to the sink, weeping, silently, one hand supporting her chin as she stared down at the cockroaches that came and went with their hideous broken speed, now a pause, now a rush.

I don't recall her wearing anything but a faded, stained brown house dress. Her breasts looked like poorly stuffed small pillows. In one of them her death began. She developed cancer before her forty-fifth birthday and, after months of suffering, died of it.

When I was eight, I had lived in Cuba with my grandmother on a sugar plantation that belonged to an ancient relative, Tía Luisa, who was not my aunt at all but a distant cousin. Because of that and because of my grandmother's broken English—even after decades in the United States, she spoke with a heavy accent—which obliged me to speak to her in Spanish, I was fluent by then.

One later winter afternoon when it began to grow dark around four, I stood in the kitchen a few feet away from Elpidia, watching her. At last, I ask her why she cried so.

"no sé, mi hija," she answered, turning toward me her kindly, utterly miserable face. "No sé . . ." I don't know, my daughter. I don't know.

MY PARENTS returned from Europe, after a sojourn of three or four years, when I was eleven. They slid into my sight standing on the deck of a small passenger ship out of Marseilles that docked in New York City on the Hudson River alongside a cavernous shed. They were returning home after their adventures, the most recent being their flight from the Balearic Island of Ibiza during the Spanish Civil War.

My mother had draped a polo coat over her shoulders—I supposed because it was a cool spring day—and she smiled down at my grandmother and me where we waited in the shadowed darkness of the shed. Sunlight fell in daggers through holes in the roof high above us.

It had been years since I'd seen either of them. They were as handsome as movie stars. Smoke trailed like a festive streamer from the cigarette my mother held between two fingers of her right hand. When she realized we had spotted her, she waved once and her head was momentarily wreathed in smoke. The gangplank was lowered thunderously across the abyss between the ship's deck and the pier. Passengers began to trickle across it. Suddenly my parents were standing in front of us, a steamer trunk like a third presence between them.

"Hello . . . Hello . . . Hello," they called to us as though they were far away. They pointed out pieces of their luggage for porters, speaking to my grandmother and me in voices that were deep, musical—not everyday voices like those I heard in Kew Gardens—but of unbroken suavity as though they had memorized whole pages written for them on this occasion of their homecoming.

They spoke of shipboard life, about a cave in Ibiza outside of which my father had crouched for hours, humiliated by the fit of claustrophobia that had paralyzed him not two feet from the entrance, while my mother hid inside along with other refugees before escaping the next day to the ship that carried them to Marseilles, and about the fact, ruefully acknowledged by both of them with charming smiles, that no troops from either side had especially wanted to capture them, about the behavior of the French, and British filmmaking, and such a myriad of subjects that although I stood motionless and listening ravenously, I felt I was tumbling down a mountain side, an avalanche a few yards behind me.

Unlike her brother, Fermin, my mother had not a trace of a foreign accent. But in the middle of a sentence, she switched to Spanish and bent suddenly to embrace my grandmother with nearly human warmth as if she'd all at once recalled that the elderly woman standing so submissively before her, a stunned smile on her face, was her own mother, who, with her poor grasp of English, would not have understood even a part of what was said.

My mother's eyes stared at me over my grandmother's shoulder. Her mouth formed a cold radiant smile. My soul shivered.

My father leaned toward me, reaching out a hand to push a clump of my hair behind my ear. The tips of his fingers were damp. He laughed. He murmured, "Well, pal. Well, well . . . here we all are . . ."

I HAD been told by some relative that my father wrote for the movies. During the month that followed their return from Europe, he sold a script to a Hollywood studio for $10,000, a sum beyond my comprehension.

After two days, they left the small Manhattan hotel that they'd gone directly to from the ship, and took a room at the Half-Moon Hotel on the boardwalk at Coney Island, a ramshackle pile at the best of times that burned down long ago. My father said they were too "broke" to afford the first place. Something about his tone of voice suggested to me that being "broke" was only a temporary condition, and that it was different from being poor.

He also told me that he'd written the entire movie in a week while Elsie, my mother, handed him Benzedrine tablets from the bed upon which she lay doing crossword puzzles and lighting cigarette after cigarette. My grandmother and I visited them there one afternoon. During the hour we spent with them, my father presented me with a typewriter, a Hermes baby featherweight, saying, "Don't hock it. I may want it back," and only a few days later took it back with a muttered explanation I couldn't quite make out.

During that same visit, he asked for the loan of a bequest left to me two years earlier by "la Señora Ponvert," swearing he would repay me—all this spoken as though we both understood what tomfoolery it all was, the old lady leaving it to me, the amount itself, fifty dollars, and, further, that the people in the room, my grandmother and I, he and Elsie, even the room itself, were all manifestations of a larger truth than reality could ever be—and at this vertiginous moment my mother spoke from the chair where she was sitting, looking though the pages of a magazine. "Tía Luisa," she said without glancing up at me. I had forgotten, not that it was the same person they both had mentioned to me by different names, but that there had been a bequest. I looked over at my grandmother, who was nodding her head rapidly and saying, yes, yes, in a nearly inaudible voice as though she had been considering that very matter and had arrived at the fortunate conclusion that she and I would make the journey to the bank and withdraw the money at once.

When my father sold the movie in a week or so—it was easier in those days, simpler—he didn't offer to pay me back my fifty dollars, or to return the typewriter. And I, feeling that both matters would be judged by them as trivial, never mentioned them. I hadn't cared about the money but I had liked the typewriter.

Once my father was paid for the movie, he arranged for me to meet Elsie at De Pinna's department store on 5th Avenue to buy me some clothes. There was little danger in the subways and on the streets in those days, and a child was safer, except for an occasional flasher lurking at the end of a station platform. But as I rode into the city from Kew Gardens, I felt an alarm pervading me I couldn't name.

423

I saw Elsie before she saw me. She was moving indolently toward the glove counter near the store entrance. She looked so isolated yet so complete in herself.

Then she seemed to sense my presence. She turned around as I neared her. "Oh. There you are," she said formally. Her smile was meant for great things.

The shoe department was on the second floor, and we were going to begin there. We went to the elevator, my mother keeping a distance between us. From time to time, she glanced at my shabby footwear. I felt ashamed, as though it were I who had made them unfit for her eyes.

She bought me two pairs of beautiful shoes, one black, one green suede. During the time we were together, it was as if we were continually being introduced to each other. I was conscious of an immense effort—to start anew every time I began to speak.

It took less than twenty minutes. She smiled brilliantly at me. "Can you get home by yourself?" she asked me as though I had suddenly strayed into the path of her vision. I nodded wordlessly. The shopping was over.

I watched her walk away up Fifth Avenue with her peculiar stride, so characteristic of her that in the relatively few weeks she'd been back in the United States, I'd already learned it. Half the time she would tip-toe as though she were ready to fly off the earth. For years afterwards I thought about that stride of hers, and now and then I would imitate it. It had been an expression of her strangeness, her singularity, even, if remotely, of her glamour.

I tried wearing the green suede shoes with Natalie's print dress, which, as I'd grown taller, fit me better. But they didn't work. And I had no other clothes to match the elegance of those shoes. They gathered dust in my grandmother's closet. When I left for good, I left the shoes there too.

2000

NEON EFFECTS

by EMILY HIESTAND

from SOUTHWEST REVIEW

> *At times all I need is a brief glimpse, an opening in the midst of an incongruous landscape, a glint of lights in the fog, the dialogue of two passersby . . . and I think that, setting out from there, I will put together, piece by piece, the perfect city, made of fragments . . . of signals . . .*
>
> —Italo Calvino, Invisible Cities

"Do you want to know what I think?" Tommy asks, mildly and not rhetorically but offering his customer the small window of free will, the chance to *not know* what already burdens Tommy's superior automotive mind.

What Tommy Hoo thinks has rarely been apparent in the eight years that he and Steve Yuen and their pals at Nai Nan Ko Auto Service have cared for my Subaru three-door coupe. No, normally one must urge Tommy and Steve to say what they think, posing brutally direct questions: "Do I need a new battery before winter or not?" "Is the gurgle in the transmission trouble or not?" Even when Tommy and Steve do answer, they convey a sense that the jury is still out on the beloved Western idea "cause and effect." They have a bone-deep respect for the contingency of all things, and have never before actually volunteered a definitive opinion. It is an unprecedented moment in our relationship.

"Do you want to know what I think?"

"Yes, yes," I murmur.

Encouraged, my mechanic declares, firmly and unambiguously, "Don't put it on your car."

What I want to put on my car came as a gift from my husband, Peter, who was with me the palmy summer night that I saw a medium-size UFO floating down Brighton Avenue, hovering on a cushion of clear blue light that came billowing from underneath the craft—an airy, etherealizing light, shedding a serene glow over the asphalt road and its scurrying film of detritus. Some of us have been half-hoping for this all our lives, those of us who as children crept out after bedtime on summer nights, who stood in our backyards barefoot in the mowed grass to look up at the implacable dark glittering. And we have been well prepared for the moment in the close of darkened movie theatres; the special effects teams of Spielberg and Lucas have taught us, shown us, how to experience an encounter. We grow quiet, we suspend yet more disbelief, we feel a naïve awe and a shiver of fear as the Mother Ship appears, huge and resplendent with lights beyond our ken, and again when the fragile, more-advanced-than-us beings step out into our atmosphere. But we think it will happen far away—if it happens at all—in a remote desert, on some lonely country road, to someone else. We are not prepared for this astonishment to visit our own city street, to glide publicly past the Quickie Suds and Redbone's Bar-B-Que. Now Peter has pulled up close to the hovercraft and I can see inside its glowing body. There, not abducted, are two teenage boys such as our own planet produces.

"It's a Camaro," Peter says.

It is. A late model silver Camaro to which the boys have Done Something—something that washed over me, as Philip Larkin said of jazz, the way love should, "like an enormous yes."

And now Tommy has said, "Don't put it on your car," pronouncing where Tommy has never before pronounced.

"It" is two neon tubes which mount on the underside of a car and create a ravishing fusion of color and light whenever you flick a switch on the dashboard. The effect—"The Ultimate Effect" it says on the package—is produced by an underbody lighting kit that consists of the neon tubes, mounting hardware, and a fat wad of wiring. This kit is one of the thousands of devices collectively known as "automotive aftermarket products": sound systems, sunroofs, drinkholders, mudflaps, seat covers, carpeting, coats for nose grills, and ice machines. (And, I like to think, bud vases.) One nice thing about the genre of aftermarket products is that it opens up what might have otherwise seemed closed and finite. Implicit in every aftermarket product is the idea that

426

a vehicle is never a *fait accompli;* rather, its manufacturer has merely stopped fabrication at a reasonable point and has delivered a work-in-progress—a canvas.

The present canvas has the contour of a lithe sedan, but within that contour lies a hatchback that gives the sleek sedan the carrying capacity of a pickup truck. The rear window is a marvel of the glassmaker's art, an immense, gently curving expanse that arcs snugly over the chassis like the canopy of an F-16 over its Blue Angel. I have come with this car and the kit to Tommy and Steve because I trust them, and because their shop is so nearby that I can walk over whenever Tommy calls to say "You *cah* is ready," in his crisp, then soft, muscular speech that accents unexpected syllables, often with a faint gust of air—the sounds and emphases of Chinese overlaying English and giving it a gently pneumatic texture.

It helps to be able to *walk* to the garage of an auto mechanic whose wall is covered with letters of praise and satisfaction. It is one of the village-scale civilities that can be found in the urban world, a place that can be an impersonal tale, not least because of the automobile itself, the ways it reconfigures lives, flattens the depth of space, blurs time. So I don't want to go to another mechanic across town. I want to work with Tommy and Steve on this. When we talked over the telephone, Tommy had said, "No, we don't do that." And then he paused and asked, "Is it a *pinstripe?*" and, as always, his tone conveyed that we were only beginning, together, to enter into another automotive mystery.

Seeing the opening, I replied, "Oh no, it's not a pinstripe, it's just a couple of neon tubes mounted on the undercarriage. I could almost do it myself." (An outrageous lie if taken literally, but Tommy took my meaning: that the operation would be child's play for his shop.) "But there *is* some wiring to hook up, and I wouldn't want to mess with the electrical system."

"No, we don't do that."

I didn't say anything, and then Tommy said, "Why don't you bring over. We will take look."

One look at the kit, however, and Tommy and Steve are dead against it, and the reason is rust. "Rust," they intone together, as clerics of old must have said "Grim Reaper"—capitals implied in bitter homage. Here is the problem: to install the Ultimate Effect, a row of holes must be drilled on the undercarriage of the car, and this, my clerics believe, is an open invitation to the corroding enemy. Moreover, on this car the

427

rocker panels offer the only site on which to mount tubes, which fact gives us reason to say "rocker panels" several times (and me to remember a charged scene in *The French Connection*), but it must not be a good thing because the faces of Tommy and Steve remain glum.

The men also point out that the kit instructions say: IF YOUR AREA EXPERIENCES SNOW AND ICY CONDITIONS, YOU MUST REMOVE THE SYSTEM BEFORE THE WINTER SEASON. Needless to say, New England experiences these conditions, yet it would seem simple enough to remove neon tubes each November and re-mount them in April (dark when Persephone descends, illuminated when she rises). But Tommy notes that no quick-release clamp system is provided with the kit, and points out that he is not inclined to jury-rig one.

"Half-hour to take off, half-hour to install. Each time," he says funereally.

The two mechanics and I stand and look at one another politely, the current automotive mystery now fully declared. After another moment Tommy says softly, kindly, "Miss *Hies*tan', this will not add to the *value* of *you cah*."

After a long moment peering at each other as across a gulf, I venture an explanation.

"It's for fun," I say.

"For fun," Nai Nan Ko's mechanics repeat slowly, skeptically. And then, nimbly, before my very eyes, they begin to absorb the new concept.

"For fun," they say to each other. And now they are smiling and trying very hard not to smile, nearly blushing and bashful, and unable to look at me directly. We have unexpectedly stepped over into some new and intimate territory.

Upon reflection, one knows why these men did not consider fun at the first. Commonly I appear, as all their customers do, in a stoic, braced attitude awaiting the estimate, or later in miserly ponderings: Can the brake repair be put off a few weeks? (No.) Would a less expensive battery be okay? (No.) Fun has not come up during our eight years of dealings, not once. And now optional tubes that cost a bundle to install, tubes that tempt fate, that add no value, do not strike Tommy and Steve as barrels of it.

In the new silence that steals over us as we stand about the neon kit, I mention that it is a gift from my husband, that I will have to talk with him about the rust problem. At this piece of information, the situation transforms. Immediately, Tommy and Steve are smiling at me directly and sympathetically, relieved to be able to believe that I am on a wifely errand of humoring. In a near jolly mood, Steve stows the kit in the trunk of my car, and when last I see the two mechanics they are huddled, brooding happily under the raised hood of a banged-up Civic.

I am also left to brood. Here is dull old duality, posing its barbaric polarity: radiant swoon or structural integrity. Shrinking from the horrible choice, it occurs to me that someone must know how to do this, that the fine mechanics of Nai Nan Ko may simply not know the tricks that New England's custom shops have devised to deal with neon and rust, neon and winter, even as MIT's particle physicists do not necessarily know how to keep a cotton-candy machine from jamming. Sure enough, Herb, at the Auto Mall in Revere, knew all about neon effects.

"Four tubes or two? For two tubes, lady, that will be three hours, a hundred and fifty to install." And he is emphatic about rust, roaring out "No problem!" One of America's mantras and a phrase that wants a whole essay for itself.[*]

"None at all?" I persist. "Won't the holes allow water to seep in, especially during the winter when the tubes are out?"

"Well, sure," Herb replies peevishly, "a little water is going to get in, but it's not going to rot out right away, maybe in the *future* or sometime. Hold on a minute, lady. Eddie!" Herb calls into his shop. "That guy with the black Saturn gets his CD-changer installed in the trunk." Then back to me. "Where were we?"

"About the underbody rusting," I prompt, but greatly savoring the sound of Herb's Future—a place where rust *does* occur but whose temporal locus is so indeterminate as to make precautions about it absurd.

"See," says Herb, "I use a non-acid silicon sealant and we prime the holes with a primer."

Pressing the harried Herb one more degree, I ask if he has devised a quick-release system for the tubes for winter removal.

"Naah," Herb replies. "I've never taken one off. They just leave 'em on."

"Really?" I ask. "But these instructions say that ice and snow destroys the neon tubes."

___

[*]Glancingly, one can say of "No problem!" that its subtext is often a radical laissez-faire-ism, the speaker's Mr. Magoo-esque state of mind, which triggers a semantic backfire, making you think, This guy may not only *not* solve any existing problem, he may cause an entirely new one. The term is also used now in situations where previously a speaker would have been expected to say "You're welcome." And this second usage creates a curious sensation, introducing into the exchange of simple courtesies the idea of some problem, albeit one that is, for the moment, absent.

"Yeah, maybe," says Herb. "But I've never taken them off for any-body. *Nobody* takes them off in the winter." As an afterthought, he adds, "And that's when they get wrecked."

And that's when they get wrecked. In a tone that means, Winter is the time, lady, when neon tubes on cars are *supposed* to get wrecked, Ecclesiastically speaking.

"Anything else?" Herb asks.

A hard frost comes to the old Puritan city, and then winter, and the *tubos de neon* lie in their box along with the manual in Spanish and English, the high-voltage transformer, the rocker switch, fifty feet of black cable, six nylon clamps, six black *tuberia termocontrabile,* eight hex screws, and *la cable de energia rojo.* There is a time for everything: a time for seeking a neon mechanic, and a time to just read the manual instead and wait for spring, even as gardeners all over our region are curling up under quilts with the Book of Burpee. The first instruction, printed in large capital letters at the top of page one, is SOLO PARA EL USO FUERA DE LA CARRETERA O EN EXHIBICIONES / FOR OFF-ROAD OR SHOW USE ONLY.

Taken seriously, it would void the whole project.

The scroll of warnings continues. *El transformador para el Sistema de Luz de Neón produce un voltaje muy alto. Proceda con cautela durante la instalacion para evitar una descarga electrica o heridas.* Meaning, you can die of electrical shock doing this, so seriously listen up: Do not mount the effect at all on vehicles with antilock braking systems. Do not install the wiring too close to the gas tank, in consideration of the five-to-nine-thousand *voltaje muy alto.* Always always turn off the effect at gas stations when refueling. In the same large, all-caps typeface used for its death-warnings, the manual stresses one crucial aesthetic pointer. KEEP THE NEON UNITS ABOVE THE LOWEST POINTS OF THE CHASSIS TO HIDE THEM, the manual instructs. YOU WANT JUST THE GLOW TO BE SEEN, NOT THE UNITS THEMSELVES. This is first-rate advice that the Luminists and the Hudson River Valley School would recognize at once—all those painters who knew to locate the source of their bathing light just *beyond* the dark sail, the looming crag, the fringe of native firs.

I look up from page three (how to use a cigarette lighter to melt the *tuberia termocontrabile* to make a watertight seal), and the only thing aglow outside is a streetlight in the dull gray cowl of a cold January. And yet there is a somewhere where the neon season never ends:

South Florida, whose tropical climate and car culture, whose fancy for sheen and the night were destined to have brought neon and cars together at some point in the twentieth century.

The provenance of neon on wheels is traceable to Hialeah and the dragsters who first began to substitute neon tubing for the wiring on their distributors—Whoa! That lights up the whole engine block! Maybe Steve Carpenter saw that, the photographer who rigged up some temporary tubes under a Ferrari Testarossa and took a picture of the result for the album cover of a *Miami Vice* soundtrack. The general idea had gotten into the air, and the air was being inhaled, and all awaited the brothers Efrain and Roberto Rodriguez.

During one of the boreal storms that shoulder into our region, I place a long-distance call to their shop in Miami. Deirdre Rodriguez answers the telephone and over the next twenty minutes tells me that her husband, Efrain, is out in the warehouse right now overseeing a shipment to Tokyo; that the fire-loving countries of Latin America, China, and Japan are her best new customers; that, of *course* she has neon on her car! ("What do you think, darling?!"); that she has a special pink-to-purple-to-magenta spectrum, and that her mother has one too! Mrs. Rodriguez, who speaks in the clipped accent of her native England, remembers the hour of advent.

"I will tell you a woman-to-woman comment," she says, lowering her voice. "This is how it really happened. One night, we were lying in bed reading, and my husband said, 'Deirdre dear, I am going to put neon under cars.' Well, neon is so very fragile, isn't it? Sometimes our installers cannot even transport the tubes to the job sites without breaking them. So I said to him, 'Darling, go back to sleep.' Poor thing, I thought, he has completely snapped."

But within a week, says Mrs. Rodriguez (nibbling a little crow), the brothers had one tube of purple neon installed under Roberto's car. "Incredible!" Mrs. Rodriguez recalls of the sight. "We were speechless." On the spot, she says, her husband and his brother understood that "they must do something." Over the next months, Efrain and Roberto spent hours experimenting in their sign shop, where they invented a way to encase neon tubes in heavy-gauge plastic cylinders, figured how to bundle the tubes with a compact transformer and how to lay out the wiring system under a chassis. By spring they were ready, and at the Miami Grand Prix the Rodriguez brothers presented the Glow Kit.

431

Miami saw and Miami approved in a citywide supernova of enthusiasm, which was to be expected. In less warm-blooded places, neon has been a symbol for a garish modernity: "The neon glow from those technological New Jerusalems beyond the horizons of the next revolution," sniffs Aldous Huxley. But Miami knows better. She seems always to have known, intuitively, that this emanation from a gas both noble and rare belongs most intimately to her own streets. Although Las Vegas and Tokyo both have more ostentatious neon than Miami, and Paris long ago enfolded the bright gas into the evening cascade of her amorous boulevards, no city does neon with Miami's style. Mere days after the Rodriguez invention was unveiled, Miami's salt-free vehicles had begun to glow with the same radiance that nuzzles its old Deco façades. A native Miamian muses to me that her city's neon must be a human signal back to the glossy subtropical landscape—a semaphore sent to roseate spoonbills, to pink flamingos and lurid sunsets—a friendly, natural wave, a wish to belong.

Soon after the debut at the Grand Prix, the neon effect began to migrate from South Florida westward to Texas and California. It moved northward up the Eastern Seaboard until it reached the Mid-Atlantic coast, where it began to bog down. In Maryland and Virginia, the effect was declared illegal, possibly because underbody lighting tends to wash out painted highway lines, possibly because the police are a jealous police. (Especially the police do not care for other vehicles using blue light, which is their own color.) Of all regions, New England has been slowest to respond; to find my peers I must travel to the warmer, Latin quarters of our city, undimmed by the flinty northern palette.

❧

Naturally, I am aware that a good many people are not only *not* putting neon on their cars, they have sold these cars and are going about on bicycles and subways, mentioning holes in the ozone layer. Who does not take their point? The automobile was once our super-dense icon of protean motion, of independence; was once made sensible by vastness; was a soulful chamber, its highways songlines. It was deliverance for Okies driving through dust. And then its Faustian appetite overtook farmlands and estuaries, dissolved the city in sprawl, fumed the air, spurred malls and Valhalla Villages. The car and its beds of tarmacadam possessed planners to trade in the boulevards of memory for cloverleaves and concrete ramps. It has nearly ruined the railroads (our Zephyrs, Crescents, and Coast Starlights).

The usual erasure of places—all the vanishing places that can be carried only as Baudelaire's great swan carries its natal lake through the poultry market—has been painfully accelerated by the automobile's demands. I know that. And yet I wish to adorn the suspect thing. It is one of the small canvases of a fragmented people. I know that too. And there is a credibility problem here for me, who has for years railed about the Commodification of Everything, saying, Lookyhere, Marx was right. Marx *was* right, consumer culture does insidiously invite us to think of everything, even our very own lives, as "product." And yet I am gladly shelling out $154.99 for a box of high-grade glam. Perhaps it is because these underbelly lights, while admittedly not a totally worked-out policy for transformation of culture, seem finer, truer, more heartfelt than one president's let-them-eat-cake "thousand-points-of-light" nonprogram. Because the gonzo extraterrestrial fireflies feel like descendants of Baudelaire's *movements brusques* and *soubresauts,* the strange and quick new ways of moving in the city. Because they are nite lights, sending the kind of signals—"affectionate, haughty, electrical"—of which Walt Whitman spoke. We can easily guess that the poet of the urban world would go for neon lamps: "Salut au monde!" Whitman calls across the mobile century, "What cities the light or warmth penetrates I penetrate those cities myself . . . I raise high the perpendicular hand, I make the signal."

Maybe too it is because these glow pods are a shard of the sublime, the old aesthetic of exaltation, so chastened over this century by a well-known catalogue of horrors. Maybe the sublime has turned hypermodern, calibrated its energies, and bolted the idea of ecstatic transport onto Trans Ams—is lurking underneath things. Maybe I shouldn't say much more. Maybe the ultimate effect is, after all, just fun and flash, a sassy way of saying "I'm here." But it turns a massproduced object into a carriage of light, and the light these youths bring into the city also seems to work a little as safe passage, as a visa across the often guarded lines of urban and ethnic territory. "*Es como una familia,*" one young man will say of the fraternity of neon.

❧

About the time that our ground begins to relax into spring, Annie, the tango dancer, tells me about Bigelow Coachworks. Annie has a leonine shock of gold hair, a closet full of swirly skirts, and a collection of vintage

Fiestaware. She dances the slow Argentine-style tango and I felt sure that her word about neon customizers would be trustworthy. The first thing I notice about Bigelow Coachworks (other than it being named coachworks) is that the shop is immaculate. Not one oil-soaked rag. Inside the office there is a counter and a young woman behind it whose strawberry blond hair has been teased and sprayed into what used to be called a beehive. For neon, the young woman says, I must talk with Jim Jr.

No sooner have I said the word "neon" than Jim Jr., who has the palest kind of amber eyes, has plunged into the issues: First, the switch and ways it can be wired—into the headlights or parking lights, or independently onto the dash. The independent switch is a problem, Jim says, because you can forget to turn it off and drain your battery. Next, do I want two tubes or four? Two is plenty in Jim Jr.'s opinion; in fact, having no rear-mounted tube avoids the messy matter of plastic cases melted by the exhaust pipe. Now the mounting. Am I aware that the tubes aren't really made for New England winters? And do I know that the kits don't come with dismounting hardware? Do I know that Jim has engineered custom clamps that stay in place and make it easy to pop the tubes in and out with the seasons? As for rust, a touch of silicon on each screw will suffice.

It is a virtuoso romp, all the nuts and bolts of the neon sublime known and mastered by Jim, who has installed some fifteen systems, including, he says with a shy smile, the one on his own truck. My man. Jim Jr. levels with me about the thirty-six-inch tubes.

"These are going to give a *lame* effect," he says, examining the kit. "There isn't enough *juice* here for the effect we want."

Fortunately, the fifty-four-inch tubes for the effect we do want can be had right up the street, at Ellis The Rim Man's Auto Parts store, a temple to the aftermarket product where a beefy salesman shows me the selection (all made by the Rodriguez brothers) and then says, in the tone of a man who wants to have a clear conscience,

"You know, it's really dying out."

"Dying?"

"I think the kids just got tired of being harassed by the police." The salesman now pauses, glances at the two young salesclerks at the counter, and clues me in: "It's only boys who buy this stuff—you know, ethnics, Hispanic boys."

As the present contradiction occurs to him, he studies me evenly.

When the young men at the counter see what I am buying, one of them asks politely, "Is this for your son?"

My son, I think, not the least insulted, only feeling the sudden sensation of having one, and being the kind of mother who would get a top-of-the-line neon kit for him.

"No, it's for me," I say, smiling.

"Al-*right*," the boys say, and shoot me the hubba-hubba look. Now they want to talk neon.

"*Si, si,*" of course they have it on their *caros*. Enrique has green and José has aqua. They have neon *inside* their cars too—under the dash, on their gear shift knobs. The store has a demonstration model. José gets it out, plugs it in; we stand around it to ogle the colored coils zooming around inside the clear plastic handle.

What do Enrique and José like about having neon on their cars? What *don't* they like! It's way *chevere*, way cool, it's like being inside a nightclub! Man, it lights up your whole body and everything you go by, and makes things look really, really bright. When José and Enrique hear that I saw my first neon car near the store, they cry out in unison.

"That was *us!*"

"You drive a silver Camaro?"

"Oh, no" they cry again, just as pleased. "Oh, no, that *wasn't* us, that was Alberto. That's Alberto's spaceship!"

Now they want to tell me something way-way *chevere*: the festival is coming. That's where we can see all the best neon cars and also the low-riders slow-dancing their cars down the road, each spotless vehicle also booming with salsa.

"So neon hasn't died out?"

"No way," gapes Enrique, incredulous at the thought. Wait and see! Much lighting-up in the streets before summer is over.

The boys hold the door as I exit the showroom—carrying a long cardboard box of glass, transformer, and rare gas under my arm. They step out with me onto the broad sidewalk of our city's Commonwealth Avenue. It is about nine at night, July, prime time, and while we are standing there a boy that Enrique knows comes billowing by in a Cougar with some brand-new magenta light to spill. He creeps almost to a stop.

"*Hola!*" he calls.

"*Hola!*" the boys call back. "*Que lindo se ve.* How nice it looks. *Que bufiao! Miraeso.* Look at that. *Ooouuu, la luz.*"

2000

435

TOWARD HUMILITY

by BRET LOTT

from FOURTH GENRE

5

ONCE IT'S OVER, you write it all down in second person, so that it doesn't sound like you who's complaining. So it doesn't sound like a complaint.

Because you have been blessed.
You have been blessed.
You have been blessed.
And still you know nothing, and still it all sounds like a complaint.

4

You are on a Lear jet.

It's very nice: plush leather seats for which leg room isn't even a matter, the jet seating only six; burled wood cabinets holding beer and sodas; burled wood drawers hiding bags of chips, boxes of cookies, cans of nuts; copies of three of today's newspapers; a stereo system loaded with CDs.

Your younger son, age thirteen, is with you, invited along with the rest of your family by the publicist for the bookstore chain whose jet this is. When you and your wife and two sons pulled up to the private end of the airport in the town where you live, there on the tarmac had sat a Lear jet, out of which came first the publicist, a young and pretty woman in a beige business suit, followed by the pilots, who introduced themselves with just their first names—Hal and John—and shook hands with each member of your family.

"You're all welcome to come along," the publicist had said, and you'd seen she meant it. But it was an invitation made on the spot, nothing you had planned for. And since your older son, fifteen, has a basketball tournament, and your wife has to drive, it is left to your younger son to come along.

Your younger son, the one who has set his heart and mind and soul upon being a pilot. The one whose room is plastered with posters of jets. The one who has memorized his copy of Jane's Military Aircraft.

"I guess we can get you a toothbrush," you'd said to him, and here had come a smile you knew was the real thing, his eyebrows up, mouth open, deep breaths in and out, in his eyes a joyful disbelief at this good fortune. All in a smile.

Now here you are, above clouds. In a Lear jet, your son in the jump seat—leather, too—behind the cockpit, talking to Hal and John, handing them cans of Diet Coke, the publicist talking to you about who else has ridden in the corporate jet. Tom Wolfe, she tells you. Patricia Cornwell. Jimmy Carter. And a writer who was so arrogant she won't tell you his name.

This is nowhere you'd ever thought you might be. Sure, you may have hoped a book you wrote might someday become a bestseller, but it wasn't a serious hope. More like hoping to win the lottery. A pretty thought, but not a whole lot you could do about it, other than write the best you knew how.

But getting on a list wasn't why you wrote, and here, at 37,000 feet and doing 627 miles an hour over a landscape so far below you, you see, really, nothing, there is in you a kind of guilt, a sense somehow you are doing something you shouldn't be doing.

Riding in a Lear jet to go to a bookstore—four of them in two days—to sign copies of your book.

Your book: published eight years before, out of print for the last two. A book four books ago, one you'd thought dead and gone, the few copies left from the one-and-only hardcover print run available in remainder bins at book warehouses here and there around the country.

A book about your family, based on the life of your grandmother, who raised six children, all of whom were born in a log cabin your grandfather built, the last of those six a Down's Syndrome baby, a

437

daughter born in 1943 and for whom little hope of living was held out by the doctors of the time. It is about your grandmother, and the love she has for that baby, her desire to see her live, and her own desire to fix things for her daughter as best she can, if even at the cost of her other children and, perhaps, her husband.

A book recently anointed by a celebrity talk show host. Not a celebrity, but an icon. Not an icon, but a Force. A person so powerful and influential that simply by announcing the name of your book a month ago, your book has been born again.

Bigger than you had ever imagined it might become. Bigger than you had ever allowed yourself even to dream. Even bigger than that. And bigger.

Guilt, because it seems you're some kind of impostor. Even though it is based on your family, you had to reread the novel for the first time since you last went through it, maybe nine years ago, when it was in galleys, you sick of it by that time to the point where, like all the other books you have published—there are eight in all—you don't read them again. But this one you had to reread so that you could know who these characters were, know the intricate details of their lives so that if someone on the television show were to have asked you a question of an obscure moment in the whole of it all, you would have seemed to them and to the nation—Who would be watching? How many people? As many as have bought the book? And more, of course—to be on close terms with the book, with its people, its social context and historical and spiritual significance.

You wrote it ten years ago.

And yesterday you were on this talk show host's program.

Tom Wolfe, you think. Jimmy Carter, and you realize you are dressed entirely wrong, in your dull green sweater and khaki pants, old leather shoes. Maybe you should have worn a sport coat. Maybe a tie. Definitely better shoes.

You can see the soles of your son's skateboard shoes, worn nearly through at the balls of his feet, him on his knees and as far into the cockpit as he can get. He's got on a pair of cargo shorts, the right rear pocket torn, and a green T-shirt. He'd been lucky enough to wear a polar fleece jacket to the airport this February morning in the sunny South.

This is all wrong.

The publicist continues on about who has ridden in the corporate jet, and you nod, wondering, How did I get here?

All you know is that you wrote this book, and received a phone call the first week in January, a call that came on a very bad day for you, a call that found you out a thousand miles from your home, where you were teaching others how they might learn to write. A job in addition to the daily teaching job you have so that you might make ends meet, and so that your wife wouldn't have to work as many hours as she has in the past.

The Force found you there, on a very bad day, and gave you unbelievable news. And now your book is on the lists.

You think about that day. About how very bad it was, how empty, and hollow, and how even the news that was the biggest news of your life was made small by what happened.

And now the plane begins its initial descent into the metropolis, and your son returns to the seat beside you, still with that incredulous smile, though you have been airborne nearly an hour. Hal and John happily announce you'll be landing in moments, the landscape below hurrying into view—trees, highways, cars, homes. Nothing different from the view out any airplane window you have looked before, but different all the way around.

Everything is different.

The jet settles effortlessly to the ground, taxies to the private end of an airport you've flown into before, the public terminal out your window but far, far away, and you see, there on the tarmac as the jet eases to a stop, a Mercedes limousine.

Yep. A Mercedes.

You look at your shoes, and at your son's. His cargo shorts. This sweater you have on.

"When we were here with Jimmy Carter, the lines were all the way out the store and halfway around the building," the publicist says. "This is going to be fun," she says, and smiles, stands, heads out the door past smiling, nodding Hal and John.

Then John asks, "What would you guys like for dinner?"

You and your son look at each other—he's still smiling, still smiling—and then you look to John, shrug, smile. "Subs?" you say, as if the request might be too much to manage.

"No problem," John says, and both he and Hal nod again.

Here is the store: brick, tall, a presence. A single store in a huge bookstore chain, every store complete with a coffee bar and bakery, a gift shop with coffee mugs and T-shirts and calendars.

And books.

You climb out the limousine before the chauffeur can get around to open your door, because you don't want to make him feel like you're the kind of person who will wait for a door to be opened. Then you and your son, the publicist in the lead, make your way for the front doors.

Inside is a huge poster in a stand, the poster two feet by four feet, advertising your being at this store for a signing. In the center of the poster is your picture, formidable and serious, it seems to you. Too serious. This isn't you, you think. That person staring pensively off the photographer's left shoulder is somebody posing as an author, you think.

There are a few people in the store, and you wonder if the line will form a little later on, once the signing gets underway, and you are ushered by a smiling store manager in a red apron to the signing area.

It's in the middle of the store, and is a table stacked with copies of the anointed book, and with reprints of the earlier three books, and of the four that have come out since the anointed one first appeared all those years ago. Your books, you see, are piled everywhere. Books, and books.

"Look at this!" the manager exclaims, and points like a game show hostess to a rack of paperback books beside you, the Bestseller rack. "You're the number one book," the manager says, and you see the rows of your book, beneath them a placard with #1 printed on it.

You look at your son to see if he's as impressed as you are beginning to be.

He smiles at you, nods at the books, his eyebrows up.

He's impressed.

You take your seat behind the table laden with your books, and see between the stacks that there is a kind of runway that extends out from the front of your table to the other end of the store, a long and empty runway paved with gray-blue carpet. Big, and wide, and empty.

"We'll get you some coffee and cookies, if that's all right," the publicist says to you, then, to your son, "Hot chocolate sound good?" and your son says, "Yes ma'am," and, "Thank you."

You are here. The signing has begun.

But there are no customers.

You wait, while the manager announces over the in-store speakers your presence, fresh from yesterday's appearance on national TV. This drives a couple of people to the runway, and they walk down the long corridor of gray-blue carpet toward you. It seems it takes a long time for them to make it to you, longer even than the flight up here from your hometown, and you smile at these people coming at you: a young man, tall and lanky; a woman your age with glasses and short brown hair.

They are smiling at you.

You know them. Students of yours from the program where you teach a thousand miles from home. They are students of yours, friends, writers. Both of them.

You stand, hug them both, introduce them to your son, to the manager back from the announcement, and to the publicist returning now with that coffee and hot chocolate, those cookies. Then the three of you remark upon the circumstance of your meeting here: they live in the same city, and have been waiting for your appearance at the store; how wonderful and strange that your book has been picked, what a blessing!; when Jimmy Carter came here, the line was out the door and halfway around the building.

You talk, sip at the coffee, don't touch the cookie. There are no other customers, and the manager promises they will come, they will come. She's had phone calls all day asking when you will get here, and if the lines will be too long to wait through.

You talk more, and more. Talk that dwindles to nothing but what is not being said: where are the customers?

Now, finally, fifteen minutes into a two-hour signing, you see an older woman rounding the end of the runway. She has bright orange hair piled high, and wears a tailored blue suit. She's pushing a stroller, and you imagine she is a grandmother out with her grand-child, the child's mother perhaps somewhere in the store right now, searching out children's books while Grandma takes care of the baby.

It's an expensive suit, you can tell as she moves closer, maybe thirty feet away now, and you see too the expensive leather bag she carries with her. The baby is still hidden under blankets, and you smile at the woman as she moves closer, closer, a customer heralding perhaps more customers, maybe even a line out the store and halfway around the building by the time this is all over.

Maybe.

Then here is the woman arriving at the other side of the table, and you see between the stacks she is even older than you believed.

441

Heavy pancake make-up serves in a way that actually makes her wrinkles bigger, thicker; watery eyes are almost lost in heavy blue eye shadow; penciled-in eyebrows arch high on her forehead.

And you are smiling at this person, this customer, as she slowly bends to the stroller and says in the same moment, "Here's the famous writer, Sophie, the famous writer Mommy wants you to meet," and she lifts from inside the blankets, the woman cooing all the while and making kissing sounds now, a dog.

A rat dog, a pink bow in the thin brown fur between its pointy ears.

"Sophie," the woman says to the dog, "would you mind if Mommy lets the famous writer hold you?" and her arms stretch toward you between the stacks of your books, in her hands this dog with a pink ribbon, and without thinking you reach toward her, and now you are holding Sophie.

The dog whimpers, shivers, licks its lips too quickly, tiny eyes darting again and again away from you to Mommy.

You don't know what to say, only smile, nod, and let your own eyes dart to your students, these friends, who stand with their own smiles, eyes open perhaps a little too wide, and then you glance behind you to the publicist, whose chin is a little too high and whose mouth is open, and to the manager, who stands with her arms crossed against her red apron. She's looking at the gray-blue carpet.

And here is your son. He's standing at the end of this line of people, hands behind his back, watching. He's not smiling, his mouth a straight line, and your eyes meet a moment.

He's watching.

"Sophie would love it," the woman begins, and you turn to her. She's plucked a copy of the anointed book from one of the piles, has opened it to the title page. Those watery eyes are nearly lost in the wrinkles gathering for the force of her smile. "I know Sophie would absolutely love it," she continues, "if you were to sign this copy to her."

You swallow, still smiling. "For Sophie?" you say.

The woman nods, reaches toward you for the dog, and you hand it out to her while she says, "She'll love it. She'd be so very proud."

Here is your book, open and ready to be signed.

You look at your students. Their faces are no different, still smiling. They are looking at you.

442

You look at the publicist, and the manager. They are both looking at you, too.

And you look to your son. He has his hands at his sides now, his mouth still that thin, straight line. But his eyes have narrowed, looking at you, scrutinizing you in a way that speaks so that only you can hear, This is what happens when you're famous?

These are the exact words you hear from his eyes, narrowed, scrutinizing.

"She would be so very proud," the woman says, and you look to her again, Sophie up to her face now, and licking her cheek, that pancake make-up.

You pull from your shirt pocket your pen.

3

Everyone is here, your living room choked with friends, maybe fifty people in all, all there to watch the show. You and your wife have laid out platters of buffalo wings, fresh vegetables, jalapeño poppers, various cheeses and crackers and dip; there are bowls of chips, a vast array of soft drinks. Cups have been filled with store-bought ice, paper plates and napkins and utensils all spread out.

They are here for the celebration. You, on the Force's talk show, your book the feature.

Kids swirl around the house and out in the yard, their parents laughing and eating and asking what it was like to meet her, to be with her, to talk with her. Some of them tell you, too, that they have finally read your book, and tell you how wonderful your book was.

You've known most of these people for years, and there are moments that come to you while these friends tell you how wonderful your book was when you want to ask them, Why didn't you read it when it came out eight years ago? But you only smile, tell them all the same thing: thank you, thank you, thank you.

You tell them, too, that the Force was incredibly intelligent, disarming, genuine, better read than you yourself are. A genuine, genuine person.

This was what she was like when you met her, when you taped the show for three hours two weeks ago, you and her book club guests— four women, each of whom wrote a letter about the effect of your book on their lives that was convincing enough to get the producers

443

of the show to fly them in, be these book club guests—and there were moments during that whole afternoon when, seated next to her and listening to one or another of the guests, you stole a look at her and told yourself, That's her. That's her. I'm sitting next to her. Moments that startled you with the reality of this all, moments that in the next moment you had to shut down for fear that thinking this way would render you wordless, strike you dumb with celebrity were the conversation to turn abruptly to you.

Then the show begins. Kids still swirl, and your wife has to pull two preschoolers from the computer in the sunroom off the living room, where they are banging two-fisted each on the keyboard, no one other than you and your wife seeming to notice this, everyone watching the television. There are no empty chairs left, no space on the sofa, the carpet in front of the TV spread with people sitting, paper plates in hand heaped with buffalo wings and jalapeño poppers and veggie sticks, and you have no choice but to stand in the back of the room, watching.

Here is what you were warned of: this episode of the book club show—your episode—happens to fall during sweeps month, when ratings are measured so as to figure how much to charge for advertising time, and since the viewership for the monthly show featuring the book and the author always plummets, the producers have decided to spend the first half of the hour with bloopers from past shows. "Forgettable moments," these fragments have been called by the promotional ads leading up to the air date.

This was what you were warned of, two weeks ago when you were through with the taping. Officials from the show told you all this, and you'd nodded, smiling, understanding. What else was there for you to do? Demand equal time with everyone else?

No. You'd nodded, smiled, understood.

Now the Force introduces video clip after video clip of, truly, forgettable moments from past episodes: two people argue over whether the toilet paper is more efficiently utilized if rolled over the top or out from beneath; a woman tells a Viagra joke; the Force marches down the street outside her studio in protest of uncomfortable panty hose.

Your guests look at you.

"I had nothing to do with this," you say, too loud. "It'll be on the last half of the show," you say, too loud again.

They are quiet for a while, then return to ladling dip onto plates, loading up wings and poppers, pouring soda, until, finally, you are introduced, and the book, and there you are for two minutes talking about your grandmother, and your aunt with Down's Syndrome, your voice clear and calm, and you are amazed at how clear and calm you are there on the television, when you had wanted nothing more than to jump from the sofa you were seated on in the studio and do jumping jacks to work off the fear and trembling inside you. Now comes a series of family photos, a montage of images with your voice over it all, calm and smooth, the images on the screen pictures your family has had for years.

Pictures of your grandmother, and of your aunt.

The people you wrote about, whose lives are now here for the world to see, and you realize in this moment that you had nothing to do with this. That these photos—of your grandmother, your aunt, and your grandfather and aunts and uncles and your father too, all these family photos that have existed for years—simply bear testament to the fact they were lives lived out of your hands, and all you had to do was to write them down, getting credit for all those lives led.

You think about that bad day in January. About how this all began, and how all this credit has come to you.

Yet you are still a little steamed about losing the first half of the show, when every other author you've seen featured on the show has gotten most of the program. You are a little steamed, too, about not having some place to sit here in your living room, and about those kids banging on the keyboard. You are a little steamed.

Then the discussion with you and the four women and the Force begins, and you see, along with everyone in your house, and everyone in the country, the world, a discussion that had lasted three hours squelched down to eight minutes, and six or so of those given to a woman who gave up her Down's Syndrome child at birth because of the "life sentence" she saw being handed her. You see in your living room choked with your friends this woman crying over her life, her decision, and see her somehow thank you for your book and the meaning it has given her life.

You knew this would be what was included on the air. You'd known it the moment her voice wavered and cracked that afternoon two weeks ago, there in the studio. You knew it then, and now here it is: this woman, crying over giving up her baby, and thanking you for it.

And you see yourself nod on the air, looking thoughtful.

445

She makes great TV, you think. This woman who missed the point of your book entirely.

2

You are answering the phones for a while, because of the terrible thing that has happened this bright, cold January day.

"We'll send you a brochure," you say to someone on the other end of the line, no one you know, and as she tells you her address you do not write it down, only sit with your back to the desk, looking out the window onto the late afternoon world outside: snow, sky.

A little after lunch, this day turned very bad, a turn that has led to you here, in the office of the program in which you teach a thousand miles from home, to answer the phone for the administrative director.

She is in the other room, too much in shards to answer the phone, to field the bonehead questions that still come to a program such as this one no matter what bad things happen and when. People still call to ask about the program, about costs and applications, about credits and teachers. About all things.

Earlier today, before you began answering the phone, before lunch, your agent called here, where you are teaching others to write because it seems you know something about writing, to tell you the novel you have just finished writing is awful.

You are here for two weeks, in workshops and seminars, lectures and readings, the students adults who know what is at stake. Though they have lives away from here, just as you have your own, you and they converge on this New England campus from all over the country, the world, twice a year to study the word and all it can mean. They come here to study writing, because they want to write, and some of them become friends to you and to the other writers teaching here, because it is this love of the word that unites you all.

Some of them become your friends.

Your agent said to you this morning, "What happened to this?" She said, "Where was your heart?"

Her call, you'd recognized with her words and tone, had not surprised you. You knew it was coming. You knew the book was dead and gone to hell in a hand basket, had known it for the last month as you'd tried to get to the end of the thing. You knew it had gone to hell in a hand basket even before you missed the deadline last week.

You knew.

The novel: a sequel to the last one you published, early last year. That one had done well, better than any of the others you've published this far. A novel you'd had a tough time trying to get published, seeing as how your books have never done that well. You're a literary author, and publishers know that means you don't sell many books. You're not a bestseller, they know. You write well enough, but you're just not a bestseller, a fact you reconciled yourself to many years ago.

But the first hardcover run of this latest book—a run in the low five figures—sold out in a few months, the publisher electing not to reprint. They'd sold as many as they'd believed they could sell, had also sold it to paperback with another publisher.

Everything was great, with selling out the print run. So great they asked ten months ago if you would write a sequel to it, and you agreed, though it wasn't anything you'd thought much about. Not until you saw how well the book was selling.

Now, here you were, ten months later, teaching people to write on a day cursed with the sad and empty curse of a startlingly blue winter sky. A day in which you have been informed of what you have known all along: this one didn't work.

You know nothing about writing.

But this is not the bad thing. It had seemed bad enough to you, walking across campus to lunch after the phone call, three hours long, from your agent, a phone call in which you both reconnoitered the train wreck before you, pieced out what was salvageable, shrugged over what was lost.

The day seemed bad enough then.

And then.

Then, after lunch, one of the students was found in his room, dead. Not one of the students, but one of your students.

Not one of your students, but a friend.

Some of them become your friends.

You were to have had dinner in town with him tonight, to talk about the novel he is writing, the novel you had been working on with him all last semester, when he was a student of yours and during which time he became a friend. A big, ambitious, strange and haunting novel.

A novel that will go unfinished now.

He was found in his dorm room, sitting at his desk, having gone to

447

his room the night before, students have said, complaining of a headache.

He was found sitting at his desk, reading a copy of one of your books. A novel. A lesser known one, one it seemed no one really cared for.

Your friend was reading it.

He was found at 1:30 on this blue and cursed January afternoon. Now it is 4:00, between that time and this a somber and hushed chaos breaking out all over campus. Everyone here knows everyone here. No one has ever died here before. He was too young. He was your friend.

And now you are answering phones for the administrative director who is in the other room. You told her you wanted to answer the phone to give her time away from the bonehead questions, but you know you offered as a means to keep yourself from falling into shards of your own. You offered, so that you would have something to do, and not have to think of this very bad day, when the loss of your own book, you see, means nothing. A book means nothing.

You have lost a friend. A friend who is here, a thousand miles from home, too. A friend not much older than you, his death a complete and utter surprise. He lives with his mother, you know, where he takes care of her, an invalid, and where he is writing a big, ambitious, strange and haunting novel.

The phone rings. You are looking out the window at the afternoon sky growing dark, the blue gone to an ashen violet, and you turn to the phone, watch it a moment as though its ringing might change how it appears, like in cartoons when the phone jumps from its place and shivers.

It rings, and nothing happens, rings again, and you pick up the receiver, hold it to your ear knowing another bonehead question is on its way.

"May I speak to _____ _____?" a man says, all business, a solid voice that carries authority with it, and you think perhaps this is an official from the college, calling on business. Not a bonehead.

"Hold on," you say, and place the phone down, go to the room next door, where she is sitting, gathering herself.

"Can you take a call?" you ask, and try to smile. "It's for you," you say, and she nods, sniffs, tries at a smile herself. She stands, and you follow her back into her office, her domain, you only a brief tenant this afternoon of a very bad day.

448

She picks up the phone, says, "Hello?" and her eyes go immediately to you. "You were just talking to him," she says, and hands you the phone, trying to smile.

You take the receiver, bring it to your ear, say, "Yes?"

"I'm calling from Chicago," the businessman's voice says to you, "and my boss is working a project she needs to talk to you about. I need to break her from a meeting. Can you hold?"

A meeting, you think. My boss. What is this about?

You say, "Sure," and now music comes on the line, and you glance up at the director, who is looking at you, wondering too, you can see, what this might be about. You don't live here. You're a thousand miles from home. Who knows you are here, and why?

You shrug at her in answer to her eyes, and then the music stops with a phone connection click, and a voice you think you may recognize says your name, then her own, then shouts, "We're going to have so much fun!"

Who is this? Is this who you think it is? Is this who she says she is? Is this her?

"Is this a joke?" you shout. "Is this for real?" and your eyes quick jump to the director, who sits in a chair across from you, watching you in wonder.

This makes the woman calling—her—laugh, and she assures you this is no joke, this is for real, and that she has chosen a book you have written as her book of the month next month.

It's a book four books ago, a book out of print. A book about your grandmother, her Down's Syndrome daughter, your family.

This isn't happening. It hasn't happened. It will not happen.

But it has happened: you have been chosen. Your book has been anointed.

"This is secret," she says. "You can't tell anyone. We'll announce it in twelve days. But you can't tell anyone."

"Can I tell my wife?" you manage to get out, and she laughs, says you can, but that's all, and she talks a little more, and you talk, and you cannot believe that you are talking to her, you here a thousand miles from home and with a secret larger than any you have ever had lain upon you. Even bigger.

Yet all you can think to say to her is, A friend of mine died today. A friend of mine died. Can I tell you a friend of mine died?

But you do not say it. You merely talk with her, her, about things you won't be able to recall five minutes from now.

449

And then the phone call is over, and you hang up, look at the administrative director.

She knows who it was, you can tell. She knows, but asks, "Was it her?"

"It's a secret," you say, your words hushed for fear someone else in the office might hear. "You can't tell anyone," you say, and you are standing, and you hug her because she is the closest person to you and you have this secret inside you, and because she is the only other person on the planet to know.

You will call your wife next. You will call her and tell her of this moment, of this delivery. Of this news beyond any news you have ever gotten.

You let go the director, and see she is crying, and you are crying now, too. You are crying, and you are smiling, and you look back to the window, see the ashen violet gone to a purple so deep and so true that you know none of this is happening, none of it. This is what you finally understand is surreal, a word you have heard and used a thousand times. But now it has meaning.

A friend has died. The Force has called. The sky has gone from a cold and indifferent blue to this regal purple. A secret has been bestowed. A novel has been lost. Another gone unfinished.

This is surreal.

You go to the window, lean against the frame, your face close enough to the glass to make out the intricate filaments of ice crystals there.

You want to feel the cold on your cheek, want evidence this is real, all of this day is real. You want evidence.

You listen again to her voice on the phone, the words exchanged. You feel this cold.

A friend has died, and you did not record his passing with the Force.

And now you cry openly, watching the sky out there in its regal color, regal not for anything you have done. Only assigned that value by your eyes on this particular January day. That color has nothing to do with you, exists as it does as a kind of gift whether you are here to see it or not.

What does a book matter?

Still you cry, and do not know if it is out of sorrow or joy, and decide in the next moment it is out of both.

1

Your newest book is pretty much going to hell. In a hand basket.

Late afternoon, December, and you and your wife are in lawn chairs at the soccer field, watching your younger son play in one of the last games before Christmas.

Christmas. Your deadline for the next novel. The advance you were given, a sum the same as you were paid for your last book, even though it sold out its print run and sold to paperback as well, was spent months ago. Ancient history. Now here's Christmas coming hard at you, the novel going to hell.

Your son, a wing, is out on the field, your wife sitting beside you on your left, your older son a few feet farther to your left and in a lawn chair too, and talking to a schoolmate sitting on the grass beside him. Long shadows fall from across the field toward you, cast by the forest there. Other parents, schoolmates, brothers and sisters are spread across your side of the field, those shadows approaching you all. Maybe thirty or forty people altogether. It's a small school, new and with no field on campus, this one a municipal field at a city park. Lawn chairs is the best anyone can do.

And of course here with you, too, is your book pretty much going to hell, and this fact, its lack of momentum in your head and heart coupled with that looming deadline, might as well be a dead body propped in yet another lawn chair sitting next to you for all its palpable presence in your life. The world knows, it seems to you, that you are flailing.

You are cranky. That's what you would like to think it is. But it is more than that, and you know it, and your wife knows it, and your children do too. You are angry, resentful. You are in the last fifty pages, but the book is leaving you, not like sand through your fingers, but like ground glass swallowed down.

You believed you had something, going in to the writing of it nine months ago. You believed you were headed somewhere.

You thought you knew something: that you could write this book.

So, when you see your son lag behind on a run downfield, you yell at him, "Get on the ball! Run! Get in the game!"

It's too loud, you know, with the first word out of your mouth, and you turn to your wife, say, "Why doesn't he get into the game?" as though to lend your outburst credence. As though to find in her some kind of agreement that it's your son slacking off, when you know too well it's about a book you are writing going down like ground glass.

She looks at you out of the corner of her eye, says nothing.

Your older son gets up from his lawn chair, and moves even farther away with his friend, and you look at him, too. He's got on sunglasses, a ball cap on backwards. He's embarrassed by you, you know.

You would have been, too, were you him.

But the book is dying. It is dying.

You yell, even louder, "Let's GO! Get in the GAME!" and feel your hands in fists on the arms of the lawn chair.

This time your younger son looks over his shoulder, though far downfield, and his eyes meet yours. Then, quickly, they dart away, to others on the sidelines, then to the ground, his back fully to you now, him running and running.

"He's always just hanging back like that," you say to your wife, quieter but, you only now realize, with your teeth clenched. "It's like he's always just watching what's going on." You know your words as you speak them are one more attempt to give your anger, your resentment a clear conscience: you're yelling because of your kid. Not because of you.

And now your wife stands, picks up her lawn chair, moves away, settles her chair a good fifty feet from you.

This is no signal to you of the embarrassment you are. It is nothing cryptic you are meant to decipher. It is her truth and yours both, big and dumb: you are a fool.

And it is because of a book. A stupid book. There are more important things, she is shouting to you in settling her lawn chair that far from you. There are more important things than a book.

You are here in your chair, alone with yourself. And the corpse of your book propped beside you.

You look off to the right, for no good reason but that it's away from those you have embarrassed, and those who know you for the fool you are.

And see there near the sideline, almost to the corner of the field, a blond kid, down on one knee on the sideline, his back to you. He's maybe ten yards away, the sun falling across the field to give his blond hair an extra shimmer to it, turning it almost white.

He's talking to himself, you hear, his voice quiet but there, just there. He's got on a black T-shirt, cargo shorts, skateboard shoes, and though his back is to you, you can see he has in one hand a plastic yellow baseball bat, in the other a plastic Day-Glo orange squirt gun.

He's holding them oddly, you can see, the bat by the thick end, where the ball makes contact, the handle up and perpendicular to the ground, like a flagstaff with no flag; the squirt gun he holds delicately, thumb and first finger at the bottom of the grip, as though it might be too hot.

He's still talking, and you can see the gun and bat moving a little, first the gun, his hand shaking it in sync, you hear, with his words, then the bat, the movement small, like the sound of his voice coming to you across the grass, and over the shouts of players at the far end of the field. Then the gun shakes again, and you see too by the movement of his head that he looks at the gun when he moves it and talks, and looks as well at the bat when he moves it and talks.

What is he doing?

Then he turns, rolls toward you from the knee he is on to sitting flat on the ground. He's facing you now, still holding the bat and gun in this odd way, and you see, now, now, he is a Down's Syndrome boy: almond eyes, thick neck, his mouth open.

He speaks again, looks at the bat, moving it with his words, and you only now realize he is speaking for the bat, that the bat itself is talking, this boy supplying the words, and then the gun answers the bat.

They are talking one to the other: a yellow bat, a Day-Glo squirt gun.

The boy is about your younger son's age, you see, and see too the shimmer of late afternoon sunlight in his hair the same as a few moments before, when his back was to you, and you hadn't known. You hadn't known.

You look at him. Still they talk one to the other, the words nothing you can make out, but there is something beautiful and profound in what you see. Something right and simple and true, and just past your understanding.

It's a kind of peace you see, and can't understand, this moment.

I wrote a book about that, you think. I wrote a book about a Down's Syndrome person, my aunt, and her mother. My grandmother, you think.

That was a good book, you think. That one was a gift, given to you without your even asking.

453

A gift, you think, and you wonder who this boy is with, who his own family is, who he is a gift to, and just as you wonder this you hear a rise in the crowd.

Parents and children in lawn chairs are growing louder now, clapping, hollering, though nothing as bombastic as what you knew you let out a few minutes before, and you turn to the sound, see your son's team moving and moving before the goal down there, the ball popped to the left and then right, and now you hear from the boy the word, "Go," then louder, "Go! GO!" and you look at him, see him turned to that end of the field now too, see the bat and gun held still, this boy back up on one knee and in profile to you. "GO JOHNNY!" he yells, and you know he has a brother out there.

The gun and bat talk to one another again, while the shadows from the far side of the field grow closer to you all, to everyone, and now you know you knew nothing in writing that book. It was a gift, this story of a mother and daughter, but has it made you a better father to your son? Has it made you a better husband to your wife?

The answer, of course, is no, because here you are, chewing out the world around you because a book is going down like ground glass swallowed.

This is when the boy happens to glance up from the dialog he creates and lives at once, to see you looking at him. Your eyes meet a moment, the talking toys now still, and you say, "Hi." You say it just to be nice to him. You say it because your eyes have met, and he has seen you watching him.

But you say it to try and save yourself.

He looks at you, looks at you, and even before he goes back to the dialog at hand, his friends these toys, you know he won't say a thing.

You are a stranger.

You look beside you. There is no corpse of a book here, not anywhere around. Your wife is gone too, her to your left and away from you, your older son even farther away. And there is your younger son, out on the field and running away from you as best he can. Your son, a teammate to this boy's brother.

There is, you know, only you here with you, and though you wish it were possible, pray it might be possible, there is no way for you to stand and lift your lawn chair and walk fifty feet away from you.

Which is what you want to do. To be away from you, here.

Because you have been blessed.

You have been blessed.
You have been blessed.

0

You have everything to learn.

This will be what keeps you. What points you toward humility: knowing how very little you know, how very far you have to go. As far now, in the second person and once it's all over, as on an afternoon soccer field, shadows growing long.

I know nothing. I know I know nothing.

I have been blessed.

for Jim Ferry

2001

THE CANALS OF MARS

by GARY FINCKE

from SHENANDOAH

W HEN MRS. SOWERS, during the first week of sixth grade, showed us the canals of Mars, she traced the straight lines of them with the rubber tip of a wooden pointer. "Think of the Erie Canal," she said, holding the stick against the poster-sized map of Mars. "Better yet, think of the Panama and the Suez," she added, starting a list we were to memorize for one week's worth of geography.

"It's very likely," she said, "there were countries on Mars that fought over their technological marvels," and then she named, for our current events lesson, the nations threatening war for the Suez Canal, hissing out the names Nasser and the U.S.S.R., explaining the possible domino effect of the A-bomb.

The map, Mrs. Sowers went on to explain, had been drawn by Percival Lowell, a respected astronomer who had calculated the locations of Martian infrastructure. I believed her because up to that point I'd been relying for my information about Mars on a handful of science fiction movies I'd seen and a comic book Dave Tolley had brought to school the year before.

Through early September, before she brought us up to date on the Suez crisis, Mrs. Sowers ran a series of experiments for science. She demonstrated the water cycle; she wowed us with magnets and electric current that stood our hair on end.

Nature lessons were another matter. We fidgeted through two weeks on Pennsylvania plants. None of us liked the taste of the sassafras tea she brewed from a small tree on the hillside behind our school. It was like drinking the chewing gum our parents preferred to the sweet pleasures of Double Bubble and Bazooka.

What my friends and I wanted to know about were killer plants. Venus Fly Traps, for instance, or Pitcher Plants, or most of all, the whereabouts of those wonderfully gigantic man-eaters from the double features we watched on weekends at the Etna Theater.

All those enormous leaves. The suffocating, hair-trigger, relentless vines. Those plants were as dangerous as the giant squids created by atomic tests that left excess radiation in the ocean. If even one of their million fine-threaded leaves were brushed by careless explorers or women who wandered off from jungle camps against the advice of the guide, the horrible gulping would begin.

After one of those movies—a new Tarzan with Lex Barker— Charles Trout, the smallest boy in our class, was tossed into brambles behind the Etna Theater by boys we didn't know because our parents had saved enough money to make down payments on houses in the suburbs rather than stay in Etna, where the steel mills and railroad yards were showing signs of shutting down for good. "See?" my father would say, running his finger over his newly painted bakery wall. "See what Etna does to white?" And I nodded, thinking I could write my name and the names of all my friends with my finger through the soot.

Charles Trout laughed it off. None of us lived in Etna. We never saw those boys on the streets where we lived. And no matter, we couldn't get enough of those movies. We looked for plants in the neighborhood that might thrive on blood, dropped ants by the hundreds into any flower that grew wild, but never once did one close on the insects. It was as hard to find a carnivorous plant as it was to find quicksand. Apparently, we thought, you had to live in some steamy, forbidding place to watch anything being eaten by flowers.

Mrs. Sowers told us plants couldn't possibly get that large. She said we didn't study the Venus Fly-Trap because there weren't any in Pennsylvania. We were right, though, about one thing—they lived in bogs where other flowers seldom live. Worse, she insisted there weren't any within hundreds of miles of us.

That weekend Dave Tolley and I hiked to every marshy place we could find. It was late September, the weather, we thought, still warm enough for those traps to be working. Now that we had an important clue, we wanted to prove Mrs. Sowers wrong.

Meanwhile, we were glued to *You Asked For It*, where every Sunday on television we could see the impossible come true. Sooner or later, we thought, somebody would write in and ask to see a man-eating plant, but later that fall we settled for a man who could catch a bullet in his teeth.

While Dave Tolley and I watched, a bullet was marked by a witness from the audience so the rest of us would know it had really been fired. The camera, while the bullet was loaded, showed us the audience, all of the studio guests sitting up straight. They looked as if they were holding their breath. Every man was wearing a coat and tie, every woman a dress, and all of them were as old as our parents or older.

Even the man who could catch a bullet in his teeth was wearing a coat and tie as if he were going to church to pray for perfect timing. He furrowed his brow. He squinted. He concentrated. The marksman aimed carefully and fired. Across the studio stage the man was still standing. The camera panned in to show us it was the marked bullet he pulled from between his teeth, and we immediately set out to attempt a sort of beginners' lesson for bullet catching.

In Dave Tolley's refrigerator were bunches of green, seedless grapes. His parents played canasta on Sundays; they wouldn't be home for hours, and we threw those grapes across the living room at each other, never once catching even a lob toss between our teeth.

There were over a hundred grapes on the carpet. "Either he's a fake," Dave Tolley said, "or we're spastic." I shrugged. We had to pick all those grapes up and wash them, eating enough to make it look as if we were helping his parents rather than using their grapes as ammunition. Twenty grapes into the bowl, we decided to try one more time, and when Dave Tolley, a few minutes later, caught one of my tosses between his teeth, we shut up about impossible and decided that if somebody practiced longer than the ten minutes we'd just spent, maybe it could be done.

After all, Richard Turner, another boy in our class, could already juggle three balls. He'd learned to do it in one afternoon from his father. We thought of four balls, then five; we thought of swords and flaming sticks; we thought of increasing the speed of grapes until we could take on a bullet, how we could perform a feat so incredible that nobody would believe it.

Mrs. Sowers, of course, was no help. On Monday morning, when we told her, she said it was a silly thing to try. "Oh, that's just impossible," she said, even though we described the careful ways the program had made sure the whole thing was genuine. She shook her head and started current events, beginning with the Soviets invading

458

Hungary. "For a few days there, the Hungarians thought they were free. Nothing's the way it looks," she said, "when it comes to Communism."

She went on and on about misuse of power, how France and England had invaded Egypt. They equated power with authority, she explained, and everybody in our class wrote it down.

Dave Tolley and I had some authority. We were patrol boys. We directed traffic for a few minutes in the morning and the afternoon. I loved wearing that belt and the crossed white strap that sported the patrol badge. It showed Mrs. Sowers approved, that I was responsible and trustworthy, that even the low-readers from the Locust Grove trailer court had to wait for my signal to cross. The badges we wore were like magic that warded off danger. None of those thuggish boys had ever threatened us.

The Invasion of the Body Snatchers arrived at the Etna Theater. We'd been waiting so long, every boy in our sixth grade class but Jimmy Mason, who was thirteen and lived in the trailer court, watched it on Saturday afternoon. The Body Snatchers, it seemed, were plants. None of us could figure out how they'd changed the first human victims, but after that, people carried the big seed pods for them, placing the pods near the sleeping who woke up transformed into aliens. Sure enough, all the people in the movie who changed acted like plants. They didn't have emotions. They did anything they were told.

Just like in the Tarzan movies, it seemed scarier to be threatened by plants. You could recognize which animals were threatening. You stayed away from them. But plants? Except for poison ivy and the thorns on berry bushes and roses, there wasn't anything to be afraid of. Trees, bushes, flowers, weeds—if some of them could attack, we'd be out of luck because we were surrounded.

In the middle of November, Mrs. Sowers took Dave Tolley and me aside. "Listen, boys," she said, "I've come across a story you might enjoy. In England, a man came across a large meadow completely covered by sundews."

She looked at us for a moment. "Sundews are carnivorous plants," she said, and both of us started paying attention.

"There were a million plants," Mrs. Sowers said, and all of them, as far as the man could see, had just swallowed butterflies. An enormous flock of them had decided to settle on those flowers, and they had paid for their mistake, millions of them simultaneously eaten in minutes.

Dave Tolley and I nodded like carnival dolls. "Imagine," she said, "a whole field of insect-eating plants." We did, but like everything we wanted to see, the butterfly eaters seemed as far away as Mars.

"And as for *The Invasion of the Body Snatchers*," she said, "and all that big seed pod business, that's the Communists. Did either of you see *The Thing* a few years back? The alien in that movie was a vegetable that drank blood—it was a Communist, too. Korea and Red China—that's what all the to-do was about then. This thing in Egypt might be over for now, and all the Communists have to show for it is a canal nobody can use because it's full of sunken ships and broken bridges."

THE LAST DAY before Christmas vacation, beginning at lunch, was our party—the gift exchange, games with candy bars as prizes, mothers bringing cookies and potato chips and Coke—but first, Mrs. Sowers said, she had a surprise, flinging her arm toward a man in a dark suit who had materialized in the doorway.

"Who can remember their canals?" Mrs. Sowers said. The stranger smiled while we chorused Panama and Suez, and then pieced together the canals of Pennsylvania, pleasing Mrs. Sowers by conjuring Main Line, Schuylkill, Delaware, Lehigh and Morris.

The man in the suit, Mrs. Sowers said, had helped build the Pennsylvania Turnpike. That road had been completed, a wonderful success, nothing like that old dream we had studied in September, the Chesapeake and Ohio Canal, which was supposed to come right from the Chesapeake Bay to Pittsburgh and the beginning of the river seven miles from where we were sitting.

It turned out, after we had passed her retest, showing we remembered the long-closed canals of Pennsylvania and the still-open canals of the world, Mrs. Sowers was having that engineer show us a film on the first turnpike in America because part of that road ran through our county. And when Charles Trout, looking at the map of the turnpike, everything else in Pennsylvania blacked out, said it reminded him of the canals of Mars, the engineer told our class those lines on Mars weren't canals at all. Nobody said anything. Nobody looked at Mrs. Sowers. The engineer kept going, telling us those lines were just Martian forests that flourished on either side of the

460

canals, how irrigation would show itself to approaching spacecraft, how growth along our own lengthening turnpike system would tell the monsters coming our way we could think.

So that settled that, we thought. Mrs. Sowers wasn't wrong, but she wasn't infallible. If we knew who to ask, he'd lead us to carnivorous plants; if we talked to an expert, we'd learn to face a one-man firing squad and live to hear the applause. But when she told us, just before the gift exchange, that the troops were withdrawing in the Middle East, we all smiled because the inevitable atomic war had been postponed a while longer.

I gave her a gift-wrapped box my mother said contained a pair of stockings. "Thank you," Mrs. Sowers said, and I nodded, embarrassed, because I hadn't even seen the stockings before my mother wrapped them. Anything could have been in that box, as long as it lay flat, was light, and was less than ten inches long and six inches wide.

Because it was Friday, I got off the bus two miles from my house where a path between the Atlantic station and a car dealership made a shortcut to the Locust Grove trailer court. I walked, on Fridays, from the Atlantic station to my father's bakery in Etna. It was a mile, maybe, from that bus stop to the bakery, all of it along heavily-traveled Route 8, but there was a sidewalk most of the way, or parking lots to cut across, and I'd been walking that route once a week since fourth grade, during all that time talking to nobody who got off the bus there except Jimmy Mason after he flunked sixth grade and ended up in my class instead of the junior high school.

My mother worked until six o'clock on Fridays, but on that first official day of winter it was cold and gloomy and already nearly dark at four p.m. Instead of going up the path as he always did, Jimmy Mason fell in beside two older boys I'd never seen. All three of them caught up to me as soon as I crossed the Route 8 bridge where Pine Creek ran under the highway.

Jimmy Mason said the three of them had a job selling Christmas trees in Etna. He cut in front of me and walked backwards, slowing us down. If I had any money, he said, I should buy a tree from them, or better yet, just give the money to them and they wouldn't bother me any more.

"I don't have any money," I said, telling the truth.

"Not on you," Jimmy Mason said, but the other two boys bumped against me from either side.

461

"What's that badge for?" the biggest said. "You play cops and robbers at your school?"

"Safety patrol," I said. He turned and put his forearm against my chest, resting it across the badge. I noticed he had a mustache.

"You keep the babies safe?"

I didn't say anything. I already wished I hadn't said a word or had the stupidity to wear that patrol gear outside my winter coat. "Patrol boy," he said. "I want to cross here. Why don't you step out and stop those trucks?"

I cut to the inside, afraid he'd push me into the highway. I kept walking, down to the last section, a quarter mile of crushed cinder sidewalk, Pine Creek ten feet below us on one side, a hundred-foot cliff running down to the highway on the other.

All three lanes were patch-iced, the traffic one step from where he waved his arms. I could see the stoplight where businesses, including my father's, began. My mother would be wrapping bread and sandwich buns. In a few minutes she'd start looking out the window to see if I was coming.

He snapped the white straps crossed over my red jacket. "Safety patrol," he said. "Pussy." The badge blinked from the early sets of headlights. He pulled on a pair of black leather gloves. "Give me that badge," the boy said, "or I'll beat the shit out of you, patrol boy."

He shoved me toward the guardrail, and I looked down the hillside at the creek I could see moving beneath the thin ice. "Don't move," he said, sticking a blue pen in my face. "Patrol boy, you write this down: I died here, December 21," and then he shoved my arm toward the guardrail that made that pen skip along the metal's white and rust until I stopped where a string of *fuck yous* began.

"More darker," he said, and I went over and over the letters. "So the police," he said, "can read it when your body's found—now walk."

All four of us skidded down a path through the trees that lined the creek bank. Anybody driving a car along Route 8 couldn't see us anymore. On the other side of the creek an identical thick set of scrub trees covered a bank that sloped up and stopped where the leveled slag of the parking lot for National Valve began. Anybody in that factory, even if he was taking the time to stare out a window instead of shaping and cutting pipe, couldn't see us. Only someone overhead in a helicopter or a hot air balloon could have watched what was happening.

462

"You ever seen it hard, patrol boy?" he said. "You can fight back now or else you can kneel and suck it." I checked the bank on the other side of Pine Creek for an opening among the trees. For all I knew, nobody worked at National Valve after four o'clock. When he cocked his fist I stepped into water that ran over my shoes. "Cold?" he asked. "Wet?"

I watched his hands as I backpedaled to knee-high, the ice collapsing under me, and then I turned and slogged to the other side, eleven years old and dying at 4:15, December 21, in Pine Creek, all three of those boys screaming "Safety Patrol" across that ditch of factory run-off as I scrambled to the almost-empty lot where two cars were parked so near the edge, so close together, I thought, before I began to run toward the bakery, one driver was kneeling for another or both of them were waiting to kill me.

2001

463